The formation of Modernist literature took place in a cultural climate characterized by an unprecedented collaboration between painters, sculptors, writers, musicians, and critics on both sides of the Atlantic. Within this multifaceted movement, William Carlos Williams is a paradigmatic case of a writer whose work was the result of a successful attempt at integrating ideas and concepts from the revolutionary visual arts. This book takes up a range of questions about the deeper affinities between Williams's poetry and the visual arts (including photography) that have not yet been studied in depth. What connections, for example, inform Williams's programmatic insistence on "contact" and the "shallow" or intimate space in a Cubist painting (which, as Braque advocated, should open up toward the viewer instead of receding into the infinity of the traditional vanishing point)? Are there fruitful applications of such concepts as synesthesia or kinesthesia, much talked about in Futurism and Precisionism, to Williams's preoccupation with an "aesthetics of energy"? How does Williams successfully integrate in his poetry such fundamentally different concepts as Kandinsky's theory of expression and Duchamp's notion of the ready-made?

This book is a major step toward a fuller exploration of the connection between the visual arts and Williams's concept of the Modernist poem, and of his achievement in transcending an art-for-art's-sake formalism to create poems which both reflect their own nature as a work of art and vividly evoke the world of which they are a part. As Williams repeatedly stressed, "[I]t must not be forgot that we smell, hear, and see with words and words alone, and that with a new language we smell, hear and see afresh. . . . "

D1453765

CAMBRIDGE STUDIES IN AMERICAN LITERATURE AND CULTURE

The Revolution in the Visual Arts and the Poetry of William Carlos Williams

CAMBRIDGE STUDIES IN AMERICAN LITERATURE AND CULTURE

Books in the series

Continued on pages following the Index

The Revolution in the Visual Arts and the Poetry of William Carlos Williams

PETER HALTER
University of Lausanne

CAMBRIDGE
UNIVERSITY PRESS

CAMBRIDGE UNIVERSITY PRESS
Cambridge, New York, Melbourne, Madrid, Cape Town, Singapore, São Paulo, Delhi

Cambridge University Press
The Edinburgh Building, Cambridge CB2 8RU, UK

Published in the United States of America by Cambridge University Press, New York

www.cambridge.org
Information on this title: www.cambridge.org/9780521102667

First published 1994
This digitally printed version 2009

A catalogue record for this publication is available from the British Library

Library of Congress Cataloguing in Publication data
Halter, Peter.
The revolution in the visual arts and the poetry of William Carlos
Williams / Peter Halter.
p.   cm. – (Cambridge studies in American literature and
culture)
Includes bibliographical references (p.) and index.
ISBN 0–521–43130–1
1. Williams, William Carlos, 1883–1963 – Knowledge – Art.   2. Art
and literature – United States – History – 20th century.   3. Modernism
(Literature) – United States.   4. Modernism (Art) – United States.
I. Title.   II. Series.
PS3545.I544Z589   1994
811'.52 – dc20   93–25882
CIP

ISBN 978-0-521-43130-9 hardback
ISBN 978-0-521-10266-7 paperback

Contents

Illustrations

Acknowledgments

===

In writing (and rewriting) this book I have been helped by conversations with a great number of friends and colleagues, especially John G. Blair, Neil Forsyth, Albert Gelpi, Brian Gibbons, Peter Hughes, Elizabeth Kaspar Aldrich, Beverly Maeder, Walter Naef, Max Nänny, Roelof Overmeer, Henri Petter, Gregory Polletta, David Roscoe, Barbara Sträuli, Andrew Torr, Richard Watts, Mike Weaver, and Franz Zelger. Several of them read the entire manuscript and made valuable suggestions for revision, most notably Richard Watts, Jay Blair, and Max Nänny. Their astute criticism, unflagging encouragement, and friendship made much of my work possible. The same is true for J. Hillis Miller, whose criticism and generous support, ever since I met him when I was a young assistant at Zürich University, provided more guidance and encouragement than he can possibly know.

My heartfelt thanks also go to William Eric Williams and his wife, Mimi, wonderful hosts during several visits at 9 Ridge Road in Rutherford, visits which enabled me to go through Williams's personal library and to study in the original some of the paintings and photographs that Williams had acquired or received from his artist friends Charles Demuth, Charles Sheeler, and Ben Shahn.

The initial phases of research and writing were supported in a crucial way by a two-year grant from the Canton of Zürich; it enabled me, among other things, to spend a year as a Postdoctoral Fellow at Yale University. At Yale, my special thanks go to the librarians of the Beinecke Library of Rare Books and Manuscripts for letting me use the Williams files and various other unpublished material related to my subject. I have also greatly benefited from the editorial assistance of my two editors at Cambridge University Press, Julie Greenblatt and T. Susan Chang, as well as from the help and advice of production editor Janis Bolster and copy editor Sandra Graham. Technical support of a different kind came from Martin Heusser, who not only persuaded me to buy a Mac at the time they still cost a small fortune but helped me greatly whenever I was in trouble on my journey from the electric to the electronic age.

Finally, I am especially grateful to Doris, who believed in this book even in those moments when I had doubts whether it would ever see the light of day. Her caring and her intellectual and moral support helped me during every stage of this project, from the moment of its inception to its completion.

Grateful acknowledgment is made to New Directions Publishing Corporation and to Carcanet Press Limited for permission to quote from *The Collected Poems of William Carlos Williams*:

Volume 1: *1909–1939*. Ed. A. Walton Litz and Christopher MacGowan (1986). Copyright 1938 by New Directions Publishing Corporation. Copyright © 1982, 1986 by William Eric Williams and Paul H. Williams.

Volume 2: *1939–1962*. Ed. Christopher MacGowan (1988). Copyright 1944, 1953, copyright © 1962 by William Carlos Williams. Copyright © 1988 by William Eric Williams and Paul H. Williams.

Grateful acknowledgment is made to New Directions Publishing Corporation for permission to quote from these further copyrighted works of William Carlos Williams:

The Autobiography of William Carlos Williams. Copyright 1948, 1951 by William Carlos Williams.

The Build-up. Copyright 1946, 1952 by William Carlos Williams.

The Doctor Stories. Copyright 1934, 1962 by William Carlos Williams.

The Embodiment of Knowledge. Copyright © 1974 by Florence H. Williams.

The Farmers' Daughters. Copyright 1934, 1950 by William Carlos Williams. Copyright © 1957 by Florence H. Williams.

I Wanted to Write a Poem. Copyright © 1958 by William Carlos Williams.

Imaginations. Copyright © 1970 by Florence H. Williams.

In the American Grain. Copyright 1925 by James Laughlin. Copyright 1933 by William Carlos Williams.

In the Money. Copyright 1940 by Florence H. Williams.

Many Loves & Other Plays. Copyright 1948 by William Carlos Williams.

Paterson. Copyright © 1946, 1948, 1948, 1949, 1958 by William Carlos Williams.

Pictures from Brueghel. Copyright 1954, 1955, 1962 by William Carlos Williams.

A Recognizable Image: William Carlos Williams on Art and Artists. Copyright © 1978 by the Estate of Florence H. Williams.

Selected Essays. Copyright 1954 by William Carlos Williams.

Abbreviations

1 WORKS BY WILLIAM CARLOS WILLIAMS

A   *The Autobiography of William Carlos Williams*. New York: New Directions, 1967.

CEP   *The Collected Earlier Poems*. New York: New Directions, 1966.

CLP   *The Collected Later Poems*. Rev. ed. New York: New Directions, 1963.

*CP*1   *The Collected Poems of William Carlos Williams*. Volume 1: *1909–1939*. Ed. A. Walton Litz and Christopher MacGowan. New York: New Directions, 1986.

*CP*2   *The Collected Poems of William Carlos Williams*. Volume 2: *1939–1962*. Ed. Christopher MacGowan. New York: New Directions, 1988.

EK   *The Embodiment of Knowledge*. Ed. Ron Loewinson. New York: New Directions, 1974.

FD   *The Farmers' Daughters*. New York: New Directions, 1961.

I   *Imaginations*. Ed. Webster Schott. New York: New Directions, 1970. Contains reprints of five works:

    AN   *A Novelette and Other Prose* (*Other Prose* includes the essays "An Essay on Virginia," "Marianne Moore," and "The Work of Gertrude Stein," here abbreviated "EV," "MM," and "WGS.")

    DW   *The Descent of Winter*

    GAN   *The Great American Novel*

    KH   *Kora in Hell: Improvisations*

    SA   *Spring and All*

IAG   *In the American Grain*. New York: New Directions, 1956.

IWW   *I Wanted to Write a Poem: The Autobiography of the Works of a Poet*.

Reported and edited by Edith Heal. 1958; rev. ed. New York: New Directions, 1978.

P   *Paterson.* Rev. ed. by Christopher MacGowan. New York: New Directions, 1992.

PB   *Pictures from Brueghel.* New York: New Directions, 1962.

RI   *A Recognizable Image: William Carlos Williams on Art and Artists.* Ed. Bram Dijkstra. New York: New Directions, 1978.

SE   *Selected Essays.* New York: New Directions, 1969.

SL   *The Selected Letters of William Carlos Williams.* Ed. John C. Thirlwall. New York: McDowell, Obolensky, 1957.

VP   *A Voyage to Pagany.* New York: New Directions, 1970.

2 MANUSCRIPT COLLECTIONS

L, SUNY   The Lockwood Memorial Library, State University of New York at Buffalo.

YALC   Yale American Literature Collection, Beinecke Library of Rare Books and Manuscripts, Yale University, New Haven.

3 OTHER WORKS

CSA   Wassily Kandinsky, *Concerning the Spiritual in Art.* Ed. Robert Motherwell. New York: George Wittenborn, 1947.

Introduction

The formation of Modernism in general and of Modernist literature in particular took place in a cultural climate that was characterized by an unprecedented collaboration between painters, sculptors, writers, musicians, and critics on both sides of the Atlantic, with centers in Paris, London, Berlin, Zürich, and New York. Within this multifaceted movement, William Carlos Williams may well be the paradigmatic case of a writer whose poetics are the result of a "cross-fertilization in the arts," to borrow the expression James E. Breslin used in one of the best articles written so far on Williams and the visual arts.[1] Peter Schmidt, in an equally pertinent essay on the subject, even writes that "[o]f all the poets who have been influenced by the visual arts, William Carlos Williams may present the most complex case":

> Blake, Rossetti and Pound turned paintings into poems and saw poems become paintings. But none seems to match the combined range and depth of Williams' involvement in the arts. Blake's work represents a one-man movement in both painting and poetry. Rossetti and his fellow Pre-Raphaelites had a much more uniform style and subject matter than did the artists Williams knew. Pound's artist friends were certainly as diverse as those of Williams, but they exerted a more problematic influence, and it is not surprising that the single most important visual influence on Pound – the ideogram – was largely his own invention. Williams, on the other hand, paid close attention to three quite different art movements.[2]

The movements referred to by Schmidt are the Stieglitz school of "straight" photographers and Precisionist painters, European Cubism and its American adaptations, and Dada and Surrealism. To these one could add Postimpressionism, Vorticism, Futurism, Expressionism, and Early Abstraction – movements with which Williams was in touch through such artist friends as Pound, Demuth, and Hartley, as well as through many other channels.

Since this book is not the first to relate Williams's achievement to the revolutionary movements in the visual arts, it can rely in many ways on the material and the insights assembled and gained in previous studies.[3] (Needless to say, this

1

debt also extends to dozens of books and articles on the relationship between literature and the visual arts in a more general way, as well as to a great number of pertinent studies on Williams and on Modernism.)

With the exception of two recent publications,[4] all of the few book-length studies on Williams and the visual arts, beginning with Bram Dijkstra's pioneering study and extending to those by Dickran Tashjian, William Marling, and Christopher MacGowan, extensively document biographical influences, above all the multifaceted contacts between Williams and the New York avant-garde. All of them, with increasing complexity, also try to revaluate Williams's work in the light of their findings.

All in all, however, we still have relatively little extensive, and even less in-depth, literary analysis in this field, and many of the basic questions about the deeper affinities between Williams's poetry (or Modernist poetry in general) and painting have not yet been fully explored. If, for instance, one of the common features of Modernist poetry is the discarding of the traditional "continuous" forms in favor of the discontinuous, broken, "illogical" forms of montage, what are the deeper connections to the abandoning of the continuous space in Modernist painting? Are there fruitful applications of such concepts as synesthetic and kinesthetic art, much talked about in Futurism and Orphism, to Williams's preoccupation with verbal force within an "aesthetics of energy"? Can we establish connections between Williams's programmatic insistence on "contact" and the creation of a Cubist space that is no longer organized around a vanishing point receding into infinity but rather opens up toward the viewer? And if one can indeed relate a specific space in poetry with a specific space in painting, are the related spaces rooted in phenomenological changes that establish a common ground between some of the basic forms of Modernist poetry and Modernist painting?

The aim of this book, in the context of these and other related questions, is twofold. First, it is to contribute to a deeper understanding of Williams's poetics and to affirm his poetics as one of the important contributions to Modernist aesthetics; and second, to contribute to the continuing exploration of the common ground of the various art forms in Modernism, a ground which, of course, can only be found beyond the ineluctable differences of each artistic medium. Williams himself is a case in point here: His importance as a poet is rooted in the very fact that he was able to find in the visual arts an essential inspiration for the development of his own poetics without violating his own medium, writing.

Of the book-length studies devoted so far to Williams and the visual arts, Henry Sayre's *The Visual Text of William Carlos Williams* and Peter Schmidt's *William Carlos Williams, the Arts, and Literary Tradition* are closest to the present study insofar as they rely largely on previous scholarship and concentrate on the specific nature of Williams's Modernist poetics in light of its relation to Modernist painting. Schmidt's book, published around the time that I was about to finish the present study, can be taken in several ways as a valuable counterpart to my own approach. Schmidt tries to show "how even during the decade in which Williams wrote *Spring and All* he sought to integrate ideas from the visual arts with what in 1939 he called 'the usable past' – the full range of both American and European literary tradition." He accordingly argues that "in general Williams used the inspiration he gained from the arts not . . . to create a visual poetics, but to return to and renew specifically *literary* traditions and modes" (p. 7). Although I agree with Schmidt that Williams did not primarily create a visual poetics *as such,* I nevertheless propose that he tried to develop, by way of the visual arts, an aesthetics informing *all* Modernist art, including literature. Whereas Schmidt thus reads Williams's poems in the light of the *literary* concepts which Williams had derived from the visual arts, my own book redefines Williams's specific achievement in terms of a *basic aesthetics of Modernism* developed in direct response to the revolution in the visual arts. This difference of approach not only influences Schmidt's reading of Williams's poems (or the selection of the poems treated); it also leads to a different conception of those aspects of Dada, Precisionism, and Cubism that are considered vital or fruitful for Williams's own achievement.

The differences between my own approach and Sayre's book, on the other hand, are of another kind. Sayre fully identifies Williams's aesthetics with the formalist approach, that is, with the need to foreground in multiple ways the status of the work of art as artifact: a created object of its own that must never be mistaken for the reality it refers to. The importance of this dimension is amply confirmed in the present book, but I will argue that it must not be regarded as determining the poem to the point that it becomes irreconcilable with other important dimensions – above all Williams's conviction that there exists a deeper connection between artifact and thing-world: The work of art comes alive by sharing the life of the object it "imitates." The poem, in other words, is for Williams a product of the imagination that enables us to empathize with the world of nature because the re-creative mind and nature are correlative and extend each other.

The importance of this basic tension in Williams's poems between the referential and self-referential dimensions, between the poem as an autonomous work which yet depends on the deeper connections to the empirical world it refers to, is stressed in several recent interpretations of Williams's aesthetics, most notably Charles Altieri's *Painterly Abstraction in Modernist American Poetry* and Albert Gelpi's *A Coherent Splendor*. Both Altieri and Gelpi see Williams's achievement essentially in terms of this double fascination with the poem as a plastic medium and as an object endowed with the power of reference.

In this respect Williams's poetics anticipates what has sometimes been regarded as a typically Postmodernist attitude: a poetics of participation which, in Altieri's words, essentially "seeks to uncover the ways man and nature are unified, so that value can be seen as the result of immanent processes in which man is as much object as he is agent of creativity."[5] My own approach here, unlike Sayre's, endorses the interpretation first advanced by J. Hillis Miller in his seminal chapter on Williams in *Poets of Reality,* albeit not in the sense that the poet's self fuses with the world it mediates to the point of total obliteration.

To say therefore that Williams takes us beyond a rigid dualism of self and other, subject and object, is not to deny the existence of a separate self. With Joseph Riddel we could say that, "[o]n the contrary, it [Williams's attitude] affirms both the finite self and its finite imagination. . . . The self closes with the other; it wanders in the intimacy of a world which like itself is governed by change, growth, and decay. Neither the self nor nature has an essence, except in the necessity of their relationships."[6] This, basically, is the phenomenological stance behind Williams's famous dictum, "No ideas but in things" (*P,* 6, 9).

As a consequence of this, the most fundamental tension underlying Williams's poetics is the double awareness of the work of art as a separate reality *and* as an "imitation" of the world at large because of the essential kinship between the experiential self and the outside world. This means that both the formalist impulse and the will to establish that essential "contact" with the empirical world are constantly at work in Williams's poems, which hence are largely the result of the complex ways in which these basic forces interact with, and work against, one another.

For both of these fundamental dimensions Williams discovered important sources of inspiration in the visual arts. All of the revolutionary movements, from Cézanne and the Fauvists through Cubism, Futurism, and Vorticism to Dada and Surrealism, stressed the autonomous nature of the work of art and insisted, in the words of the Cubists, on the painting as a *fait pictural.* All of these movements, however, also eschewed total abstraction and insisted on the necessity of figuration, since all of them regarded art as a heterocosmos that loses its deeper meaning the moment it abandons its connection with the empirical world. Reference is often made in this context to the turning point in the history of Cubism. At the end of its "analytic" phase Picasso and Braque had reached the point of nearly total abstraction; at that moment they realized that to abandon representation also meant giving up the possibility of foregrounding the problems of artistic creation and of the viewer-response dimension that were so essential to them. Even Kandinsky, the only artist who had gone over to total abstraction in 1911, insisted on what we could call the isomorphic nature of his art, regarding his forms and colors as a means of representing the object-world stripped, as it were, of all accidentals in order to arrive at the pure "inner sound" of things.

Stressing the object character of the work of art, therefore, did not entail severing the ties with the outside world; on the contrary, many Modernists strove to develop an art that conveyed or embodied a *more essential* dimension of the reality referred to. In this respect Williams was inspired and/or confirmed in his own energy-oriented aesthetics by such movements as Vorticism and Futurism, as well as Kandinsky's theories of expression and Pound's concept of the ideogram, developed by way of Fenollosa's writings on the Chinese ideogram. All of these movements and theories share the notion that art should be related to a universe of process and interaction; in writing this means that, among other things, one should accurately mime these processes by using transitive verbs instead of nouns, since nouns are products of the categorizing habits of the mind, with a far too static and abstract concept of "the real."

The call for "contact" that Williams developed in this context was directly related to the need to create an indigenous American art. Genuine "contact," Williams and his artist friends believed, could be established only with one's own immediate environment; and since in all viable art sharp attention to the particulars of such an environment was identical with attention to the vital underlying processes manifest in each of them, the particular *was* the universal, as Williams never tired of stressing.

This meant that the poet can be "both local (all art is local) and at the same time . . . surmount that restriction by climbing to the universal in all art." Poetry then, like all art, can and must be the result of the artist's attempt "to lift an environment to expression" (*SL*, 286). This was a conviction, Williams discovered, that in his own particular situation had far-reaching consequences with regard to both iconography and form. The artist who tried to be "a mirror to this modernity" (*CP1*, 108) had to reflect contemporary America in all its aspects – above all the innumerable things banished from traditional art as banal or ugly. As a consequence, poetic or artistic form had to be the result of an adaptation of the revolutionary European achievements to the specific American needs – it had to highlight its own status as an artifact or *made* thing but at the same time had to be capable of accommodating the "actual" in all its manifestations. The synthetic form evolving from these needs is another version of the basic tension in Williams's poems between the concrete and the abstract, the referential and the self-referential, the one and the many, and it was once again inspired by achievements in the visual arts, ranging from Gris's Synthetic Cubism to Duchamp's ready-mades and the Precisionist adaptations of Futurism and Cubism developed by Williams's friends Demuth and Sheeler.

Thus all the subsequent chapters take up in one form or another the rich balance to be found in Williams between, on the one hand, this concept of the poem as an artifact that "deals with words and words only" (*I: SA*, 145) and, on the other hand, his fidelity to the poem as a means "through metaphor to reconcile / the people and the stones" (*CP2*, 55) – that is, fidelity to the poem as a field of action "transfused with the same forces that transfuse the earth – at least one small part of them" (*I: SA*, 121). Each chapter deals with the analogies between these basic aspects and the corresponding structural elements in the visual arts.

Invariably, the relationships between the different art media are grounded in analogy and not identity, as Williams was well aware. A case in point is iconicity, dealt with mainly in the last chapter. The iconic dimension, albeit important in many Williams poems, always interacts with the symbolic dimension (as defined by C. S. Peirce and Jakobson),[7] since Williams works with both the imitative and the systemic nature of language. Thus, to start with, he tried to exploit the analogy of poetry and painting by asserting that "a design in the poem and a design in the picture should make them more or less the same thing."[8] "Design," in both media, can be both concrete and abstract, both mimetic and nonimitative, and thus a poem, in its overall concrete or iconic design, can visually embody what it refers to in its words. But since design can also be abstract or nonmimetic, the words on the page, Williams realized, could as well be arranged in a stanzaic form that, in its arbitrariness, mirrored not only the arbitrariness of the sign but, once again, the status of the poem as artifact.

Thus on the visual or spatial level the poem, like the painting, could work with the tension between mimesis and creation. On the other hand, the generation of meaning in all language unfolds in time, and thus Williams, working with, and not against, the sequential nature of language, extended the iconic dimension into the temporal level: In the arrangement of words and lines on the page his poems reflect how the self – step by step, moment for moment – explores the environment. Williams, in other words, embodies on the iconic level not only the objects themselves but also the processes by which these objects are perceived. But on this level, too, his poems are once again imitative *and,* at the same time, part of an autonomous linguistic structure, since both the tension between lineation and syntax and the distribution of the words on the page also highlight the nature of the poem as artifact.

Thus iconicity is part of the mimetic or "imitative" dimension, rooted in an organic form that interacts with (or counteracts) the "design" imposed on the poem by "an Objectivist writer whose characteristic form is Cubist construction made of free-verse units."[9] This basic tension is finally resolved (or relinquished) in the longer poems of the fifties, which are devoted less to foregrounding the object character of the poem and more to emphasizing voice and the spoken idiom, devoted less to the enactment of sense experience and more to reveries and meditation, to explicit musing and the intense effort to explain the meaning of past events and experiences. Poems such as "Asphodel, that Greeny Flower" or *Paterson,* Book 5, mark the peak of a major change whose first occurrence, as Stephen Tapscott notes, is to be found in the second book of *Paterson:*

> The famous example of this discontinuous development, of course, is the appearance of the tri-partite line – as early as Book 2 of Paterson – in a brooding section about history, memory, and the (female) park at the outskirts of the (male) city: "The descent beckons / as the ascent beckoned." Later, by the time of "Asphodel," Williams had consolidated the formal discovery, recognizing the thematic uses to which it could be put. In this context, I think, it's clear that something

happened through *Paterson* 3 and 4; gradually the visual, Cubist form of the poem shifted toward more spoken forms. ("Williams, Sappho, and the Woman as Other," p. 30)

Paterson is thus essentially a work of transition, in which Williams gradually moves beyond the Imagist and Objectivist poetics which is the subject of the present book. Although the overall structure of *Paterson* is unthinkable without the collage form derived from Modernist painting, it in many ways leads beyond the poetics and aesthetics informing Williams's previous poetry, and it can be properly appreciated only if one takes into consideration the specific ways in which Williams's Objectivist poetics interacts with, and finally gives way to, the new style that fully emerges in the 1950s.

To conclude these opening remarks, it seems important to stress that this book is not limited to the relationship between Williams's poetry and the visual arts in the sense of clear-cut influences only. Rather, it sets out to establish some of the deeper analogies between several art forms and many artists whose achievements may be related on the basis of direct or indirect influence *or* on the basis of phenomena that exceed these categories altogether. The deeper connections are important on all levels, but to distinguish clearly between them is often difficult or downright impossible. Williams himself, and many of his artist friends of the New York avant-garde, regarded their theories and achievements largely as the result of a collective enterprise, and although there are many instances where direct influence is evident and/or acknowledged, the work of an individual artist or writer is also imbued with innumerable cultural and aesthetic stimuli that lead beyond any specific single source. In view of the speed with which, since the late nineteenth century, avant-garde publications, art periodicals, exhibitions, books, and personal contacts have disseminated artistic styles and ideas, the notion of influence, though still viable, has to be qualified and expanded. The deeper relevance of Williams as poet, after all, is rooted in the fact that his artistic achievement, beyond its personal, retraceable history, is an important embodiment of the *Zeitgeist* and thus reflects many of the fundamental issues of the age.

Prelude

Getting in Touch

On February 17, 1913, the Armory Show opened in New York. In this huge exhibition the revolutionary European movements in the visual arts, such as Postimpressionism, Fauvism, Cubism, and Futurism, were introduced to the general American public for the first time, side by side with a comprehensive show of progressive American art. The exhibition was an object of derision and amusement to the vast majority of visitors and critics alike, but it deeply impressed a number of artists and critics, who were increasingly dissatisfied with the triteness and utter conventionality of the established artistic forms. Their main reaction was one of fascination and excitement: The revolutionary European art threw the provincial and conventional character of most of their own products into sharp relief and created in turn an intense hope for an American art of equal temerity — for an art that would neither ignore what had happened outside America nor withdraw from the crass contemporary world of materialism and science into the creation of spurious idylls based on an anemic idealism. The feeling of hope for an imminent fundamental change has been well described in a number of studies, such as those by Milton Brown and Meyer Schapiro:

> About 1913 painters, writers, musicians, and architects felt themselves to be at an epochal turning-point corresponding to an equally decisive transition in philosophic thought and social life. This sentiment of imminent change inspired a general insurgence, a readiness for great events. . . . The world of art had never known so keen an appetite for action, a kind of militancy that gave to cultural life the quality of a revolutionary movement or the beginnings of a new religion.[1]

All of Williams's own comments on the Armory Show reveal this same feeling of elation:

> There was at that time a great surge of interest in the arts generally before the First World War. New York was seething with it. Painting took the lead. We were tinder for Cézanne. I had long been deep in love with the painted canvas through Charles Demuth but that was just the beginning. . . . Then the Armory Show

8

burst upon us, the whole Parisian galaxy, Cézanne at the head, and we were exalted by it. (*A*, MS version, Williams files, YALC)

In several ways Williams was ready to be deeply influenced by the show and the subsequent excitement.[2] Introduced into the world of art through his mother's still lifes, he had shown a keen interest in painting from the beginning. Even after he had begun to write, he toyed with the idea of becoming a painter for several years. His early friendship with Demuth, whom he met in 1905 in Philadelphia, was the first of several intimate relationships with painters, such as those with Charles Sheeler and Marsden Hartley. Other contacts of primary importance were those he established later in 1913 with the New York avant-garde circles in which artists from various camps – writers, painters, photographers, composers, and so on – were closely associated for the whole of the coming decade.

In the fall of 1913 Williams met Alfred Kreymborg, who was about to publish the little magazine then called *Glebe,* and who had agreed to publish Pound's *Des Imagistes.* When Pound sent Kreymborg the poems for the anthology, he told him in the accompanying letter to "get in touch with old Bull."[3] Kreymborg belonged to a group of artists who formed a little artists' colony at Grantwood near Richfield, New Jersey. In summer 1913 Man Ray and Samuel Halpert had found what Williams described as "several wooden shacks there in the woods." "Several writers were involved, but the focus of my own enthusiasm was the house occupied by Alfred and Gertrude Kreymborg to which, on every possible occasion, I went madly in my flivver to help with the magazine which had saved my life as a writer" (*A*, 135). The magazine was *Others,* successor to *Glebe,* and Williams was to meet there, among others, Orrick Johns, Malcolm Cowley, Man Ray, Alanson Hartpence, Peggy Johns, Mina Loy, and "the great Marcel [Duchamp], who would be there now and again" (*A*, 135). Through Kreymborg and Demuth, Williams was soon introduced into the two other centers of the avant-garde, Stieglitz's gallery, 291, and Walter Arensberg's apartment on West 67th Street.[4]

Together with Edward Steichen, Stieglitz had opened his *Little Galleries of the Photo-Secession* (called "291" after its address on Fifth Avenue) in 1905, and from 1908 onward he presented a series of shows by Rodin, Matisse, Toulouse-Lautrec, Henri Rousseau, Cézanne, and Picasso. It was for all of these artists their first exhibition in the United States, and Stieglitz was not exaggerating when he wrote to a friend that the Armory Show was "really the outcome of the work going on at '291' for many years,"[5] although he was not directly involved in its organization. Of equal importance was Stieglitz's famous periodical *Camera Work.* At first exclusively devoted to artistic photography, it soon developed into the most important periodical for avant-garde activities in all the visual arts.

After the Armory Show Stieglitz concentrated his efforts more and more on propagating and supporting the Americans among the early Modernists, such as the painters John Marin, Arthur Dove, Marsden Hartley, Georgia O'Keeffe, Charles Demuth, and the photographer Paul Strand.

Among the third group of artists to gather around Walter Arensberg were the New York Dadaists. Marcel Duchamp, who moved into a "studio" at the Arensbergs' immediately after his arrival in New York in 1915, was the most important of a large group that included the Frenchmen Picabia, Gleizes, Henri-Pierre Roché, and the composer Edgar Varèse. They were joined by a number of young American painters – Man Ray, Demuth, Joseph Stella, Morton Shamberg, and Charles Sheeler – and writers such as Kreymborg, Williams, Allan Norton, Mina Loy, and Amy Lowell. Among a large group of less regular callers were Alfred Stieglitz, Wallace Stevens, and Isadora Duncan. Last but not least were a few *enfants terribles*, such as the adventurer Arthur Cravan, who claimed to be a nephew of Oscar Wilde, and the Baroness Elsa von Freytag-Loringhoven. Cravan produced one of the earliest happenings at the 1917 Independents Exhibition. He was supposed to give a lecture on modern art before an audience that consisted largely of society ladies and gentlemen, but he arrived completely drunk and had hardly staggered to the speaker's desk and started his lecture when he began undressing himself. Arensberg and his friends were delighted by the resulting tumult, and Duchamp called the evening a true Dada event.

Elsa von Freytag-Loringhoven, who was over fifty at the time, was an eccentric who once shaved and painted her head and wore assorted tools as embellishments; she was one of Duchamp's protégés and made her own object-art in the wake of his ready-mades. When Williams met her, he was fascinated; for him she embodied a Europe as steeped in culture as it was decadent. On the other hand, Williams was for her a primitive American hick whom she offered to turn into a true Dionysian artist by letting him become her syphilitic lover. His refusal led to some violent scenes, which, as Williams put it, "all but finished me."[6]

Williams's immersion in the activities of the New York avant-garde movement of those years was of crucial importance for his whole future career. For the first time he had found his own people; for the first time he really felt in touch. It did not even matter that "no one knew consistently enough [what they were seeking, so as] to formulate a 'movement.' " "Here was my chance, that was all I knew. There had been a break somewhere, we were streaming through, each thinking his own thoughts, driving his own designs toward his self's objectives" (*A*, 148, 138). One thing, however, was obvious: For the really new, for the revolutionary discoveries, one had to go to the visual arts. And ultimately these discoveries were applicable to literature, too, for "impressionism, dadaism, surrealism applied to both painting and the poem" (*A*, 148).

At the beginning there was a feeling of liberation, simple and pure. " 'The Nude Descending a Staircase'," Williams wrote in his *Autobiography*, fifty years after seeing it for the first time, "is too hackneyed for me to remember anything clearly about it now. But I do remember how I laughed out loud when I first saw it, happily, with relief" (134). And elsewhere he said that at this moment he had felt "as if an enormous weight had been lifted from my spirit for which I was infinitely grateful."[7]

The weight that he felt taken from him was "the accumulated weight of a thousand voices in the past," as he wrote in an essay on Whitman some years later, voices that make up "the structure of the old," which "says no! to everything in propaganda and poetry that wants to say yes. Whitman broke through that. That was basic and good" (*SE*, 218). Thus a new reading of Whitman – his wife had given him a copy of Whitman's poems on the first of March 1913 – induced in him the same feeling of liberation that he experienced even more intensely when he was confronted with "the whole galaxy" of the revolutionary European artists:

> As I look back I think it was the French painters rather than the writers who influenced us, and their influence was very great. They created an atmosphere of release, color release, release from stereotyped forms, trite subjects. There was a lot of humor in French painting, and a kind of loose carelessness. Morals were down and so were a lot of other things. For which everybody was very happy, relieved.[8]

This passage shows that the revolution was recognized as both one of form and content from the very beginning. Williams and his friends were aware of the fact that, together with the formal and iconographical conventions in the visual arts, many of the traditional notions of ideality, of which these conventions were an expression, were also discarded. Critically or apologetically the new art introduced many hitherto ignored aspects of the contemporary world, above all the modern industrial and urban environment. Moreover, the laws of perception themselves and thus the very nature of empirical reality, as opposed to the nature of the work of art, became a basic theme; perspectival illusionism, which had reigned before the advent of late Impressionism, was replaced by a daring and often humorous exploration of the fundamental problems of artistic representation.

For Williams a similar revolution in poetry promised to overcome the "deadness of copied forms" and shatter the "tyrannies of the past" (*SE*, 218). It also promised to open up whole new spheres, such as the world he knew from his private life and daily work as a doctor – a partly suburban, partly urban and industrial environment – which contained a wealth of subject matter that so far had been excluded from poetry as "low," banal, insignificant. Williams was now fully aware that discovering its richness entailed a rejection of the traditional notions of beauty, with their inherent categories of the refined and primitive, significant and insignificant, meaningful and meaningless.

Thus "a local assertion" was an assertion of new values, and the creation of new forms was the attempt "to force [the poem] into approximation with experience rather than reading – bringing a whole proximate 'material' into view" (*A*, 148). It had taken Williams years to discover this ultimate aim of his poetry, and it was to take a lifetime to explore it.

Williams could not have achieved what he did if he had been alone. He was carried first by the tremendous "surge of interest in the arts" in the wake of the Armory Show, and by the common goals he shared with his friends and fellow combatants among the avant-garde movement. But he was unique not only in insisting that an indigenous American poetry should be created by "lifting an environment to expression," but also in his lifelong attempts to adapt the innovations in the visual arts to his own poetic needs and ends.

Chapter 1

"A Poem Can Be Made of Anything"

"The Wanderer," published in *The Egoist* in 1914, is the first poem that testifies to Williams's willingness to embrace the present-day reality of his immediate environment as his world, however repellent it may often be. Williams once described "The Wanderer" as "a reconstruction from memory of my early Keatsian Endymion imitation" (*IWW*, 25–6), a long narrative poem he had been working on while doing his internship around 1908. It was about a young prince who has been abducted at his wedding feast and is wandering about in a strange country, trying in vain to recover his past and his home. But although the later poem is based on the earlier one in its plot structure, it is entirely antithetical in its essence – whereas in the epic fragment the prince's dissociation from his environment is complete and the loss of his native land irrevocable, "The Wanderer" enacts the hero's homecoming, the ecstasy and the terror he experiences while he is being initiated into his world under the guidance of a goddess.

In the second part of "The Wanderer," this goddess is Demeter, disguised as a crone while wandering through the world on her search for her daughter Kora, who had been abducted by Hades. In the disguised goddess

> age in age is united –
> Indifferent, out of sequence, marvelously!
> Saving alone that one sequence
> Which is the beauty of all the world . . .
> (*CP1*, 28)

Williams discovers that an imaginative view of reality sees all ages in one age, all places in one place, all possibilities in a given actuality. Each age, even if it is debased and degraded, contains the past and therefore "the beauty of all the world," however hidden or distorted. In such an age a goddess disguised as a crone, "walking imperious in beggary," is the appropriate guide. Demeter searching for Kora, the goddess of spring, embodies life (or an age, a culture) in wintertime, and she helps the poet to envisage, beyond its present barrenness, its hidden significance and beauty.

Thus, "to lift an environment to expression" (*SL,* 286) entailed for Williams, among other things, to discover and recreate the timeless in the present, the universal in the local. It also meant that the poet, in a painful process of rebirth, had to find the sources of his art in the violent and chaotic energies of an ever-changing present, which he had to accept to the point of becoming a part of it:

> Then she leaping up with a great cry –
> Enter youth into this bulk!
> Enter river into this young man!
>
> Then the river began to enter my heart
> Eddying back cool and limpid
> Clear to the beginning of days!
> But with the rebound it leaped again forward –
> Muddy then black and shrunken
> Till I felt the utter depth of its filthiness
> The vile breath of its degradation,
> And sank down knowing this was me now.
>
> (*CP1,* 35)

This crucial passage makes it obvious that Williams's passionate identification with the here and now does not make him a full-fledged Futurist, as Monroe Spears, among others, maintains, although it may lead him to adopt a Futurist stance in those poems that enact the discovery of the beauties of the technological world in epiphanic moments.[1] Poems such as "The Great Figure," "Overture to a Dance of Locomotives," and "The Attic Which Is Desire:" could be called Futurist poems, but they have to be placed within the larger context of Williams's experience of the world in its totality. An empathetic identification with the world, such as it is programmatically enacted in the leap into the Passaic, entails embracing the basic polarities underlying all manifestations of reality, in order to achieve a poem whose network of interrelated polarized forces is a veritable field of action. Each word in such a poem has to be a vector, a force at the disposal of the poet, who should be

> a man
> whose words will
>   bite
>   their way
> home – being actual
> having the form
>   of motion
> (*CP1,* 339)

In those moments of revelation, in which Williams manages to transcend his empirical self, he moves beyond the Romantic dichotomy between subject and object and recognizes in himself "the same forces which transfuse the earth" (*I: KH,* 121). His self, in Joseph Riddel's words, "closes with the other; it wanders in the intimacy of a world which like itself is governed by change, growth and decay. Neither the self nor nature has an essence, except in the necessity of their relationship."[2] Williams will henceforth speak for the earth in all its aspects. Within this basic task – which he later called "through metaphor to reconcile / the people and the stones" (*CP2*, 55) – nature remains a touchstone for civilization, as does, by extension, the rural for the urban. If the city embodies civilization's desires, dreams, hopes, and aspirations, perpetually thwarted and perpetually renewed, rural life is a more elementary world, with its basic antagonistic forces less disguised. It is, moreover, Williams's personal ground: "I was always a country boy, felt myself a country boy. To me the country world was a real world but none the less a poetic world" (*IWW,* 33). Once people in the city, as in "The Wanderer," are "divorced" from nature, they have lost contact with the life-giving roots, with the godhead itself: "Nowhere you! Everywhere the Electric!" (*CP1*, 31) The poet's task, in the words of the goddess who leads him into the Jersey mountains, is to rouse the people by leading them back to the vital source:

> . . . look child, look open-mouth!
> The patch of road between precipitous bramble banks,
> The tree in the wind, the white house, the sky!
> Speak to them of these concerning me!
> For never while you permit them to ignore me
> In these shall the full of my freed voice
> Come grappling the ear with intent!
> At which I cried out with all the might I had,
> Waken! O people, to the boughs green
> With unripe fruit within you!
> Waken to the myriad cinquefoil
> In the waving grass of your minds!
> Waken to the silent Phoebe nest
> Under the eaves of your spirit!
>
> (*CP1*, 32)

Throughout Williams's work the juxtaposition between the two realms of nature and civilization, city and country, the synthetic and the natural, will be one of the basic polarities. Among the early poems exploring this juxtaposition are two with the title "Pastoral." In one of them (*CP1*, 70) the behavior of the quarreling sparrows is juxtaposed with the seemingly more civilized pursuits of humanity; the second part of the poem, in which the old man gathers dog-lime and "walks in the gutter / without looking up" with a tread that is "more majestic than / that of the Episcopal minister / approaching the pulpit / of a Sunday," is an implicit analogy to the first part. In both parts a straightforward, single-minded behavior is set against a more "refined" behavior, and in each case the values behind the traditional notions of culture are revealed as inadequate. Stylized, formalized, ritualized behavior can be empty and spurious, while its absence reveals a new dignity.

Williams's assessment of these values can be placed within the larger context of the rejection of the genteel tradition by the poets of the *Others* group. Van Wyck Brooks, who was one of the earliest critics to see the "new poetry," as it was sometimes called, within this larger perspective, noted that it attacked the general assumption that "the only hope for American society lay in somehow lifting the 'Lowbrow' element to the level of the 'Highbrow'." The new poets, on the other hand, discovered such qualities as "a certain humanity, flexibility, tangibility" in the lower levels of society and upheld them against the "glassy inflexible priggishness" of those classes responsible for "Highbrow" culture.[3] Other critics argued, as James Oppenheim did, that "perhaps the raw appetite is wiser than the 'fine taste.' If one must choose, there is much to be said for the street and the mill and the saloon, and all places where life is a hot flame, and not the curling wisp of incense."[4]

Williams's own vitalistic outlook found recurrent expression in images of fire and flame, especially in images where a fiery energy is suppressed, smothered, hidden, or contained by the dominant forces in society. The poet's task is to uncover the "radiant gist" and the "cold fire," or again – as Williams once described the purpose of *In the American Grain* – "to draw from every source one thing, the strange phosphorus of the life, nameless under an old misappellation" (*IAG*, Foreword, n.p.).

Thus one of the important aspects of raising an environment to expression was to assess the values of a less refined but more vital indigenous culture. As a result of this, the very term "culture" had to be redefined, as Williams recognized. He was possibly influenced in this respect by Kreymborg and those members of the *Others* group who had been familiar with the Stieglitz circle and *Camera Work*, the organ that had, as early as 1905, advocated a development of cultural sensibilities, so as to be able to respond favorably to the primitive quality of an America transformed by an expanding technology.[5]

Williams and Duchamp: Redefining Art and Culture

The view that there was a close connection between primitivism and technology was not shared by Williams, but it indirectly supported his own attempts at fundamentally revaluating contemporary civilization. And while the group of poets around Kreymborg and Williams were still fighting for a marginal recognition – "we were destroyers, vulgarians, obscurantists to most who read," Williams recalls in his *Autobiography* (148) – they gained important support through the enthusiasm of the French Dadaists for America's technological culture. Of special importance here were certain statements by Duchamp, whose *Nude Descending a Staircase* had been the pièce de résistance of the Armory Show, and who was therefore a celebrity from the very moment he arrived in New York in 1915. In several interviews he championed the new (and America, in its essence, *was* the new to him), declaring, "we must learn to forget the past, to live our own lives in our own time." Also he admired New York as "a complete work of art," the apotheosis of change, progress, and the "scientific spirit" of the twentieth century, of American growth as opposed to European decadence.[6] "From the very instant one lands," he declared, "one realizes that here is a people yearning, searching, trying to find something."[7]

Duchamp's attitude strengthened Williams's own rejection of the traditional notions of art and culture with their narrowly circumscribed standards of taste and artistic achievement. ("Everything, no matter what it is must be re-valuated," he wrote some years later in *The Great American Novel* [I, 172].) Duchamp's most spectacular attacks against these notions were his ready-mades – objects like his bicycle wheel, bottle rack, shovel, and urinal – which, according to his theory, were turned into works of art by the mere fact that he had chosen them. His ready-mades were broadside attacks not only against the conventional notions of suitable subject matter but against the definition of a work of art as a unique artistic creation, bearing the imprint of the artist's personal vision of reality.

Although Duchamp denied that the objects he had chosen had any aesthetic merit in themselves, he could not prevent their aesthetic dimension being discovered, through their displacement and defamiliarization, by those few who, like Williams, were not outraged but highly stimulated and exhilarated. Williams's description of Duchamp's ready-made *Fountain* (Figure 1) as "a magnificent cast-iron urinal, glistening of its white enamel" (*A*, 134) is revealing in this respect. Duchamp himself was not quite consistent in his argumentation, since almost all of his ready-mades were products of the "scientific spirit" he had hailed, products whose artistic value he pointed out in the very defense of his urinal after it had been rejected by the committee of the 1917 Independents Exhibition: "The only works of art America has given are her plumbing and her bridges."[8]

Not only do we find passages in Williams's writings that endorse this attitude,[9] but Williams's own procedure in many of his poems from 1914 onward was closely related to Duchamp's, though it was less radical and less spectacular. Such a poem as "Pastoral" (*CP1*, 64), written at a time when he had probably neither seen nor heard of Duchamp's earliest ready-mades, contains a veritable list of things that have the same value: They, too, function as *objets trouvés* whose utter insignificance from a conventional point of view clashes with the high value placed on them by the speaker:

> When I was younger
> it was plain to me
> I must make something of myself.
> Older now
> I walk back streets
> admiring the houses
> of the very poor:

      roof out of line with sides
      the yards cluttered
      with old chicken wire, ashes,
      furniture gone wrong;
      the fences and outhouses
      built of barrel-staves
      and parts of boxes, all,
      if I am fortunate,
      smeared a bluish green
      that properly weathered
      pleases me best
      of all colors.

         No one
      will believe this
      of vast import to the nation.

In this poem – as in many later ones, such as "The Red Wheelbarrow," "Between Walls," "The Great Figure," "Perfection" – the assessment of the "supreme importance" (*CP1*, 206) of the *objets trouvés* in their momentary constellations is essential. The poems are acts of affirmation *and* defiance because they all stress the value of what, from an ordinary point of view, is utterly banal. Hence titles such as "Pastoral" are much less ironic than is often assumed. These poems are enacted discoveries, and they are of the greatest importance to the poet, although (or because) "No one / will believe this / of vast import to the nation."

    Through a radical revaluation, "contact" with the immediate ground is established, and each poem is a discovery that contributes toward an indigenous art based on the appraisal of an indigenous culture. "The one quality that gives art any reason for being," Robert McAlmon wrote in *Contact*, which he co-edited with Williams, "is the exuberance and impact behind it, of a personality discovering reality for itself."[10]

    Since Williams's main goal in these poems is not a debunking of conventional attitudes but an assertion of new values, it is necessary for him at this stage to point out didactically the importance of the seemingly banal. Ideally, Williams had already recognized at this time, things should speak for themselves (*IWW*, 21), and he gradually developed subtler rhetorical means to achieve his aims; but even in his most didactic poems the clash between the value attributed to the depicted objects and their seeming triviality creates a tension that adds at least as much to the impact of the poems as it detracts from them. It is part of their basic anecdotal structure, with a narrative nucleus of the speaker/poet confronting his world. "Observations are processes here, not results," as Whitaker aptly remarks.[11]

    Whereas in the earliest of these poems Williams often starts with one or several images and then, at the end, asserts their meaning, he later often anticipates it and thus creates a specific expectation:

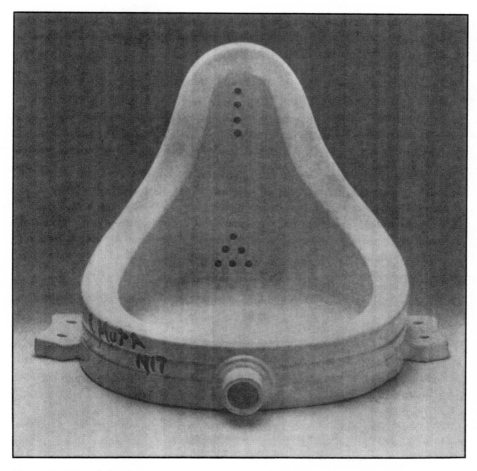

Figure 1. Marcel Duchamp, *Fountain*. Ready-made, New York, 1917. Original lost. Replica, 1964. Arturo Schwarz Collection, Milan. Reproduced by permission.

So much depends
upon

a red wheel
barrow . . .
               (*CP*1, 224)

or:

I must tell you
this young tree . . .
               (*CP*1, 266)

Another procedure is to start with lavish praise and then add a detail that takes us by surprise and lets us recognize that the poem deviates radically from a traditional attitude to the things depicted:

PERFECTION

O lovely apple!
beautifully and completely
rotten . . .
(*CP2*, 80)

Together with the title, the device of invocation and the exclamation in the first line create the expectation of a poetic world with a suitably lofty style, which is then debunked in two steps: "O lovely . . . " clashes first with "apple." The apple itself is surely not an appropriate subject for an invocation, although it is at least familiar as a classical motif in painting. But then, as soon as we have adjusted to the level of a still life, we are confronted with an even more unexpected continuation:

beautifully and completely
rotten

The poem as a whole repeats these juxtapositions in a subtler way, gradually adjusting our vision until we understand and empathize with the speaker's delight in the perfection revealed by the last stage of the cyclic process of growth and decay:

O lovely apple!
beautifully and completely
rotten,
hardly a contour marred –

perhaps a little
shrivelled at the top but that
aside perfect
in every detail! O lovely

apple! what a
deep and suffusing brown
mantles that
unspoiled surface! No one

has moved you
since I placed you on the porch
rail a month ago
to ripen.

No one. No one!

An early poem with the same device of opening invocation is "Smell!" (*CP1*, 92), where the speaker seems to evoke a sublime landscape in the first line, only to deflate those expectations by the word "nose" at the beginning of the second line. (The nose is invoked here as a kind of ersatz muse, a guide to the treasures of the world around the poet):

> Oh strong-ridged and deeply hollowed
> nose of mine! what will you not be smelling?

In his first critical essay, "America, Whitman, and the Art of the Poetry" (1917), Williams stressed the urgent need for an American poetry that was "free to include all temperaments, all phases of our environment, physical as well as spiritual, mental and moral. It must be truly democratic. . . . "[12] Forty years later, looking back on this lifelong concern of his, he said in an interview: "Anything is good material for poetry. Anything. I've said it time and time again" (*P*, 222). His 1917 essay was a homage to Whitman, the "first primitive," the "rock" and foundation of everything to come; there was no progress unless the poets had "grasped Whitman and built upon him" (29, 31).

Dada

In his own time it was chiefly painting that offered an art of equal daring, especially the Dadaists with their revolutionary acts of defiance and derision. They had perfectly understood that in the arts "there is nothing sacred. . . . There is nothing . . . but change and change is mockery" (*I: KH*, 13). At times Williams felt closely akin to this Dada spirit of mockery – "I didn't originate Dadaism but I had it in my soul to write it" (*IWW*, 60) he said later – but on the whole he was more eager to stress the "Pleasures of Democracy," as the subtitle he once planned for *Al Que Quiere!* indicates. It was important to discard Beauty with a capital B, but it was even more important to discover and assess a new beauty in the familiar but habitually rejected objects of the everyday world, to create beauty by means of that "transforming music that has much to do with tawdry things" (*SE*, 20).

In order to achieve this, one had to come to terms with the chaos of modern life, create order out of disorder, discover beauty where others perceived trash only. In one of the short stories written in the thirties there is an almost pro-grammatic statement of the process involved. The doctor-narrator, looking at the many things piled up in the living room of one of his patients, tries to find out why "the whole place had a curious excitement about it for me, resembling in that the woman herself, I couldn't precisely tell why":

> There was nothing properly recognizable, nothing straight, nothing in what or-
> dinarily might have been called its predictable relationships. Complete disorder.
> Tables, chairs, worn-out shoes piled in one corner. A range that didn't seem to

be lighted. Every angle of the room jammed with something or other ill-assorted and of the rarest sort.

I have seldom seen such disorder and brokenness – such a mass of unrelated parts of things lying about. That's it! I concluded to myself. An unrecognizable order! Actually, the new! And so good-natured and calm. So definitely the thing! And so compact. Excellent. And with such patina of use. Everything definitely "painty." Even the table, that way, pushed off from the center of the room. ("Comedy Entombed: 1930," *FD,* 327)

There is something liberating and highly stimulating in this "unrecognizable order," liberating by its very negation of "predictable relationships." Gradually, under the apparent brokenness and chaos a new order becomes visible to the discerning eye, "good-natured and calm," "compact," and "definitely 'painty'," an order that seems related to an artist's sensitivity, utterly different from the compulsively maintained and often stifling order in the traditional sense of the word.

With his reference to painting in this passage Williams might well have had in mind the Junk Art of such Dada painters as Schwitters and Janco or of such Dada-influenced Americans as Stella, Dove, and Maurer (Figure 2). The meaning of their collages and assemblages must have been apparent to him when he saw them, or heard of them, for the first time around 1920, recalling to him his own poems in which he tried to assess the beauty of the seemingly random assortment of "ugly" things. It is also true that many of the statements of the Dadaists about Junk Art reveal a similar feeling of liberation. "It remained an adventure to find even a stone, a clockwork, a small streetcar ticket, a beautiful leg, an insect, to experience the corner of your own room; all this could mobilize pure and spontaneous feelings," wrote Marcel Janco.[13] And Richard Huelsenbeck said in 1920 that although it was true that Dada was an "expression of the times," including "the despair of [finding] a meaning or a 'truth'," Dada was no less a liberation and a basic affirmation of life:

> From the everyday events surrounding me (the big city, the Dada circus, crashing, screeching steam whistles, house fronts, the smell of roast veal) . . . I become directly aware that I am alive, I feel the formgiving force behind the bustling of the clerk in the *Dresdner Bank* and the simple-minded erectness of the policeman.[14]

The same spirit of the "release of SOMETHING" (*I: GAN,* 174), as Williams put it in a passage that alludes to Duchamp's urinal, was pervasive among the New York Dadaists. "I was stimulated by everything," Man Ray recalled in an interview with Arturo Schwarz:

> M.R.: In the street, walking along, I would pick the things that would stimulate me and that nobody else would notice – especially the things that others wouldn't notice.

Figure 2. Kurt Schwitters, Merz Picture 31A, *Cherry Picture* ("Merzbild 32A, Das Kirsch-bild"). 1921. Collage of cloth, wood, metal, gouache, oil, cut-and-pasted papers, and ink on cardboard, 36⅛ × 27¾ in. Collection, The Museum of Modern Art, New York. Mr. and Mrs. A. Atwater Kent, Jr., Fund. Reproduced by permission.

A.S.:   Like the crushed tin can you picked up on 8th Street and transformed into an art object merely by giving it the title *8th Street!*

M.R.:   Exactly![15]

The similarities between Williams's attempts and those of the Dadaists should not obscure the differences in their formal means and strategies. The montage technique of the Dada collages and assemblages anticipated those of Surrealism, while Williams's poems of that period were more traditional insofar as they were still built around a coherent narrative nucleus. Moreover, Williams's poems were basically acts of affirmation, while the Dada creations were often born of nihilistic despair. "Disgusted with the World War butcheries," wrote Hans Arp, "we devoted ourselves to the fine arts. While far away the heavy firearms thundered we sang, painted, glued, nailed, wrote our poems wholeheartedly. We sought an elementary world that would heal man from the madness of the time and create a new order."[16]

But even here there are affinities. In 1920 Williams had written to a friend that disgust was his "most moving emotion" (*SL,* 146), and in almost everything he wrote there was more than a grain of the *épater le bourgeois* attitude of Dada, clearly visible, for instance, in his frequent attacks on the established cultural institutions. Some of these attacks against the current state of American poetry around 1920 were as fierce as any of that time. In "Belly Music," written in 1919 for *Others,* Williams inveighed against the stultifying concept of the beautiful which lay behind the policy of the editors and the "sophomoric, puling, nonsensical" critics: "The American editorial – and critical mind is hipped on the question of 'good stuff,' especially if it be 'lovely.' But for the reason that American editors, critics, publishers do no more than this they merit only to be branded and ignored." In opposition to an art based on past aesthetic norms of the precious and rarefied, Williams insisted on an art that was the creative product of a constant awareness of the artist's own time and hence, by necessity, always changing, always new. What was needed was "not one more lovely poem" but "the NEW, the everlasting NEW, the everlasting defiance."[17]

Thus Williams, like the Dada artists, rebelled against the narrow concepts of art and culture prevalent at that time. Their appreciation of the common and seemingly trivial things, on the other hand, can be seen as part of a counter-culture set up against the attitude of the vast majority. What is revealing in this context is the affection for things marked by time and usage, things that are worn out and show "patina of use," or objects that, with a life of their own, seem to refuse to be subjected to a rigid order. Hence Williams's delight in the houses of the poor in "Pastoral," with their roofs "out of line with sides" and their "furniture gone wrong" (*CP*1, 64). Here the poet's or the painter's approach clashes most vividly with a conventional point of view. From the latter point of view these are all objects that either function badly or have ceased to function at all and have therefore lost their raison d'être, whereas from a non-utilitarian angle they come alive the very moment their functional side is absent: Now we can be affected by them as objects qua objects and are no longer put off by seeing them as mere means to an end.

Of course, Dada artists were not the only kindred souls in this respect; among his contemporaries, it was to painters in general that Williams felt close in spirit, many of whom showed the same fascination with the world of things. Intuitively, or consciously like Williams, they saw in this lack of appreciation and reverence for common things one of the causes for the destructive spirit of their civilization. Objects were used and then discarded. For Williams and many other vanguard artists in the 1920s this destructive spirit originated in the hostility of the Puritans toward all physical forms of life, an attitude that urged Americans to exploit nature rather than enjoy it and to act "as if the earth under our feet/were/an excrement of some sky," as Williams writes in "To Elsie" (*CP1*, 218). Northern New Jersey, whose rural and unspoiled character was almost completely destroyed during Williams's lifetime, was a constant visible proof to him that "Waste! Waste! dominates the world" (*CP2*, 324). Once, Williams writes in his *Autobiography,* there were many springs in the region, some of them "kept beautifully." Later they were all gone because "the people that went there . . . actually shat in it, stole the pipe, killed the fish, dumped garbage, tramped the grass, the usual thing" (*A,* 383).

Least deformed by this mentality and therefore least estranged from the physical world, Williams discovered, were the "common people." Among them one could still find "Men intact – with all their senses waking," with a "directness . . . which reformers, that is to say, schemers, commonly neglect, misname, misapprehend as if it were anything but to touch, to hear, to see, to smell, to taste" (*IAG,* 206). Among the traits that Williams found in them were the "delicious sincerity of pioneer people" (ibid.), an admirable singleness of purpose (as shown by the old man gathering dog-lime), or a frank appreciation of the sensual or sexual that often triumphs over a false restraint. An example of the latter is the old man's behavior in "Canthara" (*CP1,* 78):

> The old black-man showed me
> how he had been shocked
> in his youth
> by six women, dancing
> a set-dance, stark naked below
> the skirts raised round
> their breasts:
> 　　　　　bellies flung forward
> knees flying!
> 　　　　　　　　　– while
> his gestures, against the
> tiled wall of the dingy bath-room,
> swished with ecstasy to
> the familiar music of
> 　　　　　his old emotion.

The tension in this poem results from the contrast between the old man's moral outrage at the beginning and the subsequent delight revealing itself in his gestures that "swished with ecstasy to / the familiar music of / his old emotion." "We are reminded," wrote Williams in a later essay, "that the origin of our verse was the dance – and even if it had not been the dance, the heart when it is stirred has its multiple beats."[18] The heart, one might add, has its own reasons; and the primitive order of the dance is, in Joseph N. Riddel's words, "anterior to consciousness" and "takes place in the world of innocence, its form dictated not by a prescribed choreography but by improvisation stimulated by the response of the whole self to another or to a thing" ("The Wanderer and the Dance," p. 55). Thus the old man, who at first seems imprisoned in a set of conventions and whose responses seem dictated by institutions and "–isms," frees himself easily by the body language of his movements – in themselves a kind of dance – in which a prereflective consciousness becomes manifest. (Similarly the old man gathering dog-lime has a body language that reveals his harmonious relationship to the "pastoral" world around him.)

The dance – one of Williams's favorite images for the poem – is form being born, meaning generated by the response of "the whole self to another or to a thing." In a poem like "Danse Russe" (*CP1*, 86), in which the poet himself is the dancer, the dance is at once the poem and the making of the poem, the dancer/poet realizing himself in his act. This means that he transcends and affirms his self simultaneously – a self that embraces, and identifies with, the other – and he realizes that his self has its essence in its relationship with the world around him and is thus "the happy genius of [his] household." As a self that generates order, on the other hand, he has by necessity a separate identity: "I am lonely, lonely./ I was born to be lonely,/ I am best so!"

Thus all of these poems are enacted discoveries, with the poet as a "wanderer" who discovers his intimacy with the other; and the form of these poems is a process that leads the poet, by his attentiveness to the silent language of things or human beings, to the revelation of a "hidden order." Each of these poems is – metaphorically and sometimes also literally – a dance, since each generates its meaning in the moment of its making.

Kandinsky's "Constructional Tendencies"

On the level of subject matter the provocative works of the Dadaists were highly stimulating for Williams with regard to the necessary ousting of all established art forms and the championing of a new art that reflected the contemporary world in all its aspects. Dada was a striking proof that "a poem can be made of anything" (*I: KH*, 70). On the formal level, Dada innovations helped Williams to discover poetic ways of tearing down the "constant barrier between the reader and his consciousness of immediate contact with the world" (*I: KH*, 88). By

inserting bits and pieces of unmediated "found" language he could insert veritable *objets trouvés,* or by building the poem around moments in which the poet
discovers things that can function as *objets trouvés* he stressed the magic inherent
in things that were previously completely excluded from poetry as trite and
therefore antipoetic.

Many further impulses came from almost all the other revolutionary movements in the visual arts. One of the great painters and theorists, Wassily Kandinsky, also exerted a considerable influence on Williams.[19] Mike Weaver was
the first to point out that Kandinsky's *Concerning the Spiritual in Art* seems to
have provided Williams not only with the subtitle "Improvisations" for *Kora in
Hell* but also with three categories that served as an outline for his own basic
poetic modes.[20] Here are Kandinsky's three categories, or "sources of inspiration":

1. A direct impression of nature, expressed in purely pictorial form. This I call an
   "Impression."
2. A largely unconscious, spontaneous expression of inner character, non-material
   in nature. This I call an "Improvisation."
3. An expression of slowly formed inner feeling, tested and worked over repeatedly and almost pedantically. This I call "Composition." Reason, consciousness, purpose, play an overwhelming part. But of calculation nothing appears:
   only feeling. (p. 77)[21]

Weaver, correctly to my mind, links Williams's pastorals and portraits – his
predominant form between 1913 and 1916 – to Kandinsky's "Impressions";
Kora in Hell, on the other hand, as the subtitle indicates, is the literary
equivalent of Kandinsky's "Improvisations." The poems that could be clas-
sified as "Compositions" are those which resulted from Williams's endeavor
to get away from "free verse" – a contradiction in terms, as he soon realized
– to a form that was neither too rigid nor so free as to become nearly amorphous. The gradual emergence of a poetic form, between the late 1910s and
the early 1920s, that was orally *and* visually patterned, testifies to this struggle. It may well have been Williams's painter's bias that led him to his dis-
satisfaction with the form of the "Impressions" and to his search "for some
formal arrangement of the lines, perhaps a stanzaic form." "I have always
had something to say," he recalled later, "and the sheer sense of what is
spoken seemed to me all important, yet I knew the poem must have shape.
From this time on [i.e., the publication of *Al Que Quiere!* in 1917] you can
see the struggle to get a form without deforming the language" (*IWW,* 23;
notice Kandinsky's corresponding effort to create "Compositions" in which
"of calculation nothing appears: only feeling").

If Kandinsky's three "sources of inspiration" provided Williams with categories for his own poetic modes,[22] it is possible that he was also influenced by

the two "constructional tendencies" which Kandinsky directly related to the
three categories quoted earlier:

> These tendencies fall into two divisions:
> 1. Simple composition, which is regulated according to an obvious and simple
>   form. This kind of composition I call *melodic*.
> 2. Complex composition, consisting of various forms subjected more or less com-
>   pletely to a principal form. The principal form may be hard to detect, and by
>   the same token it increases its inner resonance. This kind of composition I call
>   *symphonic*.
>
> Between the two lie various transitional forms in which the melodic principle
> definitely exists. The history of the development is closely parallel to that of music
> (*CSA*, 76).[23]

Williams's first attempt at writing a poem that moves, in Kandinsky's terminology, from the "melodic" to the more complex "symphonic" form is "Jan-
uary Morning" (*CP1*, 100). The subtitle "Suite" could refer to Kandinsky's
"constructional tendencies" and indicate that the poet is trying to achieve the
composite form of a suite by a succession of more or less self-contained "melodic" imagistic units. Some of these units can be related to one another by the
principle of opposition – as theme and countertheme, so to speak – juxtaposing,
for instance, inertia and movement, dreariness and exhilaration, constraint and
liberation:

XIII

Work hard all your young days
and they'll find you too, some morning
staring up under
your chiffonier at its warped
bass-wood bottom and your soul –
out!
– among the little sparrows
behind the shutter.

XV

. . . .
Well, you know how
the young girls run giggling
on Park Avenue after dark
when they ought to be home in bed?
Well,
that's the way it is with me somehow.

Other units could be called equivalents: that is, they are similar in one respect
and dissimilar in another; musically one could call them variations of a common
theme:

II

Though the operation was postponed
I saw the tall probationers
in their tan uniforms

          hurrying to breakfast!

III

— and from basement entries
neatly coiffed, middle aged gentlemen
with orderly moustaches and
well brushed coats

This overall structure is often repeated within the individual units, as in the following one where the images of winter in the first part of the unit and summer in the second are related by contrast as well as by analogy:

X

The young doctor is dancing with happiness
in the sparkling wind, alone
at the prow of the ferry! He notices
the curdy barnacles and broken ice crusts
left at the slip's base by the low tide
and thinks of summer and green
shell-crusted ledges among

          the emerald eel-grass!

Even on the level of the smallest details the organizing principles of analogy and contrast can be detected. Thus the soft movement of the "exquisite brown waves" with "long circlets of silver moving over [them]" in section IX has its equivalent in the "emerald eel-grass" of the next section, while on the level of contrast in both instances the harmony evoked by the gentle movement of these things and the play of light over them is juxtaposed with the harshness of the "crumbling ice crusts among [them]" (IX) and the "shell-crusted ledges" (X).

Ready-mades and Objets Trouvés

Kandinsky's theories were of primary importance for Williams not because of the frequent analogies to music but because they figured prominently within the multifaceted movement in the visual arts away from a mimetic mirroring of the surface of things toward an exploration of the essence of inner and outer realities in various nonnaturalistic art forms. One of the most revolutionary steps was taken by the Cubist painters, when they began to represent objects from several angles at the same time and thus achieved a multiplicity of perspectives by mounting different viewpoints. Montage after that became a structural device of crucial importance,[24] and Williams was one of the earliest poets in America who realized that it could be adapted to new uses in poetry. One possibility, he discovered, was to take words, phrases, and slogans from newspapers, billboards, and the like and insert them as ready-mades, so to speak, into his poems. If Duchamp revealed the formal properties of his bicycle wheel, bottle rack, shovel, and urinal by virtue of their displacement,[25] Williams revealed the intrinsic poetic qualities of *all* language by taking bits and fragments out of their original context and putting them into a poem just as they were found. This was, in a way, a logical extension of the procedure in those "impressions" which enacted the discovery of *objets trouvés* by the poet.

Of course the choice of his found phrases, slogans, and signs is not purely accidental. They are inserted to show the poetic qualities of precisely those things that had been considered antipoetic from a traditional point of view: advertising slogans (*CP1*, 232), a list of ice cream flavors (*CP1*, 335), street signs (*CP1*, 325), a grocery list:[26]

> 2 partridges
> 2 Mallard ducks
> a Dungeness crab
> 24 hours out
> of the Pacific
> and 2 live-frozen
> trout
> from Denmark
> (*CP2*, 208–09)

The rhythm of these bits of found language is as specifically American for Williams as the things named are part of contemporary (American) civilization. (This, of course, does not define or exhaust their meaning; the specific form of each of these linguistic "ready-mades" or *objets trouvés* entails its own effect and has to be taken into consideration if we want to assess its impact or meaning. Thus the list quoted above, on one level a simple enumeration, contains innuendos of advertising slogans which result, together with the speaker's equally implicit delight about the exotic food available on the market, in a playful – and partly ironic? – tone of its own, a tone and a meaning that is in turn modified by the context of the whole poem, as we shall see later.) Williams tirelessly pointed out that, here and elsewhere, neither the "found" language nor the things denoted are antipoetic; the fact that Wallace Stevens had used the term in connection with Williams's poems had particularly annoyed him – if Stevens did not understand what it was all about, who would?

Thus, when Williams was once asked by an interviewer to reveal the meaning of the grocery list, he pointed out that "rhythmically it's organized as a sample of the American idiom" (*P*, 222) – hence it is an *objet trouvé* which, by its inherent formal properties alone, is a tiny part of an indigenous American art. This interview – or parts of it, to be precise – was again used as a found object by Williams when he inserted it, together with other letters, quotations, newspaper passages, historical records, and the like into *Paterson*. The contrast between these ready-made passages, inserted in the manner of a collage, and the poet's own language (which, again, comprises not only both verse and prose but also imitations of other styles, historical and contemporary), is important for the poem as a whole, and neither the inserted bits and pieces nor the prose parts are "antipoetry" set against the poetic passages proper. "All the prose," Williams wrote to a friend,

> has primarily the purpose of giving a metrical meaning to or of emphasizing a metrical continuity between all word use. It is *not* an anti-poetic device, the repeating of which piece of miscalculation makes me want to puke. It *is* that prose and verse are both *writing*, both a matter of words and an interrelation between words for the purpose of exposition, or better defined purpose of the art. (*SL*, 263–64)

Ready-mades or *objets trouvés* of another sort are the "verbal transcriptions" of the spoken American idiom as Williams found it among his friends and patients, bits and pieces of conversation, overheard and recorded by the poet as vital, living speech: "The physician enjoys a wonderful opportunity actually to witness the words being born. Their actual colors and shapes are laid before him carrying their tiny burdens which he is privileged to take into his care with their unspoiled newness" (*A*, 361). In some of these poems Williams achieves a rare concentration, directness, and authenticity. In "To Close" (*CP2*, 232), for instance, the choking anxiety of the parent comes through in the last line of the poem with an immediacy that could not have been achieved by any other means:

> Will you please rush down and see
> ma baby. You know, the one I talked
> to you about last night
>
> What's that?
>
> Is this the baby specialist?
>
> Yes, but perhaps you mean my son,
> can't you wait until   ?
>
> I, I, I don't think it's brEAthin'

Others are very funny, like the following "Detail" (*CP2*, 20), but the *comédie humaine* behind it is without the faintest trace of that condescension which so often characterizes the literary usage of idiomatic language:

Doc, I bin lookin' for you
I owe you two bucks.

How you doin'?

Fine. When I get it
I'll bring it up to you.

The effect here depends not only on the idiom, with its specific rhythmic qualities, but also on the apparent non sequitur, revealing a poor man's strategy that
ensures him at least *this* doctor's sympathetic understanding.

Art as "Construction"

Thus Williams discovered, around 1920, that the poet, who works with words,
uses "prefabricated" material; hence he is a "bricklayer" who "builds" his poems
as an architect builds a house: "Yes, writing is bricklaying," he wrote to his
friend Kenneth Burke in 1921. "L'architecture c'est poser un cailloux sur un
autre. You like that? My brother handed it to me. I wish he really knew what
it means" (*SL*, 55). And whether he builds his poems from the ground up, so
to speak, or whether he works with structures that, in part or wholly, were so
felicitously prearranged when he found them that he could use them such as
they were, is not a fundamental difference but one of degree only.

Williams's friend Charles Demuth once used the same metaphor when he
was asked by an interviewer, "What would you most like to do, to know, to
be? (In case you are not satisfied.)" He answered: "Lay bricks. What it's all
about. A bricklayer."[27] This response, incomprehensible to the critics and therefore taken as a proof of Demuth's strong Dada affinities, reveals the same concept. If words were the bricks of the poet, then lines, forms, and colors were
the bricks of the painter. Creating new images, according to this theory, consisted of using the existing material as a means to new ends.

We do not know whether it was Williams, Demuth, or someone else who
created the metaphor of bricklaying; the concept of artistic creation which it
entails, however, seems to have gained wider currency in the second half of the
nineteenth century. Paul Valéry equated artistic creation and *construction* in an
essay on Leonardo in 1894, and for Cézanne the same word was a key term for
the artistic process.[28] Theories of art as construction played an important part in
various Postimpressionistic art forms, above all in Cubism and related movements. Juan Gris, whose paintings Williams especially admired and whose most
important theoretical statements he was to read in the *transatlantic review* in 1924,
stressed the notion of painting as *architecture plate et colorée*. Piero Della Francesca
was rediscovered as one of the originators of an art that stressed architectural
design: Vorticism, according to Pound, "was a renewal of the sense of construction . . . , an attempt to revive the sense of form – the form you had in Piero

Della Francesca's *De Prospettive Pingendi*."[29] And Charles Sheeler, who became Williams's close friend after the two met in the early twenties, wrote about his first encounter with Piero's frescoes: "It was a revelation to me. . . . I discovered Piero Della Francesca at Arezzo – you saw pictures that were really planned like a house. By an architect. One doesn't build a house just on impulse. They didn't start piling bricks hoping it would turn out to be a house. They really did have their blueprints."[30]

At the beginning of the 1920s Williams's notion of the poet as bricklayer or architect also helped him to blend his need for an indigenous American art based on the here and now with the current propagation of American technology and a new popular culture based on it, as was advocated by Duchamp and Picabia and by such periodicals as *291, 391, The Soil, Secession,* and (in its later issues) *Broom.*[31] In an editorial in *Contact* Williams stated that it was "by paying naked attention first to the thing itself that American plumbing, American shoes, American bridges, indexing systems, locomotives, printing presses, city build-ings, farm implements and a thousand other things have become notable in the world." Based on this he believed that "in the arts discovery and invention will take the same course. And there is no reason why they should unless our writers have the inventive intelligence of our engineers and cobblers."[32]

To the same degree that Williams developed his constructivist theory of art – a theory that would finally lead to the provocative definition of the poem as "a small (or large) machine made of words" (*CP2,* 54) – he was increasingly dissatisfied with imagistic theories. "Imagism," he said later in a talk in 1948, "was not structural: that was the reason for its disappearance" (*SE,* 289). There is no doubt that Imagism was a potent force in Williams's work in the crucial years when he abandoned his Keatsian imitations: "The immediate image, which was impressionistic, sure enough, fascinated us all," he wrote in the *Autobiography* about the years after the Armory Show. "We had followed Pound's instructions, his famous 'Don'ts,' eschewing inversions of the phrase, the putting down of what to our senses was tautological and so, uncalled for, merely to fill out a standard form" (*A,* 148). But if one were to stress the imagistic elements in Williams's poems without, at the same time, pointing out other crucial elements in his art form, one would miss the essence of his poetry. Moreover, such a poem as

> a black, black cloud
> flew over the sun
> driven by fierce, flying
> rain

written when he was eighteen (*A,* 47; *IWW,* 4), bears witness to the fact that he was writing imagistic verse at a time when Imagism was not yet inaugurated at all, and that Imagism in general and Pound's early poetry in particular helped

Williams to rediscover his original impetus toward a poetry that shared with Imagism its clarity, precision, and concentration, yet in other aspects (such as its iconography and its peculiar verbal dynamism) pointed forward to a poetic form of his own.

Chapter 2

Vortex; or, A Thing Is What It Does

In many respects Williams's imagistic poems are closer to Pound's aims and theories as outlined in his essays on Vorticism and Fenollosa than to Pound's (or anybody else's) Imagist poems. Of special relevance are Pound's increasing doubts around 1912–13 about the validity of conventional notions of metaphor and simile, doubts that were considerably increased when in late 1913 he became acquainted with Fenollosa's insistence on the verb as the essence of language and his own subsequent convictions that the predicational, verbal force was a decisive element of poetic impact. Thus he wrote to Iris Barry in 1916:

> You should have a chance to see Fenollosa's big essay on verbs, mostly on verbs.
> . . . He inveighs against "IS," wants transitive verbs. "Become" is as weak as "is."
> Let the grime *do* something to the leaves. "All nouns come from verbs." To primitive man, a thing only IS what it *does*. That is Fenollosa but I think the theory is a good one for poets to go by.[1]

In the course of his new discoveries many of his imagistic poems (which retrospectively may have appeared to him as "a flirtation with a poetic of stasis," as Hugh Kenner puts it),[2] must have become at least somewhat problematic. Thus *Gaudier-Brzeska* contains several passages that reflect Pound's attempts to come to terms with both the virtues and the drawbacks of one of the basic practices of Imagism, the "doubling" of images. The paradigmatic example for this practice is Pound's famous poem "In a Station of the Metro," in which a literal image is doubled with a metaphorical one, so that the two images together form what Pound calls an "Image" (with a capital) or "one-image poem," which he defines as "a form of super-position, that is to say . . . one image is set on top of another" (*Gaudier-Brzeska*, p. 89):

> The apparition of these faces in the crowd;
> Petals on a wet, black bough.

That the two images are indeed related on the basis of a metaphor or hidden simile is also indicated by the colon which Pound used in the first published

35

version ("The apparition of these faces in the crowd: / Petals on a wet, black bough."[3]). "In a poem of this sort," Pound explains, "one is trying to record the precise instant when a thing outward and objective transforms itself, or darts into a thing inward and subjective" (p. 89).

However, Pound's Vorticist terminology makes it clear that he was not primarily concerned with the *tertium comparationis* introduced via the metaphorical hinge but with the peculiar impact of the welding of images that turns the poem into a "cluster of fused ideas . . . endowed with energy." What Pound envisages here becomes clearer in a later chapter in *Gaudier-Brzeska,* in which the poetic theory evolving out of the one-image poem is outlined at greater length. This time the starting point is an explicit simile, namely,

The pine tree in the mist upon the far hill looks like the fragment of a Japanese armour

which Pound analyzes as follows:

The beauty of this pine-tree in the mist is not caused by its resemblance to the plates of the armour.

The armour, if it be beautiful at all, is not beautiful *because* of its resemblance to the pine tree in the mist.

In either case the beauty, in so far as it is beauty of form, is the result of "planes in relation."

The tree and the armour are beautiful because their diverse planes overlie in a certain manner.

There is the sculptor's and the painter's *key.* The presentation of this beauty is primarily his job. And the "poet"? "Pourquoi doubler l'image?" asks Barzun in declaiming against this "poésie farcie de 'comme'." The poet, whatever his "figure of speech," will not arrive by doubling or confusing the image.

Still the artist, working in words only, may cast a more vivid image of either the armour or the pine by mentioning them close together or by using some device or simile or metaphor, that is a legitimate procedure of his art, for he works not with planes or with colours but with the names of objects and properties. It is his business so to use, so to arrange, these names as to cast a more definite image than the layman can cast; in the like manner it is the painter's or the sculptor's business so to use his planes, his colours, his arrangements that they shall cast a more vivid, a more precise image of the beauty upon the mind of his spectator, than the spectator can get of himself or from a so different department of art. (*Gaudier-Brzeska,* p. 121)

Pound's ambivalent attitude in this passage toward the use of metaphors and similes is resolved for the moment by accepting the use of metaphors not for the implied resemblance between tenor and vehicle but for the specific beauty that results when the "diverse planes" of the two images "overlie in a certain manner" and thus create a fruitful tension. That the relationship between the two images need not be a metaphorical one is implied in the phrase that the poet "may cast a more vivid image of either of the armour or the pine by mentioning them close together," a phrase that recalls an earlier statement in which he conceived of words as electric poles or cones, radiating lines of force: "[T]hree or four words in exact juxtaposition are capable of radiating this energy at a very high potentiality."[4]

In Pound's theoretical writings of those years, images abound in which he conceived of art as a patterned force or energy, energy with a shape. He saw the artist as a counterpart to the modern scientist, for whom energy "has no borders" and is "a shapeless 'mass' of force." "The rose that his magnet makes in the iron filings does not lead him to think of the force in botanic terms, or wish to visualize that force as floral and extant (*ex stare*)." The modern artist, on the other hand, should be in the footsteps of the medieval "natural philosopher" who "would probably have been unable to think the electric world, and not think of it as a world of forms."[5]

Pound's concept of poetry as shaped energy is directly connected to a number of metaphors derived from sculpture and painting. He regarded "exact definition" and "clear, shape-giving bounds" as equally important in the visual arts as in poetry. Strength, energy, impact depended for him to a large extent on the "beautifully definite," while "vague suggestion" (as found in Symbolism, for instance) was linked with the "amorphous" and with "the petrified and the copying," which he regarded as typical of all art forms lacking in creative energy.

The artists Pound specifically had in mind as his models at that time were first of all Gaudier-Brzeska and Wyndham Lewis. Many of their statements offer direct parallels to Pound's own words, such as Gaudier-Brzeska's credo, "I shall present my emotions by the arrangements of my surfaces, the planes and lines by which they are defined," or Lewis's, "What made me . . . a painter, was some propensity for the exactly-defined and also, fanatically it may be, the physical or the concrete."[6]

Williams's theoretical statements between 1917 and 1923 (as outlined mainly in the "Preface" to *Kora* and the prose sections of *Spring and All*) offer numerous parallels and similarities to Pound's tenets. Williams shows an even stronger aversion to a poetry relying heavily on overt metaphors and similes:

> Although it is a quality of the imagination that it seeks to place together those things which have a common relationship, yet the coining of similes is a pastime of very low order, depending as it does upon a nearly vegetable coincidence. Much more keen is that power which discovers in things those inimitable particles of dissimilarity to all other things which are the peculiar perfections of the things in question. (*I: KH,* 18)

Thus both Pound and Williams argue in favor of a poetics of economy, objectivity, and precision, a poetics that leads – through the attempt at gaining intensity by ellipsis and a sharp, nondiscursive juxtaposition of images – to a poetry of the nonmimetic. One of the important common origins of such a poetics is found in the early theoretical justifications of nonmimetic forms in the visual arts, such as outlined by Henry van de Velde and Wilhelm Worringer as early as 1902 and 1908, respectively. Worringer maintained in his highly influential book *Abstraktion und Einfühlung* (which was also an acknowledged source of Hulme's theories) that there had been throughout history a constant alternation of naturalistic with nonnaturalistic styles; in the latter, organic nature was reduced to linear-geometric forms and represented by the interaction of lines, forms and colors.[7] And van de Velde wrote in 1902: "A line is a force acting similarly to all elemental forces; several lines brought into contact but repugnant to each other have the same effect as several elementary forces in opposition."[8]

Beyond Mimesis

Theories like these helped such painters and sculptors as Kandinsky, Klee, Lewis, Gaudier-Brzeska, and others on their way from a figural to an abstract art. Of course most of them resisted total abstraction, and poetry – with rare exceptions (as evident in some Dada verse) – was tied to the concrete. However, Pound and Williams, both excited and encouraged by what was happening in the visual arts, thought these ties very compatible with a poetic form that would go beyond the *purely* mimetic. As early as 1912 Pound had written, "In every art I can think of we are damned and clogged by the mimetic," and in 1915 Pound's friend May Sinclair wrote of Imagism (as redefined by Vorticist theories), "Presentation not representation is the watchword of the school . . ."[9]

The same fundamental opposition underlies Williams's theories in *Spring and All*. Art, he writes, is "not a matter of 'representation' . . . but of separate existence" (*I*, 117), and the poem is not to hold "a mirror up to nature" (*I*, 150), "nor is it description nor an evocation of objects or situations merely" (*I*, 149). But neither is it "to avoid reality," or to "use unoriented sounds in place of conventional words" (*I*, 150). The poet will come closest to "pure art" therefore "not when his words are dissociated from natural objects and specified meanings but when they are liberated from the usual quality of that meaning by transposition into another medium, the imagination" (*I*, 150). Hence poetry "affirms reality most powerfully" when it accepts, and works with, the referential nature of words, but makes use of them in order to create "a new object, a play, a dance" (*I*, 149–50).

Any poem by Williams is thus conceived as a new object, like the things it celebrates, such as trees, flowers, people, fragments of green glass, and so on, but at the same time it is not a completely separate entity severed from, and unrelated to, empirical reality. The poet, by raising those things to the imagination, creates a poem which is an extension of nature's processes. Nature is thus "not opposed to art, but apposed to it" (*I*, 121), and the two separate realities are related, not because the work of art is "like" the things it refers to but because it is "transfused with the same forces which transfuse the earth – at least one small part of them" (*I*, 121).

What exactly does this mean, and how does Williams attempt to achieve his goal? One of the clearest statements about this crucial point is to be found in a late letter:

> To copy nature is a spineless activity; it gives us a sense of our mere existence but hardly more than that. But to imitate nature involves the verb: we then ourselves become nature, and so invent an object which is an extension of the process. (*SL*, 297)

"We then ourselves become nature": The phrase recalls Williams's primordial union of subject and object, poet and world, inside and outside, which he described in his letter to Marianne Moore, and which is programmatically enacted for the first time in "The Wanderer," where the young protagonist plunges into the "filthy Passaic" and ties his own existence inseparably to the "utter depth of its rottenness" until he can say "I knew it all – it became me" (*CP*1, 35). Each subsequent poem is ideally a reenactment of that first union, whereby the poet's mind – and, by extension, the reader's – is "turned inside out" into the world (*I: KH*, 75), until he achieves an "approximate co-extension with the universe" (*I: SA*, 105).

One of the primary means of reaching this union in poems that are "an extension of nature's processes" is, as we have seen, the verb. By writing poems that consist of primarily verbal (i.e., active, dynamic) structures, and by thus attempting to reach the essence of the world's body – "a thing only IS what it *does*," was Pound's summing up of Fenollosa's findings – Williams creates an imaginary space of empathy, intimacy, and participation. In this space of interpenetration he tries to rejoin the severed realms of inside and outside, man and nature, urban man and man-made environment, in order to fulfill the basic task he had set himself: "to repair, to rescue, to complete" (*SL*, 147).

The most obvious way of using verbs and predicational forms as a means of conveying the energy of nature is of course a rendering of things in motion, and it is significant that this is the essence of the very early "a black, black cloud / flew over the sun / driven by fierce flying / rain" (*A*, 47). It is equally significant that, first, the metaphorical or semimetaphorical terms "flew," "driven," "fierce" and "flying" are all used to enhance the violent motion and inherent energy of nature, and that, second, the "mysterious, soul-satisfying joy" that Williams experienced immediately after having written the poem was "mitigated by the critical comment" on the use of metaphor "which immediately followed it," as he recalled in his *Autobiography:* "How could the clouds be driven by the rain? Stupid" (*A*, 47). Throughout his life Williams was to remain diffident with regard to too facile a use of metaphors and similes, but throughout his life he was to use them as a poetic device for making the energy in things manifest, in all those cases where this energy defied literal description and where it was appropriate therefore "through metaphor to reconcile / the people and the stones." At times it even became possible to move explicitly, by means of metaphors, from the particular to the generic, or from one particular field to another seemingly completely separate one:

A SORT OF SONG

Let the snake wait under
his weed
and the writing
be of words, slow and quick, sharp
to strike, quiet to wait,
sleepless.

– through metaphor to reconcile
the people and the stones.
Compose. (No ideas
but in things) Invent!
Saxifrage is my flower that splits
the rocks.

(CP2, 55)

The snake under the weed can only become the appropriate metaphor for the process of writing if the connotations and associations that go together with the traditional emblematic or symbolic snake have been discarded beforehand. (Part of the poem's effect consists of course in the very act of thwarting the reader's expectations.) "What I put down of value," Williams writes in *Spring and All*, "will have this value: an escape from crude symbolism, the annihilation of strained associations, complicated ritualistic forms designed to separate the work from 'reality' . . . " (*I*, 102). Once these obstacles are removed, once the "associational or sentimental value [which] is the false" is overcome, it becomes possible to "[lift] to the imagination those things which lie under the direct scrutiny of the senses, close to the nose" (*I: KH*, 14). To experience the snake imaginatively, therefore, is to experience its life, its energy; and the poem which is to embody it does so by means of words that are "transfused with the same forces which transfuse the earth – at least one small part of them" (*I: SA*, 121). Or, as Williams states elsewhere, "the word must be put down for itself, not as a symbol of nature but a part, cognizant of the whole" (*I: SA*, 102).

Of central importance for this poetic practice is to reveal the dynamism inherent in things that seem to be purely static and spatial. Hence the tension between the outward stillness and inward motion or hidden energy, which characterizes many of Williams's poems. "The Tree,"[10] although not one of his masterpieces, is an excellent example of that kind of tension:

The tree is stiff, the branch
is arching, arching, arching
to the ground. Already its tip

reaches the hats of the passersby
children leap at it, hang on it –
bite on it. It is rotten, it
will be thick with blossoms in
the spring. Then it will break off
of its own weight or from the pulls
of the blossom seekers who will
ravish it. Freed of this disgrace
the tree will remain, stiffly upright
                    (*CP1*, 263)

The juxtaposition of static and dynamic elements structures the poem on several levels. There is, first of all, a contrast between the "stiff" tree and the children who "leap at it, hang on it – / bite on it," a contrast which is repeated in the second part with its vision of the same tree in the coming spring, when its branch will "break off . . . from the pulls / of the blossom seekers who will / ravish it." (Note how in both instances the sequence of verbs or verbals progresses from the familiar ["leap," "hang"] to the extravagant ["bite"], or from the literal ["it will break off . . . from the pulls"] to the metaphorical ["ravish"].)

This contrast between things *outwardly* static and dynamic finds its analogy in the tension between the outward stasis and the inward dynamism of the tree itself: The opening phrase "The tree is stiff" is immediately followed by "the branch / is arching, arching, arching / to the ground," so that the very stiffness of the tree is felt as a kind of counterpull to the forces of gravitation. The precarious balance in this field of force is enhanced by the fact that the branch is "rotten" (which leads to the anticipation that it will "break off" next spring); on the other hand, the vision of this rotten branch as "thick with blossoms in / the spring" comes as a surprise; the very tenacity of the tree's life as it is envisioned here will, however, cause the branch to "break off / of its own weight or from the pulls / of the blossom seekers." Thus the whole is an intricate little network of interacting forces that lead upward to light and fruition and downward to the ground again, or, through cyclic renewal, to a new flourishing and then to decay, or, equally, through decay to renewal, as the last two lines express: "Freed of this disgrace / the tree will remain, stiffly upright."

"The poem as a field of action": Although Williams seems not to have used this phrase before the 1940s, the concept is outlined in what may be his earliest theoretical statement, the fragment "Vortex" (1915), contained in the Williams collection at the State University of New York, Buffalo. The section quoted below obviously refers directly to Gaudier-Brzeska's credo, "I shall present my emotions by the arrangement of my surfaces, the planes and lines by which they are defined"; and Williams may also have had in mind Pound's discussion of the comparison between the pine tree and the fragment of Japanese armor, in which he defines the resultant beauty of form as one of "planes in relation":

> I meet in agreement the force that will express the emotion by an arrangement of planes.
>
> By planes I take the meaning to include sounds[,] smells, colors, touch in themselves, not outlined by a literal sense.
>
> A literal sense I take to equal the line wherein I am in agreement with Brzeska that the line has no existence being merely the meeting place of planes.

In a longer version of the essay the analogy between literature and the visual arts implied here is stated more explicitly; in addition to this the passage also contains the analogy between the structure of works of art, whether they are made of words, stone, or sounds, and empirical reality itself:

> [I]n using words instead of stone I accept "plane" to be the affirmation of existence[,] the meeting of substances[,] whether it be stone meeting light or perfume striking mountain air or a sound of a certain quality against one of another or against silence.
>
> The affirmation of existence and freedom [is] in the quality of the sound or the perfume or the stone.
>
> The story, literal drawing[,] is the line that has no existence.[11]

For Williams, nature and the work of art, we recall, are not opposed but apposed to each other; both have an existence of their own, and both are, essentially, "the meeting of substances," planes, forces in relation. Predominantly mimetic art forms, such as realism or naturalism, are, according to this conception, much too preoccupied with "the story, literal drawing" or "a literal sense"; thus the line in painting and the discursive language of traditional poetry, which are used primarily for this purpose, have "no existence" artistically.

It was to the nonmimetic art forms therefore (or to the art forms that included the mimetic as one dimension in interaction with others only), such as Postimpressionism, Cubism, and Futurism, that Williams looked for a confirmation of his own poetics. It is interesting to note that Williams's first attempt to formulate a theory of the poem is at the same time the most radical, because it ignores the fact that words always *mean*, even when freed from the task of mere mimetic "copying." Thus his Vortex theory, put into practice, would eventually lead to the hermeticism of *Kora in Hell*, a book whose excellence, as Williams later maintained, was "the disjointing process" (*I: AN*, 285) but whose fault, at the same time, was "the dislocation of sense, often complete" (*I: SA*, 117). After *Kora*, therefore, Williams developed and modified his theory of the poem: It was important, he realized, to transcend the categories of simple copying by which "every common thing has been nailed down, stripped of freedom of action and taken away from use" (*I: AN*, 295–96), but it was equally important to make full use of the referential power of words.

Williams and Kandinsky: Sound and Sense

It seems that here, with regard to this tension between the abstract and the concrete, Kandinsky's theories were once again a rich source. Williams refers to them not only in the *Kora* Preface but also in *The Great American Novel*. He must have been familiar with Kandinsky's theories through the double channel of the painter's own writings and Marsden Hartley's intimate knowledge of the artist, whom he had gotten to know during his Berlin days and whom he admired tremendously. It is impossible to tell, however, whether Williams gained important insights by following Pound's suggestion to "transpose [Kandinsky's] chapter on the language of form and colour and apply it to the writing of verse" (*Gaudier-Brzeska*, p. 86), or whether the Russian painter's theories were mainly a confirmation of conclusions Williams had arrived at independently or through other sources. The latter was true of Pound, who wrote that "when I came to read Kandinsky's chapter on the language of form and colour, I found little that was new to me. I only felt that some one else understood what I understood, and had written it out very clearly" (p. 87). Either way Kandinsky's theories must have been highly stimulating for Williams and at the very least a help to him in clarifying and confirming his own ideas.

Kandinsky's theory of the "internal sound" of things revealed in art, for example, is particularly illuminating with regard to Williams's aims and procedures.[12] According to this theory, a form in painting

1) Either . . . aims at delimiting a concrete object two-dimensionally,
2) Or a form remains abstract, a purely abstract entity. Such abstract entities, which have life in themselves, are a square, a circle, a triangle, a rhombus, a trapezoid, etc., many of them so complicated as to have no mathematical formula. . . .

Between these two boundaries lie the innumerable forms in which both elements exist, with a preponderance of either the abstract or the concrete. (*CSA*, 48)[13]

For Kandinsky, abstract art is a means to reveal the inner resonance, or the "inner sound," that each abstract form possesses of its own. "In a painting, when a line is freed from delineating a thing and functions as a thing in itself, its inner sound is no longer weakened by minor functions, and it receives its full inner power."[14]

Of course, words in literature cannot be wholly abstract, and their power to denote is part of their essence. But words, too, says Kandinsky, are objects that have their own inner sound, a sound that "springs partly (perhaps principally) from the objects denoted. But if the object is not seen, but only its name heard, the mind of the hearer receives an abstract impression only of the object dematerialized, and a corresponding vibration is immediately set up in the 'heart' " (*CSA*, 34).[15] Constant repetition of a word results in forgetting the object it refers to, thus revealing the "pure" sound of the word itself. This is what Kandinsky admired in Maeterlinck (*CSA*, 34), and it is exactly the same effect that Williams praised in Laurence Sterne and Gertrude Stein: "The feeling is of words themselves, a curious immediate quality quite apart from their meaning, much as in music different notes are dropped, so to speak, into repeated chords at a time, one after the other – for themselves alone" (*SE*, 114).

According to Kandinsky, all "organic forms" in art – objects depicted by words in literature, for example, or concrete things delineated in painting – invariably possess an internal "double sound." In this "double sound (or spiritual accord) of naturalism with the abstract" the two sounds or reverberations may either enhance or weaken each other, and they may do so "either by concord or counterpoint" (*CSA*, 49).[16]

One of the texts that shows Williams's own poetics to be closely related to this conception is the interview with Mike Wallace included in *Paterson* 5, in which Williams talks about the meaning of the "fashionable grocery list" included in "Two Pendants: For the Ears." There is, Williams says, "a difference of poetry and the sense. Sometimes modern poets ignore the sense completely. That's what makes some of the difficulty. The audience is confused by the shape of words" – confused by a "shape," Williams implies, which is deliberately pointed out in such poems, as a dimension continually present in language but often ignored. "In prose," Williams adds,

> an English word means what it says. In poetry, you're listening to two things . . . you're listening to the sense, the common sense of what it says. But it says more. That is the difficulty. (*P*, 225)

This added dimension in poetry is the complex overall effect achieved by the interlacing of the individual effects of shape, sound, and meaning, similar to the interaction of the three basic elements in painting: "the action of the color of the object, of its form, and of the object *per se*, independent of either color or form" (*CSA*, 50).

Thus Williams stresses the dimension of sound and rhythm as an integral part of the overall effect of his grocery list and relates it to the language it is written in:

> We poets have to talk in a language which is not English. It is the American idiom. Rhythmically it's organized as a sample of the American idiom. It has as much originality as jazz. If you say "2 partridges, 2 mallard ducks, a Dungeness crab" – if you treat that rhythmically, ignoring the practical sense, it forms a jagged pattern. It is, to my mind, poetry. (*P*, 222)

The "jagged pattern" which Williams relates to another indigenous American art form, jazz, is part of the specific possibilities the American idiom offers to him. It is a language characterized by heavy stresses and a rhythmic vigor all of its own.[17] In such a language rhythm and sound are of special importance with regard to the tension between the individual words, which in their totality make of each poem a field of action with its "rout of the vocables" (*P*, 258), all pulling and pushing against one another at once. Words treated in this way, writes J. Hillis Miller,

> become interjections, exclamatory vocables, substances of sound divorced from any abstract meaning and returned to their primitive power as explosions of linguistic energy, each with its own precise radiance. The relations between the

words seem less those of grammatical meaning than the attractions caused by the juxtapositions of energies. (*Poets of Reality*, p. 302)

In order to assess the effects of the "double sounds" inherent in the interactions of the abstract and the concrete, each individual item has to be seen within its larger context and evaluated as a single element of a larger compositional whole. Thus Williams's grocery list is part of one of his longest nonepic poems of his later years, "Two Pendants: For the Ears" – an unusually dark poem in which Williams desperately tries to overcome one of the great crises of his life, caused by his own impending retirement and his mother's imminent death, to name only two major sources of anxiety and suffering reflected in the poem. Many of the poet's basic resources seem to fail him here or to have become precarious, above all those he shared with his mother, such as the capability of seeing all things "without forethought or afterthought but with great intensity of percep-tion," so that "whatever is before her is sufficient to itself and so to be valued" (*I: KH*, 8, 7). It was this attitude that enabled her to live in an "Eden" that was, for all its being "impoverished and ravished," as "indestructible as imagination itself" (*I: KH*, 7). In "Two Pendants" this ability, lost in his mother, seems to fail the son too, and the darkest moments of the poem record the paralyzing agony of an almost total breakdown of the communication that had existed before, through love and through that imaginative identification with the world at hand which mother and son had previously shared.

The meaning or impact of the grocery list can be assessed only in this context: It is part of Williams's desperate attempt to overcome his paralysis and lead his mother back to their common fascination with the here and now. If in Part I an intense preoccupation with the "particulars of morning" is the only means at hand to overcome the nightmare of the previous night, then in Part II even the most banal particulars of everyday life seem hauntingly desirable to the poet in his shattering helplessness at the bedside of his mother, who is in a coma. The grocery in this context points to his "eagerness for evidences of life con-tinuing like rumors elsewhere," as Neil Myers writes in his sensitive analysis of the poem. Myers's interpretation of the grocery list, however, stresses negative implications only; to him it symbolizes "the easy packaged use of death behind a false plenty of a commercial civilization."[18] It is true that Williams's usual firm foothold in reality is often replaced in this poem by a cleavage between the inside and outside, human beings and nature. The ecstasy of early spring in the first part of the poem, for instance, forms an ironic and almost threatening contrast to feelings of isolation and despair, and the cycle of the seasons is ex-perienced as a "flux (that diarrhea)" (*CP2*, 189), an onrush and transience of life in which generations merge in the poet's mind, leaving him behind:

> – their smiles vanish
> at the age of four. Later they
> sob and throw their arms about my

> waist, babies I have myself delivered
> from their agonized mothers.
>
> (*CP2*, 205)

Although the identification with nature, vital artifact, and the delights of everyday life is fragile and partly failing, it has not lost its redeeming qualities completely; in a moment of one's desperate attempt to overcome a feeling of total paralysis, even the vigor and strength embodied in the "jagged pattern" of the grocery list can be of help. For the moment, though, there seems to be no enhancement of the vigor of the abstract by the concrete; to enumerate the delights brought home by some neighbor from the market seems irrelevant if not offensive, and the list clashes with the simple, direct, and unbearable fact immediately following it: "Elena is dying." It is a refrain that appears throughout this second part, a refrain that, here and elsewhere, juxtaposes the irreconcilable which yet, somehow, has to be reconciled:

> I say to myself
> Now it is spring
> Elena is dying

A little later the trivial list suddenly becomes meaningful on another level: Elena emerges from her coma and surprises the couple looking after her by asking for . . . fish, of all things, and then amazes them by her incredible appetite:

> Has
> she eaten anything yet?
>
> Has
> she eaten anything yet!
>
> Six oysters – she said
> she wanted some fish and that's
> all we had. A round
> of bread and butter and a
> banana
>
> My God!
>
> – two cups of tea and some
> ice cream.
>
> Now she wants the wine.
>
> Will it hurt her?
>
> No, I think
> nothing will hurt her.
>
> She's
> one of the wonders of the world
> I think, said his wife.
>
> (*CP2*, 213–14)

Another level on which the grocery list is meaningful is the contrast between the homely and the exotic. Elena's lifelong dream of living in a refined cultural environment has never come true; since her Puerto Rican days she has led the life of a "despoiled, molted castaway," with her great imagination as her "sole remaining quality" (*I: KH,* 8). She had rejected the culture and environment into which she had been transplanted by her marriage:

> What snows, what snow
> enchained her –
> she of the tropics
> is melted
> > now she is dying
>
> The mango, the guava
> long forgot for
> apple and cherry
> wave good-bye
> now it is spring
> Elena is dying
> > Good-bye
> > > (*CP2,* 207)

Both the fashionable food of the grocery list and the products of the Latin American world Elena comes from contrast with the local environment she always rejected; and when her son brings her a bottle of sherry there is another of those rare moments of genuine contact between mother and son:

> I'm afraid I'm not much use
> to you, Mother, said I feebly.
> I brought you a bottle of wine
> – a little late for Easter
>
> Did you? What kind of wine?
> A light wine?
>
> Sherry.
>
> What?
>
> *Jeres.* You know, *jerez.* Here
> > (giving it to her)
> So big! That will be my baby
> now!
>
> > (cuddling it in her arms)
> *Ave Maria Purissime!* It is heavy!
> I wonder if I could take
> a little glass of it now?
> > > (*CP2,* 213)

If the vigor contained in the "jagged pattern" of the grocery list has a reassuring effect on the son — a vigor sought as an integral element of his own language, the American idiom — it is the sound of the Spanish *jerez* that leads Elena back to the world of her youth and to such childhood memories as the magic of Latin prayers. Mother and son are separated from each other by belonging to different worlds, yet are at the same time united by the son's recognition of the importance of being rooted in a specific environment.

Theories of Expression

In Kandinsky's terminology, we could say that in this poem the "double sound" or "spiritual accord," which results from the interaction of the "organic" or concrete with the abstract, is in each case codetermined by its own interaction with other elements in the larger frame of the work of art as a whole. Each detail therefore depends in its impact, in Kandinsky's words, on "(1) alterations in the relations of one form to another, and (2) alterations in each individual form, down to the very smallest. Every form is as sensitive as smoke, the slightest wind will fundamentally alter it" (*CSA*, 51).[19]

Kandinsky had gone over to total abstraction by the time he wrote this, and he was convinced that abstract painting was a basic means to dis-cover the internal resonance of forms: "The freer the abstract form, the purer and more primitive the vibration" (ibid.). Must we then, he asked,

> altogether abandon representation and work solely in abstraction? The problem of harmonizing the appeal of the concrete and the abstract answers this question. Just as each spoken word rouses an internal vibration, so does every object represented. (*CSA*, 50)[20]

In his important essay "Über die Formfrage" (1912), Kandinsky tried to outline at greater length the formal properties of an art that would, within the realm of the concrete, ideally correspond to abstract art. This "great realism," as he called it, was a nascent art form characterized by, first of all, an attempt at discarding the "superficially artful" and embodying the essence in "a simple ('inartistic') representation of the simple solid object." To discard "conventional and obtrusive beauty" and to concentrate on a straight presentation of things in their essential outward form was, in Kandinsky's view, the surest way of revealing their pure internal resonance ("On the Question of Form," p. 161).

It was of equal importance, he wrote, to render all objects in such a way as to remove them from the realm of the pragmatic and utilitarian ("das Pragmatisch-Zweckmässige"). For Kandinsky, Henri Rousseau was the great master here; equally revealing, he said, were the drawings of children. Both the great naive painter and the child are not yet prepossessed by the pragmatic and util-

itarian view of the world, for they "see everything with fresh eyes" and still
have "the natural ability to absorb the thing as such" ("On the Question of
Form," p. 174). Such an experience is at the furthest possible remove from a
conceptual approach which experiences all objects through the function they
have within the larger network of a world in which everything is seen as logically
and causally connected.

Now, each of the two constitutive traits of Kandinsky's "great realism" is
also a fundamental tenet for Williams. Kandinsky's call for an art that should
discard the traditional notions of the beautiful has its correspondence in Williams's lifelong attacks on too limited a concept of "Beauty," a concept that he
sees as inextricably linked to equally narrow notions of literature itself, or the
meaning of such terms as "tradition," "novelty," "innovation." "What then
would you say of the usual interpretation of the word 'literature'?" the narrator
in *The Great American Novel* is asked in one of the imaginary dialogues. "Per-
manence," he answers. "A great army with its tail in antiquity. Cliché of the
soul: beauty." But, the other protests, "can you have literature without beauty?"
"It all depends," the narrator says, "on what you mean by beauty. There is
beauty in the bellows of the BLAST, etc. from all previous significance. – To
me beauty is purity. To me it is discovery, a race on the ground" (*I*, 170–71).

Such a new beauty based on discovery, however, can only be achieved by
words that are free from "previous significance," words not "bound" to past
literary forms (which in turn are tied to past worlds and past values): "The word
is the thing. If it is smeared with colors from left or right what can it amount
to?" (*I: GAN*, 171). Such poets as Marianne Moore are, in Williams's view,
truly creative because they are using words in such a way as to free them from
past associations, by "wiping soiled words or cutting them clean out, removing
the aureoles that have been pasted about them or taking them bodily from greasy
contexts" (*I:* "MM," 315–16). "If one come with Miss Moore's work to a
friend" who is not familiar with it, Williams writes,

> he will perceive absolutely nothing except that his whole preconceived scheme of
> values has been ruined. And this is exactly what he should see, a break *through* all
> preconceptions of poetic form and mood and pace, a flaw, a crack in the bowl. It
> is this that one means when he says that destruction and creation are simultaneous.
> (*I:* "MM," 308–09)

In *The Great American Novel,* the image used for this necessary breakthrough is
that of a fist going "through the middle of the rose window. . . . Bing! One
accurate word and a shower of colored glass following it. Is it MY fault? Ask
the French if that is literature" (*I: GAN*, 170). The reference here of course is
to Marcel Duchamp, one of whose conversations with Walter Arensberg about
the value of novelty Williams had recalled in the *Kora* Preface: "According to
Duchamp . . . a stained-glass window that had fallen out and lay more or less

together on the ground was of far greater interest than the thing conventionally composed *in situ*" (*I*, 8). Williams shared Duchamp's belief that chance and accident are creative principles that often triumph over outworn artistic conceptions.

It was equally important for Williams to recognize that a new beauty based on discovery would necessarily assume different forms in different environments. If Kandinsky's discoveries were the appropriate ones for Europe, Duchamp's ready-mades (such as the *Fountain*, alluded to in the following passage) were, among other truly creative art forms, important in America:

> Expressionism is to express skilfully the seething reactions of the contemporary European consciousness. Cornucopia. In at the small end and – blui! Kandinsky.
> But it's a fine thing. It is THE thing for the moment – in Europe. The same sort of thing, reversed, in America has a water attachment to be released with a button. That IS art. (*I: GAN*, 173).

Kandinsky himself had pointed out that there was no such thing as an intrinsic superiority of one art form over another: "The artist may use any form which his expression demands; his inner impulse must find suitable external form." This meant that the artist had to "ignore the distinctions between 'recognized' and 'unrecognized' conventions of form," and that "all means are sacred which are called for by internal necessity" (*CSA*, 53). While the opposite principle of "external necessity" produces "conventional beauty" only, internal necessity "knows no such limits and often produces results conventionally considered 'ugly'." The traditional opposition of the beautiful and ugly was therefore untenable for Kandinsky, since " 'ugly' only means 'spiritually unsympathetic,' being applied to some expression of internal necessity either outgrown or not yet attained" (*CSA*, 54, note).

Williams, too, was convinced that genuine beauty was often diametrically opposed to the traditional notions of beauty and that the accusations against the ugliness of modern art were rooted in the modern artist's refusal to "adopt more accepted modes of expression."[21] And for both Williams and Kandinsky it was essential that the artist transcend the traditional conceptual framework that lay behind these accepted modes of perception. Hence Kandinsky's admiration for Henri Rousseau, in whose world things are often no longer logically related, and hence Williams's praise of Gertrude Stein, who had freed words "from the dead weight of logical burdens" (*I*: "WGS," 346) and who had carried to the extreme the necessary "general attack on the scholastic viewpoint, that medieval remnant with whose effects from generation to generation literature has been infested to its lasting detriment" (*I*: "WGS," 346–47). Williams came to believe that the poem especially was fatally limited as long as it was kept wholly within the Procrustean bed of "logicality" – a conceptual framework which for the vast majority of readers was identical with the "so-called research for truth and beauty" but had "the effect of a breakdown of the attention" (*I*: "WGS," 348).

In order to prevent this breakdown of the attention and to pursue the real goal of writing, poetry, in Williams's view, had to abandon "the paralyzing vulgarity of logic for which the habits of science and philosophy coming over into literature (where they do not belong) are to blame" (*I: "WGS,"* 347). It had to embody a more genuine movement – one that would anew "keep a beleaguered line of understanding which [prevents] movement from breaking down and becoming a hole into which we sink decoratively to rest" (*I: "WGS,"* 349).

Thus, together with other early Modernists, Williams reached the conviction that the artist had to transcend the "limits of perception" inherent in Cartesian or post-Renaissance rationalism. In this respect, he became one of the foremost exponents of a multifaceted movement that goes back at least to the second half of the nineteenth century, a countertradition in search of a more immanental or empathetic experience of the object-world. This alternative outlook is to be found, for instance, among the "physiognomists" (i.e., the nineteenth-century theoreticians of perception), the artists and critics in the wake of Cézanne (who was often praised as a "primitive"), as well as the Gestalt psychologists of the early twentieth century.

In all of these movements, theories of expression figure prominently, although the awareness of the expressive dimension as such is of course much older than that. "There is no theory of art, old or new, which ignores this element altogether," writes E. H. Gombrich. "The ancient theory of music, for instance, elaborated the 'expressive' character of modes and keys, orators discussed the physiognomy of words, rhythms, and sounds, and architects had something to say about the physiognomy of the various 'orders' in architecture. Even in the visual arts, the expressive properties of shapes and forms as such were by no means neglected by the writers of the academic tradition." But Gombrich, too, stresses that in this century the attention paid to the expressive dimension reaches a new climax, although he somewhat narrowly regards this change as mainly an outcome of Expressionist art theories.[22]

In addition to the increased emphasis on the importance of expression, one also finds various attempts to put the vastly differing attention paid to it in different cultures into a wider historical perspective. In this respect, Kandinsky is not alone when he relates a high awareness of the expressive properties not only to a "naive" but also to a more primordial experience of reality. "Within the larger dimension of the development of mankind," writes the art historian Hans Sedlmayr,

> as well as in the smaller one of the development of each human being, the ability to grasp the expressive character of things (their physiognomic dimension) is an older and more original way of perceiving the world than is the ability to perceive forms and colors from a purely formal point of view. The child perceives the

expressive properties of things (that is, whether they appear friendly or angry, serene or sad) before it notices colors and forms. . . . The world of the so-called primitive peoples is full of these physiognomic experiences amounting to "compressions," since they are inseparably welded to the perception of the factual characteristics.

Afterward there are two different modes of perception: a primary physiognomical one – in which things, colors, forms, in fact virtually everything, can be experienced as severe or serene, powerful or tired, relaxed or full of tension (to name only a few of the many physiognomic qualities) – and a later, secondary perception of things from a conceptual-formal-technical point of view. Each object and each characteristic can be perceived "objectively" or physiognomically; for instance, a red with so and so much blue or gray or white added would be an example of a color perceived purely with regard to its specific hue, seen as an aspect of the object bearing it. Experienced "physiognomically," on the other hand, "red" is not an optical-spectral entity but something completely different, characterized by its living, "burning," energetic, powerful expression.[23]

Kandinsky devoted an important chapter in *Concerning the Spiritual in Art* to the expressive qualities of colors: the warmth of yellow and the coolness of blue, for instance, with their inherent movement – "the warm colors approaching the spectator, the cool ones retreating from him." Equally important are the excentric and concentric movements, both of them also characteristic of warm and cold colors:

> If two circles are drawn and painted respectively yellow and blue, a brief contemplating will reveal in the yellow a spreading movement out from the center, and a noticeable approach to the spectator. The blue, on the other hand, moves into itself, like a snail retreating into its shell, and draws away from the spectator. The eye feels stung by the first circle while it is absorbed into the second. (*CSA*, 57)

In Kandinsky's view the artist has above all to be susceptible to this expressive dimension of colors and forms; he has to revert back to that primary sensitivity to the impact of all things which children and the so-called primitives alone seem to possess, in an age severely limited and impoverished by its rational-technological outlook.

Again, it is precisely this sensitivity to the expressive dimension of all things that is one of Williams's specific qualities, a sensitivity which results in that rare immediacy he advocated in such dictums as "No ideas but in things" or in his manifestoes praising "contact" in art. Due to this immediacy we find in Williams's poem, according to Kenneth Burke, "man without the syllogism, man without the parod[y], without Spinoza's Ethics, man with nothing but the thing and the feeling of that thing." Seen from this angle, he added, contact in these poems "might be said to resolve into the counterpart of Culture, and Williams thereby becomes one of our most distinguished Neanderthal men."[24]

Burke was certainly going too far in his conclusion that "[Williams's] hatred of the idea in art is consequently pronounced," but his view is of particular

interest in the light of the theories of expression that juxtapose a primary awareness of the expressive dimension in all things to a later perception dominated
by the spirit of Cartesian rationalism, with its tendency of activating perception
mainly on a logical-causal-relational level. Insofar as the latter perception lies at
the heart of modern civilization, "contact" with its attempt at closing the gap
– and the ensuing estrangement – between self and world is indeed the counterpart of (modern) culture, and Williams's vision is therefore indeed related to
that of the so-called primitives.[25]

Expressions in Color

In these poems, in which we have "man with nothing but the thing and the
feeling of that thing," colors, for instance, are forces that spread or recede, rouse
or calm – fill, together with all other things, a space that is never empty and
never static, sometimes floating in it and enveloping everything as part of the
living light:

> Yellow, yellow, yellow, yellow!
> It is not a color.
> It is summer!
> It is the wind on a willow,
> the lap of waves, the shadow
> under a bush, a bird, a bluebird,
> three herons, a dead hawk
> rotting on a pole –
> Clear yellow!
> It is a piece of blue paper
> in the grass or a threecluster of
> green walnuts swaying, children
> playing croquet or one boy
> fishing, a man
> swinging his pink fists
> as he walks –
>
> (CP1, 161)

Diverging, spreading yellow becomes the "radiant gist" of a beautiful summer
day; and the dazzling outgoing activity of nature that the color contains is embodied in the incantatory fourfold repetition of the word "yellow" itself – in
its explosive sound pattern it is "transfused with the same forces which transfuse
the earth – at least one small part of them" (I: SA, 121). This fourfold repetition
is echoed in the repetition of the anaphoric "It is . . . It is . . . It is" of the
following lines, and in the cumulative effect of the rhapsodic Whitmanesque
accretion of details throughout the poem. The all-pervading yellow becomes
identical with everything the eye, moving insatiably from one thing to another,
encounters – in a series of equations that culminate in the paradoxical identity

of yellow with "a bluebird," "a piece of blue paper," "green walnuts swaying," "a man / swinging his pink fists / as he walks," "tufts of purple grass." Yellow in this color field of action (which one might compare to a Kandinskian palette with its characteristic yellow, blue, green, red, and pink) permeates everything; it reigns supreme and forces, as it were, the other colors to submit, so that yellow is "a disinclination to be / five red petals or a rose" and the green sepals under the "four open yellow petals [curl] backward into reverse spikes."

In Williams's spring poems – poems devoted to the crucial moment of birth and renewal in a universe experienced as a never-ending process of creation and destruction, growth and decay – the drama of spring is always, among other things, a drama of colors. Thus in "Portrait of the Author" (CP1, 172) the bright green of the budding trees is full of a disturbing, maddening energy, an energy, however, that is uncannily contained and enclosed in the slow, silent, unfolding of the leaves:

> The birches are mad with green points
> the wood's edge is burning with their green,
> burning, seething – No, no, no.
> The birches are opening their leaves one
> by one. Their delicate leaves unfold cold
> and separate, one by one.

The impact of this "burning" green can be understood only if we realize that it is the extremely bright green of spring which approaches yellow, as the title of another spring poem, "The Yellow Season," indicates. The basic movement of yellow, says Kandinsky,

> that of straining towards the spectator . . . and the second movement, that of over-running boundaries, [have] a material parallel to that human energy which attacks every obstacle blindly and goes forth aimlessly in all directions. . . . If we compare [yellow] with human states of mind, it might be said to represent not the depressive, but the manic aspect of madness. (CSA, 58)

The poet in "Portrait of the Author" is possessed by precisely this manic, upsetting, nondirected energy, due to his empathetic identification with the "burning, seething" bright green trees. This feeling leads to an overwhelming desire to break through silence, isolation, and inertia and bridge the intolerable distance that separates him from all other human beings:

> O my brother, you redfaced, living man
> ignorant, stupid whose feet are upon
> this same dirt that I touch – and eat.
> We are alone in this terror, alone,
> face to face on this road, you and I,
> wrapped by this flame!
> Let the polished plows stay idle,

their gloss already on the black soil
But that face of yours –!
Answer me. I will clutch you. I
will hug you, grip you. I will poke my face
into your face and force you to see me.

But the frantic desire does not lead to action – the poet's immobility reflects
the contending forces in nature, with the almost unbearable tension between
the trees burning with their "mad" bright green and the leaves unfolding in-
tolerably slowly and coldly:

And coldly the birch leaves are opening one by one.
Coldly I observe them and wait for the end.
And it ends.

Thus the contending forces in the poet, by virtue of his "approximate co-
extension with the universe" (*I: SA*, 105), reflect the forces of nature, and an
essential part of these forces are the contending forces of the interacting colors
themselves. Green, according to Kandinsky, is the result of blending warm yellow and cool blue and thus itself generates, at least to some extent, the fundamental tension experienced by the poet in "Portrait of the Author":

An attempt to make yellow colder produces a greenish tint and checks both the
horizontal and eccentric movement. The color becomes sickly and unreal, like an
energetic man who has been checked in the use of his energy by external circumstances. The blue by its contrary movement acts as a brake on the yellow and is
hindered in its own movement, and, if more blue is added, the contrary movements cancel each other out and complete immobility ensues. The result is *green*.
(*CSA*, 57)

Williams expressed the same perception in *Kora in Hell*, although he lifted it to
the more general level of a basic underlying principle:

*Between two contending forces there may at all times arrive that moment when the stress is
equal on both sides so that with a great pushing a great stability results giving a picture of
perfect rest.* (*I*, 32–33)

In "Portrait of the Author," the bright green of springtime is of course far
away from this "great stability"; first, yellow predominates over blue, and
second, the effect of each of the two contending forces is felt separately, and
the total impact can be expressed only as a paradox: The leaves are burning
while they coldly and slowly unfold, and the poet is ecstatic and terrified at
one and the same time, "wrapped by this flame" and "peering out / into
the cold world" at one and the same moment, crying out and waiting silently
for the end.

In this, as well as in other spring poems, black and white, "the second great
antithesis" (*CSA*, 57), is also part of the perturbations of spring. The white

blossoms which virtually seem to explode out of the black of the branches are "flares of / small fire" (*CP1*, 172) joining forces with the burning green. And white, too, similar to the bright green, is a deeply disturbing color, hot and cold at once.

In another spring poem, "The Widow's Lament in Springtime" (*CP1*, 171), in which the confrontation with the awakening life is extremely painful because it throws the woman back on her own deprivation, this confrontation culminates in the experience of the overwhelming whiteness of the blossoming trees:

> Thirtyfive years
> I lived with my husband.
> The plumtree is white today
> with masses of flowers.
>
> . . . .
>
> Today my son told me
> that in the meadows,
> at the edge of the heavy woods
> in the distance, he saw
> trees of white flowers.
> I feel that I would like
> to go there
> and fall into those flowers
> and sink into the marsh near them.

A white that rouses the desire to merge with it and get lost in it is experienced as an extreme: Oppositions fuse, ecstasy leads to oblivion and annihilation, the color of joy turns – as in China – into the color of mourning. In Williams's poems, writes James E. Breslin, " '[c]rowds are white,' the sea is dark: immersion in either gives relief, a union with One, but halts the cyclic process of renewal."[26] Kandinsky in turn writes: "White is a symbol of a world from which all colors as material attributes have disappeared. The world is too far above us for its structure to touch our souls. There comes a great silence which materially represented is like a cold, indestructible wall going on into the infinite. White, therefore, acts upon our psyche as a great, absolute silence, like the pauses in music that temporarily break the melody. . . . White has the appeal of nothingness that is before birth" (*CSA*, 59–60).

Of course the meaning or impact of a color cannot be defined once and for all. Within different contexts and different juxtapositions it can elicit different, even diametrically opposed, reactions. Thus in "The Wildflower" (*CP1*, 236) white is opposed to the longing for Dionysian abandonment and sensuous immersion elicited by the

> Black eyed Susan
> rich orange
> round the purple core

In this poem white recalls things that belong to an unassuming, ordinary, and restrained domesticity, such as the common "white daisy," or "farmers / who live poorly." White is related to the bleaker aspects of the present or to one's everyday life, while the orange, purple, and black colors of the wildflower are as sensuous as the remote or past worlds whose reality cannot be separated from dreams and fantasies:

> But you
> are rich
> in savagery –
>
> Arab
> Indian
> Dark woman.

In "Queen Anne's Lace" (*CP*1, 162), a *paysage de femme* poem which fuses the white of a woman's body with a field of white flowers, a basic tension is expressed through the different impact of the two shades and textures of white embodied in the anemone on the one hand and the wild carrot on the other:

> Her body is not so white as
> anemone petals nor so smooth – nor
> so remote a thing. It is a field
> of the wild carrot taking
> the field by force; the grass
> does not rise above it.

The smooth, delicate, and pure white of the anemone petals seems passive, fragile, almost incorporeal and related to the virginal when compared to the *wild* carrot, which is not "so remote a thing" but active to the point of "taking / the field by force" – a paradox which recalls the androgynous nature of flowers.[27] With the wild carrot there is "no question of whiteness, / white as can be"; the added purple mole at the center of each flower makes it approachable. It is turned into a flower-woman that is desired by the sun-poet *and* desirous of him, caressed *and* caressing: "Each part / is a blossom under his touch / to which the fibres of her being / stem one by one."

Here, where there is desire, love, warmth, and fertility, whiteness does not reign supreme; it is not the spotless purity of the dematerialized absolute. Although it still contains the "pious wish to whiteness," it is "a pious wish to whiteness gone over –." Gone over to where? Whiteness of Apollonian clarity and restraint gone over to whiteness of Dionysian ecstasy, gone over to the climactic moment in which the field of erotic encounter is "empty" of everything but the "white desire" to collapse into the "nothing" at the very end of the poem, when the imaginative ecstatic union of the male sun-poet with the female field of flowers has reached its orgasmic height and the poet is thrown back on himself, on his own separate consciousness:

> Wherever
> his hand has lain there is
> a tiny purple blemish. Each part
> is a blossom under his touch
> to which the fibres of her being
> stem one by one, each to its end,
> until the whole field is a
> white desire, empty, a single stem,
> a cluster, flower by flower,
> a pious wish to whiteness gone over –
> or nothing.

Such a pan-erotic empathetic identification of the poet with the sun in his encounter with the field of flowers is only possible in a poem whose aesthetics of energy transcends the fixed categories of the rationalist technological outlook and makes no fundamental difference between human and nonhuman realms. The poem becomes a field of action into which the poet's consciousness enters, in the double movement of appropriating it and being exposed to it with "the mind turned inside out" (*I: KH*, 75). And the colors in this field of action are an essential part of the basic forces interacting with each other.

The specific process that gives direction to these interacting forces is often that of *form being born* out of the formless ground.[28] In this context "Queen Anne's Lace" is of particular interest because it paradigmatically enacts this process on the level of colors: It begins and ends with color being born, so to speak, through the subtlest distinction of white. The white of the wild carrot is *not* "white as can be," which, as an endpoint on a scale, turns into its own negation – into an absence of color which is an absence of life, the "nothingness that is before birth" (*CSA*, 60). Hence the sense of purity conveyed by total whiteness can only be a purity beyond fruition.

Approached from this angle, the "nothing" of the last line acquires a second meaning, which becomes clearer when we realize that syntactically it stands in opposition to the previous eight lines: "Each part / is a blossom under his touch . . . until the whole field is . . . a pious wish to whiteness gone over – / or nothing." Life begins where the sterility and nonform of absolute whiteness "[goes] over" into something else – life begins where color begins, and a color can be perceived only in its relation to another color.

Thus the interaction of colors enacts in a paradigmatic way what happens also on all other levels (that is, the level on which the sounds and forms of the words making up the poem interact as well as the level of the interaction of the things denoted). "Interaction" in this process, it is important to realize, has to be taken literally, since to bring out the expressive dimension in colors, forms, and objects means to bring out what is "adverbial, not adjectival," as Rudolf Arnheim writes. Expression applies "to the behavior of things, not to the things themselves" (*Toward a Psychology of Art*, p. 208). In this sense viable art indeed contains the universal in the particular, since it embodies something of the *natura naturans* underlying the myriad forms of the *natura naturata*. "In a broader sense," writes Arnheim,

> it is the direct expressiveness of all perceptual qualities that allows the artist to convey the effects of the most universal and abstract psycho-physical forces through the presentation of individual, concrete objects and happenings. While painting a pine tree, he can rely on the expression of towering and spreading this tree conveys to the human eye, and thus can span in his work the whole range of existence, from its most general principles to the tangible manifestations of these principles in individual objects. (pp. 69–70)

Williams said more or less the same in poetic form in "Still Lifes," written in the last years of his life. It is a poem by an artist who not only kept in fruitful touch with what happened in the visual arts throughout his life but who also never stopped pondering the mysterious way in which a particular poem or painting partakes of the universal, the mysterious way in which it is "transfused with the same forces which transfuse the earth – at least one small part of them":

> All poems can be represented by
> still lifes not to say
> water-colors, the violence of
> the Iliad lends itself to an arrangement
> of narcissi in a jar.
> The slaughter of Hector by Achilles
> can well be shown by them
> casually assembled yellow upon white
> radiantly making a circle
> sword strokes violently given
> in more or less haphazard disarray
>
> (CP2, 378)

Chapter 3

The Poem as a Field of Action

If Kandinsky was by far the most important theoretician among the early Modernists with regard to the expressive properties of colors and the canvas as a color field of action, the more general problem of the expressive properties of form was, on the other hand, widely discussed and explored by a large number of artists and critics, most notably the Cubists. Their work held a special fascination for Williams because it resisted total abstraction and tried to come to terms with the crucial problem of an art form that was nonmimetic and yet tied to empirical reality, however transformed it might appear on the canvas. Williams found in their paintings one of the basic aims of his poems, namely, "an attempt to render plastic the inner constitution of objects,"[1] instead of faithfully rendering their outward appearance only. He tried to show what this meant for poetry in one of the first programmatic poems about the lesson of Cubism and Futurism, "To a Solitary Disciple" (*CP1*, 104), written in 1916:

> Rather notice, mon cher,
> that the moon is
> tilted above
> the point of the steeple
> than that its color
> is shell-pink.
>
> Rather observe
> that it is early morning
> than that the sky
> is smooth as a turquoise.

By calling the disciple "mon cher" Williams pays tribute to the French origin of Cubism; the title itself recalls the avant-garde feeling of isolation: In 1916 he who is about to learn his lesson is still a "solitary disciple." The speaker begins by pointing out that to observe the way in which the details that make up the visual field are interrelated is more important than to create fanciful conceits or similes. Precise observation, even if at first it seems mere naming ("Rather

60

observe / that it is early morning"), takes precedence over the poetic "coining of similes," which is "a pastime of very low order" (*I: KH*, 18). Not that color or texture should be neglected, but he who begins by saying that the color of the moon is shell-pink and that the sky is smooth as a turquoise shows that he is unable to "so [construct] his praise . . . as to borrow no particle from right or left" (*SE*, 17).

But to observe a form or color precisely is not precision for precision's sake. Precise observation is, for instance, a prerequisite to experiencing the kinesthetic impact of the various forms:

> Rather grasp
> how the dark
> converging lines
> of the steeple
> meet at the pinnacle —
> perceive how
> its little ornament
> tries to stop them —
>
> See how it fails!
> See how the converging lines
> of the hexagonal spire
> escape upward —
> receding, dividing!
> — sepals
> that guard and contain
> the flower!
>
> Observe
> how motionless
> the eaten moon
> lies in the protecting lines.

Now the daring metaphor has its function. Like the Futurists, who tried to do justice to the impact of forms by visualizing them through force lines and ray lines, Williams tries to do justice to the *impact* of the hexagonal spire: He begins by carefully describing how "the converging lines / of the hexagonal spire / escape upward – / receding, dividing!" and then "[lifts] it to the imagination" by superimposing the spire (whose "dividing" and unfolding force lines above the pinnacle enfold and hence protect the moon) with the sepals of a plant that "guard and contain / the flower." The hexagonal lines of the spire are thus turned into veritable force lines for the observer who is sensitive to the dynamic pattern inherent in this visual field of action.[2] To *see*, Williams tries to demonstrate, is to perceive and feel the visual dynamics inherent in all forms and colors, and to assess the dynamic patterns that result from their interaction. This phenomenon, writes Rudolf Arnheim in *Toward a Psychology of Art*, "is perhaps more universally and more strongly apparent in art than it is in nature, because the artist fashions his pattern in such a way that the movement of form flows clearly throughout the work." Therefore "one of the most elementary statements that can be made about any work of art is that it represents a dynamic pattern" (p. 78).

One of Williams's later poems, "Raindrops on a Briar" (*CP2*, 148), indicates that he seems to have realized this, instinctively or consciously, at an early stage:

> I, a writer, at one time hipped on
> painting, did not consider
> the effects, painting,
> for that reason, static, on
>
> the contrary the stillness of
> the objects – the flowers, the gloves –
> freed them precisely by that
> from a necessity merely to move
>
> in space as if they had been –
> not children! but the thinking male
> or the charged and deliver-
> ing female frantic with ecstasies;

According to Arnheim, any description of a work of art (or, we ought to add, of a visual field in general) "in terms of static or geometric shapes ignores its main animating feature, namely, the fact that all form is primarily visual action." Sometimes this action is "organized around one dominant center, from which movement radiates throughout the entire area. In other cases, two or more centers of movement create a contrapuntal pattern. From the main arteries of the composition, the movement flows into the capillaries of the smallest detail" (p. 74).

Such a contrapuntal pattern is pointed out by the "teacher" in "To a Solitary Disciple":

> It is true:
> in the light colors
> of morning
>
> brown-stone and slate
> shine orange and dark blue.
>
> But observe
> the oppressive weight
> of the squat edifice!
> Observe
> the jasmine lightness
> of the moon.

At the beginning of the poem the narrator seems to reject not only the "easy lateral sliding" of descriptions that resort to the "associational or sentimental value" (*I: KH*, 14) of "poetic" similes, but also an Impressionist preoccupation with the specific light of the fleeting moment. But, as Thomas R. Whitaker astutely notes, "the poem's implicit strategy is to include in its own synthesis whatever it may deprecate as an abstracted quality" (*William Carlos Williams*, p. 41). The extended analogy between the force lines of the spire and the sepals of the plant is a Poundian superposition that leaves the two images intact and separate but leads us, at the same time, to an increased awareness of the analogous dynamic pattern in both of them. "The imagination," says Williams in the Preface to *Kora*, "goes from one thing to another. Given many things of nearly totally divergent natures but possessing one-thousandth part of a quality in common, provided that be new, distinguished, these things belong in an imaginative category and not in a gross natural array. To me this is the gist of the whole matter" (*I*, 14).

Similarly the color is given its due when it is embedded in the structural whole of this field of action. Once its role in the contrapuntal pattern of the light and dynamic versus the dark and heavy is felt and understood, the poet can fuse factual description with metaphors that lead to an imaginative transformation of surface reality in order to impart the full kinesthetic impact of the visual field:

> But observe
> the *oppressive weight*
> of the *squat* edifice!
> Observe
> the *jasmine lightness*
> of the moon.[3]

If "To a Solitary Disciple" is primarily an exploration of the expressive properties of geometrical form, visualized in terms of Futurist ray lines and force lines, other poems of the same time (e.g., "Virtue," "Tree," and "Dawn") are febrile fields of action that combine Futurist kinetics with Fauvist color explosions:

> Now? Why –
> whirlpools of
> orange and purple flame
> feather twists of chrome
> on a green ground
> funnelling down upon
> the steaming phallus-head
> of the mad sun himself –
> blackened crimson!
>
> (*CP1*, 89)

Some poems are transcriptions of real or imaginary paintings, such as "Spring Strains" (*CP*1, 97), with its veritable Expressionist frenzy:

> In a tissue-thin monotone of blue-grey buds
> crowded erect with desire against
> the sky –
>   tense blue-grey twigs
> slenderly anchoring them down, drawing
> them in –
>
>   two blue-grey birds chasing
> a third struggle in circles, angles
> swift convergings to a point that bursts
> instantly!
>
>   Vibrant bowing limbs
> pull downward, sucking in the sky
> that bulges from behind, plastering itself
> against them in packed rifts, rock blue
> and dirty orange!
>
>   But –
> (Hold hard, rigid jointed trees!)
> the blinding and red-edged sun-blur –
> creeping energy, concentrated
> counterforce – welds sky, buds, trees,
> rivets them in one puckering hold!
>
> Sticks through! Pulls the whole
> counter-pulling mass upward, to the right
> locks even the opaque, not yet defined
> ground in a terrific drag that is
> loosening the very tap-roots!
>
> On a tissue-thin monotone of blue-grey buds
> two blue-grey birds, chasing a third,
> at full cry! Now they are
> flung outward and up – disappearing suddenly!

As in "Virtue," energy is a sexual energy here, animating all things in their striving for fruition; this sexual–erotic dimension with its implicit empathetic identification between speaker and world (by means of such words and phrases as "erect," "tense," "vibrant bowing limbs") has its antithesis in the nonsexual descriptions of the forces at work and resolves this tension by leading us to experience the erotic dimension in many of the seemingly neutral verbs (such as "drawing them in," "chasing," "sucking in").

Equally important is the tension between words referring to the details of nature as tangible reality and those other words that obviously refer to objects as they appear in a painting, and thus to the depicted scene as preordered in a work of art. Nature is presented to the reader through the double artistic vision of an (imaginary) painting and a poem, a procedure that leaves no room for a consistent illusionistic reading of the poem as an "objective" rendering or copying of empirical reality. Phrases such as "a tissue-thin monotone of blue-grey buds" and "two blue-grey birds chasing / a third struggle in circles, angles / swift convergings to a point that bursts / instantly!" refer to an outside reality and color as paint on a canvas, and to lines and forms as a design on a picture plane.

By exploring this ambiguity Williams consciously aligns his poem with painting in the wake of Cubism, and its basic tenet to renounce the illusionistic representation of space (as well as other forms of mimetic copying) and to exploit the paradox inherent in a medium that tries to render depth on a surface. Thus, when in "Spring Strains" the sun is said to pull "the whole / counter-pulling mass upward, to the right," Williams creates a tension between "normal" perception and the mediated one of a viewer in front of a canvas. Similarly the sky appears not vast and empty but as solid and massive as anything else, bulging from behind and "plastering" itself against the limbs of the trees "in packed rifts."

The words referring to the objects in this poem as painted ones provide the poet with metaphors that are referential and self-referential at one and the same time, since they convey the drama of nature as well as the drama of paint and, indirectly, of words, as an imitation of the primary and the secondary field of action. Moreover, they enable Williams to explore some of the basic paradoxes of the visual dynamics of a painting (and, for that matter, of a poem). There is, first of all, the paradox of that "more pregnant motion" in a work of art which, being an object, seems "for that reason, static" (*CP2*, 148), a paradox which enables the viewer (as well as the reader of a poem) to experience a moment as dynamic *and* perennially present. This paradox is implied in the description of the three birds as "[struggling] in circles, angles / swift convergings to a point that bursts / instantly!" The last word, on a line by itself, embodies the here and now of such a moment, an explosion that takes place anew each time the onlooker's eye alights on the birds, or the reader's eye on the word.

A related aspect of the paradox of flux and stasis in a work of art is that the viewer can return to a part of the painting at will in order to reexperience it – in identical or different ways. Thus the speaker returns at the end of the poem to the details evoked at the beginning, but progresses now in a different, more rapid way to the poem's dynamic center. In any kind of poetry the sequential reading of words and lines entails a certain linear progression, just as the "reading" of a canvas entails, in a different way, a linear progression of the eye. But although the spatial art of painting achieves a higher degree of simultaneity of impression than a poem, the degree is variable in both art forms. And just as the Cubists try to increase simultaneity by eliminating traditional "narrative" content, Williams tries to gain immediacy and intensity by reducing traditional sequential progression. The Cubists increase the number of simultaneous im-

pressions by compressing multiple views of the same subject into one painting;
Williams in turn loosens linear narrative sequence in such poems as "Spring
Strains" and replaces it with an accretion of details out of which he gradually
builds a network of interacting forces with a complex underlying design.

Thus in "Spring Strains" there is the primary level of an empathetic identification with the energies of nature, dominated by the force and counterforce
of buds against sky and, finally, buds, twigs, and sky against the "creeping energy" of the "blinding and red-edged sun-blur." Since this network of forces
is presented in the mediated form of a painting, it interacts with the field of
action of the painting itself. On this level Williams exploits the tension between
the solidity of the painting, with its layers of paint and its tangible, static presence,
and the powerful dynamics of its imitation of the forces of nature. Whereas
these forces move mainly on a vertical axis, the visual dynamics of the painting
qua painting include movements of compression and expansion. The very solidity of the painting with its layers of paint seems to contain a centripetal
movement: The sky is tightened into "packed rifts" and the sun "welds" sky,
buds, and trees and "rivets them in one puckering hold." The movement of
the birds, on the other hand — swift, violent, explosive — is predominantly
centrifugal, culminating first in a burst and, at the end of the poem, in a whirl
that flings them out of the visual field and, as it were, out of the painting.

The Problem of Space

Thus, by presenting the forces of nature with images and metaphors which refer
to a painting in the Cubist sense of a *fait pictural* or *tableau-objet*, Williams consciously works against the illusion of an "objective" rendering of reality: "Spring
Strains," like "To a Solitary Disciple," is turned into a programmatic poem with
regard to the important "transition that took place, in the world of that time,
from the appreciation of a work of art as a copying of nature to the thought of
it as the imitation of nature, spoken of by Aristotle in his *Poetics*, which has since
governed our conceptions" (*A*, 240). It pays homage to those painters of the
late nineteenth and early twentieth centuries who "took the lead" in this respect,
who discovered that "the objective is not to copy nature and never was, but to
imitate nature, which involved active invention, the active work of the imagination" (*A*, 241). The imagination creates an equivalent for the forces of nature
that the artist "[feels] moving within himself" (*I: SA*, 105), by virtue of his
empathetic identification. Such an equivalent, whether it is a poem or a painting,
is the result of the "dynamization of emotion into a separate form" (*I: SA*, 133).
Cézanne, who saw art as a "harmony parallel to nature,"[4] is praised by Williams
as "the first consciously to have taken that step" (*A*, 240), followed by such
painters as Braque, who "is said to have taken his pictures outdoors, on occasion,
to see if their invention ranked beside that of nature worthily enough for him
to approve of it" (*A*, 240–41).

However, although it was fundamental that the work of art was conceived of and appreciated as an independent object, not any aesthetic object fulfilling these demands would suffice. The common goal of the artists following the example of Cézanne was a work of art that would transcend the duality of appearance and substance by rendering plastic the forces of nature that had shaped the things into the forms in which they appeared – a work of art, in other words, which was inextricably linked to those shaping forces in its act of imitation.

Thus Williams shared with the Cubists and other artists who followed the example of Cézanne one of their profoundest aims, namely, to dissolve "the unyielding wall between the interior force and the external mask" and to unite the inner and outer "through a plastic resolution of sensual presences."[5] "Landscape reflects itself, humanizes itself, thinks itself in me," Cézanne had said to Gasquet.[6] And Williams wrote in his *Autobiography:* "By imitation we enlarge nature itself, we become nature or we discover in ourselves nature's active part" (*A,* 240). This discovery could only be enacted in a work of art whose "sensuous presence" was an expression of a space of intimacy, empathy, and contact between subject and object, self and other.[7]

The painters in the wake of Cézanne came to realize that this space had to be radically different from the traditional one. At the threshold of Cubism was Braque's and Picasso's discovery that the "eye's normal perspective, systematized for art during the Renaissance, was neither an exclusive nor an ideal mode of vision."[8] Critics usually stress the fact that this discovery and its subsequent discarding of traditional perspective meant above all "that any three-dimensional form, be it a human head, wine glass, or hat, might be seen from two or more angles simultaneously, and that once analyzed in terms of pure volumes, of structural dynamics, its potentialities surpassed the accidents of vision."[9] But equally important (and directly related to the attempt to convey the structural dynamics of the depicted objects) was the discovery that the Renaissance perspective entailed an unwanted feeling of separation between the spectator and the depicted world. The space of the traditional painting extended from the frame (that is, the picture plane) in the foreground to the vanishing point at the furthest possible remove from the spectator, who was therefore always in front of – and outside – the picture. In contrast to this space of separation, with its "miserable tricky perspective," as Apollinaire called it – "that infallible device for making all things shrink"[10] – painters such as Braque envisaged a new intimacy between viewer and canvas. Braque wanted to replace the vanishing point, the empty space into which all painted objects receded, with a space that was solid and close to the viewer – a space with objects that would not only be visible but tangible, too:

What attracted me strongly – and what governed the development of Cubism – was the concretization of this new space which I sensed. So I began to paint still-

lifes mainly, for in nature there's a tactile space, an almost tangible space, I would
say. I've stated it before, by the way: "When a still-life is no more within arm's
length it ceases to be a still-life." This answered the desire I've had all my life to
touch the thing and not only to see it.[11]

The object in such a tactile space acquired a new importance; it was no more
the "shrunk," withdrawn object within the illusory perspectival space but an
object whose essence was brought out in paintings that concentrated on its
"thingness," its plasticity – qualities that involve our sense of touch as viewers,
as much as our sense of sight.[12] At the same time the new object should not
fool us, but rather remind us of the fact that it was painted. In other words, we
as viewers should experience the tension between the object rendered or
(re)presented and the painting as an object in itself. Thus, instead of the old
space of separation with the sharp distinction between the space in which the
painting is hung and the illusory space (the "look out of the window") evoked
in it, we have a space of interaction in which the spectator alternates between
experiencing the plasticity of the rendered objects and an awareness, as Williams
was fond of pointing out by telling the Alanson Hartpence anecdote, that ultimately it was all a matter of paint applied on a flat canvas.[13]

Ideally, according to Braque, the viewer is now much more involved than
before, spatially and (hence) emotionally. When in a Cubist painting objects are
experienced in their plasticity, when flatness gives way to depth, the painting
opens up toward rather than away from the spectator:

> Before one used the Renaissance framework, largely because of the vanishing
> point, and the depth helped the illusion. But I have suppressed the vanishing point
> which is almost always false. A painting should give the desire to live "within." I
> wanted the public to participate in my painting, for the frame to be behind one's
> back. . . . O, I didn't entirely invent that. Paul Désiré Trouillebert asked Corot
> one day, "But where is that tree you are putting in the landscape?" Corot replied:
> "Behind me."[14]

Among the Cubist painters, it was Juan Gris whom Williams admired most, for
an art that effortlessly blended construction ("design") and representation, but
in regard to the relationship of self and empirical reality it was Braque who was
closest in spirit to him. Braque sought the same intimate and empathetic contact
with the outside world; for him, too, the work of art was an expression of "the
mind turned inside out" into the world (*I: KH*, 75). Braque also sought the
silent revelation of things; once he said the idea was absurd that, in a painting,
one *began* by depicting the objects since the whole process consisted in a *gradual
approach to* them. In a statement which directly recalls Williams's well-known
letter to Marianne Moore (*SL*, 147), Braque said:

> I have made a great discovery: I no longer believe in anything. Objects don't exist
> for me except in so far as a rapport exists between them or between them and
> myself. When one attains this harmony, one reaches a sort of intellectual non-

existence – what I can only describe as a state of peace – which makes everything possible and right. Life then becomes a perpetual revelation. That is true poetry.[15]

For both Braque and Williams the new art forms were directly related to this basic phenomenological level. The vision of an artist is always related to the prevalent outlook of the times, as shaped by, for instance, science, philosophy, religion, economics, and politics, and the artist's own way of interacting with these shaping forces, be it in the sense of concurrence or – more often in modernity – antithesis. Thus Braque pointed out the connection between the development of science in the Renaissance on the one hand and that of painting on the other; the two are not only related but reflect (and codetermine) a specific relationship between human beings and the world: "The discovery of mechanized perspective by the painters influences thought. Relationships are functions of a viewpoint. Logic is an effect of perspective."[16]

Ultimately, seeing (perceiving) and thinking are related to each other, such modernists as Braque and Williams discovered; both realized that the reunion or interpenetration of self and other was impossible in a world in which "logicality" (I: "WGS," 348) and perspectivism set each human being apart from his or her environment. "Traditional perspective did not satisfy me," Braque said in conversation with Dora Vallier. "Mechanized as it is, this perspective can never give you full possession of things. It starts from a specific viewpoint and then is entrapped in it."[17] In his Cahiers he noted, "With the Renaissance, the conceptual replaced the spiritual."[18]

Braque saw central perspective as the product of a basic concept or idea that not only was deeply problematic in itself but prevented the artist from approaching the world with a fresh or new perception because of its preordained, conceptualized way of seeing.[19] For Braque, traditional painting was part of a Cartesian world of rationalism in which, as he said, people "perceive things by the intellect only, that is, as mere reflections of their concepts. One wants to define things, and the definition replaces the thing itself. As a result, one loses all contact with reality. We actually live in a world stuffed with concepts."[20]

Braque's pronouncements recall similar statements throughout Williams's writings, as, for instance: "When . . . things were first noted categories were ready for them so that they got fast in corners of understanding. By this process, reinforced by tradition, every common thing has been nailed down, stripped of freedom of action and taken away from use. This is the origin of trips to the poles, trips of discovery, suicides and the inability to see clearly" (I: AN, 295–96).

"The Innocent Eye"

It is interesting to see Braque's and Williams's theories within the larger perspective of the multifaceted movement away from naturalistic or overly mimetic art forms in the nineteenth and early twentieth centuries. This movement had one of its origins in an aesthetic theory that saw the work of art as essentially dependent on an "innocent eye": that is, on a primary emotional response to elemental stimuli – lines, colors, shapes. According to this theory it was essential that such a primary response at least partly transcend a prior "knowledge" of empirical reality, since the originality of the work of art depended on these basic non-preconceived elements of vision. Thus John Ruskin had written as early as 1856:

> The whole technical power of painting depends on our recovery of what may be called *the innocence of the eye;* that is to say, of a sort of childish perception of these flat stains of color, merely as such, without consciousness of what they signify, – as a blind man would see them if suddenly gifted with sight.[21]

Or, in another context:

> The greatest thing a human soul ever does in this world is to see something, and tell what it saw in a plain way. Hundreds of people can talk for one who can think, but thousands can think for one who can see. To see clearly is poetry, prophesy and religion all in one.[22]

Twenty years later in Germany the art historian Konrad Fiedler attacked "perception as a means to arrive at concepts," and demanded that it be conceded that "perception has a meaning independent of any [conceptual] abstraction." Man, Fiedler wrote, "is capable of achieving spiritual domination over the world not only by means of concepts but also by perception."[23]

In France the exponents of similar views were above all the Postimpressionist painters Gauguin, van Gogh, and Maurice Denis, and the critics Félix Fénéon and Albert Aurier, all usually called "Symbolists" at that time. They were largely responsible for the early appreciation of Cézanne, whom they admired as an "incomplete" or "primitive" artist, singularly devoted to his pathbreaking personal vision and adamant in his refusal to follow the traditional art forms – forms that they considered more refined and sophisticated but utterly dependent on preconceived notions of mimetic copying and thus more and more at a dead-end.

Cézanne himself insisted time and again on the importance of approaching a motif without preconceived notions. Ideally, the artist is only a receptacle of sensations, he argued in one of the conversations with Gasquet. Looking at nature, the artist has to take "from left and right, here, there, everywhere, its tones, its colors, its nuances," and then has to "fix" them, "bring them together" on the canvas. However, Cézanne said,

> if there is the slightest distraction, the minutest failure, if, above all, I interpret too much on some days, if on one day I'm carried away by a theory which doesn't go together with the theory of the preceding day, if I'm thinking while I'm painting, if I intervene, helter-skelter, all goes to pieces.[24]

Paul Valéry expounded similar views in 1894 in his essay on Leonardo, which marks his first attempt to write an aesthetic theory. In this essay Valéry contrasts modern man with the ideal universal man of the Renaissance, in whom the abilities to perceive, conceive, and construct are not yet at variance. Ideally, Valéry writes,

> before generalizing and building we observe. From among the mass of qualities that present themselves, our senses – each in its own fashion, with its own degree of docility – distinguish and choose the qualities that will be retained and developed by the individual. At first the process is undergone passively, almost unconsciously. . . . Later, one's interest being awakened, one assigns new values to things that had seemed closed and irreducible; one adds to them, takes more pleasure in particular features, finds expression for these; and what happens is like the restitution of an energy that our senses had received. Soon the energy will alter the environment in its turn, employing to this end the conscious thought of a person.
>
> The universal man also *begins with simple observation, and continually renews this self-fertilization from what he sees.* He returns to the intoxication of ordinary instinct and to *the emotion aroused by the least of real things,* when one considers both thing and instinct, so self-contained in all their qualities, and concentrating in every way so many effects.[25]

In his own time, however, Valéry argues, this balance was lost and replaced by the domination of the conceptualizing, reasoning, and abstracting activities of the mind:

> Most people see with their intellect much more often than with their eyes. Instead of colored spaces, they become aware of concepts. Something whitish, cubical, erect, its planes broken by the sparkle of glass, is immediately a house for them – the House! –, a complex idea, a combination of abstracted qualities. If they change position, the movement of the rows of windows, the translation of surfaces which continuously alters their sensuous perceptions, all this escapes them, for their concept remains the same. They perceive with a dictionary rather than with the retina; and they approach objects so blindly, they have such a vague notion of the difficulties and pleasures of vision, that they have invented *the beautiful views.* Of the rest they are unaware.[26]

It will be clear by now that all of these theories have direct phenomenological implications: A different kind of perception entails a different kind of cognition. According to Valéry, "the exercise of the opposite gift (that is, the gift for *seeing* more than one *knows*[27]) leads to analyses in the true sense." This gift is the antidote to "the weakness existing in all branches of knowledge," which is "our choice of obvious standpoints, our being content with definite systems that facilitate, that make it easy to grasp. In this sense one can say that the work of art is always more or less didactic."[28]

Some of the basic differences between genuine seeing as opposed to seeing that relies entirely on knowing (which can lead to re-cognition only) are pointed

out by Richard Shiff in the context of the attacks of the "Symbolists" on naturalistic and positivistic systems of representation in France: "The implication
of this general theory – in some of its forms called 'empathy' theory, in others,
the theory of 'expression' – is that the modern artist must turn away from overly
illusionistic systems of depiction, systems developed to create the image of an
object-filled natural world but which lack any emphasis on the abstract structure
of the expressive elements of that world."[29]

Both an empathetic identification with things and the resultant experience
of their expressive properties are stressed by Valéry as direct results of a "pure
observation of things." Moreover, we find in Valéry the same direct connection
as in Williams between intense seeing and the enjoyment of the unique qualities
of each individual object. Valéry praises those "men who feel with special delicacy the pleasure that is derived from the *individuality* of objects. What they
prefer and are delighted to find in a thing is the quality of being unique – which
all things possess." Such a delight, in Valéry's view, can be directly linked to
the faculty of empathetic identification:

> Their [i.e., these men's] form of curiosity finds its ultimate expression in fiction
> and in the arts of the theater and is called, at this extreme, the *faculty of identification.*
> Nothing seems more deliberately absurd when described than the temerity of a
> person who declares that he *is* a certain object and feels its impression – especially
> if the object is inanimate. Yet there is nothing more powerful in the imaginative
> life. The chosen object becomes as it were the center of that life, a center of ever
> multiplying associations depending on whether the object is more or less compli-
> cated. Essentially this faculty must be a means of exciting the imaginative vitality,
> of setting potential energy to work.[30]

In Ruskin's writings there are also passages that suggest a direct correspondence
between the "innocence of the eye" and the capability of experiencing, through
empathy, the expressive properties of things. The following is a description of
a tree, set down to educate the eyes of painters:

> The Power of the tree . . . is in the dark, flat solid tables of leafage, which it holds
> out on its strong arms, curved slightly over them like shields, and spreading towards
> the extremity like a hand. It is vain to endeavour to paint the sharp, grassy, intricate
> leafage until this ruling form has been secured; and in the boughs that approach
> the spectator the foreshortening of it is just like that of a wide hill-country, ridge
> just rising over ridge in successive distances.[31]

Ruskin, writes Hugh Kenner, "is tracing the tree's visible gestures. The strong
arms his fir tree holds out betoken no act of personification, in the manner of
the tiptoe posture of Romeo's dawn. They are analogies for the eye retracing
the gesture made in three-dimensional space by the piny branches." Ruskin's
half-dozen analogies and similes are "analogies not for a stolid tree but for a
tree's fancied kinetic act, and the eye's act responding" (*A Homemade World*, p.
97).

For Williams, too, the act of truly seeing a tree means tracing its visible gestures as an outward expression of its vital energies, its beauty, its life. Thus he writes in *A Novelette*:

> It is a great advantage of the winter season for the study of the sylvan nature that it enables us to see the structure of trunks and branches so much better than we can do when they are laden with summer foliage. Of all trees at this season of the year my favorite is decidedly the walnut. . . . [T]here is so much grandeur in its far-spreading, powerful arms, that it is well for us to see them during part of the year without their voluminous green sleeves. . . . The oak is inferior both in form and color, and expresses only a sturdy strength. The ash shows her grace of structure, her tall elegant limbs.
>
> Fatigue is like a tree. (*I*, 300)

Several of Williams's poems are verbal presentations of a tree's fancied kinetic act, and the attempt to see with an "innocent eye" in Ruskin's sense is as much a prerequisite for writing them as the capability of bridging the distance which sight implies by including all the other senses in a kinesthetic and synesthetic experience of the expressive or physiognomic dimension of the trees (and other natural objects) rendered.[32]

In this and other respects, Williams realized, Cézanne and such Cubist painters as Braque and Gris were close to his own aims and means. Their space is as solid as his, the objects as tangible and as near at hand. Texture of things is important in all of them, activating as it does the sense of touch and solidi ʃing space until it becomes as tangible as the objects themselves. ("The grey sky is rifted and intermediate; crushed ashes and broken glass on the frozen ground are identical with it," Williams notes in *A Novelette* [*I*, 301].)

Williams and Gris

Of course these similar aims lead to means in the two different media that can be related to each other only on the level of analogy; a tactile space in painting is not the same as a tactile space in a poem. Even the concept of analogy should not be pushed too far: The degree of fragmentation and abstraction in *Analytic Cubism* is greater than in most of Williams's works. (An exception is *Kora in Hell*, in which fragmentation, in the sense of absence of outward cohesion, is as extreme as in Cubism but different in kind, since in Cubism the smallest units – the individual objects, such as heads, hands, glasses, tables – are fragmented too, while the smallest sense units in *Kora* – words, phrases, and even sentences – remain intact. *Kora* is thus in some respects closer to Surrealism or Dada than to Analytic Cubism.)

Williams felt especially close to *Synthetic* Cubism, in which the Cubists were no longer concerned primarily with breaking up objects analytically into their essential components, but concentrated on the *tableau-objet* as an artifact exploring the spatial interaction and interpenetration of objects and planes. If Braque and Picasso were the great figures of Analytic Cubism, it is Juan Gris who became in this later phase an equally important and in some ways even leading exponent of Cubism. His paintings, Williams writes in *Spring and All,* are

> important as marking more clearly than any I have seen what the modern trend is: the attempt is being made to separate things of the imagination from life, and obviously, by using the forms common to experience so as not to frighten the onlooker away but to invite him. (*I,* 107)

Elsewhere in *Spring and All* Williams states that "nearly all writing, up to the present, if not all art, has been especially designed to keep up the barrier between sense and the vaporous fringe which distracts the attention from its agonized approaches to the moment. It has been always a search for 'the beautiful illusion.' Very well. I am not in search of 'the beautiful illusion' " (*I: SA,* 89). Neither were the Cubists. They, too, tried to remove the "constant barrier between the reader and his consciousness of immediate contact with the world" (*I: SA,* 88) by turning away from what Valéry calls *les beaux sites* and *les beaux sentiments.* Gris, Williams pointed out, painted

> [t]hings with which he is familiar, simple things – at the same time to detach them from ordinary experience to the imagination. Thus they are still "real" they are the same things they would be if photographed or painted by Monet, they are recognizable as the things touched by the hands during the day, but in this painting they are seen to be in some peculiar way – detached (*I: SA,* 110)

About Gris's painting *The Open Window* (Figure 3), a reproduction of which he had seen in *Broom,* he writes:

> Here is a shutter, a bunch of grapes, a sheet of music, a picture of sea and mountains (particularly fine) which the onlooker is not for a moment permitted to witness as an "illusion." One thing laps over on the other, the cloud laps over on the shutter, the bunch of grapes is part of the handle of the guitar, the mountain and sea are obviously not "the mountain and sea," but a picture of the mountain and the sea. All drawn with admirable simplicity and excellent design – all a unity – (*I: SA,* 110–11)[33]

The "admirable simplicity" with which Gris draws his still-life objects can be directly related to Williams's own trust in the mysterious power of words on the level of simple denotative naming. Yet, in a Gris painting, the spectator will not confuse the drawn or painted objects with the real ones; they are part of an autonomous work of art, a product of the imagination as real as the things it depicts, with its own design and structure.

In "The Rose" (*CP1,* 195) – the poem based on Gris's collage *Roses* (Figure 4),[34] – which is mounted halfway into the discussion of Gris's art in *Spring and*

Figure 3. Juan Gris, *The Open Window*. 1921. Oil on canvas, 25⅝ × 39⅜ in. Collection
Marguerite Meyer-Mahler, Zürich.

All, Williams pays tribute to a painting in which he finds some of the essential
values of truly contemporaneous art. Foremost among these values are "an escape from crude symbolism" and "the annihilation of strained associations" (*I:
SA*, 102). Gris's rose is not the traditional rose of love and beauty, which is
"obsolete." It escapes the "crude symbolism" which "associate[s] emotions with
natural phenomena, such as anger with lightning, flowers with love" (*I: SA*,
109). In this painting, the rose figures as a word should figure in a poem, "put
down for itself, not as a symbol of nature but a part, cognizant of the whole"
(*I: SA*, 102).

According to Kahnweiler, this is exactly how Gris's objects function in his
paintings. "The signs which Gris uses are 'emblems.' They *are* a knife or a glass.
They are never symbols, for they never have a dual identity, as is so often the
case with Masson. They *are* the objects which they represent, with all the emo-
tive values attached to them; but they never signify anything outside of these
objects."[35] Thus Gris, like Williams, tries to get beyond the "associational and
sentimental value" (*I: KH*, 14); no longer "labor[ing] in an old category so that
it is impossible [for him] to *see* his objects" (*I: AN*, 295; my italics), he makes
fresh use of them by exploring their visual properties within the field of action
of which they are an integral part.

Williams's poem "The Rose" is on one level an imaginative and sensitive
exploration of the visual impact of Gris's painting. *Roses* (or *Roses in a Vase*, as

Figure 4. Juan Gris, *Roses* (or *Roses in a Vase*). 1914. Oil, pasted papers and pencil on canvas, 25⅝ × 18⅛ in. Private collection, New York.

it is alternatively titled) is one of the superb examples of Gris's highly personal use of the *papier collé* technique. It consists of cutouts that cover almost the whole canvas and are so elaborately painted and drawn over that it is difficult to distinguish between the details which are part of the original collage items and those painted or drawn by Gris himself. Thus the bouquet of flowers in the vase apparently is a cutout from a wallpaper with a floral design, and over this design Gris laid his own penciled flowers. In addition he pasted on top of it and to its edge bits and pieces of red roses, cut out from what may have been an art nouveau poster or a reproduction of a watercolor painted in a fairly naturalistic style.

By this daring clash of styles and materials Gris gave new life to a conventional motif treated originally (i.e., in the cutouts) in a traditional or even trite manner. It is from this juxtaposition of the trite and the innovative that Williams takes his cue for the opening of his poem:

> The rose is obsolete
> but each petal ends in
> an edge, the double facet
> cementing the grooved
> columns of air –

Behind the obsolete symbolic rose is the flower itself, waiting to be rediscovered, a flower whose essence cannot be separated from its form and the impact of that form ("No ideas but in things"!). It is the edge, in particular, that delineates and thus defines each flower in its uniqueness. And what is true for each flower is equally true for each mediated flower in a work of art; with regard to Gris's roses, "edge" for Williams acquires a double meaning since it reflects the double nature of the created object: Gris's roses not only have an edge but also *literally* end in an edge, since the edges of the cutouts cut right through the *papier collé* flowers.

Thus the form of the cutouts alone already defies an illusionistic reading of the painting and assesses the need to become sensitive to the impact of *these* roses and *these* edges. The painting takes us into the realm of creation in which we find all the strange ambiguities of the Cubist canvas: solidity of space; an illusion of depth that is created and revoked at one and the same time; shadows that are brighter than the things casting them; incongruous overlapping of planes. Williams meets these paradoxes head-on when he calls the "mirrored" shape of the bouquet falling over the edge of the table – its "shade," as it were – "the double facet / cementing the grooved columns of air." From this image, which is as daring as it is precise, Williams moves on to the specific effects of the razor-sharp edges of the cut-out flowers: "The edge / cuts without cutting / meets – nothing." The edge, which seems to have retained the aggressive energy of the scissors or the blade that cut through the paper roses, is turned, as it were, into a force line that is resumed in the painting in its spectral counterpart or mirror image in the lower part of the picture, as well as in the multiplied circles of actual or spectral cups, saucers, glasses, and vases, until the whole picture is a field of forces that go – "whither?" Nowhere; the field is a self-contained structure of interrelated shapes, lines, and colors that "[cut] without cutting" – a structure, however, that unites the various objects in the painting not only on the level of a still life but also on the level of their individual forms. Gris created an overall "design" in his pictures – a "geometry" – by means of

a repetition of specific forms, which he called "rhymes."[36] By virtue of these
"rhymes" his pictures have an underlying cadence that structures them rhythmically and reveals to the viewer a hidden relationship between the different
objects. One could call these "rhymes" equivalences, since they reveal the similarity *and* dissimilarity of the various objects. By repeating or echoing specific
forms Gris relates the objects to one another – they "renew" each other, in
Williams's words – while each of them retains its own unique identity:

> The edge
> cuts without cutting
> meets – nothing – renews
> itself in metal or porcelain –
>
> wither? It ends –
>
> But if it ends
> the start is begun
> so that to engage roses
> becomes a geometry –
>
> Sharper, neater, more cutting
> figured in majolica –
> the broken plate
> glazed with a rose

Gris's roses, cut out and turned to new uses as a collage item, become for
Williams a confirmation of his belief that "destruction and creation are simultaneous" (*I*: "MM," 309): "The rose carried weight of love / but love is at an
end – of roses." Moreover, it is appropriate that renewal comes through a line
or edge that is part of Gris's design or "geometry":

> It is at the edge of the
> petal that love waits

Gris's act reasserts the sovereignty of imaginatively perceived form over ab-
stractly conceived object, or, more accurately, the sovereignty of a new kind of
beauty arising out of an exploration of the impact inherent in the formal values
of the object, and no longer out of an object as mere vehicle of a fixed symbolic
meaning. As soon as this "associational or sentimental value" (*I*: *KH*, 14) is
disregarded, the rose can be *seen* again and become anew a fascinating and
wondrous thing:

> Crisp, worked to defeat
> laboredness – fragile
> plucked, moist, half-raised
> cold, precise, touching
>
> What

The rose here is full of paradoxes, full of qualities that elicit tensions and con-flicting emotions: It is delicate and powerful, light and hard, tender ("touching") and cold, retaining its fragility and transience while taking on new and different qualities through its artistic transformation. Out of these tensions the mind cre-ates images that unite what seems mutually exclusive: "Somewhere the sense / makes copper roses / steel roses –."

There is no doubt that Williams's poem transcends the descriptive dimension of rose and rose painting alike, and Rob Fure is right to a certain extent when he maintains that "language in [this] poem represents an apprehension of its subject far more imaginative than ocular," and that "the poet in his quest to define and discover fresh associations *begins* only from careful observed physical reality."[37] But even the veritable flight of the imagination at the end of the poem comes out of an immersion into Gris's painting, whose "transparencies and echoing forms create a synthesis entirely fluid, almost aerial."[38] This mys-terious feeling is enhanced by the dark blue of the background (which appears black in a black and white reproduction), of which – to take up Williams's own phrase – the sense makes somewhere a vast infinite night sky, into which

> From the petal's edge a line starts
> that being of steel
> infinitely fine, infinitely
> rigid penetrates
> the Milky Way
> without contact – lifting
> from it – neither hanging
> nor pushing –
>
> The fragility of the flower
> unbruised
> penetrates space

Williams does not attempt to give his poem a "unity" or "design" by imitating Gris's spatial "rhymes"; he works *with* (and not against) the linearity (and hence the temporality) of language by entering the visual field in several consecutive attempts. Each time he traces some of its conflicting qualities as they impress themselves on the searching mind. Structurally the poem is related to the enacted discoveries of his earlier "impressions," and what Whitaker says about those poems can also be applied to "The Rose": "Observations are processes here, not results" (*William Carlos Williams*, p. 40). The dynamism of the painting (in which the fluid or aerial interacts with the solid, the geometric with the organic, the painterly with the photographic, the nonillusory with the *trompe l'oeil*) finds its equivalent in the dynamism of the poem, in which the self gradually feels its way deeper and deeper into this field of action.

These exploratory sections of the poem are interspersed with programmatic statements in calm, factual two-line stanzas, in which the traditional symbolic rose is contrasted with the rose in the present poem, where it is seen concretely, in its singleness – a complex object, an agent, a force. In the longer, exploratory passages, on the other hand, the mind pushes language as far as it will go, through an accretion of multiple characteristics of the object under scrutiny, partly incongruous and antithetical, to the point where it hesitates, peters out, or breaks off. These are moments of silence in which the imagination lingers over paradoxes and ambiguities, holding and trying to fuse them in the mind. The white spaces on the page are an expression of these pregnant moments of integration in which "the intercrossing of opposed forces" establishes "centers of stillness" (I: "EV," 321).

At the end the poem moves from successive antitheses to the rapture of an effortless contraction and fusion of the "infinitely fine" and "infinitely rigid," of the very small and the infinitely large:

> The fragility of the flower
> unbruised
> penetrates space

"One could define it," writes Gaston Bachelard, "as one of the basic postulates of the imagination: in reveries, things never keep their size, it is impossible to stabilize them in any dimension. And the reveries that really take hold of us, those that *give* us the object, are the lilliputian reveries. . . . When you are dreaming of, or thinking within, the world of small things, everything becomes bigger and bigger. The phenomena of the infinitely small take a cosmic turn."[39]

The supreme form of this dialectic of the small and large is for Bachelard the dialectic of intimacy and expansion: "Everything treasured which is small and intimate has a way of endlessly enlarging the interior space it occupies."[40] In one of Rilke's poems, Bachelard notes, all the skies are contained within the space of a rose.[41] In Williams, even the solar system cannot contain the expanding edge of the rose as it reaches out until it "penetrates / the Milky Way." Bachelard quotes Max Jacob – a poet also greatly influenced by Cubism – who wrote in *Le cornet à des:* "Le minuscule, c'est l'énorme." "To find out that this is true," writes Bachelard, "all you have to do is to go there in your imagination and live in it."[42]

The Problem of Abstraction

For the Cubists a work of art was a completely autonomous object; "a painting imitates nothing and has its *raison d'être* in itself" was a key sentence in Gleizes's and Metzinger's *Du cubisme*. However, the Cubists agreed with one another that it was of crucial importance to escape total abstraction and keep up references to external, visual reality, since the tension between the objects referred to (which the viewer can still make out) and their artistic transformation was understood to be an integral part of the impact of these paintings. "Indeed," writes Edward Fry, "the persisting fascination of . . . 'analytical' cubist paintings . . . is precisely the result of an almost unbearable tension experienced by the viewer. He is delighted by the intellectual and sensuous appeal of an internally consistent pictorial structure, yet he is also tantalized by the unavoidable challenge of interpreting the structure in terms of the known visual world."[43]

In his famous "deductive method" Gris presented his own attempt at perfecting this tension between the referential and the abstract:

> I work with the elements of the intellect, with the imagination. I try to make concrete that which is abstract. I proceed from the general to the particular, by which I mean that I start with an abstraction in order to arrive at a true fact. Mine is an art of synthesis, of deduction, as Raynal has said. . . . I consider that the architectural element in painting is mathematics, the abstract side; I want to humanize it. Cézanne turns a bottle into a cylinder, but I begin with a cylinder and create an individual of a special type: I make a bottle – a particular bottle – out of a cylinder. Cézanne tends toward architecture, I tend away from it. That is why I compose with abstractions (colours) and make my adjustments when these colours have assumed the form of objects . . . [W]hat I mean is that I adjust the white so that it becomes a paper and the black so that it becomes a shadow.
>   This painting is to the other what poetry is to prose.[44]

Is there any need at all in such an art, Gris asks himself, to "give these [abstract] forms the significance of reality, since a harmony already exists between them and they have an architectural unity?" Indeed there is, he says, since "the power of suggestion in every painting is considerable. Every spectator tends to ascribe his own subject to it. One must foresee, anticipate and ratify this suggestion, which will inevitably occur, by transforming into a subject this abstraction, this architecture which is solely the result of pictorial technique."[45]

Here affinities as well as differences between Gris and Williams become apparent. Williams, too, stressed that the work of art was an autonomous object, created "to separate things of the imagination from life" (*I: SA,* 107), but such leitmotifs as "No ideas but in things" or "contact" are indicative of a poetics that starts from the experience of concrete entities which are then "dynamiz[ed] . . . into a separate form" (*I: SA,* 133) and, as a work of art, become "a new object" (*I: SA,* 150). The "realization" of those experiences is "the made poem" which "calls [them] into being" (*CP2,* 275); in and through the poem the mind is freed and energized to pierce "through the fantastic overlay with which our lives so vastly are concerned, 'the real', as we say, contrasted with the artist's 'fabrications' " (*SE,* 231; *RI,* 140) to the essence of things, so that "with a new language we smell, hear and see afresh" (*SE,* 266).

Thus, although Williams's basic objective is "not abstractions but the thing itself as a palpable dimension of experience,"[46] a genuine experience of "the thing itself" is possible for him only when the mind is liberated by, and through, the "abstractions" of the work of art, provided that these abstractions are "transfused with the same forces which transfuse the earth" (*I: SA,* 121). Ultimately, therefore, each work of art is referential for Williams: "Modern painters . . . have been afraid of the horrible word 'representational'; they have run screaming into the abstract, forgetting that all painting is representational, even the most abstract, the most subjective, the most distorted. The only question that can present itself is: What do you choose to represent?" (*RI,* 197)

With regard to this relationship between the realm of the imaginative and the realm of the actual, Williams's concept is closer to Cézanne's than to Gris's. Cézanne stressed that the artist must have both a genuine ability to see and a concept for a pictorial structure – what he needed was, in short, *une optique* as well as *une logique.* "There are two things in the painter," he said in one of the conversations with Bernard, "the eye and the mind; each of them should aid the other. It is necessary to work at their mutual development, in the eye by looking at nature, in the mind by the logic of organized sensations, which provides the means of expression."[47] And a few days before his death he confirmed once more: "I simply must realize after nature. The sketches, my pictures, if I were to do any, would be *construction d'après.*"[48] A painting for Cézanne was a made object that would parallel nature in its harmony and take its cue from it in structure. *Une optique,* true vision, obviously comprised more than genuine perception; it included the "sensations" of which Cézanne spoke so often and which, according to Lawrence Gowing, "comprised not only the data of sight but of feeling also" ("The Logic of Organized Sensations," p. 62). By developing his *optique* (which included the "sensations") the artist could reach a state in which he had the life of nature inside him and was able to construct and harmonize as nature did.[49]

Cézanne's notion of *une optique* corresponds exactly to Williams's idea of an empathetic identification with the object world, an "interpenetration, both ways" (*P,* 12), in which the separate realms of the inside and outside are rejoined so that the mind can grasp "the essence [which] lies in the thing and shapes it, variously" (*RI,* 144). "In the composition," Williams writes in *Spring and All,* "the artist does exactly what every eye must do with life, fix the particular with the universality of his own personality" so that he will "feel every form which he sees moving within himself" (*I,* 105). In this sense, both Williams and Cézanne not only saw art as a harmony parallel to nature; they also showed throughout their lives and careers "an undiminished concern with the existent world."[50] Cézanne remained a painter of objects, Williams a poet of things.

Thus Cézanne was for Williams and his artist friends of the Stieglitz and Arensberg circles a figure of the utmost importance. He was the prime example of an artist who not only thought of the work of art as an act of creation instead of a "reproduction," but who also saw it as a product of "direct expression out of direct experience."[51] Marsden Hartley's praise of Cézanne in his book *Adventures in the Arts* is a firsthand document of what Cézanne stood for in those artistic communities so eager to create an indigenous American art that would reflect their own civilization. "We shall find him striving always toward actualities," Hartley wrote, "toward the realization of beauty as it is seen to exist in the real, in the object itself, whether it be mountain or apple or human, the entire series of living things in relation to one another" (p. 30).

Williams and Demuth

Charles Demuth, a friend of Hartley's and one of Williams's closest friends, belonged to this group of artists who, each in his or her own way, tried to achieve a Cézannean balance between a "realization of beauty as it is seen to exist in the real" and a nonillusory pictorial structure that would explore the tension between three-dimensional forms and two-dimensional picture-planes. In Demuth's still lifes, this resulted in an intriguing interaction of referential and self-referential elements. Fruits and flowers are delineated with the utmost delicacy and precision, bearing witness to the conviction Demuth shared with Williams that "the essence lies in the thing and shapes it, variously." Moreover, the depicted still-life objects often stand out from an unpainted ground. By this means Demuth enhanced the impact of the few details in fruits and flowers. At the same time the unpainted background refers to the painting as an act of nonillusory representation, an effect that is accentuated by the way in which in each still life certain parts – often such important elements as petals or sepals – are delineated by pencil only and left unpainted.

Through this *non-finito* technique Demuth achieved a high degree of concentration on the features that he regarded as essential; at the same time he presented his still life to the viewer as a *fait pictural* – a picture of fruit or flowers made with pencil and water color on a white sheet of paper. Moreover, this allowed the viewer to experience the creative *process:* The penciled details recall the initial phase of delineation before the application of color, and the transition from colored to deliberately noncolored parts within the same details evokes the moment the artist decided to stop coloring an individual leaf or petal.

Another important effect of this *non-finito* technique can be related to the basic Cubist endeavor to replace a static view of nature by a dynamic one that would present all things as agents and all forms as diagrams of forces.[52] Thus Williams describes in his beautiful homage to Demuth, "The Crimson Cyclamen" (*CP1*, 419), the effect of the "glow[ing]" petals emerging from an unpainted, bare ground as that of color awakening from emptiness and silence:

> It is miraculous
> that flower should rise
> by flower
> alike in loveliness –
>
> . . . .
> silence holds them –
> in that space. And

color has been construed
from emptiness
to waken there –

The Cubists tried to achieve such a dynamism by creating "a system by which they could reveal visually the interlocking of phenomena," as John Berger expresses it. He calls Cubism "an art entirely concerned with interaction . . . : the interaction between structure and movement; the interaction between the unambiguous signs made on the surface of the picture and the changing reality which they stand for."[53] To these one could add other interactions, such as those between painted forms and textures glued onto the canvas; the interaction between elements that create a consistent space and those that revoke it; or – as in Demuth's watercolors – the interaction of colored or "finished" planes with others left unpainted.

The close ties between Williams and Demuth found their expression in, among other things, the fact that Williams dedicated *Spring and All* to his friend and used one of Demuth's watercolors for the second poem in the book, later called "The Pot of Flowers" (*CP*1, 184). Bram Dijkstra seems to have been the first to point out that the poem is based on the watercolor *Tuberoses* (Figure 5), which Williams had acquired from his friend shortly after its completion in 1922. For Dijkstra, the poem is "a literal rendering into poetry of Demuth's watercolor" (*Hieroglyphics*, p. 172). James Breslin, in a lucid analysis of poem and painting ("William Carlos Williams and Charles Demuth"), refuted Dijkstra's too facile formula and traced a more complex relationship between the two works, taking stock of similarities *and* dissimilarities. There are, first of all, some obvious differences on the level of subject matter – Williams mentions a lamp nowhere evident in the painting, and he has a single pot of flowers while Demuth has three. But there are more fundamental differences which have their roots in Williams's awareness that the different artistic media had to be viewed in their own right, even if one could relate their aims and formal procedures. Thus he wrote in *Spring and All:* "It must be understood that writing deals with words and words only and that all discussions of it deal with single words and their associations in groups" (*I,* 145). Actually, it was this very awareness of the necessity to remain conscious of the specific possibilities and limitations of a given artistic medium that Williams, together with other Modernists, had learned from the painters. "Comparison of means among the arts and the learning of one art from another can only be successful when the application of the lesson is fundamental," Kandinsky had written in a programmatic statement in *Concerning the Spiritual in Art:*

> One art must learn how another used its method, so that its own means may then be used according to the same fundamental principles, but in its own medium. The artist must not forget that each means implies its proper application and that it is for him to discover this application. (p. 40)[54]

Figure 5. Charles Demuth, *Tuberoses*. 1922. Watercolor, 13½ × 11½ in. Private collection.

Thus Breslin is right to stress that "The Pot of Flowers" is "not simply a literal transcription of the painting, though the painting apparently provides the subject; what the poem does is to recreate in words many of the effects of Demuth's watercolor. An independent work of art, the poem (to adopt one of Williams' own distinctions) is not a mere copying but an imitation of his friend's work" (p. 251).

As in "Spring Strains" and "The Rose," the deeper affinities between the poem and the painting have to be found on the level of their basic structuring principles: that is, on the level on which both poet and painter regard their

works as a field of action, a field that deals with processes instead of static states
of being and contains, as a product of an "aesthetics of energy" (Grogan, p.
274), the expressive properties of things instead of faithfully recorded surfaces.

Such an increased emphasis on things as forces in interaction leads in both the
painting and the poem to dropping the links that, in more traditional art forms,
connected the various forms and details into a unified, mimetic whole. Instead
of this we find an accretion of details which at first appears as mere accumulation
but gradually turns out to be a careful montage, based on the principle of clash
or juxtaposition.

Demuth's *non-finito* technique, for instance, can be seen as one of those principles, opposing color with absence of color in a double interaction: painted
still life against the whiteness of the blank sheet, and the whiteness of the merely
penciled flowers or blossoms surrounded and enfolded by those that are fully
painted ("flowers and flowers reversed"). Williams builds up his entire opening
stanza on this contrast:

> Pink confused with white
> flowers and flowers reversed
> take and spill the shaded flame
> darting it back
> into the lamp's horn.
>   (*CP*1, 184)

White, in the midst of other colors, expands; the darker colors of the painted
flowers and the background, on the other hand, seem to counterbalance white,
entering into an antagonistic interaction with it of expansion and contraction.
This clash is intensified by the forms of the flowers themselves: The diagonally
ascending white flowers are licking flames, as it were, "shaded" by the darker
colors which try to "take [in]" the white flames but cannot prevent them from
"spill[ing]" themselves and "darting back" – where to? – "into the lamp's
horn": a lamp above the pot of flowers, perhaps, lighting it and intensifying the
dramatic interplay of colors and forms, a lamp which becomes a part of the field
of expanding whiteness and contracting darkness, so that the flaming white darts
back into the source out of which it seems to come.

In the next section the poem moves on from the interaction of brightness
and darkness to the interaction among the colors themselves; it moves, in other
words, from a "drama of the light"[55] to a drama of the colors:

> petals aslant darkened with mauve
>
> red where in whorls
> petal lays its glow upon petal
> round flamegreen throats
>
> petals radiant with transpiercing light

The section begins with a stately long line divided rhythmically into two identical halves with stressed end syllables: "pétals aslánt dárkened with máuve." Here the potential dynamics of the petals' form and position ("aslant") is checked by the sedate rhythm, which in turn corroborates the expressive properties of the "darkened mauve" – subdued, self-contained, drawn inward.

After this line the poem rises quickly to a climax of ecstatic motion. The colors, in rapid succession, become brighter and more active, from "darkened mauve" to glowing red and flaming green, in a reverberating "whorl" of red petals upon red petals around the core of the "flamegreen throat," a veritable vortex that seems to fuse the contending forces of centrifugal expansion and centripetal contraction. In this image, as well as in the climactic line following it ("petals radiant with transpiercing light"), luminous color becomes light again, a light which is experienced at once as emanating *from* the "radiant" petals and illuminating them from the outside, "transpiercing" them and giving them depth, transparency, substance.

In the second part of the poem, an initially covert linear progression becomes more overt:

> petals radiant with transpiercing light
> contending
>   above
>
> the leaves
>
> reaching up their modest green
> from the pot's rim
>
> and there, wholly dark, the pot
> gay with rough moss.
>   (*CP*1, 184)

The poem contains a downward movement, from the flowers to the leaves, from the leaves to the pot. This "topographical" or iconic dimension becomes clearest in the image of the petals

> contending
>   above
>
> the leaves

which embodies, visually and rhythmically, the eye's movement as it descends from the flowers to the leaves beneath, moving along the undulating forms of the plant.

As in "The Rose," however, linear progression entails much more than a more or less orderly presentation of an object under scrutiny, in order to work with, rather than against, the linear nature of language, which can only refer to one thing at a time. Once again linearity coincides with the *process* of the gradual exploration of a field of action by the self entering it.[56] However, since this field consists of multidirectional patterns of force and counterforce, the linear progression itself is counteracted in many ways. Thus, at the moment the downward movement becomes most obvious (in "petals . . . / contending / above // the leaves"), it is stopped by the opposite movement of the leaves "reaching *up* their modest green / from the pot's rim." And throughout the poem syntax, rhythm, and overall patterning with short broken lines and several one- or two-line stanzas work against smooth progression and create a considerable tension between elements that push the act of reading forward and others that slow it down and entail moments of pause.

One example of these opposite tendencies is the frequent combination of trochaic and dactylic short lines with masculine endings (i.e., lines in which both the first and last syllables are stressed). The pounding rhythm of these lines creates a mood of energy and excitement urging us onward; at the same time we are held back by the heavy pauses at the end of these lines, many of which can be read as syntactic units in their own right. This tendency is counterbalanced by the fact that, while reading on, we discover that many of the lines are actually run-on lines, or that they can at least be read as such. Thus "white" at the end of the first line appears to be a noun; in the next line we discover that it can also be read as an adjective belonging to "flower." Similarly "mauve" in line 6 is first interpreted as a noun, then as an adjective modifying "red"; and "round" in line 9 appears first to be a preposition, then the first of two adjectives belonging to "throat."

In each of these cases the resulting ambivalence creates a tension which we try to eliminate subsequently by excluding the less likely of the two alternate possibilities. But even when we arrive at the stage of giving one reading a clear preference over another, the syntactic openness is still there, eliciting a new effort to close it in each subsequent reading. This effort should ideally lead the reader to the point of abandoning a "logicality" (*I:* "WGS," 347) that rigidly defines words and word units, so that we become receptive to poems in which words are "vectors of energy" attracted or repelled by others in this "rout of the vocables" (*P,* 219), interacting with them in multiple combinations.

Cubist Painting and Cubist Poetry

The tension created by such a syntactic ambiguity can be directly related to the Cubist technique of including the ambiguous or contradictory overlapping of planes, or of fusing, or metonymically displacing, the material qualities of objects, so that a pipe becomes transparent while a glass or a carafe is opaque.[57] With those devices the Cubist painters had several aims in mind. One of them was the attempt to activate viewers by eliciting their effort to sort out the identities of objects and their positions in space. Another — a direct outcome of the first — was to confront viewers, once again, with the painting as a *fait pictural,* a work of art that foregrounds the problems of pictorial representation, such as depth, space, and artistic illusion. By thwarting attempts to read and enjoy a painting as one enjoys the view from a window, the Cubists led viewers to experience a work of art as a *made thing,* highlighting both the interactions between its painted forms and the interactions between art and life.[58]

Thus, looking at a Cubist painting we are radically prevented from identifying the painting with the objects it depicts, since we are inevitably led from the referential to the self-referential: At first sight the remaining realistic elements seem to be remnants of a mimetic art by which the artist achieves an illusion of reality. But, looking twice, we are confronted with the ambiguities and contradictions, and what at first appears as a remnant of illusionism turns out to be part of a complicated and often very witty game, ruled by the possibilities of constantly creating and debunking illusions.

The various techniques employed here are brought to a head in the *trompe l'oeil* effects. A brilliant example is Picasso's first collage, *Still Life With Chair Caning* (1912; Figure 6). The painting seems at first sight to contain a painted detail of chair caning; on closer inspection, however, one discovers that Picasso pasted a strip of oilcloth on the canvas. Now the oilcloth is demonstrably more real than the painted still life details surrounding it, but on another level it is as "false" as anything else in the painting, for it pretends to be chair caning but is only a piece of oilcloth with a *trompe l'oeil* chair-caning pattern. In a way one could say that the detail in the painting that is most mimetic is the most false — neither real chair caning nor painted chair caning but imitation chair caning on oilcloth glued onto a painting — but in the end it serves the same purpose as all the other elements. All are valid means for the painter to assess, in Rosenblum's words, "the independent reality of the pictorial means by which nature is transformed into art upon the flat surface of a canvas."[59]

Williams achieves a similar effect in those poems that consist basically in what Breslin calls a "halting, disjunctive sequence of sharply defined images" (*William Carlos Williams,* p. 82). Like the Cubist paintings, they are referential as well as self-referential. Words in them denote, but they cannot be regarded as completely identical to their referents, since they often denote different things when related to different word groups. Thus words are assessed as independent things, and, adapting Rosenblum's statement about the Cubist paintings, one could say that Williams asserts "the independent reality of the linguistic means by which nature is transformed into art upon a sheet of paper."

By these and other devices — such as absence of connectives, absence of punctuation, line breaks that do not correspond to semantic or syntactic units — Williams loads his words to the utmost with energy. They are no longer exclusively vehicles of meaning but appear as things endowed with a power of

Figure 6. Pablo Picasso, *Still Life With Chair Caning*. 1912. Oil and printed oil-cloth on canvas, 11⅞₆ × 14⅝₆ in. Musée Picasso, Paris. Reproduced by permission.

joining other words or clashing with them. They have a potential to mean, which is activated by the reader, who, in the act of ideation, tries them out in a continuous process of forming images and again abandoning them to form others.

In these acts of ideation the reader tries to complete what the poet has begun. Out of the formless ground the poet has created a form whose meaning is not fixed once and for all, but must be assessed in each reading and rereading. Often such a poem enacts a creative process in a double sense: The reader is a witness of form being born in the poet's or speaker's struggle with "a mass of detail," explored, step by step, in the attempt to "interrelate [it] on a new ground, difficultly" (*P*, 19); and the reader then continues the same process by trying to "close," for the moment, what is still open, giving meaning to words and realizing at the same time that the poem defies a definitive closure. For words are then loaded with energy when they are used by the poet in such a way as to be free – free "from all previous significance" (*I: GAN*, 171) and free from "the aureoles that have been pasted about them" (*SE*, 128), both of which would reduce words to triggering off standardized habitual modes of thought and perception.

For Williams, it is in such acts of re-creation (and co-creation by the reader) that the world comes once again alive. What lies normally "unintelligible on all sides" comes into existence when it is transformed imaginatively in the poem. For "[the world] only exists [in those moments of creation] when its emotion is fastened to it."[60] In a universe of perennial ascent and descent, creation and destruction, "a truth twenty years old is a lie because the emotion has gone out of it."[61] Therefore in art, as Williams wrote to Musja Sheeler, "the greatest difficulty comes from the necessity always to find a new formal alternative, always the new, always the nascent (the freshly born), that is why the Greeks stressed THE BIRTH OF VENUS (of beauty) from the sea which is formless except in its undulations from which all poems spring anew" (Sheeler Papers).

Thus each poem is for Williams the enactment of the permanent necessity to create new forms out of the formless ground.[62] The birth of Venus became for him one of the supreme images from the past which he adapted and transformed – made new – in his own poems. Venus is the central image for "one" (*I: AN*, 282), for the "fierce singleness" of the fully realized form. She is the direct opposite of "the senseless/unarrangement of wild things" (*CP1*, 361), of chaotic multiplicity, of "flux (that diarrhea)" (*CP2*, 189). Venus is the classic wholeness to be found everywhere, since "[a]nywhere is everywhere" (*P*, 231). Thus Williams's wife becomes Venus in *A Novelette*, since "the aberrant is the classic" (*I*, 283): "So she – building of all excellence is, in her single body, beautiful; enforcing the mind by imperfections to a height. Born again, Venus from the confused sea. Summing all the virtues. Single. Excellence. Female" (*I*, 282).

Another all-important image for the perfection of form is the flower. "The Flower is our sign," writes Williams in "To All Gentleness" (*CP2*, 68):

> Milkweed, a single stalk on the bare
> embankment . . .
>   . . . .
>   Slender green
> reaching up from sand and rubble (the
> anti-poetic they say ignorantly, a
> disassociation)
>   premising the flower,
>   without which, no flower.

The Kora myth provides Williams with a recurrent image for this important renewal through descent and reimmersion. The *opposite* movement, out of the life-sustaining ground and darkness into the light of the fully realized form, is often found in the flower or tree poems. It is a movement of expansion, from root to branch and flower, to adopt Williams's working title for his autobiography, the movement of tracing the unfolding form and empathizing with its life force when it "enter[s] into the singleness of the moment" (*I: AN,* 282) and attains its "peculiar perfection" (*SE,* 16).

"The Pot of Flowers" is one of the poems in which Williams reverses this movement, starting with the radiance of the finished form and descending downward to the leaves and the dark ground out of which the perfection of the flower springs:

> the leaves
>
> reaching up their modest green
> from the pot's rim
>
> and there, wholly dark, the pot
> gay with rough moss.

It is perfectly appropriate for Williams to end this poem by focusing on a detail that belongs to the "half [of] the world" that is "ignored" in poetry, as he states grimly in "To All Gentleness": the pot with the soil, the dirt, the "rubble . . . premising the flower, / without which, no flower" (*CP2,* 72). The concluding stanza is in several ways related to the previous ones. One first notices the contrast: The darkness and sedateness of the the pot (which is correspondingly described in a quieter, heavier rhythm) is antithetical to the preceding ecstatic radiance. But by means of a pun – wholly dark / holy dark – the poem takes us back to such words as "glow" and "radiant." This pun, which was first noticed by Breslin, seems at first farfetched, but on second thought one realizes that it is completely in accordance with Williams's insistence on the importance of the life-sustaining ground. The word "gay," too, recalls "radiant" (because of the latter's figurative sense "bright with happiness"), so that we can say that the previous ecstatic experience of light and color is echoed in the more subdued but still "gay" darkness of the pot with its "rough moss." Such echoes are even operative on the level of the form of the "objects" described, since the roundness of the pot recalls the many other round forms and circular expansions, from "the lamp's horn" to the centrifugally spreading light of the "radiant petals" and the climactic passage

> red where in whorls
> petal lays its glow upon petal
> round flamegreen throats

By means of all these homologues (which one could regard as the poetic equivalents of Gris's "visual rhymes," down to the many o's in such words as "horn," "whorls," "glow," "round," "throats," "pot") Williams indeed "gives his poem over to the flower" (*SE,* 17), that is, to the expressive properties – and concurrent emotional impact − of light, form, color, and movement, to the point where in a dramatic interaction everything is related to everything else. Each element echoes, supports, enforces, or fights and counteracts the others in a process that does not end when the poem ends but reverberates in the mind, as does the painting that inspired the poet to write his poem in the first place.

Chapter 4

Soothing the Savage Beast
Cubist Realism and the Urban Landscape

PART 1

The lifelong close friendship between Williams and Charles Demuth was the happy outcome of intimate personal *and* artistic ties. Judging from Williams's accounts in the *Autobiography* and in *The Great American Novel,* the two took to each other from the very first moment they met as young men in a boarding house back in 1903. They were both interested in painting and literature; if Williams had repeatedly toyed with the idea of becoming a painter, Demuth could not quite make up his mind whether to become a painter or a poet until as late as 1914. Personal bonds and artistic interests in mutual interaction were to a large extent responsible for the two friends developing a very similar view of the goals of Modernism and the American scene, and for their both becoming associated with the three avant-garde circles around Arensberg, Kreymborg, and Stieglitz.

Among the artists and critics forming the New York avant-garde of the 1910s and 1920s, Demuth, Williams, and Marsden Hartley were the three who were perhaps most keenly interested in, and encouraged by, the close ties established between painting, poetry, and the other art forms after the Armory Show. And each of them in his own way tried to move toward an indigenous American art. They were exhilarated by what was happening around Stieglitz, Arensberg, and Kreymborg, and excited about the stir that such new periodicals as *The Soil* or *The Seven Arts* caused, with their enthusiastic promotion of all that was regarded as typical of American civilization. But they also opposed a too facile embracing of the so-called American values and all things technological, all the more so since this often happened at the expense of ignoring or belittling what had happened in Europe.

Thus both Williams and Demuth, together with Stieglitz, Hartley, Sheeler, Marin, Stella, and others, sought "a middle ground," as Dickran Tashjian put it in *Skyscraper Primitives,* "on the entire question of emulating current European modes of expression" (p. 84). In their manifesto in the first number of *Contact,*

Williams and Robert McAlmon wrote: "We will be American, because we are of America. . . . Particularly we will adopt no aggressive or inferior attitude toward 'imported thought' or art." And in a "Comment" for the second number, Williams asserted that the Americans had to become aware of their own culture, lest they "stupidly fail to learn from foreign work or stupidly swallow it without knowing how to judge its essential values."[1]

This was also precisely Demuth's position. He was keenly interested in all aspects of contemporary American civilization, including those that were anathema to the defenders of a traditional "high culture": circus, vaudeville and the (night) life and entertainment of the *demi-monde* and the *bohème* in the big cities. With Williams he shared a keen sense for the comic, especially when it stemmed from debunking the solemn high-mindedness and reverence for Art that they found omnipresent in the conservative public around them. Hence they were both equally delighted by the consternation Duchamp's ready-mades aroused, not to speak of their appreciation of the deeper import of ready-mades and *objets trouvés*.

There were, of course, obvious differences between the two men as well. Williams felt part country hick and part avant-garde artist, deeply involved in the latest artistic developments that were totally unknown in the small town in which he lived and had his medical practice. He tried to live with these tensions and bring the two worlds nearer to each other in his art, which was so deeply rooted in the mundane and the local. Demuth, on the other hand, was more aloof and less passionately involved than his friend. He cultivated his image of a dandy and was much drawn to the inscrutable and ironic detachment of his friend Duchamp. For a long time Demuth seems to have been more doubtful than Williams about the possibilities of advancing an indigenous American art − if he frequently confirmed his commitment he would also voice his doubts. Thus he wrote to Stieglitz from his last prolonged stay in Europe in 1921: "I never knew Europe was so wonderful − and, never knew, really, − not so surely, that New York, if not the country, has something not found here." The same ambivalent feelings are expressed in a letter he sent Stieglitz some weeks later: "I think that I will stay on for another month or two, − and then come home. Had I stayed when I first came over, − I was only twenty, − well, I might have gotten into it. Now it would take years, − and work would seem so only on the surface of the scene during that time."[2] In a letter to Williams a few days later he expressed his surprise that the French suddenly took notice of what was happening in America: "France thinks a great deal of our art, − of course it seems strange, − never knowing we had one!"[3]

Demuth obviously shared with Williams that sharp sense of being surrounded by a larger public that was either distinctly hostile to them or not interested at all in what they were doing. But while for Williams this feeling had on the whole the effect of an additional incentive, it made Demuth often doubt whether the effort was really worthwhile. Nevertheless, in 1921 the decision was final – he would stay in America and devote himself to an art that was to be the result of the joint effort of the avant-garde to respond to, and cope with, the contemporary civilization to which they belonged. "Together," he wrote Stieglitz, "we will add to the American scene. . . ."[4]

The result of his decision was, among other things, a number of important paintings in oil and tempera on the landscape of the machine, and a series of "poster portraits," as he called them, done as homages to his artist friends. Almost all of these works were completed between 1920 and 1930; after that time his bad health – he suffered from diabetes – prevented him from working for a prolonged time on larger canvases.

On one level, Demuth's industrial landscapes are fundamentally affirmative, since by the very choice of his subject matter the artist documents that the classic, time-honored theme of the landscape is now by definition urban and industrial, or at least always a landscape that shows "the hand of man," to quote Stieglitz's title of one of his famous photographs. These paintings are Demuth's contribution to an art whose universals are to emerge out of the local. Moreover, they are, within his own art form of painting, his proof that Williams was right with his repeated dictum that "Anything is good material for poetry. Anything" (*P*, 222). In these paintings, Demuth seeks the confrontation with his age head-on, an endeavor that leads in part to the discovery of a new beauty: details of barns, factories, frame houses, watertanks, grain elevators, smokestacks. They are the carefully outlined and meticulously rendered motifs of a distinct landscape, as unmistakably modern as they are American, and they form the realistic basis of an art that has been labeled Precisionism or Cubist-Realism.

It is to an equal extent an art of discovery and of invention or imaginative transformation. The discovery includes veritable *objets trouvés,* such as the gigantic "Eshelman" sign in the magnificent painting *Buildings, Lancaster.* The imaginative transformation, on the other hand, is achieved by the exploration of the visual dynamics of the buildings, steeples, smokestacks, flagpoles, and lightning rods. Their dynamism is rendered visible through the Futurist network of ray lines and force lines which one could regard as the macrostructure of these paintings. The resulting beauty partly refers the viewer back to the beauty of the rendered motifs themselves, and partly points to the artist's presence and achievement. Thus the paintings are at once *mimesis* (rendering of a recognizable contemporary environment, faithful in many details) as well as *aletheia* (revelation of a hitherto hidden beauty), and *creation* (the making of artifacts that have value as objects of their own).

The Figure 5 in Gold

Demuth's famous homage to Williams, *I Saw the Figure 5 in Gold* (see Figure 8), done in 1928, is a typical painting in this respect. That Demuth based his

"poster portrait" on Williams's poem "The Great Figure" is not surprising when
we recall that the group feeling among the New York avant-gardists was rooted
in their common conviction that an indigenous American art had to make
"contact" first and foremost with those aspects of their environment that had
up to then been largely or even completely ignored. For Williams's friends,
"The Great Figure" (*CP1*, 174), with its sensitivity to things completely outside
the confines of Art, Beauty, and Culture, was a paradigmatic achievement. It
was this poem in particular that Kenneth Burke singled out for praise in one of
the earliest appraisals of Williams's art in 1922: "What, for instance, could be
more lost, more uncorrelated, a closer Contact, a greater triumph of anti-
Culture, than this poem" ("William Carlos Williams," p. 50):

> Among the rain
> and lights
> I saw the figure 5
> in gold
> on a red
> firetruck
> moving
> tense
> unheeded
> to gong clangs
> siren howls
> and wheels rumbling
> through the dark city.

The image of the firetruck racing through the city in the midst of the frenzy of
"gong clangs" and "siren howls" evokes the enthusiasm of the Futurists for the
dynamic chaos of the modern urban civilization. The poem is, together with a
few others (e.g., "Overture to a Dance of Locomotives"), clearly related to the
fascination that the metropolis held for the Futurists, the epitome of a teeming
life force with myriad nodes of energy. But when we compare "The Great
Figure" with, for instance, *The Farewells*, Boccioni's famous Futurist painting of
1911, the elements that separate the two works turn out to be as important as
those they have in common. In *The Farewells* (Figure 7), the golden figures on
the locomotive shine out in the midst of a confused whirl of bodies, which are
identifiable as embracing couples only because of the title of the painting. The
golden 5 in Williams's poem has a similar function; it, too, is the focal point in
a dynamic contemporary environment and embodies the technological nature
of the things that make up this world. The relationship between man and environment, however, is fundamentally different in the two works. Boccioni is
an apologist for a new society that envisions a mass identity for modern man,
whom the Futurists see as sustained and enveloped by an environment of overwhelming energy. The full title of the painting – *States of Mind I: The Farewells*
– clearly points in this direction. The plural implies that each individual's state

Figure 7. Umberto Boccioni, *States of Mind I: The Farewells*. 1911. Oil on canvas, 27¾ × 37⅞ in. Collection, The Museum of Modern Art, New York. Gift of Nelson A. Rockefeller. Reproduced by permission.

of mind merges into a mass experience and mass identity, as the indistinguishability of the various couples in the painting indicates. The ambiguity of the title points in the same direction, since we can also interpret it in the sense that the couples have to say farewell to their old states of mind – they have to discard, in other words, the traditional and now obsolete notion that each human being has his or her own unique *état d'âme*.

In Williams's poem, on the other hand, the environment is the dramatic setting that enhances the epiphanic effect of the golden figure on the "I," the individual whose special sensitivity enables him to be thrilled by something that is "unheeded" by all the others around him. As the 5 flashes by, large and prominent against the red background of the racing firetruck, it produces an intense moment of revelation. The golden figure is suddenly much more than a mere number; it becomes one of the new heraldic signs that are part of the specific beauty of the modern age.

"The Great Figure" is also one of the poems that recall Duchamp's influence, in particular that of his ready-mades: The golden figure 5 is a veritable *objet trouvé*, discovered by the poet among the innumerable things that belong to the neglected "soulless" present-day technological environment so systematically bypassed by the more traditional artists.[5] It is evident that Williams's poem belongs within the wider context of Duchamp's praise of American technology and the new self-confidence that this praise instigated in the American avant-gardists. In addition to that, as pointed out earlier, the Frenchman's provocative ready-mades undoubtedly helped Williams to come to the conviction that a poem, like any other work of art, "can be made of anything" (*I: KH*, 70). The very title of "The Great Figure" contains this conviction in a nutshell: In 1920, when the poem was published for the first time, a reader probably expected it to be about a figure of public importance rather than about a number, or immediately realized the clash between what one could generally expect to find in poetry and what one found here – a poem that violated the basic poetic conventions by almost any standard.[6]

Apart from influences from the visual arts, there are of course also literary ones. The poem, like many others in *Al Que Quiere!* and *Sour Grapes,* shows how Williams adopted Imagist techniques for his poems of discovery, as one could call them. It reflects some of the basic tenets of Imagism, such as the utmost concentration on one or a few central images, and the total absence of "verbiage" or outworn poetic diction. But here, too, there are differences; it is characteristic of Williams that he refuses to invariably "poeticize" the details on which the poem focuses by means of overt metaphors and similes. Hence Williams hardly ever takes up the Imagists' haiku-inspired practice of linking up an "outward" image to an "inward" metaphorical one but tries to remain as faithful as possible to the immediate sensory experience. This might, but as often did not, necessitate the introduction of overt metaphors and similes. The procedure is programmatically outlined in the Preface to *Kora:*

> A poet witnessing the chicory flower and realizing its virtues of form and color so constructs his praise of it as to borrow no particle from right or left. He gives his poem over to the flower and its plant themselves, that they may benefit by those cooling winds of the imagination which thus returned upon them will refresh them at their task of saving the world. (*I: KH,* 19)

Thus in "The Great Figure" only one word – "tense" – is used metaphorically: The poet, in an empathetic identification with the tenseness of the firemen and the whole situation, projects it onto the firetruck and the golden 5 itself.

The short lines are another device that can be related to Imagist tenets, since they direct the attention to each single detail; only when these details stand out in utmost clarity can they fully display their "virtues of form and color." The effect, however, is not noticeable to the same degree throughout the poem, as the various lengths of the lines indicate. Even in this short poem there is a clear progression from beginning to middle and end. The opening lines focus on two details of the city and night – "rain" and "lights" – and in very few words create the atmosphere of a specific setting. Then the poem moves on quickly to the center of interest. Once its focus is fully on the number 5, the even shorter lines slow it down and arrest our attention by throwing each detail of the seemingly trivial object into relief. The most striking element is, of course, the gold, which "jolts the poem into life," as James Breslin remarked in his excellent analysis of the poem, "seeming to leap out at us and demand our attention."[7] Part of this effect is rhythmic: If we take the first two lines as a unit – "Among the rain / and lights" – we get, together with the third line, two completely iambic lines with three accents in each of them:

> Among the rain / and lights
> I saw the figure 5

Coming after this, the exclamatory "in gold" receives the greatest possible emphasis, with the sole beat of the line on "gold" and a pause after it (or a fermata, musically speaking) that adds to its impact. In addition to this, the lines following ("on a red / firetruck") mark a complete rhythmic change; "in gold" thus becomes the climactic endpoint of the first iambic part of the poem, which is followed in the second part by a more complex and tenser rhythm.

This change in rhythm coincides with the change in focus – the view is gradually enlarged from the gold to the "red / firetruck" and from the truck to the hectic movement and the nerve-racking sounds, in a series of powerful syncopated double-beat lines:

> to góng clángs
> síren hówls
> and whéels rúmbling
> thróugh the dárk cíty.

In the end, when the dramatic moment is over, the poem is also over, with the firetruck disappearing into the night. Thus the last line takes us back to the beginning; the poem opens and closes with a wide-angle shot, so to speak, of the dark city with its rain and lights, a background which very effectively frames the sudden appearance of the golden figure in an exciting flash of color, sound, and movement.

If "The Great Figure" is one of Williams's most memorable and delightful early poems, the painting by Demuth which it inspired is undoubtedly one of the artist's masterpieces. *I Saw the Figure 5 in Gold* (Figure 8) is the last and most famous of his "poster portraits." Demuth obviously tried to render as dramatically as possible the sudden appearance of the number and its equally rapid disappearance, the dramatic impression of the 5 that looms large before the eye for a moment before the red firetruck vanishes into the night and darkness. This led to the daring and ingenious idea of painting the 5 three times. The largest figure, filling the whole canvas, seems to float in the air right before our eyes; the second and third recede into the background, drawing the eye to the center

Figure 8. Charles Demuth, *I Saw the Figure 5 in Gold*. 1928. Oil on composition board, 36 × 29¾ in. The Metropolitan Museum of Art, New York. The Alfred Stieglitz Collection, 1949 (49.59.1). All rights reserved, The Metropolitan Museum of Art. Reproduced by permission.

and creating a sense of rapid motion and the depth of space into which the firetruck and the 5 disappear.

In order to enhance the striking effect of the golden 5, Demuth laid out the second of the three numbers in gold leaf, turning it literally into a figure 5 in gold. By means of this collage item he introduced an additional tension by counteracting the viewer's experience of depth and motion, since the rapid transition from the largest to the smallest 5 (and back to the largest) is partly blocked by the middle 5. It acts as a veritable eye-catcher and evokes the flatness of the picture plane onto which the gold leaf is glued. As in a Cubist collage, Demuth thus forces us to realize that what we are seeing is a made thing, a *tableau-objet* or a *fait pictural*.

The dynamic use of counterpoint is one of the basic structural principles of the painting. Thus, just as in Williams's poem, the dark city frames the numbers and the firetruck; a dynamic feeling of expansion, almost explosion, is conveyed by the centrifugal force lines and ray lines of the skyscrapers in the background and the prismatic ray lines in the foreground. All these lines, one feels, have to converge somewhere in the background, a background, however, that is blocked from view by the firetruck. This truck is much more static in its mainly horizontal and vertical intersecting planes, but it nevertheless conveys force and aggression by the way it thrusts, as it were, the surrounding buildings out of its way so that they seem to recede and tilt backward.

Another important contrast is that between the sweeping curves of the numbers with their rounded-off endings, which are echoed in (or "rhyme" with) the circular street lamps, and the geometric grid of the ray and force lines. These lines have an additional important function: They hold everything together, fuse it, so to speak, into a dynamic whole, since they structure not only background and foreground but also run across the firetruck and the numbers. By breaking them up prismatically, they dynamize and consolidate the space at one and the same time. They integrate the daring juxtaposition and montage of such diverse elements as the extremely stylized firetruck, the golden numbers floating in and through the pictorial space, and the dark Cubistic skyscrapers in the background.

Now, it is interesting to note that this prismatic grid of ray and force lines running over the whole picture was probably intensified by Demuth after he had shown the more or less finished picture to Williams. His friend responded enthusiastically, telling Demuth in a letter that he considered it "the most distinguished American painting that I have seen in years." But, in a manner quite characteristic of his candor and frankness, he immediately went on to point out what bothered him. What he disliked was, above all, "the blankness of the red in the center." He suggested a revision that should "take the hint from the picture itself." By this he meant that Demuth should

> use the overlapping planes, one contour passing into the next. If that were used more through the solid red center. . . . the whole would gain by a unity of treatment which would cast a unity of feeling over it all. (*SL*, 97)

Thus Demuth probably added the finishing touches by following Williams's advice. This may well have been an additional reason for his signing the painting not only with his own initials but also with those of Williams. He also included

"Bill" and "Carlo[s]" – the two names by which Williams was addressed by his friends – as illuminated signs in the painting.

The basic aims of Demuth's picture were the same as those of Williams's poem – they were meant to be a reflection of the contemporary American scene, an expression, ideally, of an essential aspect of the world in which the artists lived and with which they had to cope. Both Williams and Demuth were convinced that this was a world that could not, and should not, emulate the more refined and/or more decadent culture of Europe, a world, however, that had a vitality all its own, and offered many new, unexpected beauties. All this is implied in the few words Demuth wrote to Stieglitz when he sent him *I Saw the Figure 5 in Gold*: "I hope you like it. It looks almost American."[8]

Williams and Demuth: Urban Landscapes

The fact that Williams's own works and those of his artist friends devoted to their own age and environment were rooted in a spirit of affirmation did not mean for them that this world had to be swallowed wholeheartedly. Viable art, for the avant-gardists, had to reflect all tempers and all climates of an age, had to deal with the wondrous and the beautiful as well as the doubtful and detestable. And often, as in Duchamp or Demuth (who was fascinated by his friend's "meta-irony"), the stance taken to the subject matter was ambivalent or complex in the sense of inviting different, and partly contradictory, responses. Many of Demuth's urban landscapes become ambiguous because of the clash between the impact of the painting and of its title. The seemingly affirmative presentation and aesthetic transformation of the world depicted is counterbalanced by the ironic detachment signaled by the title of the painting. But usually the paintings themselves contain elements that imply a more complex response to the subject matter, although this does not mean that negation ever has the upper hand over affirmation.

Among the details that signal ironic detachment are the remnants of nature that we find in some of the urban scenes, above all the trees. They almost invariably appear as some strangely distorted, crippled forms, tiny and yet tumescent, shrunken and yet rampant. (Examples are *The Tower, or After Sir Christopher Wren* and *Box of Tricks*.) Though dwarfed and incapable of effectively opposing the geometrization of space, they stubbornly refuse to be integrated and maintain themselves as elements surviving from another world. This world of nature has been almost completely wiped out, but what is left of it reminds the viewer of the price paid and renders the new urban space slightly equivocal, preventing the dynamism of the angular forms and lines from ruling triumphant. The dynamic pattern of interpenetrating planes, ray lines, and force lines is turned into a field of energy whose source is revealed as nonnatural or antinatural.

This tension between the natural and the artificial, the organic and the mechanic or geometric is, in one way or another, characteristic of almost all art coping with the city and the technological world since the gradual introduction of the new iconography in the second half of the nineteenth century. The urban world is experienced by the individual as a place of liberation and self-fulfillment, and simultaneously as a threat to his or her identity, since the chaotic energies of the new age threaten to drown the individual in the anonymity and insignificance of a mass identity.[9]

From this perspective we can regard the titles that Demuth gave to his paintings as a means to assess his individuality. These titles, which are either puzzlingly ambiguous or downright ironic, force us to ponder the artist's personal stance with respect to the world depicted. As a result of this, they also indirectly confront us with our *own* evaluation of both the world depicted and the attitude to it taken by the artist.

A famous example is *My Egypt* (Figure 9). The title contrasts the grain elevators of contemporary America with the splendors of Egypt and thus juxtaposes the pragmatic and utilitarian present with an ancient culture whose monuments belong to the greatest achievements of mankind. Visually, the title could also refer to the transformation of the Sphinx – traditionally depicted from below and rising monumentally into the sky – into the towering cylindrical shapes of the grain elevators.

This juxtaposition can be interpreted as an ironic reference to an impoverished present. On the other hand, an affirmative interpretation is equally plausible when the picture is related to the spirit of the New York avant-garde in the twenties. Within this context, the painting is one of Demuth's contributions to an art that was to make people aware of their own civilization, in a spirit of critical appreciation. The fact that Demuth called the painting *My Egypt* also points in this direction. This is my world, he seems to say, so let's have a good look at it, for what it's worth, and you'll discover with me that it has its undeniable beauty, just as any other before or beside it. Thus the equation between ancient Egypt and contemporary America implies without doubt that one can regard the grain elevators as modern American monuments. Moreover, as Tashjian points out in *Skyscraper Primitives,* one can also interpret them as "a reminder of the American soil, as fertile as that of the ancient Nile" (p. 214).

But again, the rhetoric of the painting itself is as ambivalent as that of its title, and it contains tensions that lead the viewer to a complex reaction toward both the painting and the world it refers to. The towering grain elevators convey a feeling of the sublime and create a clash between the wondrous and the banal, the romantic and the commercial. This tension is partly created and partly enhanced by the colors, mainly a deep blue that turns in the shades into a murky, almost threatening darkness.

End of the Parade: Coatesville, Pa. (Figure 10), a painting that Williams bought from the Daniel Gallery shortly after its completion in 1920, is another example

Figure 9. Charles Demuth, *My Egypt*. 1927. Oil on composition board, 35¾ × 30 in. Collection of The Whitney Museum of American Art, New York. Reproduced by permission.

of the intriguing tensions that Demuth achieves by juxtaposing elements that attract and irritate at one and the same time. The title signals ironic detachment – when the show is over, Demuth seems to say, you are once more left with a reality you may have forgotten or ignored for awhile, but you had better face it, one way or another. The title also brings to our attention the fact that there is not a single soul present in this industrial site, and if people *were* present they

Figure 10. Charles Demuth, *End of the Parade: Coatesville, Pa.* 1920. Tempera and pencil on composition board, 19⅞ × 15¾ in. The Regis Collection, Minneapolis.

would appear tiny in front of the gigantic smokestacks. Even the factories in the left-hand corner and in the background to the right are dwarfed by the smokestacks and the dark high-rise buildings that extend, upward and outward, beyond the picture frame. The sky is far away and only slightly alleviates the awesome atmosphere. In addition to this the billowing fumes of the smokestacks do not float upward but are pressed down, filling the space between the walls of the buildings and invading the streets.

Yet the overall impact of the painting is far from oppressive. The highly stylized pattern of the interacting forms, echoed as well as dramatized in the ray and force lines, is strikingly beautiful. In addition, the dominant colors are a series of rich and warm brown hues, counterbalancing the black smokestacks and dark windows, and the gray-white trails of smoke are brighter than the sky and appear as stylized clouds rather than as poisonous fumes.

In another painting, *Incense of a New Church* (1921; Figure 11), the title takes up the smoke as central motif. Once again it is ironic on one level and nonironic on another, and once more it juxtaposes the needs of the mind with the needs of the body, the spiritual with the material or materialistic. On the ironic level, the title can be read as a reference to the American Dream and its transformation from the religious to the mercantile; on another level, it can be interpreted as a refusal to look backward only, and hence as an assessment of the need to turn to one's own age, to its ugliness as well as to its beauty, to the disappearance of the visionary as well as to the advent of a new prosperity for the masses.

Clouds of smoke that recall clouds in the sky are a characteristic device in several of Demuth's urban landscapes, a device that, in its own way, evokes a nature otherwise absent. Once more the effect of this presence-as-absence of the world of nature is ambiguous. The irony is obvious when the clouds in the sky turn out to be puffs of smoke or poisonous fumes; on the other hand, they are always depicted as being beautiful and form an integral element of the aesthetic transformation of the actual into the artifact. Moreover, Demuth implies, they refer to an industrial world which the artist can ignore only at the price of an untenable escapism. Hence he consciously juxtaposes the industrial with a counterforce, be it the natural, the recreational, the erotic, or the religious. By means of these juxtapositions he confronts two domains which are in many ways antagonistic and not easily reconcilable. The strategies of titles and paintings suggest, however, that it will not do to simply pit one against the other. The artist has to create an order on new grounds, since he can neither revert to a celebration of an idyllic landscape of the past nor embrace the technological present wholeheartedly in the totally uncritical manner of the Futurists.

In Williams's *Spring and All,* dedicated to Charles Demuth, we find not only the same basic device of juxtaposition but even the same clashes between the natural and the industrial, the organic and the mechanistic, the sublime and the banal, the religious and the secular, the idealistic and the vitalistic. And in Williams's poems, too, the relation between the juxtaposed realms and their respective values is highly complex; the reader approaching them with too simplistic a scheme of values will be unable to come to terms with them. The mind has to abandon the traditional categories, so as to prevent "the so-called natural or scientific array [from becoming] fixed, the walking devil of modern life" (*I: KH,* 14). It is all too "easy to slip/into the old mode" (*CP1,* 191), to oppose, for example, light and darkness and to believe that

Figure 11. Charles Demuth, *Incense of a New Church*. 1921. Oil on canvas, 26 × 20⅛ in. Columbus Museum of Art, Ohio. Gift of Ferdinand Howald. Reproduced by permission.

Hate is of the night and the day
of flowers and rocks. Nothing
is gained by saying the night breeds
murder – It is the classical mistake

What is needed, difficult as it may be, is "to cling firmly to the advance" and to accept the fruitful tension of light and darkness, opening oneself to a universe of constant interaction and cyclic renewal, a universe in which all life leads to death and all life emerges out of death. If this is true for all life in the biological sense, it is equally true for all the other dimensions, be they spiritual, cultural, artistic, or civilizational in the broadest sense of the word. Williams opens *Spring and All* with an exploration in its most radical form of the conviction that "destruction and creation / are simultaneous": The apocalyptic vision rules triumphant, the violent mind destroys everything to arrive at the supreme moment when – for a fraction of a second – the imagination envisions the chance to create *ex nihilo,* when, once more, "THE WORLD IS NEW."

Some of the poems about cyclic renewal as the interaction of growth and decay, light and darkness have striking counterparts in Demuth's urban landscapes. Thus the opening lines of "Light Becomes Darkness" (*CP*1, 213) immediately recall Demuth's *Incense of a New Church,* with its reference to the modern world as one in which the factory has replaced the church:

> The decay of cathedrals
> is efflorescent
> through the phenomenal
> growth of movie houses
>
> whose catholicity is
> progress since
> destruction and creation
> are simultaneous

As we have seen, the strategies of Demuth's painting lead the viewer toward a critical appreciation of the depicted world; one should take the painting neither as a celebration of the modern world nor as its condemnation. (Once again, the impact of the clouds of smoke billowing forth is ambiguous – strikingly beautiful as ornamental shape but alarming as an insidious force creeping in from below and expanding inexorably.) Similarly, in "Light Becomes Darkness" the transition from cathedrals to movie houses – with its implicit replacement of old myths by new myths – is first of all neither bad nor good but points to a perennial change and renewal that is as natural as it is inevitable:

> woe is translatable
> to joy if light becomes
> darkness and darkness
> light, as it will –

The decay of cathedrals is "efflorescent" because it leads to the "phenomenal/ growth" of movie houses into which the people now come with their dreams and desires. By means of the implicit pun *efflorescent/fluorescent* Williams links up the "flowering" of the movie houses with their lighted façades; he thus not only contrasts the darkness of the decaying cathedrals with the lights of the nocturnal city, but also juxtaposes (and fuses) once more the natural with the technical. "Images [in *Spring and All*]," writes James Breslin, "rather than bearing fixed significances, are fluid, constantly dissolving into their opposites, just as in nature 'light becomes / darkness and darkness / light.' Instead of a mind that categorizes, abstracts, excludes in affirmation of the light alone, we have one that can yield to the moment, accept the generative tension of light *and* darkness."[10]

The fact that Williams's urban landscape poems and Demuth's paintings are in many ways related to one another should not, on the other hand, obscure the major differences that one can find in other respects. They are obvious, for example, when we compare Demuth's landscapes to the more radical montage poems in *Spring and All,* such as "At the Faucet of June," "Rapid Transit," "The Agonized Spires," or "Young Love." Both poet and painter create a field of action, as we have seen, by a series of interacting elements – elements that create tension or conflict by clashing with one another, or fuse with others to create harmony. But Demuth, unlike Williams, keeps the tensions that result from these juxtapositions subordinate, integrating them in an overall coherence by means of his unified subject matter as well as his artistic treatment. Although the overall impact of his paintings is highly complex and partly ambiguous, the dominant impression is that of the impressive aesthetic transformation of the actuality presented on the canvas. Their beauty and the accompanying basic sense of affirmation is the direct outcome of Demuth's goal to contribute, together with his artist friends, to the American scene. As we have seen, however, this basic affirmation does not exclude ironic distance, nor other formal devices leading to a more complex attitude and defying any simplistic readings of the paintings.

The more hazardous and difficult order of Williams's montage poems, on the other hand, consists of violently clashing images, abrupt stops of unfinished clauses, and a seemingly random accretion of details that breaks up any spatial or narrative continuity. Details of entirely different realms are yoked together, partly by a syntactic continuity that clashes with the semantic discontinuity and thus creates additional tension through the resulting incongruities. The syntax, in other words, postulates a coherence that the content defies; if there is sense and coherence, it is of a different nature and can no longer be contained within the traditional categories of logical thought and the related formal conventions of language in general and poetry in particular:

> Crustaceous
> wedge
> of sweaty kitchens
> on rock

overtopping
thrusts of the sea

Waves of steel
from swarming backstreets
shell
of coral
inventing
electricity . . .

(CP1, 211)

It is by no means accidental that in "Young Love" Williams refers to John Marin's "skyscraper soup"; the montage poems dealing with the awesomeness of the metropolis are closely related to Marin's oil paintings and watercolors of New York. Marin was intensely preoccupied with the teeming life of the city and tried to express it by painting his skyscrapers and the street life as tumbling about the canvas, as if the whole place was simply exploding before the viewer's eyes (Figure 12). It is true that Marin regarded these paintings primarily as a celebration of the energies abounding in the big city, but underneath the ecstatic dimension there also lurks an apocalyptic feeling – his city bursts with energy to the point of collapsing.[11]

The montage technique in Williams's urban landscapes is the analogous attempt to cope with the chaotic energies of the metropolis, its intoxicating promises and bitter disillusionments, its enchantments and sobering disenchantments. It seemed to Williams and some of his contemporaries that only a radical montage technique (if any form at all) could reflect the energies at work here in all their vigor, harshness, and downright violence.

In the montage poems of *Spring and All,* a basic tension underlies the many juxtapositions and clashes, namely, the dialectics of accepting or offering resistance to the forces that make up this world. On the one hand, they are welcomed as being full of an exuberant vitality, turning the city into a place of infinite possibilities of self-fulfillment for the individual:

Thither I would carry her

among the lights –

Burst it asunder
break through to the fifty words
necessary –

(CP1, 187)

On the other hand, the dominant forces can also appear malignant, making the city a place of mad, violent, chaotic activities, cancerous in their growth and inimical to the individual, who is always on the brink of being torn into the torrents of life – submerged, sucked up by the "dynamic mob" that fills the

Figure 12. John Marin, *Lower Manhattan (Composing Derived from Top of Woolworth).* 1922.
Watercolor and charcoal with paper cutout attached with thread on paper. 21⅝ × 26⅞
in. Collection, The Museum of Modern Art, New York. Acquired through the Lillie P.
Bliss Bequest. Reproduced by permission.

"swarming backstreets," stadiums, and movie houses "with the closeness and /
universality of sand" (*CP1*, 214). This mob is moved by its own spirit and
imposes its own order; it has many faces, "beautiful" as well as "terrifying" (p.
233), and extends from cheering crowds at ball games to the "Inquisition, the
/ Revolution." Again, to come to terms with these forces means to acknowledge as well as to oppose them, to face them as a life force "to be warned against
// saluted and defied" (p. 233).

The poet, too, as a paradigmatic individual, is threatened with being over-
whelmed by a mass society. There are moments when it seems utterly futile to
him to set his own poems against the omnipresent language of the metropolis,
the countless bits and pieces of advertising slogans, warnings, and newspaper
headlines which turn the city into a gigantic collage of texts:

> Somebody dies every four minutes
> in New York State –

To hell with you and your poetry –
You will rot and be blown
through the next solar system
with the rest of the gases –

What the hell do you know about it?

AXIOMS

Don't get killed

Careful Crossing Campaign
Cross Crossings Cautiously

THE HORSES   black
          &
PRANCED   white
        (*CP1*, 232)

In a world, however, in which "destruction and creation / are simultaneous," the poet realizes that this language has its own vigor and its own beauty and that he can integrate it into his poems in the form of *objets trouvés*. For the poet as well as for the painter, the details that will be relevant can, and must, be discovered all around him, readily available to the artist who genuinely sees and hears – "It fell by chance on his ear but he was ready, he was alert!" the narrator notes in *The Great American Novel* (*I*, 171). Things can suddenly fall into place in the momentum of a new language, as in "Rapid Transit" or in "Shoot it, Jimmy!" (*CP1*, 216), in which the jazz musician easily assimilates and transcends all the clichés in the vigor of his powerful syncopated slang. He is a fellow artist who also scorns the "sheet stuff" of rehashed old art forms and who does indeed "get the rhythm," to "soothe // the savage beast":

Our orchestra
is the cat's nuts –

Banjo jazz
with a nickelplated

amplifier to
soothe

the savage beast –
Get the rhythm

That sheet stuff
's a lot a cheese

Man
gimme the key

and lemme loose –
I make 'em crazy

with my harmonies –
Shoot it Jimmy

Nobody
Nobody else

but me –
They can't copy it

"Here, in the center of the book," writes Neil Myers in his pertinent essay on
Spring and All, "chaos is given speech, measure, caught unobtrusively and fully
up in the momentum of language. . . . The jazzman has the artist's natural
equilibrium: his talk is that of violence contained" (p. 227).

Another way of defining Williams's urban landscapes (which ties in well with
my own view) is to see them as modern versions of the pastoral and to locate
the basic underlying tension in the opposition of the values of city and country.
According to Peter Schmidt, several of the basic topics of the bucolic tradition
inform Williams's urban landscapes, as well as many of the paintings and photographs of the members of the Stieglitz circle. These traditional topics are
already present in a number of the poems in *Al Que Quiere!* and remain basic
elements in the many later poems that juxtapose the rural and the urban realms.
Schmidt points out that, for instance, Williams opens his early poem "Pastoral"
("When I was younger . . . ") with a condensed version of the classical debate
between the values of city and country, with the poet abandoning the prospects
of a career in favor of the more contemplative values of the country, and that
this debate is again present in a less overt form in several later poems. One can
also find such standard bucolic topics as the debate between the natural and the
artificial, or the "invitation to love," the song of sexual desire and envisioned
fulfillment ("Modernist Pastoral," 395–99).

   Thus "Flight to the City" (*CP*1, 186) is for Schmidt a conscious variation
of such a song, with the speaker "attempting to lure his maiden with the bounty
of a New York department store window":

              a crown for her head with
       castles upon it, skyscrapers
       filled with nut-chocolates –

                       dovetame winds –
       stars of tinsel
       from the great end of a cornucopia
       of glass.

We might add to this that in the same poem the lines "Thither would I carry
her // among the lights – // Burst it asunder / break through to the fifty words

// necessary –" also contain the topic mentioned by Schmidt as being part of the debate on the values of city and country: the question of (abandoning) a career. Here this motif is reversed, as the title indicates, but at the same time it is at least partly reaffirmed, since it is obvious that the vision of the city in the opening lines – "The Easter stars are shining / above lights that are flashing" – is a vision that will not come true. The reversal with its mood of disillusionment, however, is not the "true" mood either; from its dialogical opening with the two voices of the poet – the romantic stargazer versus the ironist looking for someone to support his cynical view of the luring lights of the distant city ("Nobody / to say it –/ Nobody to say: pinholes") – the poem moves on to a vision that blends both views and holds them in abeyance. This, however, is a delicate balance, and the poem, open and dynamic as it is, can easily be read in either a predominantly affirmative or an ironic way. Thus James Breslin maintains that the poem moves "toward a view of the city as sham – empty and sterile" (*William Carlos Williams,* p. 72), while Schmidt argues that "critics too readily assume that because 'glass' is modern and artificial, Williams' juxtaposition with the traditional bucolic horn of plenty must be ironic" ("Modernist Pastoral," p. 399).

It is characteristic that the same ambivalence reappears in a later poem that is closely related to "Flight to the City," the much longer "Perpetuum Mobile: The City" (*CP1,* 430). (Here the title itself relates the perennially changing city to the impossibility of arriving at a stable, fixed attitude toward it.) "There is no end / to desire," says the dreamer haunted by the distant lights on the horizon. "Let us break / through / and go there – // in // vain!" Dream and disillusionment belong together; both have to be accepted, both are part of life, and one does not exist without the other – neither as concept nor as experience. Polarities, in other words, are forces in a field of action, and whereas the names we give them create an order, the underlying reality is the field itself: "The dream / is in pursuit!" says Williams at the end of *Paterson* (p. 219), identifying process and end, search and goal, journey and destination.[12]

Thus, although the mind conceives of the two poles as separate entities, they are part of an indivisible dynamic whole, in which the envisioned goal must not be "divorced" from the pursuit of it, just as the flower, Williams's central image of perfection, cannot come into existence without the "rubble" (*CP2,* 72) of the life-sustaining ground. Hence one has to be wary of the lures of the dream, which by definition is always the unrealized or not yet realized, the there and then complementing the here and now, the potential complementing the actual. To identify dream and pursuit, therefore, is a decision for the here and now, or, more precisely, for the perennial effort to accept the world one lives in, with the everpresent tension between what is and what could be: "Be reconciled, poet, with your world, it is / the only truth!" (*P,* 84).

PART 2

One of the most remarkable examples of Williams's radical montage poems in
Spring and All is "At the Faucet of June" (*CP1*, 196):

> The sunlight in a
> yellow plaque upon the
> varnished floor
>
> is full of a song
> inflated to
> fifty pounds pressure
>
> at the faucet of
> June that rings
> the triangle of the air
>
> pulling at the
> anemones in
> Persephone's cow pasture –
>
> When from among
> the steel rocks leaps
> J.P.M.
>
> who enjoyed
> extraordinary privileges
> among virginity
>
> to solve the core
> of whirling flywheels
> by cutting
>
> the Gordian knot
> with a Veronese or
> perhaps a Rubens –
>
> whose cars are about
> the finest on
> the market today –
>
> And so it comes
> to motor cars –
> which is the son
>
> leaving off the g
> of sunlight and grass –
> Impossible
>
> to say, impossible
> to underestimate –
> wind, earthquakes in

Manchuria, a
partridge
from dry leaves.

On first reading the poem seems to consist entirely of a series of strange and
fantastic hybrid objects that are mounted in spatially and logically impossible
constellations, leading us into a world that seems not Cubist but patently Surrealist in character. According to André Breton, Surrealist art relies heavily on
the juxtaposition of the most unlike objects that are taken from what Pierre
Reverdy calls "two distant realities,"[13] such as Lautréamont's accidental but
"fortuitous meeting of a sewing machine and an umbrella on an operating table."[14] The clash or combination of such objects should ideally create an illuminating shock: " . . . from the fortuitous juxtaposition of the two terms . . .
a particular light has sprung, the *light of the image*. . . . The value of the image
depends on the beauty of the spark obtained; it is, consequently, a function of
the difference of potential between the two conductors."[15]

Such a statement recalls Williams's own definition of what may happen
through the juxtaposition of seemingly unrelated terms or objects, as set down
in his review of Marianne Moore's poems in 1925:

> . . . from all angles lines converging and crossing establish points . . . [A]p-
> prehension perforates at places, through to understanding – as white is at the
> intersection of blue and green and yellow and red. It is this white light that is the
> background of all good work. . . . As a phrase, in its slightest beginning, [such
> work] is more a disc pierced here and there by light; it is really distressingly broken
> up. But so does any attack seem at the moment of engagement, multiple units
> crazy except when viewed as a whole. (*I:* "MM," 309–10)

For a better understanding of the structure of "At the Faucet of June," Roman
Jakobson's distinction between metaphor and metonymy may be helpful. Metaphor, according to Jakobson, establishes a connection between entities on the
basis of their similarity or dissimilarity, while metonymy links entities on the
basis of their contiguity, that is, on the basis of a spatial or temporal relationship
between them. Thus for Jakobson the *metaphorical* juxtaposition of unlike objects
or of objects with hidden similarities is typical for Surrealist practices, while in
Cubist procedures objects are related to each other primarily *metonymically* on
the basis of contiguity, since in Cubism "the object is transformed into a set of
synecdoches."[16]

Now in Williams's poem such hybrid objects and phrases as "faucet of June,"
"triangle of the air," "steel rocks," and "Persephone's cow pasture" are the
result of a complex interaction of both metonymical and metaphorical relations.
The poet, in other words, seems to combine the Surrealist technique of welding
the most disparate details with devices that turn the poem into a kind of Cubist
montage driven to its extreme.[17]

On the metonymical level, Williams connects (1) the details that are taken from his own contemporary and personal environment and (2) details from the past, above all from the mythological world of classical antiquity. All of these details in turn have a potential metaphorical relationship to each other (in the sense of a hidden similarity), most obviously in the suggested similarity between the details of the past and those of the present. Here, however, Williams's procedure seems as much related to Joyce's *Ulysses* as to the practices of Surrealism: On a tiny scale, the poem juxtaposes past and present in a way that recalls the manner in which Joyce implicitly relates his Dublin of 1904 to the Homeric past.

This means that although the heap of oddly connected details seems at first to consist entirely of the random debris of some world "distressingly broken up," there are enough clues to enable the reader to realize that they might be the constituent parts of some meaningful "whole." It appears, however, that this "whole," with its order behind the apparent disorder, is built on dissonance, clash, and tension rather than on a traditional concept of wholeness, which is largely defined as the result of a *harmonious* interaction of its constituent parts. Thus the realm of nature is from the very beginning related to the realm of the urban and technological in such a daring way that the semantic anomaly finds its counterpart in the poetic anomaly (i.e., in the violated genre expectation): The poem is neither an urban landscape poem nor a pastoral but blends or welds fragmented elements of both into what one could call an "urban pastoral."[18]

One way to discover the underlying order is to place the heterogeneous details in the realm they originally come from – that is, to reconstitute their original contexts. In a Williams poem, writes Robert Creeley,

> you get apparent juxtapositions . . . that would not be understandable unless one were to take [the poem] *literally* as the context in which the mind has shifted to another point of contact in the very writing. There is no unity of view . . . in the more classical sense.[19]

Thus we may ask whether the sunlight on this June day is "full of a song/ inflated to fifty pounds pressure" because it is full of the "singing" inflated tires of the cars passing in the street. And does the faucet of June "[ring] the triangle of the air" because the sound of spouting or flowing water is part of the music of this summer day?

Such an attempt to reconstitute the original contexts – which is also an attempt to reconstitute "meaning" in a traditional sense of the word – seems at least justified insofar as it exactly corresponds to what David Lodge calls "the appropriate response to the metonymic text which would seem an attempt to restore the deleted details, to put the text back into the total context from which it derives."[20] On the other hand, we are confronted with the fact that it often seems difficult, if not well-nigh impossible, to do this here because the poem at least partly resists such filling in; thus we become conscious of – and begin to question – a process of interpretation that we usually do not reflect upon.

Are there alternative ways of reading? Attempting to remain more faithful to the radical poetic transformation of the actual, we could regard the title image of the poem as the central node of the first four stanzas, which express a movement from accumulation to release: All the multiple sensory details that make up this summer day as well as the associational inward responses are, as it were, conflated, accumulated, and compressed in their simultaneous presence in the poet's mind until they are released in an outpour of the imagination. The result is one big image cluster in which the natural interacts with the man-made, the rural with the urban, the nearest with the remotest, the timeless with the modern, the elemental with the mundane.

This cluster, moreover, also includes the meta-poetic dimension: lines 6–12 connect air/wind, which is the mythological image for poetic inspiration, with water (through "faucet") and summer ("June"), so that the whole cluster can also be seen as an image of poetic inspiration coming to fruition. Even Williams's favorite image for artistic and cultural fruition, the flower, is embedded in it, since the wind is pulling at the anemones (which in Greek means "wind flowers") in Persephone's cow pasture.[21]

The Reader as Co-creator

Thus the efforts to interpret the poem leave us torn between attempts to attain meaning by looking for coherence on the metonymical level and attempts to abandon this literal interpretation in favor of a coherence at a higher, nonmimetic or nonlogical level. Since these attempts are not only partly incompatible but also partly inconclusive, the reader becomes aware of the fact that interpretation leads to co-creation. Interpreting the poem means playing a part in the constitution of the aesthetic object. This is a phenomenon that is characteristic of all art but appears in its most radical form in Modernism and Postmodernism.[22] Williams himself was apparently fully aware of this, as an entry in one of his notebooks shows:

> . . . always in a work of the imagination, leave a large part of the thing to the imagination of the spectator; this to arouse, also to give him work to do. For that is the prime destiny of the thing produced: to have the beholder *take part* in it thus completely. Thus and thus only to complete it.[23]

In "At the Faucet of June" this co-creation can become in some instances a kind of hide-and-seek game – it seems, for instance, that the inferred image of the singing tires is indeed something like a missing link which is revealed later in the poem when song and cars are for the first time explicitly related to one another by means of a wordplay (son/song):

And so it comes
to motor cars –
which is the son

leaving off the g
of sunlight and grass –

Such a "legitimization" of the attempt to connect the disparate details provides an encouragement to have another look at the complicated network of images in the poem. In the first five stanzas, we find not only a fusion of the details of nature with those of technology but also a blending of the domestic sphere ("varnished floor") with the rural ("cow") and the pastoral proper ("cow pasture"). This rural and/or pastoral world in turn is peopled with figures from contemporary America (J.P.M.: John Pierpont Morgan) and mythology (Persephone/Kora). At this point the mythological past and the present become related through the way in which the figures from both realms begin to merge: Persephone becomes one of the young women sought out by J.P.M., "who enjoyed / extraordinary privileges / among virginity," and this J.P.M. in turn, leaping "from among / the steel rocks," is not only the powerful and ruthless financier but also a faunlike Pluto (Plouton, "the Rich One"), who abducted Persephone as she was plucking flowers in the pastures of Enna in Sicily. The steel rocks, on the other hand, are a wonderfully evocative superposition of rocks in the pastoral underworld and the gigantic piles of dollars ("rocks") heaped up by the plutocrat J.P.M., who with United States Steel had established the first billion dollar company.

These images are further enriched and complicated by the way in which Williams not only mounts them in the manner of a Cubist painting but also perceives some of the details with the eyes of a Cubist: forms that oscillate between denoting concrete, three-dimensional objects and remaining abstract, geometrical shapes, painted or glued onto the canvas. Seen in this way, the sunlight becomes a "yellow plaque upon the / varnished floor," and the sunbeams falling through the window into the room indeed form a "triangle of the air." "Triangle," in another superposition, is at once the musical instrument (in the context of the extended metaphor about the music of this summer day) and a precisely observed detail – the form "painted" by the sun – within the metonymical chain.

In the first of these two images, the words "plaque" and "varnished" are also of particular interest. "Varnished" not only evokes the shining surface of the floor and thus adds to the impact of the light; it also contains the tactile dimension, giving us, as it does, a distinct feeling of the surface, hard and smooth in its sealed gloss. Moreover, although the pun is not exploited, "to varnish" also means "to coat a painting"; hence the shining floor is implicitly linked to the shining texture of a finished canvas.

"Plaque" usually refers to either something made of metal or porcelain, or something that is solid and not formed by light only. The image of the sunlight in a yellow plaque thus conflates something solid and something created by light, something material and something immaterial. When sunshine transforms itself into a yellow plaque, light creates one of the *trompe l'esprit* effects (as Picasso called them) of which the Cubist painters were so fond. The clear-cut divisions between the realistic and nonrealistic, the factual and the imaginary break down here. Momentary constellations in reality, when closely observed, are as "artificial" as those in art itself, and the "real" turns out to be as much a fabric of the mind as the constructions of those art forms that do not hide the fact that they are something *made*. In addition to that, paradoxically, an art that foregrounds the fact that the real, as it presents itself to us, is always half perceived and half created, has, for the Modernists, more to say about the real than an art that still hopes, like Stevens's ghosts, to "step barefoot into reality."[24]

Thus Cubist poems, like Cubist paintings, are always concerned with the nature of the "real," because both foreground the complex interaction of perception and creation in the perceiving mind. *All* art, as well as all (re)cognition, is a creation rooted in perception. In this respect, too, Williams may have taken his cue from the Cubists, whose paintings are a match to the re-creative mind of the viewer, and who offered the canvas, often in a witty manner, as a field of action where figure and ground, depth and flatness, the concrete and the abstract are in an ambiguous or contradictory (and hence intensely dynamic) relationship.

In many of these paintings the hide-and-seek game that also plays a role in "At the Faucet of June" is an integral, though often ignored, dimension. "The roguish game played by the Cubists," writes Reinhold Hohl,

> is based on the fact that where something seems to be, there is nothing. Nonfigural elements give the impression of representing a nude, a portrait of a man, bottles, glasses, dice, a guitar or a violin, as well as space and light. . . . But the moment you really want to grasp the concrete images, they dissolve into lines and dim forms, and one gets lost in the maze of an abstract composition.[25]

In Cubism, in other words, the viewer is confronted with a process of creation that either stops midway between abstraction and figuration or confounds the viewer in the active role of making out what is given, of reading and interpreting the signs that seem to bring about things (and yet do not, on closer inspection) – a nude, a portrait, or a consistent space. It is this very absence of a traditional kind of coherence that allows us to become aware of the elements that *create* objects in our minds – the dark form that we read as a shadow, the strings that synecdochically stand for the guitar, the moustache that creates the face.

In an analogous way the reader of montage poems perceives *and* creates a reality out of the words and phrases at his or her disposal. Montage poems are in a similarly dynamic state. They, too, confront the reader – the co-creator – with the power of words which at once fascinate and frustrate. They form more or less well-made phrases and yet are absurd; they evoke things but jar and clash in interaction and stubbornly refuse to yield a well-built unified whole in the traditional sense.

Ideally, for Williams, such montage poems convey both the sense that writing "deals with words and words only and that all discussions of it deal with single words and their association in groups" (I: SA, 145), and that on the other hand it is through those very words that we "revive the senses" and are enabled to "re-see, re-hear, re-taste, re-smell and generally revalue all that it was believed had been seen, heard, smelled and generally valued."[26] In poems, Williams insists, it is the words and their constellations that contain and convey the sense of life in things, their natura naturans; hence language in such poems should, as Williams says in "A Sort of Song,"

> be of words, slow and quick, sharp
> to strike, quiet to wait,
> sleepless.

If language fails to embody something of the essence that animates the manifestations of life the poem speaks about, then we lose contact with our life and culture and finally end up in a civilization of "divorce," in which self and other, mind and body, the realm of humanity and the realm of nature, language, and culture fall apart.

Iconicity: The Sense of Sound

One of the means to establish this "contact" with the underlying forces at work consists in including the iconic dimension. The poet enables the reader to coexperience empathetically the life and impact of things by embodying this impact in his language. The poet creates, in other words, an analogue to what he refers to in the word bodies – their sounds and shapes – in the text.[27] Thus in "At the Faucet of June," as my definition of it as an urban pastoral in itself implies, a basic polarity among the forces in interaction is that of the urban versus the pastoral, with its clash between the sense and feeling of the dynamic, energetic, and aggressive on the one hand and the lyrical, peaceful, and serene on the other. The conflicting (and blending) moods that result from this interaction contain tension as well as elation, a sense of the energetic and vitalistic as well as a sense of the relaxed, harmonious, and incantatory.

Thus the feeling of elation on this sunny June day "full of a song" is iconically conveyed by the "ringing" sound of such words as "June," "song," "rings," "triangle," and "air," while the energy and nervousness of the urban and technological world is expressed in the accumulation of sibilants, fricatives, and plosives in, for example, the second and third stanzas:

> is full of a song
> inflated to
> fifty pounds pressure
>
> at the faucet of
> June . . .

Similarly, the potential of energy – creative as well as destructive – embodied in such a half-mythical figure as J.P.M. (who is thus a very appropriate figure in the Hades context) is expressed in the second and third lines of the fifth stanza:

> When from among
> the steel rocks leaps
> J.P.M.

The two lines contain seven consecutive monosyllabic words and, discounting the unstressed "the," six consecutive beats ("steel rocks leaps / J.P.M."), paired off as two lines with three beats in each, and with a symmetry and a near symmetry of assonances (/iː/ – / / – /iː/; /ei/ – /iː/ – /e/) that adds to the impact and counterbalances the staccato rhythm by an element of incantation.

This interaction of rhythm and sound produces a complex cluster of impressions which is deepened and at the same time modified in stanzas six to nine:

> J.P.M.
>
> who enjoyed
> extraordinary privileges
> among virginity
>
> to solve the core
> of whirling flywheels
> by cutting
>
> the Gordian knot
> with a Veronese or
> perhaps a Rubens –
>
> whose cares are about
> the finest on
> the market today –

Here the incantatory element is much more pronounced, above all by means of sonorous and exclamatory words such as "enjoyed" or "extraordinary," as well as by the accumulation of stressed words with long vowels and diphthongs ("solve," "core," "whirling flywheels," "Gordian knot," "Veronese," "Rubens," "car," "finest," "today"). This effect is deepened by the metric and assonantal similarities of the first lines of stanzas five, seven, and eight:

When from among

to solve the core

the Gordian knot

With regard to the assonantal o's, the third of the above lines ("Gordian knot") contains an inversion of the second ("solve . . . core"), so that, taken together, they form a chiasmus, with the two half-open o's (/ :/) in the middle and the open ones (/ /) at either end.

All of these assonances are part of a larger chain of assonantal o's that can be regarded as a manifold echo of the key word "song," the word that *says* song and *is* song, the word that epitomizes the dimension in this poem where sound is sense and sense is sound, where the poem is "sounding sense." It is no accident, therefore, that the most incantatory passages contain an accretion of stressed o's (the four stanzas five through eight contain as many as the remaining nine stanzas together).

Of course, sense is always the result of a complex interaction of word meaning on the semantic level with all the other elements that make up the total form. This means, with regard to the middle section of the poem, that the literally high-sounding portrait of J.P.M. is subverted and partly shifted to the satiric or mock-heroic. Women appear victimized in this modern America; Kora, flower girl and corn maiden, goddess of fertility and nature in its cyclic ascent and descent, Kora is in hell when women and the unspoiled land (which are an identity) become prey to the voracious entrepreneur with his unbounded energy and enormous financial power.

The basic spirit is one of violence and domination; J.P.M. solves the "core / of whirling flywheels" – that is, the problem of taming the energies unleashed by technology – "by cutting / the Gordian knot" rather than by trying to untie it. Again, the pun core/Kora implies that modern technology is a transformation of the basic forces of nature embodied and worshipped in the Greek goddess, so that, as Henry Adams suggested in his autobiography, the cult of the dynamo has indeed replaced the reverence for the virgin. And it is in the same imperialistic spirit that the art collector J.P.M. (who is mockingly aligned here with Alexander the Great, the man who cut the Gordian knot) solves the problem of an indigenous American art: If you don't have it, you can always plunder the treasures of the Old World and import it.

At the end of the poem, we are suddenly confronted with a few details of nature without any explicit reference to civilization, contemporary or otherwise:

Impossible

to say, impossible
to underestimate –
wind, earthquakes in

Manchuria, a
partridge
from dry leaves.

Trying to establish an order that is also based on clash and juxtaposition, we could say that the general and all-encompassing, namely, "wind," is juxtaposed with the unique or particular ("earthquakes in / Manchuria"), and the earthquakes in turn as the catastrophic or extraordinary are juxtaposed with the barely noticeable, be it banal or idyllic: "a / partridge / from dry leaves."

Another reading of "wind" and "earthquakes" could take its clue from the fact that earlier in the poem wind appears in the mythological context, "pulling at the / anemones in / Persephone's cow pasture." Since Persephone is a goddess of growth and fruition, and since the winds were worshipped by Greeks and Romans not only as agents of poetic inspiration but also as agents of fertility and impregnation, "wind" and "earthquakes" could embody creation and destruction, the two basic poles whose inevitable and perennial interaction is one of the recurrent themes of *Spring and All*.

But how should we interpret the three lines preceding this passage (beginning, in stanza eleven, with "Impossible // to say . . . ")? Can we regard them as a wry comment on what follows, in the sense that it is "impossible" to speak of such natural processes and yet "impossible / to underestimate" them? Yes, perhaps, in the sense that it is impossible to underestimate nature in all its manifold manifestations, and yet impossible, in our time, to write nature poems that rely on the evocative power of the sheer naming of a few details: "wind, earthquakes in // Manchuria, a / partridge / from dry leaves."

On the other hand, one could also take the three lines as a meta-statement about the whole poem, or, more precisely, about the revolutionary form of the present poem which is "impossible" from a traditional point of view but also impossible to underestimate because it opens up entirely new vistas for those willing to go along with it.[28]

If, however, one is right in assuming that the "freeplay" of all the details in the poem is at least partly the result of deleted connectives, any additional knowledge of context and background should somewhat narrow the openness of the poem. A case in point is the discovery that the last lines – "a / partridge / from dry leaves" – contain a reference to the painting *Male Ruffed Grouse in the Forest* by Gerald H. Thayer, painted in 1907–08 and acquired by the Metropolitan Museum of Art in 1916 (Figure 13).[29] Thayer's watercolor of a partridge merging with the dry leaves and winter trees behind it is related to the Audubon tradition of accurate and loving observation of the American fauna which Williams so highly valued – an American painting, in other words, that can be seen in direct contrast to the European and exotic masterpieces that J.P.M. accumulated, both as private collector and as president of the Metropolitan Museum.

Moreover, Thayer's painting is a kind of picture puzzle: Based on the sys-

Figure 13. Gerald H. Thayer, *Male Ruffed Grouse in the Forest.* 1907/8. Watercolor on cardboard, 20¼ × 20¼ in. The Metropolitan Museum of Art, New York. Rogers Fund, 1916 (16.167). All rights reserved, The Metropolitan Museum of Art. Reproduced by permission.

tematic exploration of mimicry in animals,[30] it depicts a partridge that is indeed difficult to tell "from dry leaves."[31] On this level, the implicit reference to the picture ties in well with the idea that the last seven lines of the poem can also be read as a meta-statement. Williams may well have singled out Thayer's painting as a work of art that, not unlike his own poem, explores ambiguity and foregrounds the problem of figure and ground. Both painting and poem are about what has to be "figured out"; both contain, in other words, the hide-and-seek dimension that asks for the viewer's or reader's active participation.

These analogies should not obscure the differences. Williams goes much further in replacing the static by the dynamic and in replacing a fixed order by a structure that is polyvalent rather than unequivocal. The result is a poetic form that remains hermetic when we approach it with traditional ideas and demands of coherence.³² If, on the other hand, we willingly join the poet in his attempt to explore *les mots en liberté,* such a poetic form can lead us into the fascinating state of mind in which we hold in abeyance several, partly incompatible meanings, all equally suggestive, and try to come to terms with a host of images and feelings that are to a good extent beyond the logical or rational but hold a power and fascination of an entirely new kind.

This new state of mind is one in which the poet has broken the "tyranny of the image" (*PB,* 137) in its apparent unequivocalness and fixed relation to all the other images surrounding it. We, as readers, in our role as co-creators, should ideally reach the same "fluid" state in which we are able to "[move] at will from one thing to another," a state that for Williams in many ways resembles the special consciousness one has of the world in the moments before falling asleep:

> At first all the images, one or many that fill the mind are fixed. I have passed through it and studied it for years. We look at the ceiling and review the fixities of the day, the month, the year, the lifetime. Then it begins; that happy time when the image becomes broken or begins to break up, becomes a little fluid – or is affected, floats brokenly in the fluid. The rigidities yield – like ice in March, the magic month. (*SE,* 307)

Chapter 5

The Virgin and the Dynamo

It is self-evident that for the American avant-garde, with their concept of an indigenous art, the urban landscape had to become one of the dominant subjects. It is equally evident that within this context of urbanity and technology one motif in particular – the machine – had to acquire a specific importance. And since the machine in many ways epitomizes this world, it is also not surprising that we find the same equivocation in its treatment that prevails in most art dealing with the urban landscape or the modern city in general.

One of the machine paintings that exemplifies this equivocation and is of particular interest in our context is Demuth's *Machinery (or for W. Carlos W.)* (1920; Figure 14). It shows a large factory ventilating system in front of a wall-like assembly of windows that are typical of colonial architecture. The painting is an intriguing combination of faithfully observed details and semiabstract mechanical forms, mounted in a Cubistlike fashion in an empty space, and thus combining, in a way that is typical for Demuth, the realistic, Cubistic, and imaginary. The specific tension in the painting also results from the clash between the delicate architectural grid of the window framework in the background and the bulky tank that spreads in the foreground with its sinuous, somewhat obtrusive, snakelike tubes.

According to Dickran Tashjian, the painting is close in spirit to the works of Duchamp and Picabia, mainly because of its "sinuous and erotic tubing," which relates it to the tradition of the "myth of the female machine" that is so prominent in the work of the two Frenchmen (*Skyscraper Primitives,* pp. 210, 33). Based on this notion (which is plausible so far), Tashjian finds it difficult to say why Demuth inscribed the painting to Williams:

> The two had, of course, been friends since school days, which might account for the inscription. Yet the painting's kinship to the sardonic tone of Picabia and Duchamp at a time when Williams was growing hostile to their influence suggests that Demuth might have gained a perverse pleasure from his dedication. Moreover, in an essay of the previous year, Williams had vehemently declared, "I don't give a damn about airplanes and airplane poetry but I do give a damn about the dis-

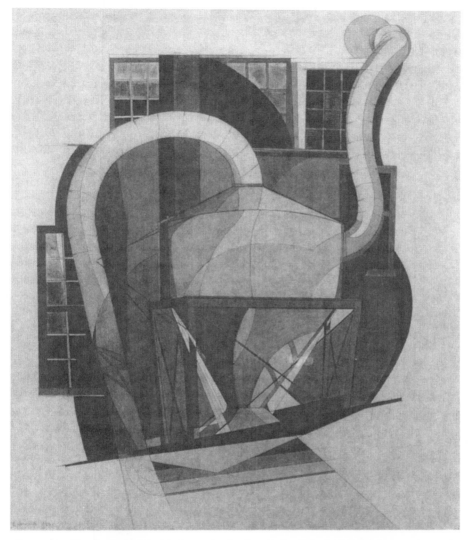

Figure 14. Charles Demuth, *Machinery* (*or For W. Carlos W.*). 1920. Tempera and pencil on cardboard, 24 × 19⅞ in. The Metropolitan Museum of Art, New York. The Alfred Stieglitz Collection, 1949 (49.59.2). All rights reserved, The Metropolitan Museum of Art. Reproduced by permission.

traught mind that must find its release in building gas motors and in balancing them on cloth wings in its agony."[1]

From all that is known about the lifelong friendship between the two artists it seems highly unlikely that Demuth should have inscribed the painting to Williams in a mocking or deprecatory spirit. There are a number of reasons that suggest themselves as an explanation for the dedication. The juxtaposition of windows characteristic of New England and Pennsylvania frame houses with the machinery belonging to an industrial plant focuses on two architectural details which were both typical for the America the artist knew and lived in. Moreover, although the two details are taken from different realms, they were both equally neglected by those adhering to traditional ideas about what is worth being treated as a motif in art. Both Williams and Demuth had discovered the beauty of the indigenous architecture years ago, and both subsequently made it part of their iconography. It figures in many of Demuth's paintings, especially in his Provincetown series and in his studies of churches in the style of Sir Christopher Wren. For Williams it was inseparably tied to his lifelong fight against "the thing that stands eternally in the way of good writing," namely, "the virtual impossibility of lifting to the imagination those things which lie under the direct scrutiny of the senses, close to the nose" (*I: KH*, 14). *Spring and All*, the volume dedicated to Demuth, begins with the complaint that there is "a constant barrier between the reader and his consciousness of immediate contact with the world. If there is an ocean it is here. Or rather, the whole world is between: Yesterday, tomorrow, Europe, Asia, Africa, – all things removed and impossible, the tower of the church at Seville, the Parthenon" (*I*, 88).[2]

In *Machinery*, Demuth does exactly what Williams and other artist friends from the Stieglitz and Kreymborg circles called for: He meets his own world head-on, juxtaposing two of its essential aspects – a great and still viable architectural tradition, and an industrial present that shapes the age, irrespective of the fact that most artists continued to ignore its existence.

On the other hand, the fact that Demuth eroticizes the machine (albeit in a playful and unobtrusive manner) must have been richly allusive to Williams. Demuth was of course familiar with Williams's efforts to move toward an empathetic, immanental experience of the world, an experience that entails, as I have shown, moving beyond the abstract-visual perception to a kinesthetic and synesthetic perception by means of all five senses. In such an experience the erotic plays an important role, since the desire for a fusion of self and world is a kind of embrace, an affirmative appropriation or possession of the world. "If there are spaces appropriate to the muscles and to each of the five senses," writes J. Hillis Miller, "there also exists a sexual space, perhaps even more important than the others. A man's body is endowed with a sexual sense which has a unique power to polarize the world. Close to the kinesthetic way of knowing, but not identical with it, the sexual sense too takes the world into the body and recreates it there, giving it a special balance and weight according to its erotic values" (*Poets of Reality*, p. 321).

Both Williams and Demuth shared this sense of the importance of experiencing and expressing the erotic dimension. Demuth's still lifes are often imbued with a sense of the erotic similar to that in Williams's poems of landscapes, trees, and flowers, some of which are, as we have seen, veritable *paysages de femme*. This common dimension strengthened not only their personal ties but also those to the other artist friends around them, for Williams and Demuth were far from being alone in this respect.[3] The erotic and sexual dimension is obvious in many landscape paintings of Marsden Hartley and Arthur Dove, as well as in the landscapes and flowers of Georgia O'Keeffe. Their nature eroticism became the nonironic counterpart of the satirical or playful machine eroticism of Duchamp and Picabia, with which it entered into a complex dialogue. In this respect, Demuth is a particularly interesting painter insofar as he used the erotic in both its affirmative and ironic mode.

In Duchamp's and Picabia's case, it seems important to note that in spite of their basically ironic stance they belong at least partly to the same camp, approaching, as it were, the same goal from the opposite direction. Thus Duchamp admitted later that the role of the erotic in his work was "enormous." Statements such as the following make it clear that his meta-ironic treatment of the erotic is in fact a satirical comment on the age, since the erotic for him is "the basis of everything," although "no one talks about it":

> I believe in eroticism a lot, because it's truly a rather widespread thing throughout the world, a thing that everyone understands. It replaces, if you wish, what other literary schools called Symbolism, Romanticism. It could be another "ism," so to speak. . . . It's really a way to try to bring out in the daylight things that are constantly hidden.[4]

The last sentence of this blandly satirical *and* serious statement recalls one of Williams's finest essays, "A Matisse," in which the painter's uninhibited celebration of the beauty of the naked woman means to the poet exactly that: "to bring out in the daylight [what is] constantly hidden." From that time on Williams was to repeatedly identify the sun and the artist as the male shaping principle at work, with the work of art as the outcome of a kinesthetic interplay of the male and the female:

> It was the first of summer. Bare as was his mind of interest in anything save the fullness of his knowledge, into which her simple body entered as into the eye of the sun himself, so he painted her. So she came to America.
>
> No man in my country has seen a woman naked and painted her as if he knew anything except that she was naked. No woman in my country is naked except at night.
>
> In the french sun, on the french grass in a room on Fifth Ave., a french girl lies and smiles at the sun without seeing us.(*SE*, 30–31)

In photography, which played an important role in this context, Stieglitz was the great innovative figure (with an enormous influence on other photographers as well as painters), followed in the twenties by, among others, Imogen Cunningham and Edward Weston. In Stieglitz, the relation between his landscapes and the series of photographs he took of his wife, Georgia O'Keeffe, over the years is of particular interest here. On the one hand, he celebrated the erotic in many of his nature photographs; on the other hand, he discovered and expressed the landscape in the many semiabstract pictures he took of Georgia O'Keeffe's body.

In her turn, his wife – the most daring of all avant-garde artists in this respect – turned many of her flower paintings into undisguised celebrations of the female body and the female genitals (Figure 15). Her gigantic blossoms, often approaching a Dionysian whorl in their dynamic double movement of expanding and contracting, unfolding and enfolding, bridge the distance between viewer and painting by virtually taking the viewer into the immense flowers, to the point where the viewer becomes the body-flower, so to speak, experiencing its being, its flowering, from the inside out, feeling the double movement of entering and approaching its core *and* of opening up and expanding from within. (It is this double movement of immersion and expansion that Williams describes in "The Poem" [*CP2*, 74], in which he immerses himself in a woman's eyes to the point where he becomes her eyes, her mind, the moment she wakes up and looks round – to "take in," absorb the room, the world outside: "a lady's / eyes – waking / centrifugal, centripetal.")

Thus Williams and Demuth knew that they shared with their mutual friends a fundamental goal, namely, an art that expressed a spiritual and sensual union of man and nature, an art that reflected one's sense of being-in-the-world as an immanental indwelling.

The unabashed eroticism in many of these works was of course partly responsible for the openly hostile reaction or the silent consternation of many contemporaries, but this reaction in turn helped Williams and his artist friends to come to a clearer view of the deeper rift separating them from the more conservative artists and the bewildered public. One of the main reasons for this rift, they realized, was the still deeply rooted Puritan tradition. The resulting anti-Puritan attitude, widespread among the avant-garde, found its clearest and most vehement expression in the writings of D.H. Lawrence, Randolph Bourne and the other *Seven Arts* critics, and, of course, Williams himself.

For Williams the influence of the Puritans was devastating, above all because of their fear of nature and sexuality. Their pernicious reign began with the destruction of Red Indian culture; since then the Puritan kept, as Williams put it in the magnificent prose of *In the American Grain*, "his frightened grip upon the throat of the world" (*IAG*, 167), preventing a new "great flowering" of American civilization.

Williams's heroes of *In the American Grain* have, as critics often pointed out, all the virtues that the Puritans lack. They are "men intact – with all their senses waking" (p. 206) – who dared to discover, accept, and *touch* the New World.

Figure 15. Georgia O'Keeffe, *Black Iris*. 1926. Oil on canvas, 36 × 29⅞ in. The Metropolitan Museum of Art, New York. The Alfred Stieglitz Collection, 1949 (69.278.1). All rights reserved, The Metropolitan Museum of Art. Reproduced by permission.

Williams sets their morality against that of the Puritans, a morality born of fear: "It is *this* to be moral: to be *positive,* to be peculiar, to be sure, generous, brave – to MARRY, to *touch* – to give because one HAS, not because one has nothing" (p. 121). The Puritans, on the other hand, totally rejected the land into which they came, and all their values emerged out of that fundamental negation:

"[T]hey looked back at the world and damning its perfections praised a zero in themselves" (p. 65). They saw themselves surrounded by the " 'squallid, horrid American Desart' " (p. 82), and they were thus "without ground on which to rest their judgments of this world, fearing to touch its bounties . . . " (p. 80):

> These were the modes of a people, small in number, beset by dangers and in terror. They dared not think. If frightened by Indians or the supernatural, they shook and committed horrid atrocities in the name of their creed, the cost of emptiness. All they saw they lived by but denied. And *this* is overlooked. (p. 112)

In such a spiritual climate the pioneers were totally incapable of "giving their fine energy" to the "great New World." Yet they could not "quite leave their hands off it but must TOUCH it, in a 'practical' way, that is a joking, shy, nasty way, using 'science,' etc., not with the generosity of the savage or the scientist but in a shameful manner" (p. 157). This attitude led directly to Benjamin Franklin's and Hamilton's doctrine of thrift and the industrial exploitation of natural resources. The world is now dealt with in a spirit of inquisition born of fear, and in a spirit of acquisition born of prudence – one has to understand, control, exploit and, finally, accumulate:

> Delay, all through youth, halt and cessation, not of effort, but of touch, all through life as it is learned: no end save accumulation, always on the way to BIGGER opportunity; we keep realization from the mind with a purpose till men are trained never to possess fully but just to SEE. This makes scientists and it makes the masochist. Keep it cold and small and under the cold lens. (p. 175)

Thus one ends up with a civilization in which "through terror, there is no direct touch; all is cold, little and discreet – save just under the hide" (p. 176). What the Puritans unconsciously headed for was a "deanimated" world which provided in every situation "a mechanism to increase the gap between touch and thing, *not* to have contact": "Deanimated, that's the word; something the sound of 'metronome,' a mechanical means; Yankee inventions. Machines were not so much to save time as to save dignity that fears the animate touch" (p. 177).

The Myth of the Female Machine

The direct connection that Williams establishes here between the fear, and the subsequent repression, of the sensual and sexual on the one hand, and the development of technology on the other, is the most forceful and explicit version of an idea that intermittently had been voiced before and found its clearest artistic expression in the myth of the female machine. One of the first writers who related the absence (or repression) of sexuality to the presence (or fascination) of the machine was Henry Adams. In "The Dynamo and the Virgin," written in 1900 but published for the first time in 1918 as a chapter of *The Education of Henry Adams,* he tried to come to terms with the strangely different role that "the Woman" played in Europe and in America.[5] In Adams's view, the Woman – in the mythical embodiment of Venus and/or the Virgin – was "the highest energy ever known to man" (p. 1071):

> The force of the Virgin was still felt at Lourdes, and seemed to be as potent as X-rays; but in America neither Venus nor Virgin ever had value as force – at most as sentiment. . . .
>
> The Woman had once been supreme; in France she still seemed potent, not merely as sentiment, but as a force. Why was she unknown in America? Anyone brought up among the Puritans knew that sex was sin. In any previous age, sex was strength. Neither art nor beauty was needed. Every one, even among the Puritans, knew that neither Diana of the Ephesians nor any of the Oriental goddesses was worshipped for her beauty. She was goddess because of her force; she was the animated dynamo; she was reproduction – the greatest and most mysterious of all energies; all she needed was to be fecund. (p. 1070)

According to Adams, the dynamo had replaced the Virgin in America, and thus Europe and America had become "two kingdoms of force which had nothing in common but attraction" (p. 1070). Thus Adams regarded the dynamo, the most attractive of the "thousand symbols of ultimate energy" at the "Great Exposition of 1900" in Paris, as the American equivalent to the force of Venus and the Virgin in Europe, and as indicative of a civilization in which even art, "like the American language and American education, was as far as possible sexless" (pp. 1067, 1072).

Among the New York avant-garde, Duchamp and Picabia were the first to relate repressed sexual energy to the creation of the machine.[6] In *Nude Descending a Staircase* Duchamp undercuts and eliminates the erotic appeal of the nude by presenting it as a series of overlapping views, thus turning the painting into a Cubistic and Futuristic version of the scientific photographs of Marey and Muybridge. Duchamp's famous *The Bride Stripped Bare By Her Bachelors, Even* can also be directly related to his view of the modern age as epitomized by America, an age which, as he predicted upon his arrival in New York, "is to be still more abstract, more cold, more scientific."[7] Although the *Bride* or *Large Glass,* as it is also called, is in many ways an inscrutable work, it is evident that it dramatizes the failure of love in our time, confronting the viewer not only with a work whose title clashes with the total absence of any kind of erotic or sensuous impact but also with a bride who is eternally separated from the Bachelors. Thus the mechanistic woman (who is more like a scientific apparatus of an undetermined order than a human being) and her suitors are forever barred from sexual consummation and sexual fulfillment.

Francis Picabia, on the other hand, frequently presented the machine as a hermaphrodite, or as a female capable of autocreation. One of his machine drawings, *Voilà elle,* appeared in the magazine *291* in 1915 (Figure 16). It shows an abstract, elegant machine, consisting of wheels, rods, screws, pipes, and wires attached to a central receptacle. Tubes and rods are clearly phallic in nature,

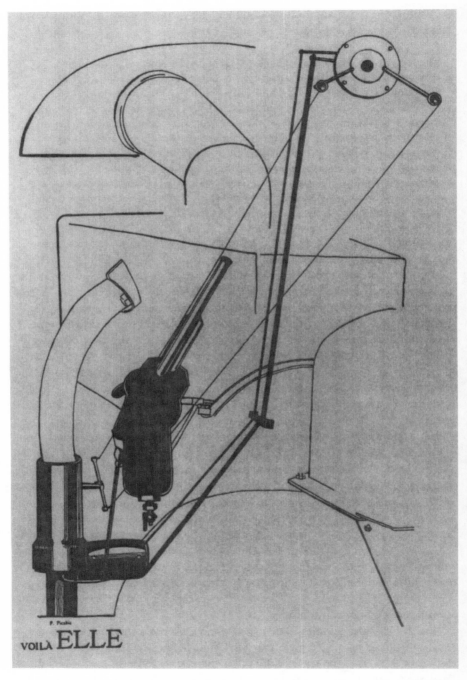

Figure 16. Francis Picabia, *Voilà elle*. 1915. Drawing, from *291*, No. 9 (Nov. 1915).

whereas receptacle and wheel are suggestive of womb and vulva. One of the phallic forms can be regarded as a pistol aiming at a wheel that becomes a target; pistol and target are connected by wires in such a way as to suggest that the pistol (or phallus) can be triggered off by the target (or vulva) when the latter moves, and vice versa. Thus the drawing can be read as a witty and satirical presentation of the idea of the sexual union – and spiritual wholeness – of man and woman: Elle, the machine, is a new mechano-morphic embodiment of this wholeness, with the male and the female tied to each other, each able to trigger the other – a sex automation that is autonomous and autocreative. Once created, Picabia implies, the machine will procreate itself.

Voilà elle is the last of a series of drawings by Picabia in *291* on the myth of the female machine, a series that began with *Fille née sans mère* in No. 4 (June 1915) and was continued with *Portrait d'une jeune fille américaine dans l'état de nudité* in No. 5-6 (July–August 1915). With the title as reference point one can make out in *Fille née sans mère* a more or less organic structure consisting of rods, springs, and billowing parts that could belong to a female body – a machine woman or monster whose parts, however, cannot be logically related to each other and serve no discernible function. The title suggests that it is the weird offspring of the unholy marriage between man and technology. In an untitled essay in the next number of *291*, Paul Haviland tried to explain the rational grounds of Picabia's Dadaesque drawings:

> We are living in the age of the machine.
> Man made the machine in his own image. She has limbs which act; lungs which breathe; a heart which beats; a nervous system through which runs electricity. The phonograph is the image of his voice; the camera the image of his eye. The machine is his "daughter born without a mother." That is why he loves her.[8]

Picabia's *Portrait d'une jeune fille américaine dans l'état de nudité* (Figure 17) in the same number is a variation on and an inversion of the same theme. If the first drawing of the "daughter without a mother" refers to the creation of the (female) machine, the second satirizes the sexual nature of the American female as cold and mechanical: a true product of the new scientific spirit, the American woman is nothing but a spark plug when stripped to her essence ("dans l'état de nudité"). Even in a Puritan civilization in which man keeps "his frightened grip upon the throat of the world" (*IAG*, 67), sex cannot be suppressed altogether. It can, however, reveal itself at the most as "acid passion" (*IAG*, 183), or, more often, as something performed dutifully. Thus the girl, like the spark plug, will do her duty under the proper conditions FOR-EVER, as the brand name of the spark plug promises – sex is taboo outside marriage but the woman will give herself to the man within bonds that last "forever." The result of these strict morals is a society in which "[p]eople married and became the parents of children and were driven to seek divorce before they had even scraped the surface of intimacy."[9]

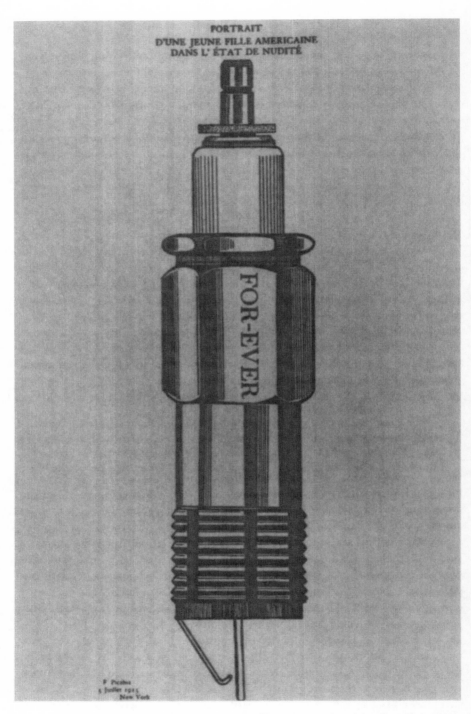

Figure 17. Francis Picabia, *Portrait d'une jeune fille américaine dans l'état de nudité*. 1915. Drawing, from *291*, Nos. 5–6 (July–Aug. 1915).

The phallic quality of the spark plug, on the other hand, can be taken as a sign of the masculinity of the emancipated American woman, who, in Lewis Mumford's words, "widened her political scope . . . at the expense of her sex life. Instead of ruling with and through her sex, the American woman, despite her studious attention to her own beauty, her figure and her dress, learned to preserve her freedom and power by keeping sex at a distance" ("The Metropolitan Milieu," p. 54). "Oh," writes Williams, "men have had women, millions of them, of course: good, firm Janes. But one that spouted any comprehensive joy? Never. Dolly Madison was a bright doll. At best they want to be men, sit and be a pal. It's all right. How could they do anything else with the men brutally beaten by the life −" (*IAG*, 179).[10]

Portraits of Women

Turning to Williams's poems about women in America we find that, in a manner characteristic for him, they run the whole gamut from grim indictment to high praise: indictment of the destructive Puritanism that prevents Americans from accepting the female principle, and hence prevents them from bringing about a new "great flowering" of the land; and praise, on the other hand, for the women figures who embody the "radiant gist," the "Beautiful Thing" which in a civilization "divorced" from the ground is repressed, maimed, or disregarded, but which reemerges everywhere and can be encountered at all times and in all places for those whose eyes and souls are not closed to it.

In Williams's poems, too, the role of woman is sometimes related to the opposition of nature and technology. In "At the Faucet of June," for instance, J.P.M., enjoying "extraordinary privileges / among virginity," is a figure whose attractiveness is as understandable as it is dubious; the easy shift, however, from "virginity" to "whirling flywheels" suggests that in such a world − although women may be "enjoyed" − woman as force is indeed replaced by the dynamo.[11]

Usually, however, the women who are victimized are being subjected to hostile forces of a more basic kind, albeit forces which are − as is made clear in *In the American Grain* − at the root of the strange craze for all things technological. As a consequence of this, disintegration, decadence, and violence appear more often in the urban than in the rural world, although women in the latter are almost as liable to become victims, since society as a whole has not turned to, but against, the life-sustaining ground. Thus one of the most memorable poems about victimized woman, "To Elsie" (*CP1*, 217), is a pastoral gone awry. No longer rooted in "peasant traditions," girls such as Elsie easily succumb to the attractions of the city, the world of "cheap / jewelry" and "rich young men with fine eyes." Hence it is true that Elsie's abuse, too, is "clearly a metaphor for the social dislocations brought on by rapid industrialization," as Peter Schmidt puts it, so that "Williams' bitter and frightened poem ends in despair,

with America's motorized Arcadia careening out of control: 'No one / to witness / and adjust, no one to drive the car' " ("Modernist Pastoral," p. 402).
Williams, however, does more than simply oppose the rural and urban realms
with their respective values; the land itself in its most isolated rural areas has
never been Arcadia, at least not since the white settlers set foot on it, the

>   mountain folk from Kentucky
>
>   or the ribbed north end of
>   Jersey
>   with its isolate lakes and
>
>   valleys, its deaf-mutes, thieves
>   old names
>   and promiscuity between
>
>   devil-may-care men who have taken
>   to railroading
>   out of sheer lust of adventure –

Elsie (and girls like her) can only succumb to the dubious dreams of the industrial
world because she belongs to those "so desolate / so hemmed round / with
disease or murder // that she'll be rescued by an agent –." The others stay out
there, to be seduced or even raped,

>   succumbing without
>   emotion
>   save numbed terror
>
>   under some hedge of choke-cherry
>   or viburnum –
>   which they cannot express –

The destiny of those nameless girls in the backwoods is clearly related to Elsie's,
down to the "choking" alliterative consonants /tʃ/ and /dʒ/ in the preceding
passage, which are echoed in the sound of "cheap / jewelry and rich young
men." The sound of the names of the trees and bushes is loaded with as much
disgust as that of the treacherous seductions of the city; there is no genuine
pastoral world left when people behave "as if the earth under our feet / were
/ an excrement of some sky."

Hence even the famous opening lines of the poem become ambivalent: "The
pure products of America / go crazy" is an outcry against a mentality that
destroys the best and most sensitive human beings before all the others, an outcry
that might have been present in Ginsberg's mind when he wrote the famous
opening line of Howl: "I saw the best minds of my generation destroyed by
madness, starving hysterical naked." But "pure" can also mean "genuine," "un-
adulterated," with a cynical undertone: The trueborn offspring of Puritan America are doomed, raised with a religion that denies the rights of the body and

turns the wilderness in which they find themselves into the "squallid, horrid American Desart." This rural America is a cruel parody of any genuine pastoral vision. It is a world in which all things physical and natural have been for so long bedeviled that the Promised Land has been turned into a prison and its fruit into "filth," so that mind and body, spirit and senses alike now starve:

> and we degraded prisoners
> destined
> to hunger until we eat filth
>
> while the imagination strains
> after deer
> going by fields of goldenrod in
>
> the stifling heat of September

There is an element of self-mockery in these lines; the poet is not only acutely aware of the clash between an ideal pastoral world and the actual life in the regions still untouched by rapid urbanization and industrialization; he is also aware of the dangers of trading off the actual world for a romantic ideal that remains fictional. He has to remain true to his vocation of being "a mirror to this modernity," he who had jumped into the filthy Passaic and had "felt the utter depth of its filthiness, / The vile breath of its degradation, / And sank down knowing this was me now" (*CP1*, 28, 35).

This means that it is all too easy to forget that "destruction and creation / are simultaneous," and that one cannot have the "slender green" of the milk-weed without the "sand and rubble" from which it reaches up, because they are "premising the flower" (*CP2*, 72). Likewise, one cannot have gentleness without violence, because each is conceived and born out of the opposition to the other: "Violence and / gentleness, which is the core? Is gentleness the core?"

Thus the tension between the ideal and the actual, the gentle or violent is a perennial one, and the "divorce" of the times is to be found not so much in a degraded present compared to a flowering past but in a civilization that opts for one side (spirit, the so-called good) against the other (matter, the "bad") and goes astray, losing one with the other because they cannot be separated.

And yet a different, more complex order reemerges, against all odds. Thus, in "Horned Purple" (*CP1*, 221), the actual seems deplorable when set off against the ideal: The passionate but courteous shepherds of the classical pastoral have become "dirty satyrs," "vulgarity raised to the last power." It is "the time of the year / when boys fifteen and seventeen / wear two horned lilac blossoms / in their caps − or over one ear," and the poet asks, "What is it that does this?" Beyond their own doing, something does it, does it to them, and suddenly they are turned into satyrs who "stand in the doorways / on the business street with a sneer / on their faces" − but also "adorned with blossoms"! Once more, one could say, this is a pastoral gone awry, with "courtships" that leave little to be hoped for by the girls courted; but again, the lines from "To All Gentleness" are a more appropriate expression of the ambivalent feelings elicited by the drives and deeper needs embodied in the "dirty satyrs": "Violence or gentleness, which is the core?"

One way of demonstrating how this ambivalence is embedded in the structure of the poem is to set off the stanzas that consist of two to four lines against the interspersed single lines. The stanzas contain the narrative elements proper, with the sordid details and the poet's comment ("Dirty satyrs . . . "), which explicitly relates the poem to the bucolic tradition; the single lines, on the other hand – which receive a special weight by the way they stand out – ask for the universal behind the particular and then concentrate on the spell created by the flowers:

> What is it that does this?
>
> Horned purple
>
> Lilacs –
>
> adorned with blossoms

At the end of the poem, the last two lines superimpose the two levels of the repellent and the magical, with a surprising twist, however, to the idyllic, which in itself sets up a kind of tension to what has come before:

> Out of their sweet heads
> dark kisses – rough faces

That these "portraits of the times" are often more than just pleasant must not prevent us from realizing, Williams insists, that the satyrs live. And so does Kora, although she is in Hell, and even Venus, for that matter. All it takes to recall this is to guard against falling into the old trap of opposing, as irreconcilable opposites, creation and destruction, love and hate, gentleness and violence, presence and absence. Instead of just mourning the absence of the "great flowering" in an impoverished present, Williams wants us to keep in mind that presence and absence are two concepts distilled from an indivisible one, as we have to keep in mind that the concept of the ideal beauty cannot be opposed to the more or less imperfect beauty we find in each individual human being: "The aberrant is the classic: as she" (I, 283), writes Williams in A Novelette, the moment he rediscovers all women, Woman, in his wife:

> And what is a beautiful woman?
> She is one.
> Over and over again, she is one. . . .
> So all things enter into the singleness of the moment and the moment partakes
> of the diversity of all things. . . . So she – building of all excellence [–] is, in her

single body, beautiful; enforcing the mind by imperfections to a height. Born
again, Venus from the confused sea. Summing all the virtues. Single. Excellence.
Female. (I: AN, 282)

The perfection is an envisioned – and only in the act of envisioning also actual
– endpoint on a scale, inseparable from imperfections because it is these very
imperfections that "[enforce] the mind . . . to a height."

The ending of *A Novelette* contains in an intriguing way this irreducible
tension in all things that has its origin in the polarized forces indivisibly contained
in them, forces that within binary thinking are usually conceived of as separate
entities but which become part of an indivisible One the moment we regard
them as "points on the same scale, distinctions of the same energy":[12]

Or to sum it all up there's the legend in gold letters on the window of the abandoned saloon:

OL   M P I

(*I*, 304)

What is present here points to what is absent; what is absent, on the other hand,
is part of the present. What is both present and absent is a "legend," a legend
in the sense of a mythology (that is, a fiction, an order, a "design") and a thing
of the past (classical antiquity), but a legend also that is part of the present, an
object referred to, gold letters saying O L   M P I. And what is absent, moreover, is also present in an additional sense, because only when we can read the
sign *with* the missing letters do we know what it "means." What is there in the
narrow sense of the word is indeed meaningless, as is presence without absence,
absence without presence. The resulting tension is ineluctable and irreducible:
not because the present "is only the sign of a lost significance"[13] set against a
haunting order of the past but because the tension between life and "legend"
(or created order) is omnipresent, in the past as well as in one's own world.
Hence the order of the old myths and Gods is not invoked to redeem the chaos
of the present, as Eliot once suggested of Joyce's *Ulysses* and, indirectly, of his
own *Waste Land*. The disorder of the present is of a different sort; it is, in Joseph
Riddel's words, "a failure of recognition, a failure to read what is there, dispersed
and concealed in the chaos of common speech" (*The Inverted Bell*, p. 105). It is
a failure to understand that the Word is (only) there within the words, that it is
present in spite of its absence, and that one's own culture has to take it up, as
any other, in the never-ending process of a renewed re-cognition and re-
creation of order, out of the life and speech at hand. Hence in language (and in
art in general) the classic is neither of the past nor of an order opposed to the
disorder of the present. All one has to realize is that literature "is and must be
constantly in revolution, being reborn" perennially (*I: AN*, 283) until, one day,
one has finally understood that "the dream / is in pursuit" and the essential

problem is "how to begin to begin again." This is the moment when one will understand that "exactly *that* is the only classic" (*I: AN*, 283).

Thus presence and absence, order and disorder, seed (or rubble) and flower, the timebound and the timeless, the aberrant and the classic, become two in one, in an indivisible *conjunctio oppositorum*. As a result of this, Williams's gods and goddesses are a part of his own world, although they are rarely named. Sometimes he names them indirectly, as in "A Negro Woman" (*PB*, 123), where his black Kora appears "carrying a bunch of marigolds / wrapped / in an old newspaper." What else is she, the poet says,

> but an ambassador
> from another world
>
> a world of pretty marigolds
> of two shades
> which she announces
>
> not knowing what she does
> other
> than walk the streets
>
> holding the flower upright
> as a torch
> so early in the morning

Many of his Kora or Venus figures he meets in the street, chance encounters that become epiphanic moments, often sparked by gestures or movements that enable him to empathize with them on a deeper level, perhaps because their movements convey a complete absence of masks and role playing, and give him the impression that these women have the center of gravity in themselves. One of them is

> THE GIRL
>
> with big breasts
> under a blue sweater
>
> bareheaded –
> crossing the street
>
> reading a newspaper
> stops, turns
>
> and looks down
> as though
>
> she had seen a dime
> on the pavement
> (*CP2*, 444)

When Williams published the first version of this poem in a little college periodical, he accompanied it by a short commentary: "But there is a dignity in this girl quite comparable to that of the Venus (de Milo). Why not imagine this girl Venus? Venus lives!. . . . [The poem] presents a simple image in the same sort of light that the Athenians placed Venus – only not in the same context."[14] The revised version of the poem is shorter, more concentrated, and changed in its stanzaic form: Instead of the irregular free verse of the first version we now have regular two-line stanzas. In addition to that, Williams eliminated some of the details that firmly placed the girl in the poverty-stricken working-class world of the Depression. It seems that he felt the need to bring the "aberrant" and the "classic" a bit closer together, fearing that the beauty he saw and wanted to bring out in the girl had been lost on his readers in the first version.

It is interesting to see the poem and commentary in comparison to Rilke's poem "Archaischer Torso Apollos." Here are the first two stanzas:

> Wir Kannten nicht sein underhörtes Haupt,
> darin die Augenäpfel reiften. Aber
> sein Torso glüht noch wie ein Kandelaber,
> in dem sein Schauen, nur zurückgeschraubt,
>
> sich hält und glänzt. Sonst könnte nicht der Bug
> der Brust dich blenden, und im leisen Drehen
> der Lenden könnte nicht ein Lächeln gehen
> zu jener Mitte, die die Zeugung trug.
>
> (We never knew his phantastic head
> Wherein the eyes' apples ripened. But
> his torso glows yet like a candelabrum
> in which his gaze, turned inwards, keeps on
>
> shining. Otherwise the stern of his chest
> could not blind you, and in the gentle twisting
> of his loins the smile could not attain
> that center which bore the procreative seed.)[15]

Rilke is struck not so much by the beauty of Apollo's torso as by the fact that the beauty of his head and gaze is still present in his torso. The beauty of what is absent is contained in what is present; head and body, in their emanation, cannot be separated, even for those who have never seen the head or gaze.

Another paradox of equal importance is that of motion and stillness. As the body glows with the beauty of the gaze, so the motionless torso is full of the "gentle twisting of his loins." Motion is stillness here; stillness is motion. "The eye sees nouns and verb as one: things in motion, motion in things," says Ernest Fenollosa.[16] The eye and the mind can transcend the fixed categories of language, as they can transcend the fixed categories of time and space, motion and stillness, in a painting, a photograph, or a sculpture.

The fact that there is no punctuation at the end of Williams's poem "The Girl" indicates that it contains a similar reification of time or motion in stillness, although we first have motion itself and then motion distilled in a pose, so to speak. It is a pose that is also full of erotic power, contained in the girl's bodily presence and reverberating, as it were, in the "still" at the end, as Apollo's erotic power is present in his torso, particularly in that magic "gentle twisting of his loins."

For Williams, as for Rilke, it is a body's presence and the expressiveness of bearings, gestures, and movements that allow it to come alive, and that enable the artist to empathize with the human beings portrayed in a kind of "negative capability." In all of Williams's poems devoted to people, especially women, we find this desire to reach their "core" by an experience that conflates inside and outside, and appropriates them by way of a language activating all the senses, in an act which is identification, embrace, and possession all at once. Ideally, this leads to a deeper, intuited knowledge, in which the experience of the mind fuses with all the other senses, including the erotic. In accordance with his own tenet, "a thing known passes out of the mind into the muscles" (*I: KH*, 74), the other is known in a holistic experience in which a woman or a man is "a physical presence waking the poet's body in response to her [or his] body's life," as J. Hillis Miller succinctly puts it (*Poets of Reality*, p. 322).

> . . . what a blessing it is
> to see you in the street again,
> powerful woman,
> coming with swinging haunches,
> breasts straight forward,
> supple shoulders, full arms
> and strong soft hands (I've felt them)
> carrying the heavy basket.
>   (*CP*1, 66)

Many of these poems, among them "The Girl," "A Negro Woman," "To a Poor Old Woman," "Proletarian Portrait," and the poem from *Paterson* 5, "There's a Woman in Our Town," are about women from the working class. Williams finds these women admirable for their ability to live outside the stifling constraints of middle-class values, which all too often put a blight on a woman's capacity to live in accordance with her deeper feelings and needs and to express them through her body. The attitudes expressed by the gestures and actions of these women bespeak simplicity, care, earnestness, single-mindedness, and intensity. Their senses are indeed "intact, awake": "To a Poor Old Woman" (*CP*1, 383), for example, is one of Williams's most delightful poems about taste, with the old woman "munching a plum on / the street a paper bag / of them in her hand":

> They taste good to her
> They taste good
> to her. They taste
> good to her

The poem becomes, as it were, the woman eating the plums; its rhythm is that of munching, tasting, thoroughly enjoying plums, with subtle variations in the lineation of the same phrase that create a constant shifting of emphasis, from the good taste of the plums to the act of tasting itself and then to *this woman* who enjoys them so much that she "gives herself / to the one half / sucked out in her hand." In the end, the enjoyment takes over and the tasting pervades all the senses, changes the mood, and even permeates the space to envelop observer and woman, self and other, in a common realm:

> Comforted
> a solace of ripe plums
> seeming to fill the air
> They taste good to her

In "Proletarian Portrait," sense of touch (which here leads literally to "contact" with the ground) is conveyed by the little detail that this "big young bareheaded woman" is standing in the street with "[o]ne stockinged foot toeing / the sidewalk" while she looks intently into the shoe in her hand and "pulls out the paper insole / to find the nail // That has been hurting her" (*CP*1, 385).

"Venus Lives": Williams and Stieglitz

The self-containedness and quiet self-assurance of these women also comes from a total absence of anxious observation of decorum, of what one is allowed to do and what one must not do. The word "bareheaded," for instance, which appears in "The Girl," "A Negro Woman," and "Proletarian Portrait," is highly revealing in this respect. It implies that all these women do not hide their sex, that they dare to show their head and their hair. The full relevance of this detail, which we are likely to miss more than half a century later, is contained in a letter that Alfred Stieglitz wrote about the street life of Paris as he experienced it when visiting the city in 1911:

> Paris is the only place I saw at the time that had stallions on the street instead of geldings, and women going through the streets without hats. The women are free, feminine. The men, very male, all going about their work. All simple, alive. Each one arranging his wares with love, with a sense of order, with gaiety.[17]

The passage is striking for its rapid transition from stallions to the "free, feminine" hatless women,[18] the "very male" men, and the wares arranged "with love, with a sense of order, with gaiety." Stieglitz obviously relates these details because they all express for him a basic affirmation of sexuality which leads to an affirmation of life. Moreover, we discover that, once more, both Stieglitz and Williams consciously or unconsciously connect the urban scenes and portraits with the pastoral tradition. Affirmation of sexuality is related to naturalness and simplicity, to a conscious or intuitive recognition and acceptance of the basic needs of both mind and body, in an environment where humanity is in harmony with the world.

Thus not only Stieglitz's commentary on his Paris experience but also the two photographs that he published of his stay there can be seen as a blending of the urban with the pastoral world. Like almost all of Stieglitz's urban landscapes they are based on the opposition of nature and city, a structural trait they share with the work of the other artists of the Stieglitz circle and with many of Williams's poems. In Stieglitz's famous early photographs of New York, taken between 1895 and 1915, the awesome or sublime impact of the metropolis is usually softened by such natural or pastoral elements as trees, snow, horses, sleighs, water, sky with clouds. His two Paris photographs, on the other hand, are street scenes focusing on people and animals in an urban, but not distinctly metropolitan, environment. One of them shows a man grooming a horse, in a dark street with a pile of wood in the foreground, the other a young, bareheaded woman crossing a wide street at an oblique angle, framed by pedestrians on a sidewalk and by trees, people, and carts in the background.

Stieglitz obviously felt that in order to catch the essence of a place and its people that were to him "all simple, alive" and impressive for their "freedom to be natural," he had to take pictures that were as direct and uncontrived as possible. To stress this informal character he called such pictures "snapshots." The second of the two Paris pictures (Figure 18) is particularly interesting in this respect. The random constellation of figures in the street justifies the title; but embedded in the accidental and momentary is a significant opposition, with the woman as the picture's unmistakable center – a dark, graceful figure standing out against the shining backlit street – set against all other people who are walking or riding in carts, in the background and to the left on an elevated sidewalk. The group on the sidewalk forms a counterpoint to the other people, and in particular to the young woman in the street. It conveys the feeling of being fenced in by the railings, in marked contrast to the spacious, bright, open street, which the young woman has almost to herself. The pedestrians to the left all wear hats; one of them is a woman with a big, heavy hat that catches all the light in what seem to be gauze flowers and ribbons, darkenening or blotting out the face underneath. This woman is a counterpoint to the bareheaded woman in the street, not only with regard to their heads but also to their figures, their bodies, gaits, and postures, all enforcing the contrast between a way of life that is "simple, alive" and natural on the one hand and constrained, weighed down, or even blighted by constricting notions of decency and decorum on the other hand.

Figure 18. Alfred Stieglitz, *A Snapshot – Paris*. 1911. Photogravure, 13.8 × 17.4 cm. *Camera Work*, 41 (Jan. 1913). The Metropolitan Museum of Art, New York. Gift of J. B. Newman, 1958 (58.577.36). All rights reserved, The Metropolitan Museum of Art. Reproduced by permission of the Georgia O'Keefe Foundation and The Metropolitan Museum of Art.

The Sense of Touch

The fact that so much that was crucial for Williams can be found in Stieglitz and the other artists of the Stieglitz circle is of course by no means accidental. Bram Dijkstra goes so far as to maintain that Williams was directly indebted to Stieglitz for his fundamental tenets, such as the need for an indigenous American art based on genuine "contact" – contact with the ground, the local, the here and now, the *Ding an sich* – or the fight against an art that imposed a symbolic import on things instead of being "free to recognize the living moment when it occurs, and to let it flower, without preconceived ideas about what it *should be*, so that you really *are* the moment."[19] One need not subscribe to Dijkstra's somewhat simplistic notions of influence to see that Williams was indeed in many ways indebted to Stieglitz and the artists of the Stieglitz circle.[20] Thus one of the important notions that Stieglitz and Williams shared was that of the importance of touch.[21] It is possible that here, too, Williams was influenced by Stieglitz, although the fact that Stieglitz

came to place increasing emphasis on touch rather late in his life might indicate
that the idea originated elsewhere. But more important than the frequently debated point of who had taken something from whom is the fact that such artists as
Braque, Stieglitz, and Williams all greatly emphasized touch, spawning the question: How does the concept of touch affect their work, and what importance does
it have in the larger context of Modernism? Thus Stieglitz himself, with a growing
awareness of the importance of conveying the sense of touch, became an adherent
of "straight" photography and moved more and more away from a photography
that still showed clear affinities to Pictorialism, although these affinities were for a
long time obscured because of his revolutionary iconography.[22] Chiaroscuro effects with comparatively soft, dark printing increasingly gave way over the years to
lighter tones and the sharpest possible focus; all this, in conjunction with semi-
longshots and closeups, led to a dramatically increased visibility of texture, and
hence of sense of touch.[23]

For his part, Williams from early on made, in J. Hillis Miller's words, "soft
closeness the primary characteristic of his world." Edges, contours, textures, and
other small details involve the haptic sense even in all those instances where
things are described as being *seen* only and not actually touched. "Proper seeing
is tactile, not abstract," says Miller, and he quotes Williams's affirmation that
the "eye awake" "seizes" the world (*CP1*, 148), as in that poem where "[t]he
eye comes down eagerly" to grasp "the contours and the shine" of the sea-trout
and butterfish on a white plate, down to the minute detail of the "fine fins'
sharp spines" (*CP1*, 353; *Poets of Reality,* p. 320).

Sometimes Williams achieves an extraordinary immediacy from the very beginning by opening a poem with a closeup, so to speak, in which the sense of
touch, combined with an unflinching directness of "naming," creates an immediate contact in the very first words. "The Girl," for instance, begins with a
close focus which is only gradually enlarged to include posture, movement, and
environment. The erotic appeal of the girl is met head-on, with a frankness that
reflects (and thus pays homage to) the frankness and absence of squeamishness
that the poet senses in the young woman herself. There is an interpenetration
between *what* is described and *how* it is described that blends *natura naturata* and
natura naturans, so that the poet "translates" what he sees and feels into a poem
in which naming is description and appropriation at one and the same time.
The poem is an appraisal that becomes praise because it is the result of possessing
through empathetic identification.

Another important element in this context is the use of the definite article
in the title.[24] A title such as "The Girl" takes the reader both *in medias res* and
inside the poet's mind, since he names what he observes without bothering to
provide the context, which the title implicitly contains. The reader joins the
poet from the start in his poetic act of discovery or revelation; he takes part in
– becomes a part of – the poet's experience in a "fraternal embrace," as Williams
calls it in *Spring and All* (*I,* 89). In such poems as "The Girl" this characteristic

device – there are ninety poems in *The Collected Earlier Poems* whose titles name persons or objects with the definite article – is driven as far as it can go, since title and poem are one syntactic unit. Williams discards the title as a meta-statement; it becomes identical with the first word of the poem and thus takes the reader from the very first moment right into it. The poem is thus turned into an icon of the epiphanic moment of discovery, a created object that re-presents in its words with as much immediacy as possible the experience that occasions it.[25]

Both this iconicity and the sense of touch are crucial devices to bring about the envisioned "contact" or empathetic identification between the minds of the poet and reader and the objects or people depicted. Tactile seeing in particular bridges the gap between self and other. It is a way of perceiving that is as much muscular as it is visual, and hence involves the whole body. This is what Williams meant when he wrote that "a thing known passes out of the mind into the muscles" (*I: KH*, 74), or that "a woman must see with her whole body to be benevolent" (*IAG*, 182). Sight as an isolated sense on its own, Williams realized, prevents genuine contact because it always keeps one at a distance.

The attempt to overcome this unwanted sense of separation is, as we have seen, an important aspect of the revolution in the visual arts, and it is an aspect that became crucial for Williams in the formation of his own poetics. Indeed, all the painters that were dear to him, from Cézanne, the Cubists, and the American Modernists to Brueghel and the anonymous artists of the Millefleur tapestries, had either turned against, or were not yet fully part of, the tradition governed by what Braque called the "catastrophe of the mechanical perspective."[26]

The prevalent attitude in Western civilization, however, which found per-haps its clearest expression in Platonism and Cartesian rationalism, has always been an attitude rooted in the prevalence of sight – to the point where seeing and knowing have become almost identical, as the figurative use of "to see" for "to understand" indicates. This visualism, as Don Ihde, William Spanos and others have begun to call it lately, is an expression of the supremacy of intellect over emotion and intuition, of head over heart, mind over body, critical distance over indwelling, seeing over touching, control over letting be.[27] Knowing, an-alyzing, controlling, and dominating entail a vantage point above and beyond, as they entail a conceiving of the world as something that is opposite – opposed to – the analyzing and controlling subject, something essentially other as well as something fixed and stable (or if subject to change, then only within a closed system).

Dürer's woodcut *The Drawer of the Reclining Woman* (Figure 19) is one of the earliest works that forcefully expresses some of the fundamental implications of the closer alignment of the arts with the scientific discoveries of the Renaissance and the subsequent development outlined earlier. Scientific correctness of per-spective is the touchstone of truth, and the frame with the grid helps to achieve

Figure 19. Albrecht Dürer, *The Drawer of the Reclining Woman*. 1538. Woodcut, 8 × 22½ cm. From *Unterweysung mit dem Zirckel und Richtscheyt*, Nürnberg 1538. Kunsthaus Zürich.

the task. But the picture also points to the price paid for the breakthrough: Whatever the artist represents is now part of a separate realm, a separate space. And the fact that the naked woman has the traditional piece of cloth drawn up over her thigh to cover her pudenda is as understandable as it is pathetic when we look at the artist staring at – not her, but the contours of her body as they appear on the grid of the frame in front of him.

Thus Dürer's woodcut is a striking example of the problematic advancement of the specific "visualism" that the Renaissance brought about and that those Modernists with whom Williams sided tried to counter with a kinesthetic and synesthetic art that would foster a "benevolence" rooted in seeing "with [one's] whole body." Unlike the attitude resulting from Cartesian rationalism, this tactile seeing or bodily knowing, through its heightened awareness of interaction and interpenetration, knows no clear-cut boundaries between inside and outside, between human life and any other form of life, the animated and the so-called deanimated. Ideally, human beings then become participants in natural processes rather than rulers of the universe who grasp, analyze, and use what they find outside themselves. A generation later, now deep in the new (or rediscovered) world of immanence, Gary Snyder writes that "we live in a universe 'one-turn,' in which, it is widely felt, all is one and at the same time all is many. The extra rooster and I were subject and object until one evening we became one."[28]

In such a universe, difference is as important as sameness, clash and juxtaposition as important as analogy and homology. It is for this reason that Williams stresses the importance of "that power which discovers in all things those inimitable particles of dissimilarity to all other things which are the peculiar perfections of the thing in question" (*I: KH,* 18), while he points out at the same time that the imagination "seeks to place together those things which have a common relationship." The latter comes "from a hidden desire for the dance, a lust of the imagination, a will to accord two instruments in a duet." But as one should not cover up differences between things by the "coining of similes," so one should not attempt "by the ingenuity of the joiner to blend the tones of the oboe with the violin. On the contrary the perfections of the two instruments are emphasized by the joiner; no means is neglected to give each the full color of its perfection" (*I: KH,* 18–19).

The swing of the pendulum here is not a dialectical step-by-step procedure toward a synthesis, but is meant to once more disclose the irreducible but fruitful tension between one and many, many and one. Part of this tension has its origin in the sameness and difference of human and nonhuman life. That the mind can experience a "co-extension with the universe" points to the fact that on the level on which all is one the object-world, too, is perceived as being alive and active. Activating this deeper knowledge is for Williams one of the most important aspects of art in general and poetry in particular. It is a knowledge that, in a basic or more peripheral way, is part of the revolutionary movements that began with late Impressionism and Postimpressionism and that is an integral aspect of the turn away from positivism and scientism based on Cartesian rationalism. Artists sought and found it in such diverse phenomena as Eastern thinking, the arts and rites of the so-called primitives, the beginnings of modern psychology, the works of the new "physiologists," and post-Newtonian science, to name only some of the main fields and influences. Pound, moving away from Imagism to the more dynamics- and process-oriented Vorticism, discovered it in Fenollosa's view of Chinese writing, a view that in turn related Eastern and "primitive" attitudes in the conclusion that Pound found so striking and that Williams must have found equally revealing: "To primitive man, a thing only IS what it *does.*"

That is why Williams, who was so strongly against an indiscriminate use of metaphors and similes, has an abundance of hidden metaphors in his poems. They are of the utmost importance because it is through them, basically, that we experience the life in all things, the forces that they embody and exert on other things and beings, as well as the forces that they themselves in turn are subject to – forces that shape them, so that it is indeed their forms that contain their essences. This is what Williams meant when he said, "The essence lies in the thing and shapes it, variously" (*RI,* 144).

To label these hidden metaphors personifications or "pathetic fallacies," as many critics still do, is to argue from the traditional Cartesian point of view, a view which ignores that, ultimately, all language is metaphorical, and that to recognize this and to draw on the hidden metaphorical dimension is to take an important step toward bridging the gap between self and other, human kind and environment. Hence Williams's poems are indeed an attempt "through metaphor to reconcile / the people and the stones." They are an attempt to pit the language of poetry against "the language of S[cience] and P[hilosophy]"

(*I:AN*, 304), whose neatly separated realms or "fixed categories" are "the walking devil of life." Thus one of the fundamental goals of poetry, as of art in general, is to counterbalance this "language of S. and P.," which brought about a rational and utilitarian outlook at the price of a profound alienation.

Chapter 6

The Search for a Synthetic Form

PART 1

Perhaps the most fundamental connection between the Cubist painters and Williams (as well as other "Cubist" writers, such as Gertrude Stein, Pierre Reverdy, and Max Jacob) lies in the fact that they all abandoned the concept of mimesis, a concept that had provided the arts with a basic goal since the Renaissance, namely, the desire to achieve an ever-refined rendering of "reality." Reality in this case was an unquestioned absolute, a tangible world that was simply there, given.

The Cubist painters moved beyond this unquestioned concept of the real and abandoned the traditional one-viewpoint painting in favor of an art that foregrounded the fact that each work of art was a *creation;* that there are different ways of *perceiving* reality and hence also different ways of *ordering* it; and that ultimately perception and creation cannot be separated, as the term "vision" in itself already implies.

Taking his inspiration from such premises, Williams pushed the new art as far as it would go in such texts as *Kora in Hell* and the montage poems of the early twenties. He realized, however (as the Cubists themselves did toward the end of Analytic Cubism), that an art that has abandoned illusionism might go too far in the other direction of abstraction. Hence Williams came to the conclusion that it was essential to achieve a balance of sorts between the representational and the abstract, the act of "naming" and the creation of a "design," the "particulars" and the "mathematics" behind them.

This basic concern was shared by all "Cubist" writers in one way or another; even Gertrude Stein, who had perhaps gone furthest in emptying words of meaning in the traditional sense, denounced abstract art as "pornographic."[1] Stein, too, was convinced that only an art that keeps in touch with the "real" can make the recipient aware of the way in which all vision invariably mediates it, shapes it while it is shaped by it. It is only thus that art can "decreate" the real, to use Stevens's term:[2] destroy the old, naive, notion of reality and replace it with a more complex approach. Such an art is by essence both referential and self-referential; it points at one and the same time to the world it mediates and to itself as mediator – a mediator, moreover, that is invariably also a created object in its own right.

Thus for a Cubist painter a painting conjures up objects, but the Cubist will not let the viewer forget its status as artifact by including contradictions or ambiguities in the depiction of space and objects – ambiguities that, moreover, also oblige the viewer to share in the (re)creation of the objects in the painting. In an analogous manner, the writer inspired by Cubism uses words that denote, and yet the violations of syntactic or semantic conventions make the reader aware that the text is made of words that are objects themselves, black letters on a white page, put together according to rules that can be observed or broken. Hence each work of art in the wake of Cubism is, in Wendy Steiner's words,

> most essentially both a sign of the thing-world and a part of the thing-world. It thus points to itself and to the object-world. And the cubist work insists on our awareness of the double relation. Thus it is both self-referential – irritatingly so, at times – and profoundly concerned with the object world. This dynamics . . . is fundamental to cubist art. Moreover, it has come to be equated with modernism as a whole. Jan Mukařovsky develops the idea extensively in "Dialectic Contradictions in Modern Art," and it lies behind most treatments of the problematic nature of modernism.[3]

Williams regarded this double relation with its inherent tension as an integral aspect of all viable art in this century. In the context of language he sometimes referred to it as the crucial element that distinguished the poetic from the non-poetic use of language. But Duchamp's ready-mades taught him that the difference was far from being absolute: The mere displacement of bits and pieces of language into a poetic context could bring out their language qua language dimension, so that the poetic potential of *all* words that one heard or read daily waited to be discovered.

The poetic potential of all language in general and of the American idiom in particular was the perhaps clearest proof for Williams that the *degree* to which language in the poem differed from language outside it was not a means to assess its success or failure. It was a fallacy, in other words, to believe that the more the language in the poem differed from the language outside it, the more "poetic" it became. There were endless possibilities to be explored from utmost simplicity to extreme versions of "language art" (to use David Antin's term),[4] and the challenge of how much concreteness one should or could combine with how much abstraction, how much literal "transcription" with how much poetic transformation, had to be met in each single case in a new way.

One particular way of resolving this tension, to which Williams came back time and again, consisted in including as much direct, undistorted reference to the "actual" as possible while still keeping the reader aware of reading *words*, parts of a poem that, "like every other form of art, is an object, an object that in itself formally presents its case and its meaning by the very form it assumes" (*A*, 267).

This specific combination of direct "naming" and artistic shaping in a form characterized by a "simplicity of design" was what he treasured in all art and found in an exemplary way in some of the great Modernist painters; in Gris, above all, among the Cubists, and in Demuth and Sheeler among the Americans. Late in his life, he was to add some of the old masters, above all Brueghel, whose artistic vision was rooted in the faithful recording of the peasant faces he saw around him, or the anonymous artist(s) of the Unicorn tapestries, whose *mille-fleurs* were not only an integral part of the carpets' design but also depicted with such precision that hundreds of them could be named later by botanists.

Throughout his life Williams came back to this need of achieving a balance between the concrete and the abstract, a balance that would do justice to both the myriad details that made up the world around him and the formal necessities of a work of art that did not hide its status as artifact. And in many statements about this need we find both a high awareness of the fact that the visual arts had provided him with the exemplary models as well as the insight that these models were not simply to be copied since his own material was language, was words.

A case in point is the passage in the *Autobiography* in which he reflects on his decision to become a writer rather than a painter:

> . . . I was still undecided whether or not I should become a painter. I coldly recalculated all the choices.
> Words it would be and their intervals: Bam! Bam! (*A*, 52)

Or consider this passage from *The Embodiment of Knowledge*:

> The writer is to describe, to represent just as the painter must do – but what? and how?
> It is the same question of words and technique in their arrangement – Stein has stressed, as Braque did paint, words. So the significance of her personal motto: A rose is a rose – which printed in a circle means two things: A rose is, to be sure, a rose. But on the other hand the words: A rose is – are words which stand for all words and are very definitely not roses – but are nevertheless subject to ar-rangement for effect – as are roses. . . . In this case the words are put there to represent words, the rose spoken of being left to be a rose.
> Let it be noted that these two phases, writing and painting, occurred synchro-nously. (*EK*, 22–23)

This is one of many passages that shows how Williams could take his clue in several ways from painting without ever ignoring his own medium. Words, which are "definitely not roses" nor any other object they name, are "subject to arrangement for effect" just as painted objects are. Or, as he says elsewhere, all language is "made up of words, the spaces between words and their configurations" (*EK*, 17). But words in language also unfold in time, so there is rhythm, and hence the spaces between words also become "intervals." So, for the poet, "Words it would be and their intervals: Bam! Bam!"

Thus Williams could indeed "never think of language apart from painting," as Joseph Riddel puts it,[5] and the exploitation of the visual dimension that became so central for his poetics is as much tied to Modernist painting as his belief in the need to foreground the artifact character in *all* works of art. But it also seems important to stress, before turning to the visual dimension proper, that Williams never failed to include the aural and temporal dimensions in his reflections on the nature of the poem either.

For Henry Sayre, this is a defect rather than a virtue of Williams's poetics; Williams, he believes, was never "fully able to articulate his discovery of a form based on the eye and not the ear, the discovery of what I have come to call his 'visual text' " (*Visual Text*, p. 3). In contrast to Sayre I would argue that Williams was fully conscious of the importance of the visual text *and* aware of the necessity to see it in its interaction with the other dimensions, since he was convinced that ultimately the spatial and the temporal, the visual and the aural were not to be separated from one another.

A prime example of this interaction is the juxtaposition of verse and prose in *Spring and All* and *Paterson:* In both texts, in different ways, verse and prose enhance each other not only visually but also rhythmically, by way of contrast or counterpoint. Another example would be the way in which in *Paterson* the visual dimension in the punctuation – the doubly spaced "delayed" full stops, for instance – turn the page into a musical score, as it were, suggesting a slowing down of the reading pace or standing for pauses, or even moments of silence.

It is true, however, that the importance of the visual dimension in Williams can hardly be overestimated. Thus it is remarkable that at several crucial moments in his development Williams achieved breakthroughs by means of discoveries in the realm of the visual organization of the poem. While the initial impetus to write a poem seems to have come frequently from the aural – the language he found about him, what he came to call the American idiom – the structural problems that had to be overcome lay in the need for an "architectural" form, the organization of the poem on the page. Thus one of the important turning points came in the early twenties when Williams realized that he had to go beyond the imagistic "impressions" of *Al Que Quiere!* and *Sour Grapes*. Of the latter he said:

> This is definitely a mood book, all of it impromptu. When the mood possessed me, I wrote. Whether it was a tree or a woman or a bird, the mood had to be translated into form. To get the line on paper. To make it euphonious. To fit the words so that they went smoothly and still said exactly what I wanted to say. That was what I struggled for. To me, at that time, a poem was an image, the picture was the important thing. (*IWW*, 34–35)

Imagism, as well as the first of Kandinsky's three basic categories, the so-called "Impression," provided Williams for a time with the necessary framework for the "impromptu" poems. At the heart of these impressions was "the picture [which] was the important thing," and Imagist concentration and precision ensured that the words "went smoothly and still said exactly what [he] wanted to say." The larger form of *Kora in Hell,* on the other hand, corresponded to Kandinsky's second category, that of the "Improvisation."

Both forms, however, had their drawbacks. While the "excellence" of *Kora* lay, as Williams later wrote, in the "disjointing process," its fault was "the dislocation of sense, often complete" (*I: AN,* 285; *SA,* 117). The imagistic impressions, in turn, were modeled on a form which had been highly helpful for a time but "ran quickly out." Imagism had been "useful in ridding the field of verbiage" but at the same time, Williams insisted, it had "no formal necessity implicit in it":

> It had already dribbled off into so-called "free verse" which, as we saw, was a misnomer. There is no such thing as free verse! Verse is a measure of some sort. "Free verse" was without measure and needed none for its projected objectifications. Thus the poem had run down and become formally non extant (*A,* 264).

Therefore an art form that deserved its name and was viable in America at that particular time had to achieve a synthesis that would fuse the two extremes of the imagistic "impressions" and the *écriture automatique* of the "improvisations." It must have form (or would become a mere "unarrangement of wild things," as he warns in "This Florida: 1924"), but it still had to reflect the artist's environment. From the European masters – Cézanne, the Cubists, Kandinsky – one could learn the lesson of form; the example of, say, Whitman, on the other hand, showed that art in America must be "free to include all temperaments, all phases of our environment, physical as well as spiritual, mental and moral."[6]

Another artist whose work was of utmost importance in the context of this search for a synthesis was Duchamp, the Frenchman who had come to America and truly responded to the new environment. In *The Great American Novel* Williams sets him off against Kandinsky, the great Russian whose art reflected the spirit of the day in Europe:

> Expressionism is to express skilfully the seething reactions of the contemporary European consciousness. Cornucopia. In at the small end and – blui! Kandinsky.
> But it's a fine thing. It is THE thing for the moment – in Europe. The same sort of thing, reversed, in America has a water attachment to be released with a button. That IS art. Just as one uses a handkerchief. (*I,* 173)

"Work which bridges the gap between the rigidities of vulgar experience and the imagination is rare," Williams noted in *Spring and All* (*I,* 134). Duchamp's ready-mades were exactly of that sort – while leaving his mundane objects intact, his gestures were creative acts that transformed the impact of these objects by transferring them to another realm. Thus they corresponded exactly to the definition of art that Williams gave in a letter to Horace Gregory: a "transference – for psychic relief – from the actual to the formal" (*SL*, 226).

The imposition or creation of form by a simple displacement of the object was a paradigmatic means to remain faithful to the object while "lift[ing] it to the imagination." Williams's own use of words as *objets trouvés* was an analogous procedure. Words were taken *tel quel* and transposed to "that 'special place' which poems, as all works of art, must occupy," a place which is "quite definitely the same as that where bricks or colored threads are handled" (*I: AN*, 312). And the art of such painters and photographers as Demuth, Sheeler, Stieglitz, and Strand could also be related to Duchamp's procedure. They all worked with what they discovered around themselves, trying to transform, without deforming, the same "rigidities of vulgar experience." Each of them in his own way tried to achieve a form of that "admirable simplicity" that Williams had praised in Gris's Synthetic Cubism.

Henry Sayre rightly points out that much work done by the early American Modernists in the wake of Cubism was often mistaken for a watered-down or misunderstood form of Synthetic Cubism, while in fact it constituted the conscious effort of adapting an artistic revolution to the different needs and circumstances of the American scene. American Modernists frequently became the victims of

> a general trend in art-historical discussions of American modernism which see the American artists' interest in objective reality as a "dilution" of the formal necessities they had inherited from European modernism. Abraham A. Davidson, for instance, argues that such American painters as John Marin, Charles Demuth, and Charles Sheeler were "unable to reconcile themselves to or even understand the ambiguities which were at the heart of European Cubism. . . . What emerges . . . is an uncertain melange of Cubist passages which are never completely digested or integrated . . . , a style marked by severe simplifications." To the contrary, the Americans' return to the object can be read more productively as the extension, rather than the dilution, of European formal exploration. (Sayre, *Visual Text,* p. 45)

It was exactly this faithfulness to the object that Williams admired in his artist friends and fellow combatants. Combined with the proper regard for the necessities of form it could lead to results that were as remarkable as those of any of the revolutionary movements in Europe.

"The Steerage" and the American Scene

One of the artistic forms that was particularly well suited to meet these needs for a "return to the object" was photography, a medium that had been a major force in the formation of the American avant-garde from its very beginnings. The pivotal figure here was of course Stieglitz. Looking back on the particular achievement of Stieglitz as photographer, Williams wrote in the important essay "The American Background":

> The photographic camera and what it could do were particularly well suited to a place where the immediate and actual were under official neglect. Stieglitz inaugurated an era based solidly on a correct understanding of the cultural relationships. . . . The effect of his life and work has been to bend together and fuse, against whatever resistance, the split forces of the two necessary cultural groups: (1) the local effort, well understood in defined detail and (2) the forces from the outside. (*SE*, 160–61)

Stieglitz, in other words, was for Williams one of the exemplary figures who had both learned the lesson of Modernism coming from Europe and understood that it was necessary to adapt and transform it in order to create a viable form of Modernism in America.

Around 1910, Stieglitz achieved one of his important breakthroughs as a photographer with a series of pictures about New York that were marked by an unprecedented directness of vision and formal complexity. In these photographs, all traces of Pictorialism that had been present in his earlier urban landscapes were eliminated.

It is not only the subject matter that is entirely modern here – skyscrapers under construction, ferryboats, airplanes, and other icons of the technological present; what is also striking is the extent to which formal concerns replace the former interest in atmosphere. A neutral light now throws the complex pattern of interacting shapes into relief, in contrast to the former New York photographs which were dominated by dense atmospheric conditions (the city transformed by nocturnal illumination or shrouded in drizzly rain or snowstorms), conditions that were part of an overriding attempt to soften the harshness of the cityscape by naturalizing it.

It was also at that time that the full implication of the photograph *The Steerage* (Figure 20) dawned on Stieglitz. (He had taken the picture in 1907 but only published it four years later in *Camera Work*.) Whenever Stieglitz talked later about the particular importance of that photograph, he referred to formal concerns that became otherwise apparent for the first time only in his 1910 New York photographs:

> In June, 1907, my wife, our daughter Kitty and I sailed for Europe. My wife insisted on going on a large ship, fashionable at the time. Our initial destination was Paris. How distasteful I found the atmosphere of the first class on that ship, especially since it was impossible to escape the nouveaux riches. . . .
>
> By the third day I could stand it no longer. I had to get away. I walked as far forward as possible. . . . Coming to the end of the deck I stood alone, looking down. There were men, women and children on the lower level of the steerage.

Figure 20. Alfred Stieglitz, *The Steerage*. 1907. Photogravure, 13⅛ × 10½ in. *Camera Work*, 36 (1911). The Metropolitan Museum of Art, New York. The Alfred Stieglitz Collection, 1933 (33.43.420–469).

A narrow stairway led up to a small deck at the extreme bow of the steamer. A young man in a straw hat, the shape of which was round, gazed over the rail, watching a group beneath him. To the left was an inclining funnel. A gangway bridge, glistening with fresh white paint, led to the upper deck.

The scene fascinated me: A round straw hat; the funnel leaning left, the stairway leaning right; the white drawbridge, its railings made of chain; white suspenders crossed the back of a man below; circular iron machinery; a mast that cut into the sky, completing a triangle. I stood spellbound for a while. I saw shapes related to one another – a picture of shapes, and underlying it all, a new vision that held me: simple people; the feeling of ship, ocean, sky; a sense of release that I was away from the mob called "rich."[7]

Neither this account nor the importance that *The Steerage* acquired – it was in many ways singled out restrospectively as Stieglitz's most seminal single photograph – can be explained without considering the impact of modern art. The trip to Paris brought Stieglitz in contact with Postimpressionism and Cubism for the first time, and it was after his return to New York that he turned his gallery 291 into a center for avant-garde activities. In 1908 he began a series of exhibitions of the European Modernists with a Rodin and a Matisse show, and in 1910 he arranged an exhibition of "Younger American Painters" that included works by Dove, Marin, Hartley, and Weber, all of which had been strongly influenced by Cézanne and the European avant-garde.

The Steerage can be called the first photograph by Stieglitz that was not only fascinating for the New York avant-garde from a formal point of view – in the context of the new confrontation with the latest European movements – but also in view of the burgeoning attempts to create an indigenous American art that would do more than merely emulate the revolutionary Europeans. Taking for his subject "the common people," as Stieglitz later put it, *The Steerage* was a striking example of the Whitmanian democratic inclusiveness that was a basic concern for the American modernists. The photograph indeed showed the attempt "to include all temperaments, all phases of our environment, physical as well as spiritual, mental and moral," which Williams had asked for in his early essay on Whitman. Like Whitman before him, writes Eric Himmel,

> Stieglitz saw himself as a prophet of a new age in America: By focusing his artistry on everyday facts of American life, he hoped to express through them a life force, a spirituality with which others in the land of soulless commerce could commune. In *The Steerage* he found outside his own social class – as have many bourgeois photographers – a sense of community and values he could respect. *The Steerage* was the strongest expression of his aspirations for a democratic American art: It invited the viewer to imagine that this crowd of unruly people had been caught, mid-passage, en route to a new world of the spirit. The camera lens, blurring the highest tier of figures into the ocean sky, abetted these intimations, as did the expectant air of the people crowding against the railings.[8]

Both Stieglitz's reminiscence and Himmel's analysis make it evident that the impact of *The Steerage* depended on the way in which its innovative iconography interacts with its equally innovative form, that is, on the manner in which the life force embodied in this "crowd of unruly people" is expressed in a photograph whose aesthetics are based on tension and dissonance rather than on harmony. The nervous angularity of funnel, beam, stairs, drawbridge, and rails contrasts with the equally dissonant rhythm of the crowd and creates a complex interplay of clashing forms, of the angular and the curved, the mechanic and the organic, down to the complex interaction of postures, heads, and hats among the individual figures themselves. In addition to this, the tension in the picture is heightened by the way in which the white drawbridge intersects it into two halves. This was a compositional device so daring at that time that Stieglitz's colleague Keiley is reported to have exclaimed: "But you have two pictures here, Stieglitz, an upper and a lower one!" (Himmel, p. 38).

The response to a photograph with so subtle and precarious a balance between order and chaos could not be unambiguous. For such critics as those writing for *The Soil* or *The Seven Arts,* for example, the picture sustained the conviction that the future of America was founded upon the vitality contained in its unique cultural diversity. Paul Rosenfeld, on the other hand, regarded it as an example of Stieglitz's courageous attempt to face the darker implications of the machine age. *The Steerage,* with its crowd enmeshed and imprisoned in the boat's machinery, expressed for Rosenfeld the "strange brazen human emptiness" of the modern industrial age: "If human forms and faces appear at all, they are terribly separate, remote, passive. Aeons of time separate the nose-picking men and dwarf-mothers of *The Steerage* from the white glittering bridge with its chains of fine links."[9]

American Modernism: The Role of Photography

In 1913 Marius de Zayas, the chief theoretician on Modernism in the Stieglitz circle, published two influential articles in *Camera Work* on the nature of photography, which were obviously based on the stylistic change in Stieglitz's work that became apparent with *The Steerage* and the New York photographs of 1910. De Zayas made a basic distinction between artistic and nonartistic photography: "Photography is not Art, but photographs can be made to be Art." Although de Zayas refrained from explicitly placing one category over the other, naming Stieglitz as the exemplary figure of the first and Steichen of the second (artistic) kind, it is clear that he was fascinated by the prospects opened up by the first kind.

While all art, including artistic photography, was for de Zayas "the expression of the conception of an idea" and thus a medium for the artist's personal, subjective vision, photography qua photography was celebrated as a completely new means to penetrate "the objective reality of forms." The photographer tries to arrive at a "comprehension of the object." His aim is not to give aesthetic pleasure but to "acquire a truth":

> The artist photographer in his work envelops objectivity with an idea, veils the
> object with the subject. The photographer expresses, so far as he is able to, pure

objectivity. The aim of the first is pleasure; the aim of the second, knowledge. The one does not destroy the other.[10]

Apparently, the boundaries between the two approaches were not absolute for de Zayas. Cubism, for example, was an art form that also explored the "reality of forms." Thus Picasso, de Zayas wrote in his introduction for the first Picasso exhibition at 291, "receives a direct impression" from external nature which he then "analyzes, develops and translates." Picasso is called the *analytic* artist par excellence, and Stieglitz becomes his counterpart as the exemplary artist in search of a *synthetic* form: "Stieglitz has begun . . . to search for the pure expression of the object. He is trying to do synthetically, with the means of a mechanical process, what some of the most advanced artists of the modern movement are trying to do analytically with the means of art."[11] As a "straight" or "pure" photographer who leaves the forms that he selects intact, Stieglitz was for de Zayas uniquely endowed to brush aside a stale perception of form molded by artistic conceptions of the past.

Stieglitz was in full accord with these ideas – which apparently were at least partly the result of the conversations between the two men – and they seem to have inspired or corroborated similar notions in other vanguard artists, including Williams himself. Williams, too, was in search of a "synthetic" art that would grow out of the artist's ability to use the expressive forms by which he was surrounded ("No ideas but in things"!). This search is evident in many of Williams's theoretical writings, such as the Whitman essay, the manifestoes about "contact" in art, the Preface to *Kora in Hell*, the prose of *Spring and All*, the essay on Marianne Moore, and many others.

In a talk in 1941, in which Williams spoke about what he called "the structural approach," he once again made the same fundamental distinction between two different procedures: the first, traditional, procedure consisted in "the selection of forms from poems already achieved, to restuff them with metaphysical and other matter," while the second entailed "parallel[ing] the inventive impetus of other times with structural concepts derived from our own day. . . . The first is *weak* and the second is *strong*."[12]

It is obvious that the first procedure violates the material, while the second tries to do it justice by finding forms for which the artist took his clue from contemporary concepts of order – Einsteinian physics, for instance, or Cubism, which in itself is related to a critical reevaluation of a visual order of the past (Renaissance perspective) and its replacement by contemporary theories of perception.

This protest against a reiteration of past artistic forms is also, as we have seen, part of de Zayas's essays, and it is interesting to notice that de Zayas regards this reliance on past forms as a "deformation" of the subject in the art of his own day. After the passage quoted earlier, in which he calls form in contemporary art "nothing but the result of the adaptation of all the other forms which existed previous to the conditions of our epoch," he concludes: "Nevertheless we cannot rightly say that a true eclecticism exists. It may be held that this combination constitutes a special form, but in fact it does not constitute anything but a special *deformation.*"[13]

Now Williams, looking back on his imagistic poems, mentioned in his talks with Edith Heal that at that time he was trying to find "a form without deforming the language" (*IWW,* 23). It is not unlikely that this juxtaposition of "form[ing]" versus "deforming" is related – directly or indirectly – to de Zayas's own distinction, and that Williams, like de Zayas, used it primarily in the sense that the old forms, since they were tied to old values, deformed the contemporary work of art.

In this context it is also interesting to note that Williams was appreciated by his artist friends as a poet whose work was distinguished by the marked absence of this specific "deformation." Thus Kenneth Burke wrote in his *Dial* review of 1922 that "contact" in Williams's manifesto could be taken to mean "man without the syllogism, . . . without Spinoza's Ethics, man with nothing but the thing and the feeling of that thing." Williams's poetry, he added,

> deals with the coercions of nature – and by nature I mean iron rails as well as iron ore – rather than with the laborious structure of ideas man has erected above nature. His hatred of the idea in art is consequently pronounced, and very rightly brings in its train a complete disinterest in form. (Note: Form in literature must always have its beginnings in idea. In fact, our word for idea comes from a Greek word whose first meaning is "form.")[14]

Burke's review, meant as high praise, may well have aggravated Williams's doubts about his imagistic "impressions" and confirmed him in his attempts to find a poetic form that would prevent the reader from pigeonholing him as a poet with a "complete disinterest in form." If Burke was an exemplary reader, Williams must have concluded, the openness for and receptiveness to the expressive properties of his environment in his poems was strong enough to be appreciated, whereas the same, it seemed, could not yet be said of his sense of form.

Both Williams's search for a synthetic form and the reception of his work can thus be related to analogous concerns and developments in the realm of photography. Those photographers who were involved in the Modernist enterprise also tried to render "the very substance and quintessence of the thing itself," as Edward Weston once put it.[15] And form, for the photographers, was not less of a problem, although it seemed at times that it would emerge out of the very endeavor itself if only the vision of the object under scrutiny was intense and pure enough. Stieglitz, for example, was more and more preoccupied, particularly in the late 1910s and the early 1920s, with a form that, while expressing a personal vision, should not be achieved at the expense of the task to register the object-world directly and undistortedly. He believed that he had come closest to this goal in his series of photographs called *Song of the Sky* and *Equivalents,* the pictures of clouds that fused the concrete and the abstract, the object-world and the expression of states of mind. In the terminology of Kandinsky, whose writings also had a great impact on Stieglitz, one could say that these photographs are as much related to the "great abstraction" as to the "great realism," although Stieglitz still respected the essential characteristics of "straight" photography.

Paul Strand, in turn, tried to achieve a similar balance in some of his famous early photographs by taking his inspiration from Cubism. In such pictures as *Wall Street* or *Abstraction: Porch Shadows,* Strand makes use of the play of shadow and light to create images that oscillate between figure and ground, the two-dimensional and the three-dimensional, concrete forms and abstract patterns, with the result that the viewer is both aware of *what* is photographed and *that* it is photographed, what is represented and what is transformed.

In an article in the last number of *Camera Work* in 1917, Strand argued in the wake of de Zayas and Stieglitz that photography "finds its raison d'être . . . in an absolute unqualified objectivity," and that the photographer who was aware of this showed "a real respect for the thing in front of him, expressed in terms of chiaroscuro . . . through a range of almost infinite tonal values which lie beyond the skill of the human hand." Strand maintained that it "is in the organization of this objectivity that the photographer's point of view toward Life enters in." Trying to account for his "Cubist" photographs, he juxtaposed two principles of form (which differ in emphasis rather than in kind): "The objects may be organized to express the causes of which they are the effects, or they may be used as abstract forms, to create an emotion unrelated to the objectivity as such."[16]

Strand's essay was one more attempt to describe that field of polarized forces in which the early American Modernists felt pulled in both directions, in a double effort to remain faithful to both representation *and* creation, to the object-world *and* their medium of expression, the double effort of doing justice both to the still widely ignored contemporary environment and the artifact nature of the work of art itself.

Charles Sheeler

Of all the American Modernist painters, it was Charles Sheeler who was most concerned with fruitfully exploring this tension. Although Williams must have been familiar with some of Sheeler's paintings and photographs by the mid-teens – a *Bucks County Barn* drawing, for example, hung in Walter Arensberg's living room – the two men did not meet for the first time until 1923 when Matthew Josephson arranged a meeting "over a Dutch-treat dinner in a New York speakeasy."[17] After that, they became close friends for life.

Sheeler was one of the first painters to discover indigenous traditions of design and architecture, such as the furniture and tools of the Shakers and the Pennsylvania barns and farmhouses. In addition, Sheeler was among the first who turned to the contemporary urban and technological world in a spirit of appreciation. Thus in the early twenties he made a series of paintings, drawings, and photographs of New York, cool and elegant studies whose peculiar tension stems from the fact that they transcend the sheer celebration they were meant to be. Fascinated by the monumentality of Manhattan, Sheeler turned its architecture into rhythmically orchestrated forms of light and shadow – forms, however, which also evoke a distinct sense of distance or even alienation by confronting the viewer with a completely empty cityscape delineated with cold clarity and uncanny precision.

Williams's essays on Sheeler express his conviction that the painter and photographer was among the few American artists who had achieved an exemplary fusion of the concrete and the abstract, the local and the universal. "He sees the universal in our midst with his eyes," Williams wrote in a draft of his essay for the 1939 retrospective at the Museum of Modern Art, "and makes it up for us in detail from those things we know, with paint on a piece of stretched cloth" (*RI*, 142).

For Williams, this was a rare achievement in this analytic age in which understanding – insight – was felt to come only from taking apart what is offered to the senses:

[T]he world is always seeking meanings! breaking down everything to its 'component parts,' not always without a loss. The arts have not escaped this tendency, nor did Sheeler whose early work leaned toward abstraction, in the drawing and composition, the familiar ironing out of planes. Something of it still lingers in his color.

Later Sheeler turned, where his growth was to lie, to a subtler particularization, the abstract if you will but left by the artist integral with its native detail. (*RI*, 142–43)

For Sheeler himself such a synthesis was an ultimate goal, as his statement about the important painting *Upper Deck* (1929; Figure 21) shows: "This is what I had been getting ready for. I had come to feel that a picture could have incorporated in it the structural design implied in abstraction and be presented in a wholly realistic manner."[18]

Design or form was a must, but so was the presence and impact of the particular in its irreplaceable uniqueness. Williams summed up this credo in the final version of the Sheeler essay:

To be an artist a man must know his materials. But in addition to that he must possess that really glandular perception of their uniqueness which realizes in them an end in itself, each piece irreplaceable by a substitute, not to be

Figure 21. Charles Sheeler, *Upper Deck*. 1929. Oil on canvas, 29⅛ × 22⅛ in. Courtesy of The Fogg Art Museum, Harvard University Art Museums. Louise E. Bettens Fund.

broken down to other meaning. Not to pull out, transsubstantiate, boil, um-glue, hammer, melt, digest and psychoanalyze, not even to distill but to see and keep what the understanding touches intact - as geapes are ruond and come in bunches. (*RI, 143*)

PART 2

This is 1939, and the last sentence, with its reference to grapes (which are never far away when Williams champions an art that works *with* the real against an art that pretends to be identical with it), takes us back to 1923 and the passages in *Spring and All* about Juan Gris, the Cubist who paints "things with which he is familiar, simple things – at the same time to detach them from ordinary experience to the imagination":

> Here is a shutter, a bunch of grapes, a sheet of music, a picture of sea and mountains (particularly fine) which the onlooker is not for a moment permitted to witness as an "illusion." One thing laps over on the other, the cloud laps over on the shutter, the bunch of grapes is part of the handle of the guitar, the mountain and sea are obviously not "the mountain and sea," but a picture of the mountain and the sea. All drawn with admirable simplicity and excellent design – all a unity – (*I*, 110–11)

This passage appears in a volume whose twenty-seven poems include as number twenty-two:

> so much depends
> upon
>
> a red wheel
> barrow
>
> glazed with rain
> water
>
> beside the white
> chickens
>   (*CP*1, 224)

Emphasizing in Williams what Williams emphasizes in Gris, we could say that the poet evokes things with which he is familiar – simple things – and detaches them from ordinary experience. Here are a few details: a wheelbarrow and chickens in a chance conjunction, the wheelbarrow "glazed" with rain, which brings out texture (touch!) and color (sight), a few details which the reader is not for a moment permitted to witness as an "illusion." One word stands against the other: "red" against "wheel," "wheel" against "barrow," "rain" against "water." What we have before us are obviously not these things but the words in a poem referring to them: wheel, barrow, red, white, chickens, rain, water – words, moreover, which, set up in a specific order or conjoined in compounds, fuse a colored object (a red wheel) and another object (barrow) to a new and different thing (a red wheelbarrow), or give us a color (white) that suddenly loses its abstract and generic character and becomes part of some specific animals (white chickens).

Words are unmistakably things here. To start with, they look innocent enough: Each, taken by itself, means something, conjuring up an object or a color. But as soon as it is connected with the words surrounding it, it can suddenly, magically, change its meaning. Thus, we are prevented from identifying it with a specific, single meaning – it becomes an object itself, assuming varying functions within a language system that has a separate reality all by itself.

Moreover, if words are things they are also things in the sense of being black letters on a white page, words that can be arranged so as to form a pattern or design, not unlike the design in a painting by Gris, who used objects with related or recurrent forms (the circular shapes of saucers, grapes, and bottles, for instance) to create his "visual rhymes." Late in his life, looking back, Williams said in an interview:

> As I've grown older, I've attempted to fuse the poetry and painting to make it the same thing. . . . to give a design. A design in the poem and a design in the picture should make them more or less the same thing.[19]

Thus in this poem, by means of the typographical arrangement and with the barest of syntactic "manipulations" – the hyphens after "wheel" and "rain," which would indicate that the two words are parts of compounds, are omitted – Williams turns a single sentence of sixteen words into a poem with four identical stanzas. Each of them has four words, three words on the first line and one on the second. Moreover, the single words that make up the second lines are all dissyllabic ("upon," "barrow," "water," "chickens"), and the last words of the first lines in each stanza with the exception of the first one are all monosyllabic with a long vowel or diphthong ("wheel," "rain," "white").

The fact that we are predominantly concerned here with the visual effects does not mean that the aural dimension is unimportant; very often, as they do here, the two enhance each other, by analogy or counterpoint. Thus the juxtaposition of the monosyllabic words at the end of the first lines in stanzas two to four ("wheel," "rain," "white") and the dissyllabic words that make up the second lines of these stanzas ("barrow," "water," "chicken") is emphasized rhythmically by the fact that all three monosyllabic words appear in stressed position at the end of the lines (and thus form masculine line endings), whereas all the dissyllabic words are stressed on the first syllable and thus provide the line in each case with a feminine ending (i.e., an ending terminating the line on an unstressed syllable: "bárrŏw," "wátĕr," "chíckĕn").[20] This sets off, visually, *and* aurally, the "concrete" stanzas two to four from the "abstract" opening stanza, which stands somewhat apart as a "meta-statement."

Part of this denser visual and aural organization of stanzas two to four is the analogy of the chiasmic and assonantal first lines of the third and fourth stanzas: "glazed with rain" and "beside the white." Based on this, we could say that the visual and aural design of the poem is gradually increased by means of a denser network of correspondences between, first, stanzas two to four and, second, stanzas three and four.

This progression within the poem is set off against the visual design, which is identical in all four stanzas, and against an ABA pattern of the focus. In cinematographic terms, one could say that after the abstract opening stanza the focus is on the "red wheel/barrow" by means of a semi-long shot, then switches to a closeup of surface and texture in the next stanza before it enlarges the view again at the end of the poem.

In his discussion of Gris's painting Williams points out the peculiar transformation that the objects in Gris's still life undergo while they continue to be "recognizable as the things touched by the hands during the day." Similarly, in his own poem the mundane objects undergo a strange change while they, too, are still "the same things they would be if photographed or painted by Monet" (*I: SA,* 110). One way of measuring this peculiar change is to take the sixteen words that make up "The Red Wheelbarrow" and read them aloud as a prose sentence. "Try an experiment," writes Hugh Kenner:

> Try to imagine an occasion for this sentence to be said:
>
> > So much depends upon a red wheelbarrow glazed with rain water beside the white chickens.
>
> Try it over, in any voice you like: it is impossible. It could only be the gush of an arty female on a tour of Farmer Brown's barnyard. And to go on with the dialogue? To whom might the sentence be spoken, for what purpose? Why, to elicit agreement, and a silent compliment for the speaker's "sensitivity." Not only is what the sentence says banal, if you heard someone say it you'd wince. But hammered on the typewriter into a thing made, and this without displacing a single word except typographically, the sixteen words exist in a different zone altogether, a zone remote from the world of sayers and sayings. (*A Homemade World,* p. 60)

Henry Sayre seems to approach the poem in a similar manner when he writes:

> As Hugh Kenner has pointed out, when read as a simple statement of fact . . . anybody could justifiably call the poem trivial in the extreme. But as a poem . . . the scope of this trivial statement of fact is enlarged. So much depends upon the *form* into which Williams molds his material, not the material itself. . . .
>
> It is crucial that Williams' material is banal, trivial: by placing this material in the poem Williams underscores the distance the material has traveled, and the poem defines a radical split between the world of art and the world of barnyards,

between a world which crystallizes the imagination and a world which is a mere exposition of the facts. (*Visual Text*, pp. 65–66)

Sayre's distinction, which at first sight seems more or less the same as Kenner's, is of a different kind. In lieu of Kenner's opposition of the poem and the banality of the prose statement, we have here the opposition of the poem and the banality of the material. The prose statement, however, is *not* identical with the material of the poem but is itself a form of language. Therefore, instead of equating the triviality of the prose statement with that of the material or subject matter, one should rather say that the prose statement (which Williams never wrote) trivializes the subject matter while the poem achieves the opposite.

Hence, if Williams's poem "defines a radical split between the world of art and the world of barnyards," it does *not* do so in the sense that all that matters is the world of art. A poem like "The Red Wheelbarrow" is an object in its own right but also – as a recreation – a revelation (aletheia), concerned with the "radiant gist" of the world referred to. If it works, it sends us back to the world of barnyards and backyards, flowers and factories, people and stones. Its formalism is not of the art for art's sake kind but is concerned with foregrounding language as the fundamental mediator between human beings and their world: "[W]e smell and hear and see with words and words alone, and . . . with a new language we smell, hear and see afresh" (*SE*, 266).[21]

It is therefore of fundamental importance that the simple and ordinary material in Williams's poems is not regarded as either banal or inessential, but that the traditional distinction between important and unimportant themes and motives as such is abandoned. Otherwise we are back to Stevens's distinction between the poetic and antipoetic which so infuriated Williams,[22] or back to the distinction between "good" and "bad taste" (leading straight to an art in which "[h]alf the world" is "ignored" [*CP2*, 68]), which Williams singled out for an attack when he came across it in a Joyce review by Rebecca West ("A Point for American Criticism," *SE*, 80–90).

For Williams, the world around him could only be "new" again when approached in, and through, an art that leaves all these hierarchies behind. Only then can the "constant barrier between the reader and his consciousness of immediate contact with the world" be torn down (*I: SA*, 88). Williams would have fully subscribed to Valéry's dictum that true seeing, in regard to nature, entailed completely abandoning *les beaux sites* ("beautiful views"), in favor of *un coin quelconque de ce qui est* ("any old corner of what is"),[23] or to Monet's contention that *tout ce qui existe est beau, . . . tout est à peindre* ("everything that exists is beautiful, . . . everything is here to be painted").[24]

If all things are equal to one another and no longer part of a traditional hierarchical frame of reference, then each thing is liberated from the traditional modes of seeing and begins to exist in its own right. It is only then that value, in Roy Miki's words, "is no longer . . . dependent upon external frames of reference (such as 'Art,' or 'Science', or 'Philosophy'). Instead, this new sense of the particular functions as an extension of what Hartley [in *Adventures in the Arts*] calls 'the brilliant excitation of the moment' (p. 249), the same living present that excites Williams."[25]

The Poem as Still Life

What is remarkable about such Williams poems as "The Red Wheelbarrow" is the seemingly effortless way in which, beyond the traditional hierarchical frame of values, a deeper order emerges out of the juxtaposition of a few ordinary details. Not unlike Duchamp's ready-mades, these simple things are found and taken over intact into the different realm of the poem. There each word seems to reacquire its original power of naming, and each thing named appears in its pristine unique thingness, first by itself and then, even enhanced, by its juxtaposition with the other details surrounding it.

It is out of this juxtaposition that a deeper underlying order emerges, ranging from the archetypal power of this particular color combination with its junction of opposites – comprising activity and passivity, innocence and experience, the sacred and profane, and so on – to the coming together, in this barnyard, of nature and culture, earth and water, the domestic and the pastoral. To quote Kenner once more, who feels the necessity to talk about this deeper order in spite of his warning that such reflections might well be "penumbral to the poem" or "even external to it":

> [R]ed goes with white, in a simple bright scheme, and "chickens" with "barrow" for an ideogram of the barnyard, comporting with the simplicities of rain; and the rain glazes a painted surface but (we are left to imagine) does not glaze the chickens, merely soaks them if they are chickens enough to stand in it. (And yet they need it, and may not be wise enough to know how much depends, for them, on the rain.) So much depends on all that pastoral order: food, and the opportunity to touch actualities (while trundling a wheelbarrow), and the Sabine diastole to counter the urban systole. (*A Homemade World*, p. 59)

Unlike Kenner I would argue that this dimension – which is in many ways related to still-life painting, though not exhausted by it – is of central importance. "Still-life," writes Meyer Schapiro in his penetrating article, "The Apples of Cézanne,"

> consists of objects that, whether artificial or natural, are subordinate to man as elements of use, manipulation and enjoyment. . . . These objects are smaller than ourselves, within arm's reach, and owe their presence and place to a human action, a purpose. They . . . are instruments as well as products of his skills, his thoughts and appetites. While favored by an art that celebrates the visual as such, they appeal to all the senses and especially to touch and taste. They are the themes par excellence of an empirical standpoint wherein our knowledge of proximate objects,

and especially of the instrumental, is the model or ground of all knowledge. It is in this sense that the American philosopher, George H. Mead, has said: "The reality of what we see is what we can handle."[26]

It is also in this sense, one can add, that Williams writes, "Say it! No ideas but in things" (*P*, 9) and insists that so much depends upon our genuinely perceiving, seeing, living with whatever we are surrounded by. The few randomly juxtaposed objects in this poem are thus related to a tradition in which, in Schapiro's words, "the belief in the dignity of still-life and landscape as themes and their equality to historical subjects has appeared as a democratizing trend in art that gives a positive significance to the everyday world and the environment" (p. 44). Part of Western art for centuries, this belief and its concomitant forms of art have reached a new importance in the painting of Chardin, Cézanne, and the Cubists. But throughout a long period, down to the present day, artists in this tradition have had to fight against the prejudice that their art is of a lower order because of the "inferiority" of its contents. And we find an (unintentional) variant of this prejudice in the formalist approach that singles out still-life paintings or poems as the paradigmatic examples of an art that places all emphasis on form and none on subject matter.

The artists in this tradition express in their works "a commitment to the given, the simple and dispassionate – the impersonal universe of matter," writes Schapiro, whose essay can also be read in large part as an extremely pertinent analysis of Williams's art:

> Once established as a model domain of the objective in art, still-life is open to an endless variety of feelings and thoughts, even of a disturbing intensity. It can appeal to artists of different temperaments who are able through the painting of small objects to express without action or gesture the intimate and personal. They may be instruments of a passion as well as of cool meditation.
>
> Still-life engages the painter (and also the observer who can surmount that habit of casual perception) in a steady looking that discloses new and elusive aspects of the stable object. *At first commonplace in appearance, it may become in the course of that contemplation a mystery, a source of metaphysical wonder.* Completely secular and stripped of all conventional symbolism, the still-life object . . . may evoke a mystical mood like Jakob Boehme's illumination through the glint of a metal ewer. (p. 44; my italics)

It is exactly this revelation that Williams seeks and achieves in his best poems. And it is in this sense that his statement "A poem can be made of anything" has to be read: *not* as a formalist credo in the narrow sense that says the subject is insignificant, but as a credo stressing that *any* common object, transformed in the creative act, can become "a mystery, a source of metaphysical wonder."[27] The world of art sends us back to the world at large, and although the two are different, they are mutually interdependent, with the work of art affirming reality by its flight, as Williams says in *Spring and All*. Life, when "named" in the work of art, exists again, is again perceived. In many of his statements Williams stresses both sides, perception and creation, and in some of them he also speaks, as Schapiro does in the passage quoted above, of the revelation that, magically, can result from it:

> When a man makes a poem, makes it, mind you, he takes words as he finds them interrelated about him and composes them – without distortion which would mar their exact significances – into an intense expression of his perceptions and ardors that they may constitute a revelation in the speech that he uses. (SE, 257)

Does all this mean that Williams's still lifes are a version of what Herbert Schneidau calls "sacramentalism" in Modernist art, rooted in a vision that "allows representation of divine things only if, paradoxically, the signifying figures are sufficiently humble and unremarkable"?[28] Yes, if one adds that in Williams the things named do not *stand for* something else but contain the "radiant gist" in themselves and their momentary constellations. In this respect, Williams's art is close to Pound's. In both of them, a traditional symbolism in which objects point beyond themselves to an abstract deeper level is replaced by an often bewildering "literalism." With regard to Pound, this literalism is pertinently analyzed by D. S. Carne-Ross:

> [I]n Pound's best verse . . . [t]he green tip that pushes through the earth in spring does not stand for or symbolize man's power of spiritual renewal. It is not polysemous. Pound's whole effort is . . . to give back to the literal first level its full significance, its old significance, I would say. That green thrust is in itself the divine event. . . . Persephone is in that thrusting tip, and if man matters it is because he too has a share in that same power, he too is part of the seasonal, sacred life of nature. But only a part.[29]

The distinction between poems in which the particulars contain or embody the universal and poems in which they stand for it cannot be overemphasized (and if Williams's poems are taken to be the second kind, then Kenner's warning is indeed justified). Both Pound's and Williams's vision is characterized by a "radical immanence" that proceeds "not by the old 'polysemous' technique but by collapsing the so-called levels of significance; Persephone is not 'symbolized' by the green tip, but is in it, and nowhere else."[30]

In a similar manner the details in Williams's still lifes are no longer part of a surface whose predominant function is to point to a depth. If the universal comes in, then it is because the particulars in interaction partake of it, as the words in interaction do on the page, and as we do when we experience this interaction in the act of reading or looking. Thus, writes Kenner,

> "No ideas but in things" meant that the energy moving from word to word would be like that of the eye moving from thing to thing. . . . And . . . though [Williams] did not need the convention that Nature was speaking, he was untroubled by any sense of its remote exteriority because he sensed his own biological kinship with

processes of struggle and growth. A way to be part of the world is to consider that through the world as through yourself moves the energy of a cellular dance. . . ." (*A Homemade World*, p. 87)

The fact that the metonymical dimension in these poems often dominates to the virtual exclusion of the metaphorical pole points in the same direction: If the details that make up the poem form a predominantly metonymical unity – that is, if they are brought together on the basis of their contiguity – then they have, as Jakobson noticed, "no capacity to assume additional shifted meanings associated by similarity with their primary meaning."[31] They ask, in other words, to be grasped literally and not metaphorically.

Again, Williams's metonymical bias is much like Pound's, whose "whole effort is not to be polysemous," and who thus moves away from a poetry that "[f]or the last two thousand years" has had "to point away from the first, literal level to further levels of meaning," a poetry in which "the thing, however concretely rendered, always 'stands for' something else supposedly more important."[32]

It is interesting to note in this context that, according to Roland Barthes, this attempt to forego a metaphorical or polysemous reading by writing a "flat" form of poetry is a fundamental aspect of the Japanese haiku. The haiku should first and foremost lead to a liberation from our incessant attempts to find a meaning beyond the denotative dimension:

> [T]he haiku functions at least with a view to obtaining a *flat* language which nothing grounds (as is infallible in our poetry) on superimposed layers of meaning, what we might call the "lamination" of symbols. . . . All of Zen, of which the haiku is merely the literary branch, thus appears as an enormous praxis destined to *halt language*, to jam that kind of internal radiophony continually *sending* in us, even in our sleep. . . . [33]

Pound's and Williams's poetry not only shares this desire for a self-sufficient denotation that would stop what Barthes calls "the vicious infinity of language" (*l'infini vicieux du language*);[34] it also shares the goal, inherent in the haiku, for utmost compression and concentration, a compression, however, that – again like that in the haiku, according to Barthes – does not aspire to a maximum of depth, polysemy, or substance. It strives for "demystifying the vertical, paradigmatic world of depth, spirituality and metaphor," as Max Nänny puts it, by restricting itself to the "horizontal, syntagmatic world of surfaces" ("Context, Contiguity and Contact," p. 396). On this level, compression and concentration means restriction to what Pound called the "luminous detail," whose "radiant gist" has to be dis-covered in the random and momentary constellation of things.

Ultimately, of course, the attempt to break the "vicious infinity of language" remains a dream. If one achieved it, then indeed one would arrive at the point where here is everywhere, the local the universal, where the tension between the literal and the metaphorical, the flat and the multilayered polysemous language would be suspended. But, as Williams noted in *Paterson*, "The dream is in pursuit" – a pursuit that has taken him a long way toward a poetic form that would stop what Barthes calls "the soul's incoercible babble" (*le bavardage incoercible de l'âme*).[35] In such a form one would no longer attempt "to set values on the words being used according to presupposed measures, but to write down that which happens at that time" (*I: SA*, 120), "seeing the thing itself without forethought or afterthought but with great intensity of perception" (*I: KH*, 8). This would be the moment, finally, in which one would have arrived at a poetry of pure denotation, a poetry whose ultimate aspiration comes very close to that of the haiku as described by Barthes:

> Neither describing nor defining, the haiku . . . diminishes to the point of pure and sole designation. *It's that, it's thus,* says the haiku, *it's so.* Or better still, *so!* it says, with a touch so instantaneous and so brief (without vibration or recurrence) that even the copula would seem excessive, a kind of remorse for a forbidden, permanently alienated definition.[36]

Williams's "The Poem" (*CP2*, 74) both contains such a naming and talks about the pursuit of it:

> It's all in
> the sound. A song.
> Seldom a song. It should
>
> be a song – made of
> particulars, wasps,
> a gentian – something
> immediate, open
>
> scissors, a lady's
> eyes – waking
> centrifugal, centripetal

In this poem, the few objects come together on a purely metonymical level – the "song," as the poem programmatically declares (and proceeds to enact) should be made of "something / immediate," and the next word, "open" (which one first reads figuratively, as part of the line "immediate, open"), turns out to be something immediate indeed, namely, "open // scissors." "Scissors," in turn, is followed by "a lady's"; if we – at least for the moment – connect the two, we do so because we have a need for order (meaning) and because the two do go together. But "a lady's," we then discover, goes together with "eyes," and when we notice it after the enjambment, the words seem particularly evocative, and "eyes," coming immediately after "scissors," particularly delicate and vulnerable.

The poem is "pure Williams," with its words that are both a "centrifugal" and a "centripetal" force, reaching out for other words and interacting with them on the level of both meaning and sound, creating harmonies as well as dissonances. The rhythmic and assonantal harmony of "It's all in / the sound. A song / Seldom a song. It should // be a song" makes us sensitive to both the gentle sound of "gentian" and "a lady's / eyes," as well as the harshness and sharpness of "wasps" and "scissors," or the energy of "centrifugal, centripetal." Just as each word is a force moving in both directions, to be taken by itself and yet changing its impact and meaning in interaction with its surroundings, so is the poem as a whole centrifugally reaching out to interact with other texts and other poems, and at the same time full of a "centripetal" counterforce that tries to stop the "vicious infinity of language," insisting on the self-contained composition (song) "made of / particulars," not unlike the centri-petal design of the gentian, a song or design of words/sounds that should be experienced "without forethought or afterthought but with great intensity of perception."

For Geoffrey Hartman, it is exactly this "intensity of perception" that Williams achieves in "The Red Wheelbarrow." It is a poem in which

> [t]he cutting edge of the caesuras . . . , here turned inward, suggest an outward-turned force that excludes or could exclude all but its own presence. There is meaning, there is an object focused on, but there is also something cleaner than both: the very edge of the pen/knife that cuts or delineates these lines. . . . The red wheelbarrow moves us into the forgetfulness of pure perception.[37]

The counterforce, however, is always there, irresistible and unquenchable in our poetry, as Barthes would say. In "The Red Wheelbarrow," the self-containedness of pure denotation is opened up by its single metaphorical word, "glazed." Michael Riffaterre calls it "the real agent of the poem's efficacy" because it is by means of this one word that Williams transforms the wheelbarrow from a purely utilitarian tool into an object of aesthetic contemplation. "Glazed," he writes,

> presupposes an artistic object with the finish of fragile, delicate china. "Glazed" conjures up a vast intertext of artifacts made with aesthetic intent. The representations it evokes are everything that a wheelbarrow emphatically is not. To be sure, the barrow is an artifact but a utilitarian one – sturdy, rustic, of the lowest rank in a farmer's assortment of tools. It never enjoys the occasional literary sheen of a spade or an axe, nor does it play a symbolic role in proverbs as a cart or a plowshare may.[38]

Williams lifts his wheelbarrow out of all this, as it were, by one powerful metaphor, representing "nature in its truth through an implicit reference to its opposite, through an intertext of art and technique." By calling upon this device of "describing nature by the detour of an ostentatious artifact" (which he does frequently in his poems), Williams "undergirds a description of exemplary nature."[39]

Riffaterre's interpretation also reveals that it is through an essentially *literary* device, namely, an intertext that links the poem with the "discourse of the kind attributable to an artist," that Williams equates his wheelbarrow with the *painting* of a wheelbarrow and thus elevates it to the "centerpiece of a still-life."

There is yet another dimension in these poems dealing with the simple, ordinary, and unassuming which suggests an essential proximity to still-life painting. One could call it the dark side underlying the eulogistic dimension, a threat intimately tied up with the attempt to reveal the "radiant gist" in what is usually overlooked or relegated to the lowest level of life. As in still-life painting, this affirmation of the importance of the unimportant has to do with the contrast between the transient and the permanent or virtually timeless. Still lifes are concerned, as Norman Bryson points out, with the foundation of life, with a "creatural" dimension that changes very little from culture to culture, from one society to the next: "Though humble," writes Bryson,

> the *forms* represented in still life are virtually indestructible. Either because they come from nature, or because they are intended for purposes that do not vary, they are forms which do not change much over long periods of time. . . . Though still life can always be accused of dealing only in odds and ends, in *rhyparos,* débris, . . . yet the forms of still life have an enormous *force.* As human time flows around the forms, smoothing them and tending them through countless acts of attention across countless centuries, time secretes a priceless product: familiarity. It creates an abiding world where the subject of culture is naturally at ease and at home. (*Looking at the Overlooked,* pp. 137–38)

For Bryson, this dimension of timelessness accounts for the fact that our experience of a still life tends to be highly ambivalent, since it contains the "veiled threat" of the "annihilation of the viewing subject" (p. 138). Still-life painting – and, I would maintain, still-life poems such as "The Red Wheelbarrow," "Between Walls," "Poem," or "Nantucket" – put us as experiencing subjects squarely into a culture, provide us with the security of a habitable space, but paradoxically at the same time undermine that very sense of security which this space of familiarity instills in us. Because "the forms in the still life address the generic body, they bypass the personal body; because all human beings are destined to the same actions, of appetite or comfort or hygiene, at this basic level of material existence there is no respect for personhood. The very place where personal being takes its stand is overturned, in a radical decentering that demolishes the idea of a world convergent on the person as universal centre."[40]

  In Williams, this threat of a radical decentering is the counterpart to the empathetic identification with the world at large and with humble and ordinary things in particular, and it is this threat that surfaces in the notion of "despair" that he evokes repeatedly when he speaks of that process of abandoning the self in an empathetic identification with the "nameless spectacle" (*CP1,* 206) unfolding in front of his eyes. The self, in such a decentered world in which "anywhere is everywhere," inhabits the world, but it does so with feelings of exhilaration *and* anxiety. "Why bother where I went," says the speaker in "The Right of Way" immediately after insisting on the "supreme importance" of the "nameless spectacle" (*CP1*, 206), and the statement, which first of all expresses the joyful feeling of being at home everywhere, contains its own sense of disorientation. "The Right of Way" appropriately ends with an ambivalent, "split" image: It expresses, on one level, the poet's enchanted identification with physical well-being of the most ordinary kind, but it also expresses – by the simple device of an enjambment – his deep-seated anxiety of losing himself in this all-encompassing empathetic identification, surfacing in the phantom image of the decentered, dismembered, castrated body:

> Why bother where I went?
> for I went spinning on the
>
> four wheels of my car
> along the wet road until
>
> I saw a girl with one leg
> over the rail of a balcony

It is not accidental, therefore, that at the very moment of experiencing this deeper identification with the world's body on this basic "low" level the poet feels time and again the need to assess the importance of his experience in terms of a *personal* vision or stance: "So much depends / upon . . . "; "I must tell you / this young tree . . . "; "The supreme importance / of this nameless spectacle . . . "; "These things / Astonish me beyond words!" (*CP1*, 224, 266, 206, 43).[41] The experience is "personalized" at the very moment self-effacement and humility become the prerequisites for penetrating to a deeper order where the accidental contains the essential, the contingent the timeless, the "local" the universal, the mundane the transcendental.

There is, then, a fundamental inherent ambivalence in these still-life poems (as well as in many other Williams poems challenging the traditional notions of "high" and "low"). The attempt to create meaning by ennobling the trite and the ordinary, the radical questioning of the traditional hierarchy of values in an empathetic identification with a life force experienced with particular intensity on the lowest levels of life, this attempt seems invariably accompanied by the threat of annihilation of the individual experiencing subject. It may be that it is this very threat which gives depth and meaning to these poems that move us "into the forgetfulness of pure perception," and which is at least partly responsible for the particular power and intensity so characteristic of the best of them.

Chapter 7

The Poem on the Page

PART 1

Looking back on the poems collected in *Al Que Quiere!* Williams said to Edith Heal:

> The poems are for the most part short, written in conversational language, as spoken, but rhythmical, I think. The stanzas are short; I was searching for some formal arrangement of the lines, perhaps a stanzaic form. I have always had something to say and the sheer sense of what is spoken seemed to me all important, yet I knew the poem must have shape. From this time on you can see the struggle to get a form without deforming the language. (*IWW*, 22–23)

Here it was, in such poems as "The Red Wheelbarrow," "At the Faucet of June," "The Right of Way," "To Elsie," and many others in *Spring and All:* a stanzaic form emerging from the need to keep the directness and simplicity of "conversational language" and to find "a form without deforming the language." It was to become Williams's most fruitful single structural device for more than twenty years, giving direction to his poetics between the early twenties and the later forties, the time when he discovered the variable foot. A *visual form* was the solution to the problem of using the "sheer sense" and force of "what is spoken" in poems that even so made the reader aware at a glance that the words on the page were not to be confused with the things they referred to but were things themselves. The stanzaic form would keep the reader aware of the fact that making poems, like making pictures, meant "MAKING OBJECTS WHICH ALONE COMPLETE SCIENCE AND ALLOW INTELLIGENCE TO SURVIVE . . . by their power TO ESCAPE ILLUSION and stand between man and nature as saints once stood between man and the sky" (*I: SA*, 112).

Thus a poem like "The Red Wheelbarrow" synthesized the concrete and the abstract in an exemplary way; on the one hand it was as unmistakably recognizable an object as a Cubist *tableau-objet*, on the other hand it made full use of the denotative power of words. The very fact that its artifact nature was so evident liberated words from the necessity to be poeticized. The patterned poem could thus become an equivalent to what Williams called "simplicity of design" in Gris's Synthetic Cubism.

The answer to the problem of overcoming "the bare image haphazard-ly presented in loose verse" (A, 265) was hence once more to be found in the visual arts. It lay, in Paul Mariani's words, in "sculpting words themselves, words with hard concrete, denotative jagged edges" (A New World Naked, p. 250).

Of course, the analogies to the visual arts, particularly to Cubism, comprise much more than this particular aspect. We have seen that for Williams both a painting and a poem are fields of action, and that in both a visual and a verbal field one can, as Kandinsky has shown, distinguish between interactions on the abstract and the concrete levels. Abstract elements – colors and shapes in paint-ings, word sounds, and word shapes in poems – have their impact and elicit responses, as do the things referred to on the concrete level, and the final impact, in figurative painting as well as in poetry, is always the result of the complex interplay of both levels.

In addition to that, both the Cubists and Williams are concerned with form being born. In Cubism this aspect is related to the basic tension between the representation of three-dimensional forms on the flat picture plane, a tension which Picasso and Braque directly related to the act of perception itself.[1]

The Cubists, in other words, tried to make us aware, often in a highly playful manner, that we, the viewers, read the forms on the canvas so that the (re)creation of space and objects in space in a painting is to a large extent our own doing, in an act of cocreation which ideally also confronts us with the peculiar way in which perception and creation invariably interact in all acts of seeing. For the artist and the viewer alike the picture consists of a repertoire of signs that are both recognized (because they clearly match elements in the object world) and inferred or literally made out (on the basis of conventions, the need for disambiguation, etc.).[2]

It was apparently in close conjunction with the creation of the stanzaic form that Williams discovered the ways and means to explore analogous dimensions in his poetry. Shaping the poems in order to make the lines fit into the stanzaic mold, he discovered new and surprising possibilities with regard to line breaks. He must have realized, above all, that exploiting the tension between lineation and syntax was an important means to foreground the way in which meaning is being born – generated – in language. As a "red wheel" can be transformed into a "red wheel / barrow," so in another poem

a girl with one leg

becomes in an instant, to our delight

> a girl with one leg
> over the rail of a balcony
> (*CP*1, 206)

The neatly shaped stanzaic patterns – with two-line units, for example, in which a long line is followed by a short line, or with tercets consisting of two longer lines with a very short one in the middle – contain an arbitrariness of design that emphasizes the artifact nature of poetry. One should not, however (as Sayre does, for example), limit Williams's procedure to the simple imposition of an abstract form on the concrete material. To say that it consists in "taking the multiplicity of detail he describes and fitting it into a single arbitrary (a priori) and visual pattern" (*Visual Text,* p. 131) means to single out one dimension at the expense of others that are of equal importance. For Williams, the a priori pattern was only acceptable as a framework when it was also meaningful; otherwise it was modified or discarded. Thus a stanzaic form or an individual line unit can make sense rhythmically; or specific line breaks suggested by, or emerging from, a stanzaic pattern can make fruitful use of the tension between line unit and sense unit, and thus foreground the gestation of meaning, as outlined above. The stanzaic form proved so fruitful because it provided Williams with a framework that "sculpted" his verse while still leaving him ample room to shift his details and vary his lines or patterns, as each individual poem demanded.

One could say, therefore, that in these poems an arbitrary pattern interacts with an organic form in the sense of Coleridge, who defined the latter as a form that "shapes, as it develops, itself from within," arising "out of the properties of the material."[3] Hence, in a Williams poem, it is never visual shape alone which decides the form it finally takes, nor rhythm nor beat nor sound nor syntax alone; only a combination of all the elements of shape, sound, and sense in interaction will justify the existence of a poem and its individual words and lines.

The flexibility that such a poetic form demands also includes in many instances deviations from, or modifications of, the basic pattern. In "To Elsie" (*CP*1, 217), for example, Williams uses the tercet with a long, a short, and a long line:

> The pure products of America
> go crazy –
> mountain fork from Kentucky
>
> or the ribbed north end of
> Jersey
> with its isolate lakes and
>
> valleys, its deaf-mutes, thieves
> old names
> and promiscuity between

> devil-may-care-men who have taken
> to railroading
> out of sheer lust of adventure –

The only stanza in the entire poem that deviates from this pattern is the last one:

> No one
> to witness
> and adjust, no one to drive the car

It would have been easy in this case to remain within the given pattern:

> No one to witness and
> adjust
> no one to drive the car

It seems obvious that Williams deviated from his standard form in order to put additional weight on "No one": The negation contained in the two words finds its visual counterpart in the emptiness that the eye encounters after them. Absence is iconically embodied in the blank, and the two words are thus emphasized not only rhythmically (by the implied pause) but visually as well.

Sometimes Williams began with a stanzaic pattern which he discarded or replaced by a different form in a later version. An interesting example is "Between Walls" (*CP1*, 453), which runs as follows in the manuscript version of 1931 extant in the Beinecke Library (YALC):

> the back
> wings
> of the
>
> hospital
> where
> nothing
>
> will grow
> they have
> strewn
>
> cinders
> in which
> shine
>
> pieces
> of a green
> bottle

Compare this to the final poem, published three years later:

the back wings
of the

hospital where
nothing

will grow lie
cinders

in which shine
the broken

pieces of a green
bottle

The improvement is remarkable in a number of respects. In spite of the fact that the abstract "design" of the stanzaic form is more apparent in the final poem, the somewhat mannered effect of the first version is gone. This is partially due to the fact that in the final version the first stanza is more straightforward and gives us that sense of concreteness that must be established before we are ready to appreciate the tensions created throughout the poem by the interplay of line unit and sense unit. This difference between the two versions of the first stanza is in fact characteristic of the changes in the poem as a whole; the final version is so compact and forceful in its visual impact that it becomes a verbal still life in its own right and seems to defy any analysis except one that approaches it on purely visual terms and regards the stanzaic form mainly as a means to give maximum emphasis to the concrete and evocative words: "back wings," "hospital," "cinders," "shine," "broken," "green," and "bottle." All stand out either at the end of the longer first lines or are given a line to themselves.

But we quickly realize that "Between Walls" is also one of those Williams poems that enact in a paradigmatic way his credo that "writing deals with words and words only and that all discussions of it deal with single words and their association in groups" (*I: SA*, 145). Thus "Between Walls," highly visual in its orientation *and* a perfect embodiment of Williams's poetics, fuses in an admirable way what Marianne Moore once called the "pull of the eye" and the "pull of the sentence."[4] Each word in it is a node of energy, evoking things and/or reaching out for the next word which lies right next to it or is separated from it by the white space that opens up after each line or stanza.

Thus, in a field created by this double pull of the eye and the sentence, the poem unfolds in space as well as in time. It comes alive and exerts its peculiar power out of the tension that this double pull creates, a tension rooted in the Janus face of language which always looks both at the world and at itself, endowed with the power to refer but bound by the laws that govern it as a system, related to the world outside but only so through the relations that each word has to the other words surrounding it.

These basic and conflicting demands become apparent at the very beginning of the poem. Obeying the laws of syntax, Williams would have had to repeat the "between" of the title at the beginning of the poem: "[Between] the back wings / of the // hospital where / nothing // will grow . . . " As it is, the poem violates this syntactic demand in order to give, by means of a deictic gesture, as much presence as possible to *these* back wings, bringing into focus, with the greatest possible immediacy, the urban site of the poem, within which we descend step by step to the fragments of the green bottle that attract the eye irresistibly in the scattered black cinders.

The view, however, on which the poem focuses so firmly from the very first moment is exceedingly drab, and the words are so placed as to prevent us from passing too lightly over it. Thus the words of the first stanza

> the back wings
> of the

reach out and find – "hospital," and the negative connotations of this word are enforced when we take in the whole second stanza:

> hospital where
> nothing

It is again a fragmentary stanza that needs to be completed, and it is here, at a moment in which we do not expect to be uplifted, that the next three monosyllabic words assert their joint verbal energies in the triple beat of

> will grow lie

In this line, however, the third verb by itself checks the verbal push of the preceding "will" and "grow"; the passivity of "lie" lets them run aground, so to speak, so that the downward movement continues to its lowest point where, after the enjambment, the eye hits

> cinders

At this moment, in the center of a gray world of disease, waste, and destruction, we come across the line

> in which shine

which takes up in its three monosyllabic words the treble beat of the previous line "will grow lie" but ends this time on the magic verb "shine," a verb that radiates light and energy in the middle of this drab site. Although "shine" immediately clashes with "broken" in the next line, the "radiant gist" (*P,* 185) of the "broken // pieces of a green / bottle" triumphs at the end of the poem against all odds. In a stark urban world where "nothing // will grow" anymore the magic of light still exists, and nature's green, which is first implicitly evoked in its complete absence, asserts itself, transformed.

Stanzaic Versus "Loose" Form

Although the discovery of the stanzaic form was a major breakthrough for Williams in his search for a poetic form that was "an object (like a symphony or a cubist painting)" (*A*, 265), the stanzaic poems continued to interact, from their very first appearance in *Spring and All*, with other, less regularly patterned poems. One can account for this by the fact that counterpoint is a major structural principle in *Spring and All* (as it is later in *The Descent of Winter and Paterson*), a principle that includes not only the juxtaposition of verse and prose but within the verse also various formal principles, ranging from the rigidly patterned poems to the "loose" ones that have no consistent stanzaic shape at all. Each form contrasts with the other and throws it into relief, so to speak, just as the different cadences of verse and prose throw each other into relief when the reader changes back and forth between them.

Keeping in mind, however, that *organic* form in the sense defined previously plays a role in all of these poems, we ask ourselves on what ground each individual poem has been given its shape, on what ground in particular Williams chose a patterned or a nonpatterned verse form.

In his attempt to answer this question, Henry Sayre comes to the conclusion that Williams used the stanzaic form for a more "objective" kind of poem, and the looser form for a more "subjective" kind. "The Red Wheelbarrow," for instance, is in its "combination of formal order together with an almost total lack of the poet's subjective presence" the paradigmatic example of the first kind:

> Beginning with *Collected Poems 1921–1931*, the volume of poems Louis Zukofsky edited for the Objectivist Press, and continuing through the late 1940s, virtually every Williams poem (barring those written before 1928) which has a recognizable stanzaic pattern is an objective description of reality. (*Visual Text*, pp. 71–72)

For Sayre, the poetics behind these patterned poems are most clearly expressed in the theoretical statements of the Objectivists and Williams's own brief summary of the movement written for the *Princeton Encyclopedia of Poetry and Poetics*. The name of the movement itself is directly related to photography, as Zukofsky's opening statement in his manifesto of the 1931 "Objectivist" number of *Poetry* makes clear: "An Objective: (optics) – the lens bringing rays from an object to a focus."[5] The Objectivist poets tried to remain faithful to the "direct treatment of the thing" advocated by the Imagists while discarding the formal looseness of their verse in favor of a firmer design. Ideally, an Objectivist poem combined the plain presentation of facts with a form that clearly raised these facts into the different realm of art.

Williams wrote a large number of poems after the early twenties that tie in well with the Objectivist goals, but he continued writing loosely designed poems that seem to be the product of a different kind of poetics:

. . . it is to say as a general rule, that almost every time Williams abandons objective description – whenever the first person, singular or plural, appears in a poem after the late 1920s – the poem possesses no consistent stanzaic pattern. These unpatterned, more personal poems are generally longer, more emotional, and less controlled than the patterned objective ones, and include the likes of "Adam" (about Williams' father), "Eve" (about his mother), "The Crimson Cyclamen" (written in memory of Charles Demuth), "Elegy for D. H. Lawrence," "To All Gentleness" . . . and others in this general vein.[6]

Out of this juxtaposition, Sayre distills "two types of poems" which are based upon "competing aesthetic assumptions":

On the one hand, [Williams] would have it that the mind represents itself by the abstract designs it discovers and creates, by the order it imposes on reality. On the other hand, whenever his poems are most clearly about the mind, they tend to be disorderly. In one kind of poem the imagination is defined as the place from which form and order spring; in the other, especially in contrast to the first, the imagination seems to be disorder's natural home. (p. 74)

Many of the "disorderly" or loose poems, according to Sayre, reflect "the lack of a bridge between the chaotic world and the ordering mind," and it is this "divorce of the writing from the vision" that "seems to justify the lack of form" (p. 73).

Now it seems to me that Sayre's distinction between the two basic types of poem is highly useful but does not do justice to the second form. It is problematic, above all, to classify the patterned variant as the one that achieves a formal order and clarity while the other, looser form fails to do so and is therefore a document of Williams's frustration or despair. One argument against such a division consists in the fact that many of Williams's loose poems – among them "The Rose," "Spring and All," "Crimson Cyclamen," "A Marriage Ritual," and "Rain" – are predominantly affirmative, while a number of poems written in the stanzaic form (particularly among those written in the 1930s and the 1940s, such as "A Portrait of the Times," "You Have Pissed Your Life," "A Bastard Peace," "These") are written in a dark or pessimistic mood.

However, one may well take one's cue from Sayre's distinction without subscribing to his conclusion that the patterned form is a sign of success while the "disorderly" form denotes a declaration of defeat before a chaotic present that defies being transformed in the work of art by the ordering mind. The loose poems are indeed more concerned with the ordering mind, while the patterned poems predominantly explore the tension between the recalcitrant object-world and the "design" or order imposed on it. The patterned form often exploits the tension between object-world and work of art; the loose form on the other hand explores the tension between self and other, with the mind incessantly engaged – sometimes successfully and sometimes not – in bringing about order.

The first, patterned kind, in other words, is more concerned with the tension between the concrete and the abstract, the mimetic and nonmimetic, while the second makes of the poem an embodiment of the act of discovery or exploration. It consists essentially of the *process* of exploration, of the self entering the (new) world naked. Each of these poems enacts a new approach, since each is about a new creation of order, at least the attempt to bring it about.

The difference between the two forms emerges very clearly when we compare "The Red Wheelbarrow" with an equally exemplary poem of the second kind, "Spring and All" (*CP1*, 183). In both poems, for instance, Williams exploits the tension between lineation and syntax, in the sense that line unit and sense unit are often not identical. This means that in both poems, as we have seen, words are at one and the same time referential and self-referential; the poem becomes a network of linguistic tensions based on dissonance and clash rather than on the harmony resulting from an identity of sense unit and line unit. One of the best descriptions of this effect is in J. Hillis Miller's *Poets of Reality:*

> Conjunctions, prepositions, adjectives, when they come at the end of a line, assume an expressive energy as arrows of force reaching toward the other words: "of red and⟶." Going for the moment toward the void, they go all the more strongly, as a man in isolation reaches out in longing toward other men and women. Into the white space surrounding the word go a multitude of lines of force, charging that space with the almost tangible presence of the various words which might come to complete the central world and appease its tension. (p. 300)

The effects of enjambments as described here can be observed in both the loose and the patterned poems. However, enjambments can also have different effects in the two forms, and this difference can tell us more about the constitutive traits of each of them. Thus in "The Red Wheelbarrow," "wheel / barrow" and "rain / water" cut the compounds into their constituents, which makes us aware of the fact "that they are phenomenological constituents as well," as John Hollander put it: "The wheel plus the barrow equals the wheelbarrow, and in the freshness of light after the rain . . . things seem to lose their compounded properties."[7] Enjambment here is used as a means of defamiliarization, which gives us back something of Ruskin's "innocence of the eye" and prevents us from seeing, as Valéry would have said, with the dictionary instead of the eyes.

On the other hand, a line break such as the following from the opening lines of "Spring and All" has, at least partly, a different effect:

> under the surge of the blue
> mottled clouds . . .

"Blue" is a noun when we take the line as a unit in itself, but it becomes an adjective the moment we reach the next line. The eye of the viewer exploring a landscape – not unlike that of a viewer confronted with the ambiguous elements in a Cubist canvas – is engaged in a process of disambiguation: The poet or persona, surrounded by a somewhat chaotic landscape, sees, at first more or less disorientedly, a multitude of details and gradually sorts them out until the whole scenery is "defined," in a process that reenacts the resurgence of life in early spring. The form of the poem, in other words, iconically embodies the gradual emergence of form in, and from, a landscape which at the beginning of the poem is still "a waste of broad, muddy fields / brown with dried weeds, standing and fallen," but which moves step by step toward a greater "clarity, outline of form."

The shift from "blue" as noun to adjective is thus part of this iconic enactment of form being born and stands for one of the many moments of (re)orientation. From the spots of blue in the sky the eye is pulled to the "mottled clouds" so that "blue," at first a noun, becomes a metonymically displaced adjective – instead of a blue sky with mottled clouds we get a sky with "blue / mottled clouds." This displacement conveys the feeling of nervous shifts from one detail to another, as well as the sense of a slight disorientation, which is reinforced by the enjambments of the next two lines:

> . . . the blue
> mottled clouds driven from the
>
> northeast – a cold wind. Beyond the
> waste . . .

Both of these run-on lines leave the reader hung up for a moment with the deictic "the" at the end, with a definite article that is severed from the noun belonging to it. The first enjambment can be read as a short hesitation before relating the direction of the wind to the cardinal points, while the second enjambment contains, as it were, the fraction of a second that the mind sometimes needs before it can name what has just caught the eye.

The entire poem is characterized by these nervous shifts. All is process here, and all is motion. Almost all the sentences are either fragmentary or elliptical, and the poem consists of incessant new beginnings and reorientations. One sentence overlaps another, or one sentence fragment stops where the next begins. Adverbials such as "now," "tomorrow," "But now," "one by one" indicate temporal jumps and modifications in which the mind is continuously pulled back and forth between a (conceived) temporal or seasonal progression and a (perceived) immediate present, a present, however, which is in itself an embodiment of continuous change.[8]

PART 2

Forms of Iconicity

Whatever the poems look like that are the result of Williams's search for a synthetic form, they invariably contain the simultaneous presence of opposed energies: of "imitation" and creation, the referential and the self-referential, the concrete and the abstract. Through the "design of [the] sentences," Williams on the one hand creates a feeling of the materiality of the words and the object character of the poems; the directness and intensity of the sheer act of naming, on the other hand, endows the poems with a power of evocation that recalls Rilke's exclamation in the ninth Duino elegy:

> Sind wir vielleicht *hier*, um zu sagen: Haus,
> Brücke, Brunnen, Tor, Krug, Obstbaum, Fenster, –
> höchstens: Säule, Turm . . . aber zu sagen, verstehs,
> oh zu sagen *so*, wie selber die Dinge niemals
> innig meinten zu sein.
>
> (Are we, perhaps, *here* just for saying: House,
> Bridge, Fountain, Gate, Jug, Fruit tree, Window, –
> possibly: Pillar, Tower? . . . but for *saying,* remember,
> oh, for such saying as never the things themselves
> hoped so intensely to be.)[9]

On one level, the two basic dimensions are unassimilable opposites, while on another they curiously enhance each other. Thus much of Williams's poetics devoted to foregrounding the artifact nature of the work of art also enhance the magic of naming – his attempt to free words from the "dead weight of logical burdens" (*SE,* 115), to wipe them clean (as Marianne Moore did) from past associations, and to dissociate them from one another in order to give them back their pristine power to reach out both for the object-world and the other words surrounding them.

All of these attempts, as we have seen, are directly connected with the breaking of the flow of discursive language, a language tied to a past culture in which it was monopolized by "science" and "philosophy" and abused by the "idea-vendors" that Williams attacks in *A Novelette.* Discarding this language meant discarding the "narrative line" or the "story line," a goal that Williams shared with most of the major Modernist writers and the revolutionary painters who had "taken the lead" in this respect, beginning with Cézanne, who in his paintings had opened up the previously closed contours of the depicted objects by means of the *passages* and gradually turned the canvas into a veritable field of *taches colorantes.*

Gaston Bachelard, Roland Barthes, and other theorists have seen in this breaking up of the traditional continuous flow of discourse (and the Cartesian rationality or "logicality" to which it is related) one of the fundamental aspects of Modernism. One of the by now classic statements on this basic disjunction is to be found in Barthes's *Writing Degree Zero:*

> In classical speech, connections lead the word on, and at once carry it towards a meaning which is an ever deferred project; in modern poetry, connections are

only an extension of the word, it is the Word which is the "dwelling place," . . .
it is the Word which gratifies and fulfills like the sudden revelation of a truth. . . .
It shines with an infinite freedom and prepares to radiate towards innumerable
uncertain and possible connections. Fixed connections being abolished, the word
is left only with a vertical project, it is like a monolith or a pillar which plunges
into a totality of meanings, reflexes and recollections: it is a sign which stands.[10]

Could this be taken to mean that such writing marks a return to the logocentric
tradition in disguise, attempting to install the Word in a presence that replaces
the absence of meaning in classical writing (in which it is an "ever deferred
project")? No, since the Word in modern poetry is, as Barthes sees it, installed
at the price of a radical free play, radiating "towards innumerable uncertain and
possible meanings." Barthes – the early Barthes of *Writing Degree Zero* – finds
this free play profoundly disturbing and regards it as a basic sign of alienation.
For Williams, on the other hand, the "disjointing process" is first of all a means
to free the words from the old restrictions fettering them, a liberation akin to
the breakthrough that Cézanne and the Cubists had achieved in painting. Of
course Williams, as we have seen, soon realized that *les mots en liberté* could lead
straight away to a new hermeticism in which the delicate balance between the
concrete and the abstract was once more turned upside down. In the field of
action that his poems constitute words must not go too much toward one pole,
or the field itself with its "rout of the vocables" will collapse.

What is important with regard to words is no less important with regard to
the overall shape of the poems. Here, too, opposed energies in interaction create
the tension that is so vital for an art rooted in an aesthetics of energy. Again the
poles are those of the concrete and the abstract, of denotation and design. Words
on the page can be arranged not only into abstract shapes, as in the stanzaic
poems, they can also be turned into icons that visually embody the objects,
processes, or movements the poem talks about. The overall shape of the poem,
too, in other words, can both foreground the creative dimension and serve
mimetic purposes; it constitutes an important additional level on which the
poem can be turned into a tense equilibrium of opposed energies.

Rendering Process

Turning to the various forms that the iconic can assume in Williams's poems,
we realize that the distinction between the "loose" and the stanzaic poems is
helpful once more, because the two forms also contain different forms of iconicity. In the poems of discovery, for instance, in which a self is engaged in
relating to its surroundings, we often find an iconic representation of the hesitancies of this self, hesitancies that sometimes embody moments of bewilderment, reorientation, or feeling at a loss, and sometimes the effort to get things
right, to counteract facileness, turns toward a false eloquence. Often they also
embody the pace or rhythm of the encounter between self and object world,

denoting moments of contemplation, pauses, silences, with a rich variety of contextually defined moods.

We noted such hesitancies and pauses in the act of exploration in "The Rose" or "Spring and All"; another example, discussed earlier in a different context, is "Two Pendants, for the Ears" (*CP2*, 201). Here both the "loose" stanza form and the delayed period surrounded by white space (as often used later in *Paterson*) are used iconically. In a poem that shows the self in an unusually depressed state, the white space surrounding the words and the irregularly shaped little stanzas denote moments of inertia, distraction, and shifts of thought along associational lines (often along the "lateral sliding" of similes and metaphors):

> The wind howled still at my
> bedroom window but here, overlooking the
> garden, I no longer hear its howls
> nor see it moving
>
>   My thoughts
> are like the distant smile of a child
> who will (never) be a beautiful woman
>
>   like
> the distant smile of a woman who
> will say:
>   – only to keep you a moment
> longer. Oh I know I'm a stinker –
>
>   but
>
> only to keep you, it's only
> to keep you   a few moments
>
>   Let me have a cigarette.

Fragmentation, loss of concentration, the wavering of thoughts, inertia – all are presented not only via language but also visually in the organization of the words on the page. Semantic, syntactic, and visual levels all interact and corroborate each other. A simile, in the effort to concentrate on it for a moment, is extended but bifurcates into two opposite directions by means of a parenthetical "never" –

>   My thoughts
>   are like the distant smile of a child
>   who will (never) be a beautiful woman

and then reappears, hesitatingly, announced by the literally lost "like" at the beginning of the next stanza, only to peter out in a passage that could be either part of a monologue that the solitary self maintains or part of an imagined (or remembered?) dialogue with the woman conjured up by the simile. The self, in other words, is also shown *visually* in a state of confusion, and the scattered words on the page become disquieting, as do the "displaced," distanced periods, which depict the self's vain attempts to recover in moments of rest or recollection.

Similes and metaphors create confusion in this poem in which the consoling certainty of names and naming dissolves ("A cloud / unclassic, a white unnamed cloud") and in which the self cannot concentrate on one thing at a time, the distracted eye focusing on one thing after another and the mind wavering from details seen to details imagined or remembered. In addition, the poem wavers between literal and metaphorical naming (the "white unnamed cloud," for instance, is transformed from a literal into a metaphorical cloud – a "cloud of / small tufts of white flowers" – and then back into a literal cloud, "through which the east sun / shines, anonymous"), and it shifts not only from one to the other but also becomes entangled in catachreses ("beds! beds for the flowers"), so that the disorder in the house and the disorder of naming are mirrored in each other:

> The short and brilliantly stabbing grass
> (my son went out during that night
>   and has not returned – later
> I found that he had returned and had
> fallen asleep on the couch downstairs –
> his bed was empty)
> – marked (plotted) by the squares
> and oblongs of the flower beds
>   (beds! beds for the flowers)
> the sticks of roses that will later show
> brilliant blooms stand out
>   in rows, irregularly
>
> A cloud
> unclassic, a white unnamed cloud of
> small tufts of white flowers
>   light as wishes
> (later to give place to red berries
>   called service berries)
> – a cloud through which the east sun
> shines, anonymous
>   (a tree marked
> by the practical sense of my countrymen
> the shad bush   to say
> fish are in the river)
>
>   floating

Note that the last word in this passage *says* "floating" and *is* floating, and that the position on the page does not only iconically reflect the "floating" state of mind of the self but also the syntactic openness (which creates anxiety in this context): "floating" can be connected to the immediately preceding line ("fish are in the river // floating") but it can also be related to "A cloud / unclassic . . . " at the beginning of the stanza, taken up once more six lines later, and lost once again when the eye notices the sign on the tree. In a sense, then, the isolated "floating" also contains the stubborn attempts of the mind to find its way back to a thread of thought lost twice, to maintain at least a modicum of coherence.

Immediately preceding this section we find the only part of the poem with a stanzaic pattern, a pattern that one can read iconically, too. Functioning as a direct counterpart of the scattered or dispersed verse surrounding it, its form is an obvious icon of the "plotted" garden with its "squares / and oblongs of the flower beds." Its reassuring order — "Here everything / is clear" — should have a beneficial influence on the despondent and confused self, who tries to recover from "night's vague images" — the dream of the killer tiger that opens the poem — by contemplating its stability and order:

> The yard
> from the bathroom window
> is another matter:
>
> Here everything
> is clear. The wind
> sounds, I can make out
>
> the yellow of the flowers —
> For half an hour
> I do not move.
>
> It is Easter Sunday.

Again, the visual dimension finds its counterpart in the language: Short, paratactical units, with factual statements, are neatly laid out, in a simple progression from one to the other. The deep suffering, however, that Williams faces in this eminently autobiographical poem cannot simply be alleviated by empathetically identifying with the reassuring order of the "particulars of morning." The poem enacts, among other things, the search for a more complex poetic form which acknowledges, and reflects, the magnitude of a crisis that defies any facile cathartic resolution.

Spatial Constellations

The different functions that the iconic assumes in this poem in the regularly patterned and irregular sections can be observed in many other poems. In the "loose" poems the iconic invariably embodies the *process* of the exploring or ordering mind coping with a multitude of details, thoughts, and sensory impressions. In the stanzaic poems, on the other hand, the iconic embodies an order or design achieved. Such a design can comprise both the spatial and temporal; often, as in the first, "loose" or irregular form, the two dimensions are shown in interaction, albeit in a more orderly, tidy, or steadily progressing way.

Spatial icons are frequently found in the still-life or nature poems. An example is "The Yellow Chimney" (*CP2*, 87), a poem which, in J. Hillis Miller's words, "is a picture of what it represents, the slender column of words corresponding to the chimney, and the lines of the poem, it may not be too fanciful to say, echoing the silver rings which strap the yellow stack at intervals" (*Poets of Reality*, p. 301):

> There is a plume
> of fleshpale
> smoke upon the blue
>
> sky. The silver
> rings that
> strap the yellow
>
> brick stack at
> wide intervals shine
> in this amber
>
> light – not
> of the sun not of
> the pale sun but
>
> his born brother
> the
> declining season

One should perhaps modify Miller's statement and say that a poem like "The Yellow Chimney" *also* contains a picture of what it represents. It is *not* a concrete poem proper but is one that comes alive, among other things, through the tense interaction or fusion of its abstract (stanzaic) and concrete (iconic) design.

There are passages in Williams which virtually amount to concrete poetry. An example is the well-known opening of *Paterson* 5 (p. 205):

> In old age
>   the mind
>   casts off
>   rebelliously
>   an eagle
> from its crag

However, Williams hardly ever became iconic to the point that one might say
he "painted" with words; he must have realized that a one-sided emphasis on
the iconic properties was, if used too often, a dead end for poetry "because of
its neglect of one side of the tension essential to the literary icon – its semiotic,
mediated nature."[11] Thus Williams usually made use of the subtler iconic device
of fusing the concrete poem or pattern poem (which represents the shapes of
the object it talks about) with an abstract stanzaic form, as he did in "The Yellow
Chimney." Another example is "The Locust Tree in Flower" (in both versions,
but particularly in the shorter, to which we shall return because it combines
several iconic devices); it echoes the shape of the locust tree with its long slim
stem and the often rooflike spreading treetop in the contours made up of title
and poem together:

THE LOCUST TREE IN FLOWER

          Among
          of
          green

          stiff
          old
          bright

          broken
          branch
          come

          white
          sweet
          May

          again

                              (CEP, 93; CP1, 379)[12]

In "Navajo" (CLP, 101), which is another example, the contours of the
poem suggest the shape of the Indian woman portrayed. In an excellent article
on the iconic dimensions in the Modernist poem, Max Nänny points out that
the squaw's erect posture ("walking the desert. . . . with fixed sight / stalking,"
"walking erect") is "iconically reinforced by the straight, non-stanzaic verticality
of the left margin." Moreover, the overall shape of the poem also suggests the
outline of an "erect" woman in a long tribal costume (carrying a baby on her
back?) that reaches "to the ground – / sweeping the ground," with the first
eight lines suggesting her "mobbled" head and line one "possibly being a hint
at a feather in her hair":[13]

Red woman,
    (Keep Christ out
    of this – and
    his mountains:
    Sangre de Cristo
    red rocks that make
    the water run
    blood-red)
squaw in red
red woman
walking the desert
I suspected
I should remember
you this way:
    walking the brain
    eyes cast down
    to escape ME!
    with fixed sight
    stalking
    the grey brush
    paralleling
    the highway . . .
    – head mobbled
    red, red
    to the ground –
    sweeping the
        ground –
    the blood walking
    erect, the
    desert animating
    the blood to walk
    erect by choice
    through
    the pale green
    of the starveling
    sage

Perhaps one could even say that the moment one has discovered the contours of the woman in the contours of the poem, these contours begin to stand out, isolated, from the "desert" of the white page, so as to enforce iconically the image of the proud, unapproachable, lonesome figure in red, "eyes cast down / to escape ME! / with fixed sight / stalking / the grey brush," in a "desert animating / the blood to walk / erect by choice / through / the pale green / of the starveling / sage."

    The typographical indication of relative positions (above all of top and bottom) as well as symmetry are also part of the spatial dimension and directly

related to the iconic representation of shape. Max Nänny notes that it is Williams
in particular among the Modernists who created many icons of this sort, and
that it is "remarkable how many of his poems mirror the relative position of
top and bottom" ("Imitative Form," p. 223). One example for this form of
iconicity is "Young Woman at a Window" (*CP1*, 373; second version):

> She sits with
> tears on
>
> her cheek
> her cheek on
>
> her hand
> the child
>
> in her lap
> his nose
>
> pressed
> to the glass

The progression of the poem down the page corresponds to the lowering of
the focus from the woman's face to the child in her lap, a shift that is paralleled
by a shift from the figures and their position ("She sits with . . . // the child /
/ in her lap") to details which sharply contrast their moods ("tears on // her
cheek"; "his nose // pressed / to the glass"), in an opposition which
simultaneously intensifies the suffering of the woman and undercuts it. (As often
happens in Williams, the space of intimacy created by the "tactus eruditus"
(*CP1*, 335) leads to a seamless unity of the psychic and the physical, the mind
and the body: Tears are hot here, and the glass is cool, in both a literal and a
figurative sense.)

The spatial relationship of the two beings (out of which emerges the interaction of proximity and distance, intimacy and isolation) is foregrounded in the
prominent position of the five prepositions "with," "on," "on," "in," and "to,"
which all stand out either at the end or at the beginning of a line. Vying for
our attention in that prominent position, they make us realize that they, too,
are subjected to iconic arrangement: "On," in both instances, is placed at the
end of a stanza *above* (or *on*, as it were) the next stanza naming the prepositional
object ("her cheek"; "her hand"), whereas "in" and "to" are both situated
within the stanza that contains the object ("in her lap"; "pressed / to the glass").

Of course the poem is another example of a form that does not rely entirely
on iconic effects; again the iconic dimension interacts with the abstract stanzaic
design, so that the poem comes alive in, and through, the tension of the concrete
and the abstract, of imitation and creation. And although Williams highlights
the prepositions for the iconic descent from top to bottom, they remain particles
in a linguistic network. In this network, for example, "cheek," among the
objects related, is first an object ("tears on / her cheek") and then, in an inver-

sion, a subject ("her cheek on // her hand") instead of remaining the object within an analogical progression (tears on her cheek, her hands on her cheek).

Here and elsewhere prepositions unfold their energy between their concrete spatial suggestiveness and their abstract grammatical function; and whereas in "Young Woman at a Window" their concreteness (and through it the iconic) prevails, the scales can always tilt in the other direction, as for instance in the opening stanza of "The Red Wheelbarrow" ("So much depends / upon . . . "). Here, too, the concreteness of the preposition "upon" is foregrounded by the fact that it fills out a line and precedes a break between stanzas; its power to suggest and iconically embody spatial relations, however, is checked by the fact that it is meaningless apart from its grammatical function within the abstract opening statement.

By working with all these tensions, Williams stays within the basic domains of verbal art, in which signs invariably operate on all three levels of the "semiotic triad,"[14] namely, the indexical, iconic, and symbolic, and in which the difference between the three is one of "relative hierarchy."[15] Moreover, Williams intuitively or consciously understood that while in poetry one could make only a limited use of both the auditory and visual icon proper – in onomatopoeia and concrete poetry – one could achieve rich and varied effects by using the iconic on the relational or diagrammatic level, of which both the opposition of disorder and order in "Two Pendants" and the relative positions of top and bottom in "Young Woman at a Window" are examples.

On this level, too, the incorporation of image icons changes the impact of the poems; icons create a more immediate awareness of what they refer to than other signs because some aspect of the referent is physically present – embodied, figuring forth – in the sign. In these poems, however, in which the iconic interacts with the other, noniconic dimensions of language, it is far less conspicuous than, for instance, in the "pure" form of pattern poetry. Paradoxically, as Max Nänny notices, it was

> this very tradition of pattern poetry – that is, poetry which attempts to represent the outline of objects (e.g. an altar, wings) by means of a clever arrangement of lines, words or letters – that has blinded critics to other kinds of iconic representation. It lulled them into the false belief that iconicity in poetry is either an eccentric device or a purely accidental and, therefore, insignificant feature. But other modes of iconic representations are possible. Thus writing and printing permit verbal signs to be arranged, first, into spatial configurations. These scriptural or typographic constellations of lines, words and letters may not only mirror the shape or pattern of concrete objects but may also analogically express relative positions, symmetry, balance, size, absence, distance, notional structures such as dissociation, fragmentation, individuality and also disguise and latency.
>
> The linear sequence of verbal signs may, second, iconically render succession in time and/or space, continuity, change (growth and decay), duration, rank and motion (be it horizontal, vertical, circular or back and forth).
>
> Once literature became primarily written and printed, once writers and espe-

cially poets began to compose at the typewriter and produced texts meant for silent readers who were no longer confronted with the spoken word but with black marks on white paper, these iconic possibilities inherent in visual signs were increasingly exploited.[16]

Thus, Nänny concludes, an increasing number of poets in our century "came to realize that by adding an iconic dimension to their primarily symbolic art, by foregrounding visual elements of the text they could enhance the poeticalness of the text due to an augmented 'palpability of signs'."[17] It is obviously such a "palpability of signs" that Williams had in mind when he wrote toward the end of the *Autobiography:* "It is the making of that step, *to come over into the tactile qualities,* the words themselves beyond the mere thought expressed, that distinguished the modern" (*A,* 380; my italics).

Rendering Motion

Since poems are bound to the linear sequence of verbal signs, iconicity can also include the temporal dimension. Poems, in other words, may iconically render succession in space or time, in the sense of embodying either the movement of what is observed or the eye movement of the observer absorbing spatial constellations − both static and dynamic − detail for detail.

In all of these instances, the poem iconically embodies a spatial–temporal continuum that implies the presence of an observer. In the case of Williams, this means that even the so-called objective or objectivist poems contain a responding consciousness, albeit a consciousness or self that strives for an empathetic identification and is thus "unsullied by appetitiveness or the drive to dominion," as Thomas H. Jackson puts it, a self that is "not an ego, in short, but a presence."[18] (Once we are aware of this presence we also realize that the difference between the poems of discovery or exploration and the objectivist poems is one of degree − they represent different ways or different stages of the interaction of self and other, self and scene.)

There are many Williams poems with an iconic rendering of the eye movement of the observing self. In some of them the *degree* of iconicity varies within the poem; that is, the iconic can be present throughout but suddenly be enforced by typographical changes. In "The Pot of Flowers" (*CP*1, 184), for instance, the eye retraces the plant in a gradual downward movement, starting with the flowers and their petals and ending at the lowest point (" . . . and there, wholly dark, the pot / gay with rough moss"). At the crucial point when the eye leaves the "whorl" of the "contending" colors to move downward to the leaves and the pot, Williams foregrounds the iconic dimension by giving the word "above" a line to itself and putting it − the only instance in the poem − in a middle position, literally above "the leaves / reaching *up* their modest green" (my italics):

> petals radiant with transpiercing light
> contending
>   above
>
> the leaves
> reaching up their modest green
> from the pot's rim

A more complex iconic use of eye movement is made in "Young Sycamore" (*CEP*, 332; *CP1*, 266). The poem, which is based on Stieglitz's photograph *Spring Showers,* as Bram Dijkstra has shown,[19] records the eye's linear movement as it follows the tree from bottom to top:

> I must tell you
> this young tree
> whose round and firm trunk
> between the wet
>
> pavement and the gutter
> (where water
> is trickling) rises
> bodily
>
> into the air with
> one undulant
> thrust half its height –
> and then
>
> dividing and waning
> sending out
> young branches on
> all sides –
>
> hung with cocoons
> it thins
> till nothing is left of it
> but two
>
> eccentric knotted
> twigs
> bending forward
> hornlike at the top

A peculiar tension in this poem results from the fact that the process of reading takes us down the page while the inward eye is moving upward, so that the iconic dimension comes in via inversion. (The very last word at the bottom of the poem is "top.") This inversion has its deeper justification in the fact that the life force embodied in the tree (with which the speaker's self and we with him empathize: "I must tell you / this young tree") exists in a world of process in which growth and decay, creation and destruction are simultaneous. Thus Peter Schmidt's interpretation indicates that – perhaps unintended but nonetheless present – the movement upward contains its inversion or counterpart:

> A second reading . . . will show that the poem is hardly without personification or metaphor, although they are implied rather than stated. Williams hints that Stieglitz's sycamore is also a tree of life, starting with youth's "round and firm trunk" and then "waning" gradually until the branches are "bending forward" like the bodies of the old. Both men and trees have offspring: seed "cocoons" hang from the leafless branches. The eye's movement thus merges with the inner eye's vision of time's passage. ("Modernist Pastoral," p. 391)

In such poems as "Young Sycamore," Williams makes a particularly effective use of iconicity. It blends the sequential act of reading with the eye's and the mind's step-by-step appraisal of the object under scrutiny to the point where the linguistic force is coextensive with the life force of the tree and thus brings about an empathetic fusion of self and scene in a space–time continuum. The unfolding or expansion of the poem becomes an icon for the unfolding and expansion of the tree, and thus mirrors the process. Together with the sum total of the other poetic devices, such as the force contained in the many finite and nonfinite verbs ("rises," "undulant / thrust," "dividing and waning," "hung," "thins," "knotted," and "bending") and the words that activate the sense of touch and the sense of hearing ("round and firm trunk," "rises / bodily," "where water / is trickling"), the poem can no longer be said to simply talk *about* the tree but rather becomes an object that shares or embodies the tree's life. Such a poem is, as Williams says, not opposed to nature but apposed to it. The process of exploration and appropriation (of which the poem is an icon) and the involvement of several senses beyond the distancing sense of sight make of the poem a kinesthetic and synesthetic object in which the self relives or recreates the life of the tree, in a way that fully justifies Williams's dictum, "A thing known passes out of the mind into the muscles" (*I: KH,* 74).

On the iconic level, some poems fuse spatial configurations not only with eye movement but also with object movement. An example is "The Waitress" (*CP1,* 279), a montage of details superimposing the proceedings at a meeting of an election committee with the portrait of the waitress. In the following passage the poem, on the level of movement, contrasts the horizontal scanning of the voters at the meeting ("And aye, and aye, and aye") with the left-right and top-bottom movement of the bell-hop running downstairs:

The Nominating Committee presents the following
resolutions, etc. etc. etc. All those
in favor signify by saying, Aye. Contrariminded,
No.
   Carried.
        And aye, and aye, and aye!

And the way the bell-hop runs downstairs:
    ta tuck a
      ta tuck a
        ta tuck a
          ta tuck a
            ta tuck a
and the gulls in the open window screaming over the slow
break of the cold waves –

On the iconic level, the stairs fuse not only the visual (the outline of the stairs)
and the temporal (the bell-hop descending the stairs) but also the spatial and the
aural, since onomatopoeia is included as well. Moreover, the two lines at the
end contain an iconic dimension, too, though in a less obvious way. They mirror
the top–bottom relation of the gulls *over* the waves and the slowness of "the
slow / break of the cold waves" by means of the enjambment and by breaking
the syntactic unit "screaming over the slow / break of the cold waves" between
"slow" and "break."

In the famous "Poem" (*CP1*, 352), Williams also conveys both the spatial
and the temporal dimension iconically:

        As the cat
        climbed over
        the top of

        the jamcloset
        first the right
        forefoot

        carefully
        then the hind
        stepped down

        into the pit of
        the empty
        flowerpot

Spatially, the relative positions of high and low are embodied in the stanzaic
arrangement, with "the top" in the top stanza and "the pit of / the empty /
flowerpot" in the bottom stanza. Moreover, in lines 2–4, "over" *is* positioned
over the line with "the top," which in turn is positioned over "the jamcloset."
Similarly, "stepped down" in the second to last stanza indeed leads down –

through the hiatus of the stanza break — "into the pit of / the empty / flow-erpot."

Iconicity here also includes rhythm, pace, and syntax. Like a number of other Williams poems, it consists of a single sentence that describes an object, animal, or human being in motion, and the linguistic energy of the sentence is identical to the energy contained and conveyed in the movement described: When the movement comes to an end, the poem comes to an end, too. In "Poem," moreover, the twelve short lines, each of which ends in an enjambment, entail a slow pace and steady progression that mirrors the inimitable combination of carefulness, precision, delicacy, and unerring poise that characterizes the cat's walking over jamcloset and flowerpots. The poem, in Hugh Kenner's words, is "one sinuous suspended sentence, feeling its way and never fumbling. Its gestures raise anticipatory tensions, its economy dislodges nothing. The cat is as much an emblem of the sentence as the sentence is of the cat. It is headed 'Poem' " (*The Pound Era*, p. 399).

Thus, once again, beginning with the title, Williams insists on our double awareness that the poem about the cat and the cat itself are at once related and different things. While he manages to write a poem that embodies something like the essence of a cat in the words and their arrangement on the page — while he manages, in other words, to write a poem that is linked to the signified via the *natura naturans* — he at the same time insists on the poem's separate linguistic identity.

In "Poem," this separate identity manifests itself not only in its stanzaic design but also in its sound patterns and word permutations. On this level, Williams highlights the noniconic dimension of language, which is based predominantly on a code of arbitrary signs or symbols. Thus the sound pattern is dominated by an intricate network of fricatives and plosives — above all t, p, c, and f — many of which are given additional emphasis by placement mainly in monosyllabic words and in stressed positions: "cat," "climbed," "top," "first," "right," "stepped," "pit," "empty." (Aurally, even the few compounds fall into this category: Each of them has two stresses, and together they result in a rhythmic pattern of their own, with an alternation of unstressed and stressed line endings: "jamcloset," "forefoot," "carefully," "flowerpot.") All of these words together turn the poem on the aural level into a semiabstract musical score, with the single consonants and vowels as notes which, in different combinations, create different words: "cat," "-foot," "pit," "top," "-pot"; "climbed," "hind"; "care-," "fore-." The poem is a prime example of that attention paid to sounds which Williams had discovered and admired in Laurence Sterne and Gertrude Stein: "The feeling is of words themselves, a curious immediate quality quite apart from their meaning, much as in music different notes are dropped, so to speak, into repeated chords one at a time, one after the other — for themselves alone" (*SE*, 114).

Word transformation or permutation, in other words, foregrounds the noniconic, systemic nature of language, in a poem that employs both the iconic and noniconic side of language on several levels. On the typographical level, the vertical axis (with top versus bottom) is iconic, while the stanzaic organization is not; the progression down the page, in turn, is iconic, and so are (since they are tied to this progression) syntax and lineation, which in their specific interaction make of the poem an imitation of the cat's careful and delicate movements. The same division or tension is present on the aural level. Rhythm and pace, which are largely determined here by syntax and lineation, are iconic or imitative, while the sound of words and word patterns, as we have seen, is not. One can hardly imagine a more intricate interpenetration of the double existence of words or of the Janus face of language. Visually and rhythmically, the poem not only denotes but also contains or embodies what it names, but it does so by means of word bodies, word sounds, and stanzaic word groupings that at the same time foreground the object character of a poem which is made with words on the page as paintings are made with pigment on a canvas.

To conclude, let us turn to two other poems which, each in its own way, are icons of the specific temporal and spatial constellation that constitutes their subject. One is "The Locust Tree in Flower" (*CEP*, 93; *CP1*, 379), whose iconicity comprises much more than the shape of the locust tree mirrored in the overall design of the poem and its title. The copresence of what the speaker sees and at the same time conceives as seasonal change is reflected right at the beginning in the copresence of the two prepositions "among" and "of," the first of which refers to the spatial and the second to the temporal dimension:

THE LOCUST TREE IN FLOWER

> Among
> of
> green
>
> stiff
> old
> bright
>
> broken
> branch
> come
>
> white
> sweet
> May
>
> again

The fact that the two prepositions at the beginning are mutually exclusive foregrounds the way in which language often connects things on one level while excluding others. Williams violates a language rule in order to embody the copresence of space and time, mirroring in his linguistic network the "real" as a field of action in which any spatial configuration is also part of an ongoing process. At the same time the "disorderly" coexistence of old and new, growth and decay, is iconically rendered by means of an accretion of details which are not neatly grouped but shown in mutual interpenetration: "green // stiff / old / bright // broken." Temporal progression, on the other hand, enacting the return of spring, is iconically embodied in the way in which the poem runs down the page in rapid succession until it reaches its climactic end. Progressing word for word we finally arrive at the moment in which we have reexperienced and recreated "white / sweet / May // again."

A third iconic dimension embodies temporality on the level of the relationship between experiencing self and experienced object world. The word-for-word progression of the poem mirrors the way in which the viewer's eyes move in quick succession from one isolated detail to another, reflecting a process of perception that is both rapid and pristine to the degree that it is still sheer naming and not (yet) concerned with achieving syntactic congruity.

Once again iconicity (which is part of the "imitative" dimension in this poem) interacts with the created pattern – the "design" – of the stanzaic form, since the poem is designed as a one-word-per-line poem subdivided into four little three-line stanzas. But at the end of this "arbitrarily patterned" poem (to use Sayre's terminology) we have again a deviation that is far from arbitrary, namely, the single isolated word "again." It names, or sums up in one word, the process the poem as a whole enacts in its four stanzas and twelve lines: the perennial return of spring within the eternal cycle of the seasons.

At the same time we can say that the last word not only identifies the being it names as a be-ing or perennial becoming but also asserts its presence by arriving triumphantly at a here and now: "come // white / sweet / May // again" is not only an invocation but also an assessment of the fact that spring *has* "come . . . again," as the title of the poem itself indirectly indicates right at the beginning.

In a poem in which each word appears only in its cardinal form, "come" is as much *comes* or *has come* as it is a vocative. Words here are entirely absorbed by sheer naming in the sense of "presencing," conveying a "primitive" or absolute awareness in which man is "with nothing but the thing," in a complete identification with the detail just focused. Thus, to say "branches" instead of "branch" in this poem would loosen the attention from *the* branch named, so to speak, the very moment it catches the eye. This, however, does not mean that the reader should entirely forget the systemic or conceptual nature of language; the very violation of grammatical constraints foregrounds it and reintroduces the awareness of the irreducible doubleness of the sign.

The relationship between self and thing-world expressed in the exclamatory stance of this poem is predominantly that of an effortless – ecstatic, rhapsodic – identification. The self is in a state of rapt involvement; it dwells in the midst of a space in which it can rapidly move in all directions, and it can do so without being lost because it is contained in the cyclic return of the seasons, a timebound timelessness of growth and decay which the eye encounters wherever it looks and which the mind enacts as a recurrence of an indomitable force in the succession of little word explosions.

The beautiful late poem "Bird" (*CP2*, 414), on the other hand, presents a less easily resolved relationship between self and other, which is expressed accordingly in a quieter and more contemplative tone — a tone, however, that does not exclude celebration and revelation. (One way to approach it would be to say that both "The Locust Tree in Flower" and "Bird" are celebratory poems, but the first is a poem of spring, the second one of November.) In "Bird," the experiencing self encounters an elusive object which represents a world of perennial flux, process, change — a world, moreover, which is again both related to and yet very different from the words we have at our disposal to describe it:

> Bird with outstretched
> wings poised
> inviolate unreaching
>
> yet reaching
> your image this November
> planes
>
> to a stop
> miraculously fixed in my
> arresting eyes

Just as the eyes of the viewer are "arresting eyes" that fix the "image" of the bird planing to a stop, so words invariably create an image and arrest in it — fix, determine — what ultimately cannot be arrested. What the agent or self in the poem finally has is a "fixed" image gleaned "miraculously" from a bird which, nevertheless, defies and transcends all defining and arresting words.

The poem indeed realizes, as Thomas H. Jackson puts it, "a small-scale poetics" ("Positivism and Modern Poetics," p. 534). Sensory perception in interaction with an imaginative language defines, and thus arrests, an "object" which at the same time escapes intact, "inviolate," thanks to the scrupulous sense of distance that the self, in spite of his empathetic identification, maintains. Sense of distance and intimacy alike are expressed, for example, in the way in which the poet addresses the bird directly as his counterpart, whom he cannot, and will not, appropriate to the extent of violating its integrity by carelessly identifying it with that which he perceives and names.

This image comes closest to doing justice to the bird by recreating the complex interaction of self and other, observer and observed, flux and stasis in an analogous verbal field of action, a network of words that as a composite "image" contains "the same forces which transfuse the earth – at least one small part of them" (*I: SA*, 121).

Part of this language field of action is the tension between lineation and syntax (which turns the act of reading into an analogy of the act of perceiving the bird: the "arrested" meaning of each line is continuously modified during the process of reading); the tension that is also created by the violation of language rules ("unreaching"; "your image . . . / planes to a stop"); the use of paradox ("unreaching // yet reaching"); or the conceptual tension arising from the fact that what is flux and motion, glimpsed for a moment, is "fixed" by the observer's eye and the writer's words alike.

In addition to all this the image of the bird planing to a stop is also recreated iconically, both as a spatial configuration and as a movement coming to a halt. Thus, at the beginning of the poem, which describes the bird planing to a stop, we have the line

> wings poised

which iconically embodies in the poise of a completely balanced line with two monosyllabic words of equal stress the image of the bird with outstretched wings. And the moment of landing, too, is visualized as well as enacted in the reading process. In

> your image this November
> planes
>
> to a stop

the eye has to move down through the emptiness of the stanza break before it is halted by the line "to a stop."

Moreover, "Bird" (like "Poem" or "The Girl" and many other Williams poems) is in its entirety an icon of the process described. It consists again of one extended sentence which "carries" the linguistic energy mirroring or containing the extended energy of the bird's landing, and when the movement described comes "to a stop" the sentence comes to a stop, too.

Conclusion

Behind the iconic dimension in Williams's poems there is a fundamental mimetic desire, a desire, however, that invariably has to coexist with the other basic need to lay bare the status of each work of art as artifact. By means of the resulting perennial tension between the mimetic and the nonmimetic, the referential and the self-referential, Williams remains faithful to the irreducible doubleness of the sign and the ensuing paradoxical nature of all art. For Wendy Steiner, the awareness of this paradoxical nature is characteristic of all Modernist poets influenced by the visual arts:

> The programmatic tension between artistic medium and represented world so crucial to Cézanne, cubism, abstractionism, and surrealism has changed the meaning of the analogy [between literature and the visual arts]. By claiming that a poem is like a modern painting one is no longer stressing their mirroring function but their paradoxical status as signs of reality and things in their own right. (*The Colors of Rhetoric*, p. xii)

By including the iconic dimension Williams does not retract from this tenet; that is, he does not stress the mirroring function in the illusionist sense of the word (mimesis as "copying"). By turning the poem into an object that visually and/or aurally resembles what it talks about he comes closer to a repleteness of meaning without denying the fundamental difference between signifier and signified. He fully realizes that the poem as icon can enrich, but not transcend, language as a sign system.[1]

By means of the icon, therefore, Williams does not transcend the paradoxical status of language but rather highlights it on a new level. On the one hand, the icon embodies – and thus "presences" – the signified in a way that noniconic naming alone cannot achieve. Iconicity cannot close the gap between signifier and signified, but it can reduce it and at least somewhat transcend the arbitrariness of the sign. Particularly in those cases in which it includes movement or process it introduces a kinesthesia that leads to a heightened sense of empathetic identification between self and other, poet/reader and object world. Together with other devices grounded in an aesthetics of energy – such as a "frontal" approach that seeks nearness to things by focusing on details and on texture (which activates the sense of touch) – Williams creates a space or realm of intimacy and participation rather than a sense of distance, a realm of interpenetration of the spiritual and the physical, the psychological and the physiological, in such a manner that one not only understands but senses through mind *and* body the deeper truth of his dictum, "No ideas but in things."

On the other hand, even iconicity itself is used by Williams to foreground the artifact nature of all poetry. The majority of his visual icons are the result of a typographical arrangement of words that turns the poems visibly – often at first sight – into a form of "language art." Thus the inclusion of iconicity can be seen as a direct result of Williams's post-Cubist endeavor to pursue a non-illusionist art of construction, which stresses the materiality of words. "In order for words to become things, they need the palpability and materiality of things," writes Wendy Steiner (*The Colors of Rhetoric*, p. 199), and we have seen that it is exactly this palpability – "the tactile qualities [of] the words themselves, beyond the mere thought expressed" – that for Williams "distinguished the modern" (*A*, 380).

All of these terms – palpability, materiality, tactility – also recall the metaphor of bricklaying that Williams used more than once in this context. The poet uses words as the painter uses pigment or the architect bricks: "There is a special place which poems, as all works of art, must occupy . . . it is quite definitely the same as that where bricks or colored threads are handled" (*I*: "MM," 312). What all these forms of construction have in common is the element of design, and iconicity is nothing but one of these various forms of design. Words on the page can be arranged into a design, be it abstract or concrete (iconic). And even the most concrete among these designs, such as pattern poems or, for instance, Apollinaire's *calligrammes*, is still an abstraction, imitating the thing-world by means of an arrangement of words on the page. This is what Williams must have had in mind when he said in an interview with Walter Sutton:

> The design of the painting and of the poem I've attempted to fuse. To make it the same thing. And sometimes I don't want to say anything. I just want to present it. . . . I don't care if it's representational or not. But to give a design. A design in the poem and a design in the picture should make them more or less the same thing.[2]

Thus "design" in a Williams poem, which invariably welds the concrete (imitative, iconic) with the abstract (arbitrary), contains on the level of its overall construction a parallel to the double role of each individual word. The design of the poem as a whole, no less than the individual word, establishes an essential kinship between signifier and signified while at the same time insisting on the ineluctable difference between word and thing, work of art and world at large. It is true that the latter on one level creates a distance between word and thing that counteracts the desire for a fusion of self and other, but it does so only in the sense of rejecting the spurious identity of signifier and signified that stigmatized for Williams the traditional illusionist art forms.

Only a poetry of imaginative naming, therefore, which is diametrically opposed to a poetry of "repeating" or "copying," can for Williams do justice to both the nature of the work of art and the empirical reality it recreates. "The only means [the poet] has to give value to life," writes Williams in *Spring and All*, "is to recognize it with the imagination and name it; this is so. To repeat and repeat the thing without naming it is only to dull the sense and results in frustration" (*I*, 115). Hence a viable art of imitation both comprises *and* transcends the traditional concept of mimesis. For Williams all art is not only imitation but also creation, and only the two separate, and partly irreconcilable, dimensions together create the revelation that leads the recipient back to the mystery of both the work of art itself and the world it refers to. Thus Williams finds a way in his poetics "to balance . . . the three irreconcilable and yet inextricably connected theories of art that have dominated Western thought since the Greeks," as J. Hillis Miller puts it.[3] Art as mimesis, art as revelation, and art as creation – none is absent in Williams's concept of imitation, and none must be isolated or pushed at the expense of the others. In Williams's successful poems, words are not only highly evocative, endowed with a curious power of naming, but also things, word sounds to be heard and word bodies to be seen on the page, audible and visible presences which can be arranged into sound patterns or visual designs.

Williams, as we have seen, found the same tension or double movement in an exemplary manner in virtually all Modernist painting, beginning with the later work of Cézanne and most radically (as well as playfully) explored by the Cubists. In the visual arts, the decisive step from an art of illusion to an art that combined the referential with the self-referential dimension was undoubtedly the discarding of the consistent pictorial space established by linear perspective. In the second half of the nineteenth century, the one-point perspective established in the Renaissance, which had created for the first time a continuous and absolutely homogeneous space, was increasingly felt to be problematic. Linear perspective, as Panofsky writes in his famous essay "Die Perspektive als symbolische Form," had by way of establishing a completely consistent space also established an absolute priority of that space over all the objects in it.[4] It thus not only detaches these objects from each other – objects which are as a consequence of this for the first time free-floating, as it were, in an infinite space – but also detaches them from the viewer, who is at one and the same time both related to them as never before and kept at a distance. By means of linear perspective, in other words, the space of the painting is extended to the viewer outside the frame, who is thus included in an entirely new way, since everything is related to his or her vantage point. At the same time, on the other hand, the same perspective excludes the viewer, since the depicted space, depicted like a view from a window and enclosed by the frame, recedes into an infinite depth, leaving the viewer, literally and psychologically, outside the depicted world proper.

Thus the viewer is both included and excluded as never before (included in a continuous space while being excluded from an "immediate" contact with the objects in the painting), since the spatial continuity entails a sense of distance that invariably thematizes the gap, never to be closed completely, between what is inside and what is outside the painting, between the perceiving eye and the perceived objects.

Such a perspective both lessens the intrinsic value of the objects depicted and alienates humanity from them; it depletes them, "empties" them, so to speak, of a value that they have of their own since the presentation of each object is primarily determined by its position in the pictorial space. What Ernst Cassirer, quoted by Panofsky, says of the "points" in such a homogeneous, closed space, is thus equally true of the objects: "Ihr Sein geht in einem wechselseitigen Verhältnis auf: es ist ein rein funktionales, kein substantielles Sein" (p. 101; "Their essence is subsumed by their mutual relationship; it is thus purely functional, not substantial").

Needless to say, such an abstract, continuous, rational Cartesian space has far-reaching consequences. It is in many ways diametrically opposed to the psycho-physiological space of immediate sense experience. In such a psycho-physiological space, writes Cassirer,

> there are no equal spaces and directions; each space has an identity and a value of its own. Unlike the metrical space of Euclidian geometry, both the visual space and the tactile or haptic space are 'anisotropical' and 'inhomogeneous'; the main directions constituting them, such as foreground-background, above-below, right-left, are in both of these physiological spaces in an identical manner dissimilar.[5]

In the nonmetric space of empirical reality the richly varying impact of the individual objects depends on their momentary position in space relative to that of the experiencing self and the other objects surrounding them; linear perspective, on the other hand, dramatically reduces this impact, since objects first of all signal their relative position in space and are subjected to playing their role as parts of a subsuming whole. Thus, while normally each place has its particularity and its own value, each place now has first of all the same value, namely, that of being the constituent part of a whole, contributing to a homogeneous and infinite space of which the experiencing self ordinarily knows nothing.

Objects in such a painting, via their relative position in space, are thus primarily related to the other objects surrounding them and refer not so much to themselves and the value accorded to them but to the space that they cocreate. At the same time, they gain a new plasticity and can, to borrow an expression from Panofsky, "breathe" in space as never before, drawing attention to their three-dimensional material "objecthood." But while this could increase the value that they have on their own, they at the same time are invariably related to the vantage point of the viewer, that is, invariably presented as the viewer sees them. They are thus psychologically at the viewer's disposal as never before, part of an anthropocentric world in which everything falls into place under the scrutiny of humans, who perceive and appropriate what is unfolded in front of them. Panofsky calls this change in perception with the ensuing change in attitude "eine Objektivierung des Subjektiven," and he admirably sums up the fundamental ambiguity of the phenomenological changes that the new space brought about:

> Now, such a definition implies that the more one had solved the technical problem of linear perspective the more one was confronted with an artistic problem. For linear perspective is by definition an instrument that cuts both ways: it creates a space in which objects can freely unfold and convey movement – but it also enables the light to expand in that space and to fill it to the point where the objects are dissolved again; it creates distance between man and the objects depicted ("The one is the eye, which seeth, the other is the object, which is being seen, the third are the expanses in between," says Dürer, following Piero Della Francesca) – but it once again suspends this distance by enabling man (who is confronted with their independent thinghood) to absorb them, as it were, with his all-encompassing eye . . . Thus the history of linear perspective can be regarded with equal justification as *the triumph of a distancing and objectifying sense of reality as well as the triumph of the human drive for power negating and suspending that distance.*[6]

The new artistic form, which could have led to an increased sense of the "objecthood" of things and a heightened respect for empirical reality, strengthened humankind's sense of superiority over all that was encountered. All is now invariably related to the viewer; as soon as the viewer changes position, the positions (and, concomitantly, the aspects) of things are changed, too. Thus the new, scientific space, related to Cartesian rationalism and subsequent models of rational, scientific knowing, places the perceiving – seeing, understanding, grasping, mastering – self at the center as never before. As a consequence of this, Renaissance and post-Renaissance painting, evolving in close interaction with the new scientific spirit, promotes what Heidegger, appropriating Nietzsche, calls Western man's will to power over existence.[7]

As we have seen, one of the basic impulses behind the gradual abandoning of linear perspective in painting in the late nineteenth century and the related questioning of the "narrative line" in Modernist literature is rooted in the attempt to move beyond this fundamentally egocentric organizing principle. Many of the artists radically questioning the traditional forms not only rejected them because they were hiding their traces and presented one particular principle of organization as the only one that was true and objective, but they also sensed that the world was represented as one to be grasped and appropriated.

This is particularly true for Williams; his need to overcome artistic and poetic forms that were essentially the product of "S[cience] and [traditional] P[hilosophy]" is inextricably connected to his need to overcome the egotistical sublime, in order to accept a self that recognizes its deeper kinship to the world as it is and of which the self is essentially a part.[8] The importance of this radically different phenomenological stance cannot be overestimated, since it codetermines throughout the form of Williams's poetry. In particular, it must not be traded off against Williams's formalism – that is, his insistence on the poet as maker and the nature of the poem as artifact. To master and appropriate the world is by definition impossible if one foregrounds the irreducible difference between what is and what is being perceived, between signifier and signified, work of art and empirical reality. To discover the deeper kinship between self and other, between names and what is being named, one first has to acknowledge the ineluctable difference between the two realms. In a poem, in other words, one has to work with, and not against, the nature of words if one is to discover the common ground of self and other, language and thing-world, to be found in the *natura naturans,* beyond the inimitable particularity of all forms of existence manifest in the *natura naturata.*

Hence, Williams realized, to insist on the poet's dual fidelity to the poem and to the world entailed abandoning the spurious comprehension promised by conventional poetry ruled by "logicality." Poetic language must neither pretend to convey empirical reality *tel-quel* nor try to represent it by simply writing *about* it; rather, in a poem that does not hide the fact that it is made with words, "the world is itself drawn into the dance of the words," as John Vernon puts it, in order to create what Cézanne called "a harmony parallel to nature."[9] Thus, for the same reasons that the Modernist painters had discarded linear perspective, Williams insisted on the necessity to "kill the explicit sentence . . . and expand our meaning by verbal sequences. Sentences, but not grammatical sentences: dead-falls set by schoolmen" (*P*, 188). Similar to linear perspective, "that infallible device for making all things shrink" (Apollinaire),[10] the "grammatical sentences" of conventional syntax detract from the impact of each detail by subsuming it under the function of establishing logical coherence and spatiotemporal continuity. In other words, both traditional paintings and poems not only disguise their object character but also establish an overall coherence at the price of functionalizing (and thus trivializing) the parts constituting the whole.

It is no accident, therefore, that from the very beginning Williams insists in his theory of the imagination on the need to pay undivided attention to each particular object under scrutiny. The poet must have the power he praises in his mother of "seeing the thing itself without forethought or afterthought but with great intensity of perception" (*SE*, 5). Only thus can each thing be appraised in its inimitable particularity. Instead of coining similes, the poet should develop "that power which discovers in things those inimitable particles of dissimilarity to all other things which are the peculiar perfections of the thing in question" (*SE*, 16). It is in keeping with this credo that the metaphorical dimension, which is still important, is often introduced in the form of ideo-grammic juxtapositions of objects: similarity is discovered within dissimilarity, and meaning is often expressed as a *discordia concors*, with a potential deeper coherence emerging from the juxtaposition of dissonant things. Moreover, in a poetry that appreciates each thing as a mysterious living entity, the metaphorical dimension of all language is highlighted in the innumerable instances in which such an appreciation entails "loading" the language with verbal energies.

Thus to "kill the explicit sentence" in order to escape the "dead-falls set by schoolmen" meant for Williams to largely replace the hypotactical structures of conventional syntax with a paratactical accretion of details. Objects are ap-proached "frontally," one by one, rather than as parts in need of being subsumed under a whole. Often they lie side by side, edge to edge, as it were, as the words do on the white page, juxtaposed on a metonymical rather than a metaphorical basis – a field of action with forces both resolved and unresolved. The poet's self is engaged, implicitly or explicitly, in exploring this field and the mysterious way in which he participates in it, in acts of discovery rather than appropriation. He thus creates a space that is not only more dynamic but also more intimate, since it includes the self in a world of process, interaction, interpenetration, and participation.

Such a space is in many ways diametrically opposed to the space created by the spatio-temporal continuity and logical coherence of discursive language, which shares with painting governed by linear perspective its overwhelming visual bias. Dominated by eyesight, which is the most abstract and detached of the senses, it by definition opposes humans to a world perceived from a distance. The space thus created is a space of separation that constitutes, as McLuhan and Parker realized, the opposition of subject and object and thus widens the gulf separating self and other:

> The discovery of the fixed position for visual experience, which is perspective, forces peripheral vision upon the viewer. . . . This dualism between center and margin found its parallel in the break between the subject and the object. It is only perspective which allows for dispassionate survey and noninvolvement in the world of experience.[11]

Although eyesight is of great importance in Williams, its impact is dramatically changed in his poems because the isolated details of his world are not only focused with intense concentration but are also literally close at hand. "Eyesight is not exempt from that delicacy which predominates in Williams' way of using his senses and makes soft closeness the primary characteristic of his world," says Miller in *Poets of Reality* (p. 320). In such a realm of "soft closeness" all expe-rience is synesthetic, involving not only sight but scent, sound, taste, and touch as well. Particularly touch, the most intimate of the senses, is ubiquitous – in this haptic space of closeups even seeing is tactile, since the eye cannot but absorb textures and surfaces, noting that the wheelbarrow is "glazed with rain / water," the trunk of the sycamore "young and firm," and a stone picked up from the earth still "breathing / the damp through its pores" (*CP1*, 50). Distance, in Williams's poems, is literally and psychologically replaced by nearness, and the peripheral, detached vantage point of the encompassing eye gives way to a self "in touch" and eyes moving out in all directions, in poems that often enact both the perception of process and the process of perception.

In such a world, anything, experienced intensely, can for the moment become the center of the universe. "Anywhere is everywhere" (*P,* 231) in Williams's world. The parsley, "crisped green" beside the "clean white sink" lit by "brilliant gas light" (*CP1*, 85); the "broken / pieces of a green / bottle" flaring up in the heap of cinders; the "cylindrical tank fresh silvered" juxtaposed with "pink roses bending ragged in the rain" (*CP2*, 68) – these and innumerable other momentary constellations of things can become a source of revelation because "they enter into the singleness of the moment and the moment partakes of the diversity of all things" (*SE,* 97). "Williams' universe," writes Miller, "unlike the Platonic cosmos, has no center, no reservoir of eternal models. There is only the ubiquitous life force that gives rise to differences in objects appearing side by side or in sequence from an infinity of centers." All of these objects are "equally important, because all exist, all have sprung up from the 'unfathomable ground' [*CP2*, 68] to manifest themselves in the open" ("Williams' *Spring and All*," p. 424).

It is significant that one can observe in the revolutionary movements in painting an analogous shift away from a world-view that accords value to objects on the basis of a clear hierarchical framework, in favor of a nonhierarchical attitude that bestows a new dignity on all that is ordinary, mundane, and seemingly insignificant. Long before the mundane was acceptable subject matter for poetry, Monet had begun to devote entire pictures to haystacks, declaring that *tout ce qui existe est beau, . . . tout est à peindre,*[12] and still lifes became, together with portraits, the most important subject matter for the Cubists. Dada and the works and theories of Duchamp can be regarded in this context as the endpoint of a long development away from a hierarchically structured world, both by either turning it upside down or by playing havoc with it. As early as 1917 Williams had understood that Duchamp, maintaining that the choice of his ready-mades was entirely based on accident, had attempted to radically bypass the hierarchical aesthetic and ethical categories of the past. Fifty years later, Williams took up this principle of randomness and accident in *Paterson:*

> Loosen the flesh
> from the machine, build no more
> bridges. Through what air will you
> fly to span the continents? Let the words

fall anyway at all – that they may
hit love aslant. It will be a rare
visitation. They want to rescue too much,
the flood has done its work

                    (*P*, 142)

Both the references to the machine and the bridges as well as the advice, "Let
the words / fall anyway at all – that they may / hit love aslant," are references
to Duchamp – the first from a critical, the second from an affirmative viewpoint.
Williams now explicitly criticizes his civilization for the very reason that Duchamp had hailed it on his arrival in New York, namely, the fact that it embraces
all things technological. Technology, like traditional art, is an expression of
humankind's will to power over things (the will to "span the continents"),
alienating humans from their environment instead of leading them back to a
recognition of their deeper kinship. On the other hand, to accept the principle
of accident entails relinquishing the attempt to subject the world to a preconceived order, in favor of a radically different attitude which is both humbler and
more receptive to moments of revelation.

If nonetheless all art, in one way or other, aspires to "make a start, / out of
particulars / and make them general" (*P*, 3), the artist who tries to do so is at
least obliged to highlight his or her medium. As a poet, for instance, one has to
acknowledge the nature of the "defective means" at one's disposal – words.
Because in poetry one must not obfuscate the ineradicable difference between
the words and the things, and enlist the reader's awareness that words are things
themselves, Williams insisted throughout his life that poetry, like all art, should
be

              Not prophesy! NOT prophesy!
                 but the thing itself!
                    (*P*, 206)

An art of illusion that pretends to *be* the real, in the manner that most painting
based on linear perspective aspires to be identical with a view from a window,
generates pictures of an absent reality while pretending to the recipient that it
is present. An art that foregrounds its own medium, on the other hand, creates
an analogon for the concreteness of the empirical world in the concreteness and
tangible presence of the work of art itself:

              A rose *is* a rose
                        and the poem equals it
       if it be well made.
                    (*CP2*, 302)

That is why the poet's dual fidelity to words and the things they denote is of
such fundamental importance. To be faithful to the living world, the poet has
to be faithful to the Janus-headed language that invariably points at one and the

same time to empirical reality and back to itself. If the poet fails to do so, the reader will confuse the two dimensions, which is bound to lead to frustration.

Now, the only means that Williams has to ensure our double awareness of both word and thing, conception and perception, is to subvert art itself, be it the art of his predecessors or his own, in the sense of continuously replacing one form by another form, an old measure by a new measure. Only a new form, in other words, will lead to a fresh awareness of the difference between signifier and signified, and only such a fresh awareness will enable us to dis-cover or un-conceal the deeper connections between art and life: "Dissonance / (if you are interested) / leads to discovery" (P, 175). All truth, Williams was convinced (and was confirmed by Einstein and Madame Curie), is a matter of re-vision of former beliefs and former structures:

> Language is the key to the mind's escape from bondage to the past. There are no "truths" that can be fixed in language. It is by the break-up of the language that the truth can be seen to exist and that it becomes operative again. (EK, 19)

By breaking up language one can "break it away from its enforcements, its prostitutions under all other categories. For language that is used as a means foreign to itself is language used as an expedient . . . impurely." On the other hand, "[b]y taking language as real and employing it with a full breadth and sweep," writing "frees it from encroachments and makes it operative again" (EK, 20). To make it operative again is, as Williams's friend Pound would have said, to make it new. And to make it new, in this sense, has nothing to do with an art-for-art's-sake formalism, but much to do with Williams's dual fidelity to both the poem and the world, and hence leads straight back from the realm of words to the realm of things. For it is only out of "the necessity for constant freshness of praise" that the need arises for new words which "will have a fresh distinction of cut, of tint, of texture" (SE, 97). Or, as Williams repeatedly stressed,

> it must not be forgot that we smell, hear, and see with words and words alone, and that with a new language we smell, hear and see afresh. . . . (SE, 266)

Notes

===

INTRODUCTION

1 James E. B. Breslin, "William Carlos Williams and Charles Demuth: Cross-Fertilization in the Arts," *Journal of Modern Literature*, 6:2 (April 1977): 248–63.

2 Peter Schmidt, "Some Versions of Modernist Pastoral: Williams and the Precisionists," *Contemporary Literature*, 21:3 (1980): 382.

3 See Bram Dijkstra, *The Hieroglyphics of a New Speech: Cubism, Stieglitz, and the Early Poetry of William Carlos Williams* (Princeton: Princeton University Press, 1969); Dickran Tashjian, *Skyscraper Primitives: Dada and the American Avant-Garde, 1910–1925* (Middletown, Conn.: Wesleyan University Press, 1975); Dickran Tashjian, *William Carlos Williams and the American Scene* (New York: Whitney Museum of American Art, 1978); William Marling, *William Carlos Williams and the Painters, 1909–1923* (Athens: Ohio University Press, 1982); Henry M. Sayre, *The Visual Text of William Carlos Williams* (Urbana: University of Illinois Press, 1983); Christopher J. Mac-Gowan, *William Carlos Williams' Early Poetry: The Visual Arts Background* (Ann Arbor: UMI Research Press, 1984); Peter Schmidt, *William Carlos Williams, the Arts, and Literary Tradition* (Baton Rouge: Louisiana State University Press, 1988).

Also of special relevance are Charles Altieri's *Painterly Abstraction in Modernist American Poetry: The Contemporaneity of Modernism* (Cambridge: Cambridge University Press, 1989), Marjorie Perloff's *The Poetics of Indeterminacy: From Rimbaud to Cage* (Princeton: Princeton University Press, 1981), and Wendy Steiner's *The Colors of Rhetoric: Problems in the Relation Between Literature and Painting* (Chicago: University of Chicago Press, 1982). Further essays to be mentioned in particular are (apart from those by Breslin and Schmidt): Ruth Grogan, "The Influence of Painting on William Carlos Williams," in *William Carlos Williams: A Critical Anthology*, ed. Charles Tomlinson (Harmondsworth: Penguin, 1972), pp. 265–98; Henry M. Sayre, "Ready-mades and Other Measures: The Poetics of Marcel Duchamp and William Carlos Williams," *Journal of Modern Literature*, 8:1 (1980): 3–22; Patrick Moore, "Cubist Prosody: William Carlos Williams and the Conventions of Verse Lineation," *Philological Quarterly*, 65 (Fall 1986): 515–36; and Charles Altieri, " 'Ponderation' in Cézanne and Williams," *Poetics Today*, 10: 2 (Summer 1989): 373–99. For further bibliographical information on Williams and the visual arts see Schmidt's *William Carlos Williams, the Arts, and Literary Tra-*

dition, which contains a virtually exhaustive list of books and articles on the subject in the notes at the beginning of each chapter. Williams's own writings on the visual arts are collected in *A Recognizable Image: William Carlos Williams on Art and Artists,* ed. Bram Dijkstra (New York: New Directions, 1978).

4   Henry Sayre, *The Visual Text of William Carlos Williams,* and Peter Schmidt, *William Carlos Williams, the Arts, and Literary Tradition.* A third book, Terence Diggory's *William Carlos Williams and the Ethics of Painting* (Princeton: Princeton University Press, 1991) was published too late to be included in the present study.

5   Charles Altieri, "From Symbolist Thought to Immanence: The Ground of Postmodern American Poetics," *boundary 2,* 1 (1973): 608.

6   Joseph N. Riddel, "The Wanderer and the Dance: William Carlos Williams' Early Poetics," in *The Shaken Realist: Essays in Modern Literature in Honor of Frederick J. Hoffman,* eds. Melvin J. Friedman and John B. Vickery (Baton Rouge: Louisiana State University Press, 1970), p. 50.

7   Roman Jakobson, "Language in Relation to Other Communication Systems," *Selected Writings,* Vol. 2 (The Hague: Mouton, 1971), p. 701.

8   Walter Sutton, "A Visit with William Carlos Williams," *Minnesota Review,* 1 (April 1961): 321–22.

9   Stephen Tapscott, "Williams, Sappho, and the Woman-as-Other," *William Carlos Williams Review,* 11:2 (Fall 1985): 30.

PRELUDE: GETTING IN TOUCH

1   Meyer Schapiro, "Rebellion in Art," in *America in Crisis,* ed. Daniel Aaron (New York: Knopf, 1952), pp. 205–06.

2   In a conversation with Edith Heal, Florence Williams said that her husband had *not* been to the Armory Show: "Bill did not attend the first Armory Show, though he always insisted that he did. He went to the second one where he read along with Mina Loy and others. He wasn't himself when he swore he'd been to the first one so I gave up trying to convince him" ("Flossie," *Williams Carlos Williams Newsletter* 2:2 [Fall 1976]: 11).

Mrs. Williams's memory proved more accurate than her husband's on a number of occasions. However, it is possible here that she was herself confused by the fact that later in his life Williams associated events with the Armory Show that had taken place at the 1917 Exhibition of the Independents. Thus the poetry session at which Williams read "Overture to a Dance of Locomotives" and "Portrait of a Woman in Bed" indeed took place at the 1917 exhibition (referred to by Flossie as "the second [Armory Show]"). Williams connected the reading – first vaguely, later definitively – with the Armory Show. He made the same mistake with regard to the scandal caused by Duchamp's ready-made *Fountain,* which had also taken place in 1917 (*A,* 136; "Recollections," *Art in America,* 51 [Feb. 1963]: 52).

It is possible that Mrs. Williams, knowing her husband was wrong in both cases, came to believe that he had not attended the Armory Show at all. If she was right, then Williams would have seen several of the show's most famous pieces at the apartment of Walter Arensberg, whom he knew by late 1913 or early 1914. Arensberg had bought a number of important paintings from the show for his large collection, including the pièce de résistance of the exhibition, Duchamp's *Nude Descending a Staircase.*

3 Alfred Kreymborg, *Troubadour: An American Biography* (1925; New York: Sagamore Press, 1957), p. 157.

4 For detailed studies of the New York avant-garde scene of that time see the books by Bram Dijkstra, William Innes Homer, Christopher J. MacGowan, William Marling, and Dickran Tashjian.

5 Letter quoted in R. Doty, *Photo-Secession: Photography as a Fine Art* (Rochester: George Eastman House, 1960), p. 63.

6 *Autobiography,* pp. 164–66, 168–69. See also "The Three Letters," *Contact,* 4 (Summer 1921).

7 "Recollections," *Art in America,* 51:1 (Feb. 1963): 52.

8 Quoted in Constance Rourke, *Charles Sheeler: Artist in the American Tradition* (New York: Harcourt, Brace, 1938), p. 49.

CHAPTER 1: *"A POEM CAN BE MADE OF ANYTHING"*

1 Monroe K. Spears, *Dionysus and the City: Modernism in Twentieth-Century Poetry* (New York: Oxford University Press, 1970), pp. 149–51.

2 Joseph N. Riddel, "The Wanderer and the Dance," p. 50. The most seminal discussion of this crucial aspect of Williams's poetry is to be found in J. Hillis Miller's chapter on Williams in his *Poets of Reality.* Riddel's essay contains a slight but important modification of Miller's view.

3 Van Wyck Brooks, *America's Coming-of-Age* (rev. ed., Garden City, N.Y.: Doubleday, 1958), p. 83. Quoted from James Guimond, *The Art of William Carlos Williams* (Urbana: University of Illinois Press, 1968), p. 12.

4 James Oppenheim, "Editorials," *The Seven Arts,* 1 (Dec. 1916): 154.

5 Critics and photographers such as Roland Rood, Charles H. Caffin, and Alvin Langden Coburn showed very early what one might call a Futurist temperament when they stressed the viability of "straight" photography. They claimed that the photographer, blending personal vision with a "scientific process," was particularly well equipped to adapt to the speed and technological character of the new age, and thus was able to capture its essence. See Dickran Tashjian's chapter "*Camera Work* and the Anti-Art of Photography" in *Skyscraper Primitives,* pp. 17 ff. Williams owned a copy of Charles H. Caffin's *Photography as a Fine Art* (New York: Doubleday, Page, 1901), which is now in the possession of his son, William Eric Williams, but of course he could have acquired it much later. By 1914–15, however, he was probably acquainted with Caffin's ideas, since Kreymborg and Caffin were friends; Kreymborg had met his wife, Christine, at the home of Mr. and Mrs. Caffin, whose protégé she was (see Dijkstra, *Hieroglyphics,* p. 26).

6 "A Complete Reversal of Art Opinions by Marcel Duchamp, Iconoclast," *Arts and Decoration,* 5 (Sept. 1915): 427–28.

7 "The Iconoclastic Opinions of Marcel Duchamp Concerning Art and America," *Current Opinion,* 59 (Nov. 1915): 346.

8 Marcel Duchamp, "The Richard Mutt Case," *The Blind Man,* 2 (May 1917): 5.

9   See for instance the following passage on bathrooms in *Kora in Hell:* "It is the mark of our civilization that all houses today include a room for the relief and washing of the body, a room ingeniously appointed with water-vessels of many and curious sorts. There is nothing in antiquity to equal this" (*I*, 171).

10 "Further Announcements," *Contact*, 2 (Jan. 1921): 9–10.

11 Thomas R. Whitaker, *William Carlos Williams* (New York: Twayne, 1968), p. 40.

12 "America, Whitman, and the Art of Poetry," *The Poetry Journal*, 8:1 (Nov. 1917): 29.

13 Quoted in Willy Rotzler, "Material-Kunst, Anti-Kunst und Ready-Made bei den Dadaisten," *Du*, 29 (Sept. 1969): 637; my translation.

14 Richard Huelsenbeck, *En Avant Dada: A History of Dadaism*, trans. Ralph Manheim, reprinted in *The Dada Painters and Poets*, ed. Robert Motherwell (New York: Wittenborn, 1967), pp. 37, 42.

15 Arturo Schwarz, *new york dada: duchamp, man ray, picabia*, ed. Armin Zweite et al. (Munich: Prestel, 1974), p. 95. (Text in German and in English.)

16 Quoted in Willy Rotzler, "Material-Kunst . . . ," p. 637; my translation.

17 "Belly Music," *Others*, 6 (July 1919), Supplement, p. 26.

18 "Essay on *Leaves of Grass*," in *"Leaves of Grass," One Hundred Years After*, ed. Milton Hindus (Stanford: Stanford University Press, 1955), p. 23.

19 Excerpts from Kandinsky's book were published in *Camera Work* (April 1912) and *Blast* (June 20, 1914), where Williams must have first read the passage which he later quoted in abbreviated form in the Preface to *Kora in Hell* (*I*, 26). Kandinsky's art and theories were of great importance to Marsden Hartley, who was associated with the Blaue Reiter group during his two stays in Germany in 1913 and 1914–15. (See Homer, *Alfred Stieglitz and the American Avant-Garde*, pp. 220–33.) Hartley met Demuth in Paris in 1912; after Hartley's return to the States late in 1915 the two became close friends. Williams in turn met Hartley either through Demuth or during the summer of 1916 when all three of them were associated with the Provincetown players. Williams and Hartley became close friends, too, and through Hartley, if not before, Williams must have been intimately familiar with Kandinsky's theories.

20 Wassily Kandinsky, *Concerning the Spiritual in Art*, ed. Robert Motherwell (New York: Wittenborn, 1947), p. 77; Mike Weaver, *William Carlos Williams: The American Background* (Cambridge: Cambridge University Press, 1971) pp. 37–39.

21   1. direkter Eindruck von der "äusseren Natur", welcher in einer zeichnerisch-malerischen Form zum Ausdruck kommt. Diese Bilder nenne ich *"Impressionen"*;

        2. hauptsächlich unbewußte, größtenteils plötzlich entstandene Ausdrücke der Vorgänge inneren Charakters, als Eindrücke von der "inneren Natur". Diese Art nenne ich *"Improvisationen"*;

        3. auf ähnliche Art (aber ganz besonders langsam) sich in mir bildende Ausdrücke, welche lange und beinahe pedantisch nach den ersten Entwürfen von mir geprüft und ausgearbeitet werden. Diese Art Bilder nenne ich *"Komposition"*. Hier spielt die Vernunft, das Bewußte, das Absichtliche, das Zweckmäßige eine überwiegende Rolle. Nur wird dabei nicht der Berechnung, sondern stets dem Gefühl recht gegeben. (Kandinsky, *Über das Geistige in der Kunst*, ed. Max Bill [Bern: Benteli, 1973], p. 142)

22 This assumption is corroborated by a passage in *The Great American Novel*, that is,

in another exploratory work in which Williams tries to give full rein to the imagination in the style of the *Kora* improvisations. In an imaginary dialogue a voice – one of the poet's selves arguing for Apollonian clarity and restraint? – opts for a more controlled artistic form with an implicit reference to Kandinsky's categories: "Let us now have a beginning of composition. We have had enough of your improvisations" (*I*, 197).

23   Die Formen dieser [konstruktiven] Bestrebungen zerfallen in zwei Hauptgruppen:
    1. die einfache Komposition, die einer klar zum Vorschein kommenden einfachen Form unterordnet ist. Diese Komposition nenne ich die *melodische;*
    2. die komplizierte Komposition, die aus mehreren Formen besteht, die weiter einer klaren oder verschleierten Hauptform unterordnet sind. Diese Hauptform kann äußerlich sehr schwer zu finden sein, wodurch die innere Basis einen besonders starken Klang bekommt. Diese komplizierte Komposition nenne ich die *symphonische.*
    Zwischen diesen zwei Hauptgruppen liegen verschiedene Übergangsformen, in welchen das melodische Prinzip unbedingt vorhanden ist. Der ganze Entwicklungsvorgang ist auffallend dem in der Musik ähnlich. (*Über das Geistige in der Kunst,* p. 139)

24 Cubism, of course, is only the tip of the iceberg, as it were; it stands in a complex and much debated relationship to the contemporary philosophical and psychological theories of Bergson, Freud, and others, which led to new and more complex notions of time, experience of empirical reality, and so forth.

25 This important effect of Duchamp's ready-mades was not intentional, however. Duchamp did not want to *enlarge* the prevalent aesthetic notions (as Williams did) but wanted to discard them altogether as an artistic criterion. "When I discovered the ready-mades," he said later, "I wanted to discourage the whole aesthetic fuss. But in Neo-Dada they used the ready-made to discover their 'aesthetic values.' I challenged them with the bottlerack and I flung the urinal in their teeth, and now they admire it as the aesthetically pleasing" (quoted in Willy Rotzler, "Material-Kunst . . . ," pp. 646–47; my translation).

26 This does not mean that there is no difference between the poet's language and that of the inserted "ready-mades," but it is a difference in *degree* only, not in *kind,* a difference that reveals similarity and dissimilarity at the same time. The original impetus for these and related forms of montage came from Braque's and Picasso's *collages:* By inserting pieces of oil cloth or newspaper, for example, they created a tension between painterly and nonpainterly material (but both good for a painting!), between the artist's own formal means and that of the predesigned inserted pieces, between the illusory depth created by the painter and the real flatness of the glued bits (or the *real depth* of the glued bits when the collage pieces overlap or are partly painted over) – to mention just a few of many possible effects.

27 *The Little Review,* 12 (May 1929): 30.

28 Kurt Badt, *Die Kunst Cézannes* (Munich, 1956), p. 163. (*The Art of Cézanne,* trans. Sheila Ann Ogilvie [Berkeley and Los Angeles: University of California Press, 1965]).

29 "Paris Review Interviews," *Paris Review,* 28 (1962): 30–31.

30 Sheeler Papers (NSh-1), frame 58, Archives of American Art, Smithsonian Institution, Washington, D.C.

31 See Tashjian, *Skyscraper Primitives*, Chapters 3, 4, and 6.

32 "Yours, O Youth," *Contact*, 3 (1921), n.p. In the course of his writings on Vorticism Pound, too, once directly linked the constructivist aspect of viable art to all other forms of creativity, such as engineering: "Our community is no longer divided into 'bohème' and 'bourgeois.' We have our segregation amid the men who invent and create, whether it be a discovery of unknown rivers, a solution of engineering, a composition of form, or what you will.

"These men stand on one side, and the amorphous and petrified and the copying, stand on the other" (*Gaudier-Brzeska: A Memoir* [New York: New Directions, 1970], p. 122.)

CHAPTER 2: VORTEX; OR, A THING IS WHAT IT DOES

1 *The Letters of Ezra Pound, 1907–1941*, ed. D. D. Paige (New York: Harcourt, Brace, 1950), p. 82.

2 Hugh Kenner, *The Pound Era* (Berkeley and Los Angeles: University of Los Angeles Press, 1971), p. 159.

3 This becomes even clearer when one compares the "one-image poem" with the Japanese haiku, which Pound discusses in the same context as a related form (which obviously inspired his own practice): "Victor Parr tells me that once, when he was walking over snow with a Japanese naval officer, they came to a place where a cat had crossed the path, and the officer said, 'Stop, I am making a poem.' Which poem was, roughly, as follows: 'The footsteps of the cat upon the snow: / (are like) plum blossoms.' The words 'are like' would not occur in the original, but I add them for clarity" (*Gaudier-Brzeska*, p. 89).

4 Ezra Pound, "Technique," *New Age*, 10 (Jan. 25, 1912): 298.

5 Ezra Pound, "Cavalcanti" (1931), *Literary Essays of Ezra Pound*, ed. T. S. Eliot (Norfolk, Conn.: New Directions, 1954), pp. 154–55. For a similar but much earlier programmatic statement see his essay "The Serious Artist" (1913): "We might come to believe that the thing that matters in art is a sort of energy, something more or less like electricity or radioactivity, a force transfusing, welding, and unifying" (*Literary Essays*, p. 49).

6 Ezra Pound, *Gaudier-Brzeska*, p. 28; Wyndham Lewis, *Time and Western Man* (London: Chatto and Windus, 1927), p. 129.

7 Worringer's influential ideas are discussed in Joseph Frank, *The Widening Gyre: Crisis and Mastery in Modern Literature* (Bloomington: Indiana University Press, 1968), pp. 51 ff. and passim; and in Spears, *Dionysus and the City*, pp. 65 ff. and 121 ff.

8 Quoted in Max Bill's Introduction to Kandinsky's *Über das Geistige in der Kunst* (Bern: Benteli, 1973), p. 10; my translation.

9 *New Age*, 10 (Feb. 15, 1912): 370; May Sinclair, "Two Notes," *The Egoist*, 2 (June 1, 1915): 88.

10 Published in *The Dial*, May 1927. Not included in *The Collected Earlier Poems*.

11 For a published version of this essay, which collates the various manuscript versions, see Williams, *A Recognizable Image*, pp. 57–59.

12 Kandinsky's terminology here suggests a direct relationship between the visual arts and music. But the painter refuted too straight an equation between the two art

forms, saying, "I personally cannot possibly want to make music by painting, since I believe that such a form of painting is impossible and unattainable" (Catalogue of the exhibition *Kandinsky, 1902–1912*, Berlin, Galerie "Der Sturm," 1912, n.p.; my translation). On the other hand, Kandinsky's "internal sounds" or vibrations are more than purely metaphorical terms; all the senses, including hearing, are involved for him in the experience of a painting, or for that matter, of all art. The body is regarded as a kind of sounding board or sounding box (*Resonanzkörper*), with "strings" resonating. Experiencing a work of art is always, to a greater or lesser degree, a synesthetic experience; and the senses in turn are not to be separated from the emotions and the mental activities. This theory finds its correspondence in statements by Williams such as, "A thing known passes out of the mind into the muscles" (*I:KH*, 74), and, "Can you not hear, can you not taste, can you not smell, can you not touch – words?" (*I:GAN*, 159). For both Williams and Kandinsky there is, therefore, no such thing as a purely optical perception of the world. For both of them human beings experience a work of art with their minds and their whole bodies, synesthetically and kinesthetically alike, whereby, ideally, they transcend the inessential and reach the core – the "inner sound" of things, or their "radiant gist" (*P*, 185).

13   1. entweder dient die Form, *als Abgrenzung*, dem Ziele, durch diese Abgrenzung einen . . . materiellen Gegenstand auf die Fläche zu zeichnen, oder

        2. *bleibt die Form abstrakt*, d.h. sie bezeichnet keinen realen Gegenstand, sondern ist ein vollkommen abstraktes Wesen. Solche rein abstrakte Wesen, die als solche ihr Leben haben, ihren Einfluß und ihre Wirkung, sind ein Quadrat, ein Kreis, ein Dreieck, ein Rhombus, ein Trapez und die unzähligen anderen Formen, die immer komplizierter werden und keine mathematische Bezeichnung besitzen. . . .

        Zwischen diesen beiden Grenzen liegt die unendliche Zahl der Formen, in welchen beide Elemente vorhanden sind und wo entweder das Materielle überwiegt oder das Abstrakte. (*Über das Geistige in der Kunst*, p. 70)

14   "On the Question of Form," in *The Blaue Reiter Almanac*, ed. Klaus Lankheit, trans. Henning Falkenstein (New York: Viking, 1974), p. 168. "Wenn also im Bild eine Linie von dem Ziel, ein Ding zu bezeichnen, befreit wird und selbst als ein Ding fungiert, wird ihr innerer Klang durch keine Nebenrollen abgeschwächt und bekommt ihre volle innere Kraft" ("Über die Formfrage," in Kandinsky, *Essays über Kunst und Künstler*, ed. Max Bill [Bern: Benteli, 1974], p. 32).

15   "Wenn aber der Gegenstand nicht selbst gesehen wird, sondern nur sein Name gehört wird, so entsteht im Kopfe des Hörers die abstrakte Vorstellung, der dematerialisierte Gegenstand, welcher im 'Herzen' eine Vibration sofort hervorruft" (*Über das Geistige in der Kunst*, p. 45).

16   "In dem Doppelklange (geistiger Akkord) der beiden Bestandteile der Form kann der organische den abstrakten unterstützen (durch Mit- oder Widerklang) oder für denselben störend sein" (*Über das Geistige in der Kunst*, p. 74).

17   The difference between the comparatively "dry" or even harsh vigor of the American idiom and the more incantatory qualities of English poetry seemed especially obvious to Williams in those cases in which it was increased by a difference of personalities, as, for instance, between himself and Dylan Thomas. Thus he wrote about one of Dylan Thomas's reading tours in the States: "What they cannot see is

that American poems are of an entirely different sort from Thomas's Welsh-English poems. They use a different language and operate under a different compulsion. They are more authoritarian, more Druidic, more romantic – and they are, truly, more colorful. WE CAN'T AND MUST NOT WRITE THIS WAY" (*SL*, 288).

18   Neil Myers, "Williams' 'Two Pendants: For the Ears'," *Journal of Modern Literature*, 1 (May 1971): 487.

19   "[D]ie Formenkomposition, auf dieser Relativität ruhend, [ist] abhängig 1. von der Veränderlichkeit der Zusammenstellung dieser Formen und 2. von der Veränderlichkeit jeder einzelnen Form bis ins kleinste. Jede Form ist so empfindlich wie ein Rauchwölkchen: das unmerklichste geringste Verrücken jeder ihrer Teile verändert sie *wesentlich*" (*Über das Geistige in der Kunst*, p. 77).

20   "Je freier das Abstrakte der Form liegt, desto reiner und dabei primitiver klingt es. . . . Da stehen wir vor der Frage: müssen wir denn nicht auf das Gegenständliche überhaupt verzichten . . . und das rein Abstrakte ganz bloßlegen? Dies ist die natürlich sich aufdrängende Frage, welche durch das Auseinandersetzen des Mitklingens der beiden Formelemente (des gegenständlichen und abstrakten) uns auch gleich auf die Antwort stößt. Wie jedes gesagte Wort (Baum, Himmel, Mensch) eine innere Vibration erweckt, so auch jeder bildlich dargestellte Gegenstand" (*Über das Geistige in der Kunst*, pp. 75–76).

21   Williams, Introduction to Sidney Salt's *Christopher Columbus and Other Poems* (Boston, 1937).

22   E. H. Gombrich, "On Physiognomic Perception," in *Meditations on a Hobby Horse and Other Essays in the Theory of Art* (London and New York: Phaidon, 1963), pp. 48–49. For further reading on the theory of expression, see Gombrich's "Expression and Communication" in the same volume, pp. 57–69, as well as his chapter "From Representation to Expression" in *Art and Illusion: A Study of the Problem of Pictorial Representation* (Princeton: Princeton University Press, 1961), pp. 359–96; Rudolf Arnheim, "The Gestalt Theory of Expression" and "From Function to Expression" in *Toward a Psychology of Art* (Berkeley and Los Angeles: University of California Press, 1966), pp. 51–73 and 192–212; Rudolf Arnheim, *Art and Visual Perception: A Psychology of the Creative Eye* (Berkeley and Los Angeles: University of California Press, 1974), pp. 444–461 and passim.

23   "Dabei ist im großen in der Entwicklung der Menschheit und im kleinen in der Entwicklung des einzelnen Menschen die Fähigkeit, anschauliche Charaktere (Physiognomisches) zu erfassen, ein älteres, ursprünglicheres Vermögen als das, die Formen und Farben abgelöst von ihrem anschaulichen Ausdruck in ihrer rein formalen Beschaffenheit zu erfassen. Das Kind unterscheidet früher 'anschauliche Charaktere' (freundlich, böse; heiter, traurig) als Farben und Formen. . . . Die Welt der Naturvölker ist gesättigt mit solchen physiognomischen Erlebnissen und zugleich 'Verdichtungen', die untrennbar mit den sachlichen Eigenschaften verschmolzen sind. Später lebt sich diese einheitliche Welt auseinander.

"Von da an gibt es zwei Wahrnehmungsweisen: eine urtümliche, physiognomische – in der Dinge, Farben, Formen, ja schlechthin alles, ernst oder heiter, kraftvoll oder müde, gelöst oder gespannt erscheinen kann (um nur einige unter den zahlreichen physiognomischen Qualitäten herauszuheben) – und eine spätere, fortgeschrittenere, begrifflich-sachlich-technische. Jeder Gegenstand und jede Ei-

genschaft können 'sachlich' oder auch physiognomisch . . . gefasst werden, z.B. eine
Farbe rein in ihrer farblichen Qualität, sozusagen auf ihre Stellung am Farbkörper
hin – dann ist es ein Rot mit dieser und dieser Beimischung von Blau oder Grau
oder Weiβ – oder 'physiognomisch': dann ist 'Rot' nicht die optisch-spektrale
Qualität, sondern etwas anderes mit den Eigenschaften eines lebendigen, 'brennen-
den', energischen, kraftvollen Ausdrucks" (Hans Sedlmayr, *Kunst und Wahrheit: Zur
Theorie und Methode der Kunstgeschichte* [Hamburg: Rowohlt, 1958], p. 107; my translation). See also Sedlmayr's essay "Ursprünge und Anfänge der Kunst," in *Epochen
und Werke I* (Vienna and Munich, 1959), pp. 7–17. Sedlmayr (as well as Arnheim
in his brilliant essays on the theory of expression) points out that expression or the
physiognomic dimension should not be confused with anthropomorphism: "Es ist
ein Irrtum zu glauben, daβ die physiognomischen Qualitäten, die wir den nicht
menschlichen Dingen zuschreiben, von den menschlichen Gesichtern her übertra-
gen sind. Die physiognomische Auffassung menschlicher Gesichter ist vielmehr nur
ein spärlicher Rest einer ursprünglichen Wahrnehmungsweise, in der vormals alle
Gegenstände geschaut wurden." ("It is erroneous to believe that the physiognomic
qualities experienced in non-human things are human expressions projected into
objects. The physiognomic experience of human faces is merely a remnant of a
primary perception of all things.") With regard to colors this means that one "can
very well experience the 'sadness' of a color without feeling sad" (*Kunst und Wahrheit*, pp. 107, 108; my translation).

24   Kenneth Burke, "William Carlos Williams: Two Judgments," in *William Carlos
Williams: A Collection of Critical Essays*, ed. J. Hillis Miller (Englewood Cliffs, N.J.:
Prentice Hall, 1966), p. 49.

25   It is interesting to note that in the Preface to *Kora* Williams links three art forms
which, each in its own way, point out the expressive properties of things: Duchamp's
ready-mades or *objets trouvés*, the paintings of the *naïfs*, and prehistoric rock painting.
All three art forms are characterized for Williams by some elements that make them
"truly new, truly a fresh creation" and thus "good art": Duchamp achieves it by
taking objects out of their environment so that, deprived of their function, they
appear in a new light; or else he makes use of chance and accident to bypass all
established aesthetic and moral categories. Naive painters, on the other hand, can,
"without master or method," produce works like that painting Williams owns
which "in its unearthly gaiety of flowers and sobriety of design possesses exactly that
strange freshness a spring day approaches. . . . " Such paintings in turn are related
for Williams to prehistoric rock painting: "galloping bisons and stags, the hind feet
of which have been caught by the artist in such a position that from that time until
the invention of the camera obscura, a matter of six thousand years or more, no one
on earth had again depicted that most delicate and expressive posture of running"
(*I*, 8–9).

26   *William Carlos Williams: An American Artist* (New York: Oxford University Press,
1970), p. 75.

27   Jerome Mazzaro, *William Carlos Williams: The Later Poems* (Ithaca: Cornell University Press, 1973), p. 123.

28   A pertinent analysis of this dimension in Williams is to be found in J. Hillis Miller's
Potes of Reality: "There is . . . much drama in Williams' work, [which] lies in a

dimension appropriate to the realm of immanence which he has entered. Three elements are always present in that realm, and these must be brought into the proper relation or life will fall back to some form of inauthenticity. Yet they are mutually incompatible. . . . The three elements are the formless ground, origin of all things; the formed thing, defined and limited; a nameless presence, the 'beautiful thing' (P, 119), there in every form but hidden by it" (p. 328). On this aspect, see also Charles Doyle's excellent article, "Kora and Venus: Process and Object in William Carlos Williams," *Perspective*, 17:3 (Winter 1974): 189–97.

CHAPTER 3: THE POEM AS A FIELD OF ACTION

1 Hutchins Hapgood in *Camera Work*, 38 (April 1912): 43.

2 Force lines as a means of conveying a sense of the inner dynamism or rhythm of objects were first introduced by the Italian Futurists, who, influenced by Neo-impressionist theories, began to "think about the depiction of movement and of the inner dynamism of objects in relation to their environment in terms of the visible marking of their real or potential trajectories into space" (Christine Poggi, *In Defiance of Painting: Cubism, Futurism, and the Invention of Collage* [New Haven, Conn.: Yale University Press, 1992], pp. 170–71).

3 My emphasis.

4 Joachim Gasquet, "Ce qu'il ma dit," in *Conversations avec Cézanne*, ed. P. M. Doran (Paris: Macula, 1978), p. 109.

5 Paul Waldo Schwartz, *Cubism* (New York: Praeger Publishers, 1971), p. 70.

6 Doran, ed., *Conversations avec Cézanne*, p. 110. See also below, note 49.

7 In " 'Ponderation' in Cézanne and Williams," one of the best discussions of the importance of Cézanne for Williams, Charles Altieri maintains that in order to assess Cézanne's influence one should first find out whether the Cézanne generally invoked by Williams is "the phenomenologist described by thinkers from Braque to Merleau-Ponty or the formalist anti-empiricist popularized by Roger Fry" (p. 378). Some of the passages in *Spring and All* explicitly referring to Cézanne indeed seem to indicate that Williams mainly emphasized the formalist or constructivist dimension of art:

> Today where everything is being brought into sight the realism of art has bewildered us, confused us and forced us to re-invent in order to retain that which the older generation had without that effort.
>
> Cézanne –
>
> The only realism of art is of the imagination. It is only there that the work escapes plagiarism after nature and becomes a creation. (*I*, 111)

As soon as we put such quotations into a broader perspective, however, we realize that the crucial term "imagination" leads us back to phenomenological issues, since for Williams it is vital to ensure, in Altieri's words, that "the imagination manages to align itself with some principle of dynamic life latent in things" (p. 377), although the poet must not try to achieve this at the price of "subordinating the word to the perceptions that it facilitates," at least not to the point where the linguistic dimension of all writing becomes invisible.

Like Altieri I would emphasize therefore that both dimensions are of equal importance for Williams; the fact that in his theoretical reflections (such as in the passage quoted above) he often stresses the constructivist pole may be the result of an at times desperate attempt to secure his own modernity. But Cézanne remained for Williams and his painter friends the prime example of an artist who succeeded in transcending what Altieri calls "the romantic dichotomies between immanence and self-reflexive irony" (p. 377). To remain faithful to one dimension while losing the other, however, is fatal – an old-fashioned realism secures immanence at the cost of bewilderment and confusion, whereas a modernist work of art losing sight of the phenomenological concerns leaves us with the compositional activity essentially an end in itself and thus with a solipsistic self that has lost the world instead of reappropriating it by means of the imagination.

8　Schwartz, *Cubism*, p. 9.

9　Ibid.

10　Quoted in Tom Gibbons, "Cubism and 'The Fourth Dimension' in the Context of the Late Nineteenth-Century and Early Twentieth-Century Revival of Occult Idealism," *Journal of the Warburg and Courtauld Institutes*, 44 (1981): 130–47.

11　"Ce qui m'a beaucoup attiré – et qui fut la direction maîtresse du cubisme – c'était la matérialisation de cet espace nouveau que je sentais. Alors je commençai à faire surtout des natures mortes, parce que dans la nature il y a un espace tactile, je dirais presque manuel. Je l'ai écrit du reste: "Quand une nature morte n'est plus à la portée de la main, elle cesse d'être une nature morte." . . . Cela répondait pour moi au désir que j'ai toujours eu de toucher la chose et non seulement de la voir" (Dora Vallier, "Braque, la peinture et nous: Propos de l'artiste recueillis," *Cahiers d'art*, 29: 1 [Oct. 1954]: 16; my translation). On tactile vs. visual space in Braque, see also Poggi, *In Defiance of Painting*, pp. 97–99. Poggi relates the importance of touch for Braque to the Cubists' attempt at overcoming the limitations of Impressionism: "By privileging vision over the other senses, the Impressionists . . . created a new form of pictorial unity. . . . In the effort to render the effect of immediately perceived visual sensations, the depicted scene tended to flatten into a field of shimmering color, which denied the viewer a sense of the tactile presence of objects. . . . Reacting against Impressionist (and Neo-Impressionist) norms in his early Cubist paintings . . . , Braque rejected a purely optical mode of representation and sought instead an art concerned with volume and the tangible space between objects" (pp. 97–98).

12　Here Christine Poggi's interpretation fully corroborates my own: "[T]he important point is that Braque sought to establish a new physical relation between the spectator and the work of art. . . . Braque's notion of the tactile, then, includes not only the material properties of objects, but *the activity of the artist or spectator who must reach out to them through a materialized experience of space.* . . . This activity of reaching out to the object, of touching it, is fully indexical, implying both physical contact and knowledge. In contrast, vision could only suggest the data of the third dimension inferentially" (*In Defiance of Painting*, p. 98; my emphasis).

13　See *Autobiography*, p. 240.

14　"Autrefois . . . on employait des cadres Renaissance, beaucoup à cause du point de fuite, et la 'cuvette' aidait à l'illusion. Mais j'ai supprimé le point de fuite, qui est presque toujours faux. Un tableau doit donner envie de vivre 'dedans'. Je veux que

le public participe à mon tableau, qu'il ait le cadre dans le dos . . . Oh! je n'ai pas
tout à fait inventé cela. Trouillebert demandait un jour à Corot:

"– Mais où est cet arbre que vous mettez dans le paysage?

"Corot répondit:

"– Derrière moi" (Michel Georges-Michel, *De Renoir à Picasso* [Paris: Librairie
Arthème Fayard, 1954], p. 112; quoted in English in Schwarz, *Cubism,* p. 44).
Daniel-Henry Kahnweiler was among the first to notice this basic aspect of Cubism.
Thus he wrote in *The Rise of Cubism:* "Representation of the position of objects in
space is done as follows: instead of beginning from a supposed foreground and going
on from there to give an illusion of depth by means of perspective, the painter begins
from a definite and clearly defined background. Starting from this background the
painter now works toward the front by a sort of scheme of forms in which each
object's position is clearly indicated, both in relation to the definite background and
to other objects" ([1920], trans. Henry Aronson [New York: Wittenborn, Schultz,
1949], p. 7).

The gradual evolution of such a "tactile" or "tangible" space in Braque's early
Cubist paintings is described by William Rubin in "Cézannisme and the Beginnings
of Cubism" (in *Cézanne: The Late Work,* ed. William Rubin [New York: The
Museum of Modern Art, 1977], pp. 151–202). Rubin tries to show that Cézanne's
influence at the inception of Cubism was "even more extensive and consequential
than has been realized" and that "the *earliest* form of Cubism was less a 'joint creation'
of Picasso and Braque than an invention of Braque alone, extrapolated from possibilities proposed by Cézanne" (p. 152). An important aspect of this evolutionary
process was Braque's solution of the problem of a purely visual space that separates
objects from each other and the viewer from the objects. According to Rubin, this
was "precisely the space bridged by Cézanne's *passage.* Thus what Braque described
as a 'materialization of a new space – making space as actual, as concrete and as
perceivable pictorially as the objects themselves' – was, in effect, the explicit artic-
ulation and radicalization of a Cézannian idea" (p. 169). (By means of what is now
commonly referred to as *passage* Cézanne had opened up objects into one another
so that they cohered into a more or less homogeneous interlocked or interrelated
whole.)

Rubin shows how in the paintings of late 1907 and 1908 Braque's handling of
space and light and his linkage of objects and planes changed with the purpose, as
Braque said, of "advancing the picture toward myself bit by bit" (p. 180, with
Braque's quotation taken from J. Paulhan, *Braque le patron* [Geneva and Paris: Edi-
tions des Trois Collines, 1946], p. 35). Braque took over Cézanne's high horizon,
closed in on the motif, compressed the space, and partly eliminated the framing
device of trees and other frames that set the painting in depth. Thus he enhanced
the feeling of nearness and tangibility and created landscapes that moved "downward
and outward towards the spectator from a back plane that closes the space" (p. 165).

15 Quoted in John Richardson, *Georges Braque* (Harmondsworth: Penguin, 1959), p.
27. The quotation is part of a longer statement which, in Richardson's words, "is
based on conversations which I had at various times with Braque" (ibid.).

16 "La découverte par les peintres de la perspective mécanisée influence la pensée. Les
rapport sont fonction du point de vue. La logique est un effet de perspective"

(Georges Braque, *Illustrated Notebooks, 1917–1955,* with a translation by Stanley Appelbaum [New York: Dover, 1971], p. 108).

17 "La perspective traditionelle ne me satisfaisait pas. Mécanisée comme elle est, cette perspective ne donne jamais la pleine possession des choses. Elle part d'un point de vue et n'en sort pas" (Vallier, *Braque, la peinture et nous,* p. 14; my translation.)

18 "Avec la Renaissance, l'idéalité a remplacé la spiritualité" (*Illustrated Notebooks,* p. 54).

19 Asked by Georges Charbonnier whether one could say that in general contemporary painting was preoccupied with liberating itself from past ideas, Braque answered that he would go as far as maintaining that a painting was only finished the moment the idea behind it had disappeared: "In painting, one starts with an idea: One starts with a generating idea. Everything happens in the head before it happens in front of your eyes. It's an idea that manifests itself, isn't it? But then, in the course of the execution, the painting affirms itself. What you have is a fight between the idea – that is, the preconceived painting – and the painting defending itself." ("G.C. – En revanche la peinture actuelle n'a-t-elle pas pour préoccupation de se libérer des idées? . . .

"G.B. – Pour moi, cela va jusqu'à dire que le tableau est fini quand l'idée a disparu. . . . Pour peindre, on part d'une idée: On part d'une idée motrice. Tout se passe dans la tête avant de se passer sous les yeux. C'est une idée qui se manifeste, n'est-ce pas? Mais, en cours d'éxécution, le tableau s'affirme. Il y a donc lutte entre l'idée – c'est à dire le tableau préconçu – et le tableau qui se défend lui-même" [Georges Charbonnier, *Le monologue du peintre* (Paris: René Julliard, 1959, pp. 13– 14); my translation.])

20 "[Les gens] ne regardent les choses qu'en intellectuels: à travers leurs idées. On veut définir les choses et la définition remplace la chose. De ce fait, on perd tout contact avec la réalité. Nous vivons en plein idéalisme" (Georges Braque, in an interview published in *Zodiaque,* 18–19 [1954], p. 11; my translation).

21 John Ruskin, "The Elements of Drawing," *Works,* vol. 15, Library Edition, ed. E. T. Cook and A. Wedderburn (London: George Allen, 1903–12), p. 27.

22 John Ruskin, *Modern Painters,* vol. 3, in *Works,* vol. 5, p. 333. In *Art and Illusion* E. H. Gombrich intermittently carries on a polemical debate against the notion of the "innocent eye," declaring that it is futile to fight against preconceived notions of what one sees. The concept of the innocent eye, according to Gombrich, is "a myth" (p. 298), since ultimately there is no perception without previously acquired notions cohering into "schemata" or "formulas." This does not mean, however, that the concept of the innocent eye cannot be at least a very productive myth. Gombrich himself states, "The history of late eighteenth and nineteenth-century art became, in a way, the history of the struggle against the schema," the struggle of artists who "strove to forget the formula" (pp. 174, 175). Thus, while one will agree with Gombrich that "the inductivist ideal of pure observation has proved a mirage in science no less than in art" (p. 321), one should nevertheless point out how important and fruitful the attempts to see with fresh eyes have been. To quote Gombrich once more: "The artist cannot start from scratch but he can criticize his forerunners" (p. 321).

23 "Über die Beurteilung von Werken der bildenden Kunst" [1876], in Konrad Fiedler, *Schriften zur Kunst,* 1, ed. G. Boehm (Munich, 1971), p. 44; my translation.

24   "... si j'ai la moindre distraction, la moindre défaillance, surtout si j'interprète trop un jour, si une théorie aujourd'hui m'emporte qui contrarie celle de la veille, si je pense en peignant, si j'interviens, patatras! tout fout le camp" (Joachim Gasquet, "Ce qu'il ma dit...," in Doran, ed., *Conversations avec Cézanne*, p. 109).

25   "Mais avant d'abstraire et de bâtir, on observe: la personnalité des sens, leur docilité différente, distingue et trie parmi les qualités proposées en masse celles qui seront retenues et développées par l'individu. La constatation est d'abord subie, presque sans pensée ... : il arrive qu'on s'intéresse et qu'on donne aux choses qui étaient fermées, irréductibles, d'autres valeurs; on y ajoute, on se plaît davantage à des points particuliers, on se les exprime et il se produit comme la restitution d'une énergie que les sens auraient reçue; bientôt elle déformera le site à son tour, y employant la pensée réfléchie d'une personne.

"L'homme universel commence, lui aussi, par contempler simplement, et il revient toujours à s'imprégner de spectacles. Il retourne aux ivresses de l'instinct particulier et à l'émotion que donne la moindre chose réelle, quand on les regarde tous deux, si bien clos par toutes leurs qualités et concentrant de tout manière tant d'effets" (Paul Valéry, "Introduction à la méthode de Léonard de Vinci" [1894], in Valéry, *Oeuvres*, Vol. 1, ed. Jean Hytier [Paris: Gallimard (Bibliothèque de la Pléiade), 1957], pp. 1164–65; English translation, "The Method of Leonardo," in *Collected Works of Paul Valéry*, vol. 9, ed. Jackson Mathews [Princeton: Princeton University Press, 1968], pp. 18–19; my emphasis).

26   "La plupart des gens y voient par l'intellect bien plus souvent que par les yeux. Au lieu d'espaces colorés, ils prennent connaissance de concepts. Une forme cubique, blanchâtre, en hauteur, et trouée de reflets de vitres est immédiatement une maison, pour eux: la Maison! Idée complexe, accord de qualités abstraites. S'ils se déplacent, le mouvement des files de fenêtres, la translation des surfaces qui défigure continûment leur sensation, leur échappent, – car le concept ne change pas. Ils perçevoient plutôt selon un lexique que, d'après leur rétine, ils approchent si mal les objets, ils connaissent si vaguement les plaisirs et les souffrances d'y voir, qu'ils ont inventé *les beaux sites*. Ils ignorent le reste" ("Introduction à la méthode de Léonard de Vinci," p. 1165; "The Method of Leonardo," p. 18).

27   "L'usage du don contraire conduit à des véritables analyses (voir plus de choses qu'on n'en sait" (Ibid., pp. 1166–67 [French]; p. 20 [English translation]). The phrase in parentheses is part of a running marginal commentary to the original text which Valéry added at a later date.

28   "The Method of Leonardo," pp. 21, 20. Many of Williams's statements, especially in *A Novelette and Other Prose*, are remarkably close to Valéry's ideas: "Science (when compared to the category of art) is cruder, more directly useful, more intimate to our lives, more embedded in our errors of perception and so harder to eradicate from the mind.... Science ... is going nowhere but to a gross and minute codification of the perceptions" (*I: AN*, 303). Or, elsewhere: "The actual is another field, the field of art, which must liberate from the defects of philosophy and science, body, mind and morals. ... This sense of the actual is destructive to much that is overbearing in S. and P." (*I: AN*, 304). Notice also the striking similarity between Williams's statement, "To unlearn is as hard as to learn" (*I:AN*, 285), and Valéry's,

"The deeper education consists in unlearning one's first education" ("The Method of Leonardo," p. 20).

29 Richard Shiff, "Seeing Cézanne," *Critical Inquiry*, 4:4 (Summer 1978): 773.

30 "Certains hommes ressentent, avec une délicatesse spéciale, la volupté de *l'indivi-dualité* des objets. Ils préfèrent avec délices, dans une chose, cette qualité d'être unique – qu'elles ont toutes. Curiosité qui trouve son expression ultime dans la fiction et les arts du théâtre et qu'on a nommée, à cette extremité, la *faculté d'iden-tification*. Rien n'est plus délibérément absurde à la description que cette témérité d'une personne se déclarant qu'elle est un objet détérminé et qu'elle en ressent les impressions – cet objet fût-il matériel! Rien n'est plus puissant dans la vie imagi-native. L'objet choisi devient comme le centre de cette vie, un centre d'associations de plus en plus nombreuses, suivant que cet objet est plus ou moins complexe. Au fond, cette faculté ne peut être qu'un moyen d'exciter la vitalité imaginative, de transformer une énérgie potentielle en actuelle . . . " ("Introduction à la méthode de Léonard de Vinci," pp. 1170–71; "The Method of Leonardo," pp. 26–27).

31 Quoted from Hugh Kenner, *A Homemade World: The American Modernist Writers* (New York: William Morrow, 1975), pp. 96–97.

32 For an excellent analysis of these aspects of Williams's art, see Miller's chapters on Williams in *Poets of Reality* and *The Linguistic Moment* (Princeton: Princeton University Press, 1985).

33 Although Williams's appreciation is of course to a good extent determined by his own aims and needs, it is remarkably similar to some of Christine Poggi's astute remarks on Gris's art in her book *In Defiance of Painting*. In an appraisal of Gris's collages that could easily be extended to include Gris's oeuvre as a whole, she writes: "Two apparently incompatible worlds, one referring to a natural, everyday mode of vision, the other to the Cubist mode of reordering the elements of vision ac-cording to conceptual schemas, are thus brought into paradoxical proximity and are forced to share the same pictorial arena. If they seem to coexist harmoniously, it is because of the extraordinary sense of balance and symmetry Gris achieved in or-ganizing each composition. Nonetheless, a hierarchy exists in the relationship be-tween the order of visual facts and the order of the artist's imagination; it is the latter which takes center stage and is presented as that which has been revealed" (p. 105).

34 It was Bram Dijkstra who first asserted that the poem "The Rose" was based on Gris's painting *Roses* (*Hieroglyphics*, p. 174). Afterward, the correspondence between the painting and the poem became an accepted fact until Henry M. Sayre contested it in his article "Distancing 'The Rose' from *Roses*" (*William Carlos Williams News-letter* 5:1 [Spring 1979]: 18–19). Sayre argues that there is "insufficient evidence to support Dijkstra's original assertion," and adds that he could not trace a reproduction of *Roses* that Williams could have come across before writing "The Rose."

It is true that there is no evidence so far that Williams saw a reproduction of Gris's collage before 1924, the year in which he must have seen the painting itself at Gertrude Stein's studio in Paris. (Stein had acquired the painting shortly after its completion in 1914.) Several details in the poem "The Rose," however, suggest that Williams had either seen the painting reproduced or that he had heard about it in detail. He may have seen a reproduction when visiting Harold Loeb, who fre-quently published Gris's work in *Broom*, or he may have known about it through

Charles Demuth or Marsden Hartley, both of whom must have seen the painting on one of their visits to Gertrude Stein; see William Innes Homer, *Alfred Stieglitz and the American Avant-Garde* (Boston: New York Graphic Society, 1977), p. 226; Alvord L. Eiseman, *Charles Demuth* (New York: Watson-Guptill, 1982), pp. 11, 16; Donald Gallup, "The Weaving of a Pattern: Marsden Hartley and Gertrude Stein," *Magazine of Art*, 41 (1948): 256–61. As Christopher MacGowan writes, the poem "possibly plays homage to both Gris and Stein. While it punctuates the prose discussion of Gris's *The Open Window*, the hackneyed word that the poem liberates is 'rose' – an example that Stein had made her own" (*William Carlos Williams's Early Poetry*, p. 112).

One detail in particular in "The Rose" offers almost incontrovertible evidence that Williams used *Roses* for his poem, namely, the image of the "grooved / columns of air." This is not only a highly imaginative but also uncannily precise "reading" of the spectral shadow of the bouquet of roses falling over the edge of the table and thereby creating the phantom image of a column whose shaft is "grooved" with the so-called flutes. Looking at this detail in the painting I find it difficult to imagine that Williams's image did not originate in this source. Another interesting detail is the dark blue background of *Roses*, which oscillates between something that is flat and something that opens up into the infinite depth of, say, a night sky. This effect may well be the origin of the daring image with which Williams concludes the poem.

35   Daniel-Henry Kahnweiler, *Juan Gris: His Life and Work*, trans. Douglas Cooper (New York: Valentin, 1947), pp. 99–100.

36   Ibid., p. 100.

37   Rob Fure, "The Design of Experience: William Carlos Williams and Juan Gris," *William Carlos Williams Newsletter*, 4:2 (Fall 1978): 13–14; my italics.

38   Schwartz, *Cubism*, p. 131.

39   "On peut énoncer comme un postulat de l'imagination: les choses rêvées ne gardent jamais leurs dimensions, elles ne se stabilisent dans aucune dimension. Et les rêveries vraiment possessives, celles qui nous donnent l'objet sont les rêveries lilliputiennes. . . . Dès qu'on va rêver ou penser dans le monde de la petitesse, tout s'agrandit. Les phénomènes de l'infiniment petit prennent une tournure cosmique" (Gaston Bachelard, *La terre et les rêveries du repos* [Paris: José Corti, 1948], p. 13; my translation).

40   "Toute richesse intime agrandit sans limite l'espace interieur où elle se condense" (ibid., p. 53).

41   The passage Bachelard quotes is from "Das Rosen-Innere," *Gesammelte Gedichte* (Frankfurt: Insel, 1962), p. 378:

> Welche Himmel spiegeln sich drinnen
> in dem Binnensee
> dieser offenen Rosen . . .
>
> (O the skies reflected inside,
> in the inland lake
> of these open roses . . .)

In another poem by Rilke, "Die Rosenschale" (p. 308), we even find the very same image of the infinite expansion of the infinitely subtle ray or force lines starting from the edge of the petals:

Und die Bewegung in den Rosen, sieh:
Gebärden von so kleinem Ausschlagwinkel,
dass sie unsichtbar blieben, liefen ihre
Strahlen nicht auseinander in das Weltall.

(And then the movement in the roses, look:
gestures deflected through such tiny angles,
they'd all remain invisible unless
their rays ran streaming out into the cosmos.)

English translation from Rainer Maria Rilke, "The Bowl of Roses," *Selected Works: Poetry* (London, 1960), p. 196.

For a comparative study that relates the *Ding*-poetry of Rilke, Williams, Francis Ponge, and Pablo Neruda, see Nancy Willard, *Testimony of the Invisible Man* (Columbia: University of Missouri Press, 1970).

42   "Pour en être sûr, il suffit d'aller en imagination y habiter" (*La terre et les rêveries du repos*, p. 13).

43   Edward F. Fry, *Cubism* (New York and Toronto: Oxford University Press, 1978), p. 20. See also Robert Rosenblum, *Cubism and Twentieth-Century Art*, rev. ed. (New York: Abrams, 1976), pp. 44–45: " . . . one of the basic meanings of Cubism [is] that a work of art depends upon both the external reality of nature and the internal reality of art. . . . It is . . . essential to realize that, no matter how remote from literal appearances Cubist art may at times become, *it always has an ultimate reference to external reality, without which it could not express the fundamental tension between the demands of nature and the demands of art*" (my emphasis).

44   "Je travaille avec les éléments de l'esprit, avec l'imagination, j'essaie de concrétiser ce qui est abstrait, je vais du général au particulier, ce qui veut dire que je pars d'une abstraction pour arriver à un fait réel. Mon art est un art de synthèse, un art déductif, comme dit Raynal. . . . Je considère que le côté architectural de la peinture c'est la mathématique, le côté abstrait; je veux l'humaniser: Cézanne d'une bouteille fait un cylindre, moi, je pars du cylindre pour créer un individu d'un type spécial, d'un cylindre je fais une bouteille, une certaine bouteille. Cézanne va vers l'architecture, moi j'en pars, c'est pourquoi je compose avec des abstractions (couleurs) et j'arrange quand ces couleurs sont devenues des objets . . . , je veux dire que j'arrange le blanc pour le faire devenir un papier et le noir pour le faire devenir un ombre. Cette peinture est à l'autre ce que la poésie est à la prose" (Daniel-Henry Kahnweiler, *Juan Gris: Sa vie, son oeuvre, ses écrits* [Paris: Gallimard, 1946], p. 277; *Juan Gris: His Life and Work*, p. 138).

45   "On peut m'objecter ceci: Quel besoin aurait-on de donner des significations de réalités à ces forces puisqu'elles sont déjà accordées entre elles et qu'elles forment une architecture? Je réponds: le pouvoir de suggestion de toute peinture est considérable. Chaque spectateur tend à lui attribuer un sujet. Il faut prévoir, devancer et ratifier cette suggestion qui va fatalement se produire en transformant en sujet cette abstraction, cette architecture due uniquement à la technique picturale" ("Des possibilités de la peinture" [1924], in Kahnweiler, *Juan Gris: Sa vie, ses oeuvres, ses écrits*, pp. 286–87; *Juan Gris: His Life and Work*, p. 142).

46   Tashjian, *William Carlos Williams and the American Scene*, p. 59.

47   "Dans le peintre il y a deux choses: l'oeil et le cerveau, tous deux doivent s'entre-aider: ils faut travailler à leur développement mutuel; à l'oeil par la vision sur nature,

au cerveau par la logique des sensations organisées, qui donne les moyens d'expression" (Doran, ed., *Conversations avec Cézanne*, p. 36; English version quoted from Lawrence Gowing, "The Logic of Organized Sensations," in *Cézanne: The Late Work*, ed. William Rubin [New York: Museum of Modern Art, 1977], p. 62).

48   Cézanne, letter of October 13, 1906, *Letters*.

49   See Joachim Gasquet, "Ce qu'il ma dit . . . ," in Doran, ed., *Conversations avec Cézanne*, pp. 109–10: "[Le peintre] doit faire taire en lui toutes les voix des préjugés, oublier, oublier, faire silence, être un écho parfait. Alors, sur sa plaque sensible, tout le paysage s'inscrira. Pour le fixer sur la toile, le métier interviendra ensuite, mais le métier respectueux qui, lui aussi, n'est prêt qu'a obéir, a traduire inconsciemment, tant il sait bien sa langue. . . . Le paysage se reflète, s'humanise, se pense en moi. Je l'objective, le projette, le fixe sur ma toile. . . . " ("[The painter] has to silence in him all the voices of prejudice, he has to forget, forget, become silent, become a perfect echo. Then, the entire landscape will inscribe itself on his sensitive plate. To fix it on the canvas, craft will intervene then, a respectful craft, mind you, which, too, is ready to just obey, to translate unconsciously, knowing its own language well. . . . Landscape reflects itself, humanizes itself, thinks itself in me. I objectify it, project it, fix it on my canvas. . . . "). See also Gowing, "The Logic of Organized Sensations," p. 64; and Shiff, "Seeing Cézanne," p. 807: "Cézanne's art . . . seems to have broken down the barrier between 'sensation' as feeling and 'sensation' as seeing."

50   Gowing, "The Logic of Organized Sensations," p. 55.

51   Marsden Hartley, *Adventures in the Arts* (New York: Boni and Liveright, 1921), p. 36.

52   This attitude finds appropriate expression in Rudolf Arnheim's statement about visual dynamics: "[The] dynamic properties, inherent in everything our eyes perceive, are so fundamental that we can say: Visual perception consists in the experiencing of visual forces. . . . Any observer not hopelessly spoiled by the practice of static measurements, which dominates our civilization, will confirm Henri Bergson's observation: 'C'est que la forme n'est pour nous que le dessin d'un mouvement' " (*Art and Visual Perception*, p. 412).

53   John Berger, *The Success and Failure of Picasso* (Harmondsworth: Penguin, 1965), pp. 59–60.

54   "Dieses Vergleichen der Mittel verschiedenster Künste und dieses Ablernen einer Kunst von der anderen kann nur dann erfolg- und siegreich werden, wenn das Ablernen nicht äusserlich, sondern prinzipiell ist. D.h. eine Kunst muß bei der anderen lernen, wie sie mit *ihren* Mitteln umgeht, sie muss es lernen, um dann *ihre eigenen* Mittel *prinzipiell* gleich zu behandeln, d.h. in dem Prinzip, welches *ihr allein* eigen ist. Bei diesem Ablernen muß der Künstler nicht vergessen, daß jedes Mittel eine ihm geeignete Anwendung in sich birgt und daß *diese* Anwendung herauszufinden ist" (Kandinsky, *Über das Geistige in der Kunst*, p. 55).

55   Breslin, "Williams and Demuth," p. 256.

56   This process of exploration also makes clear that one should not regard Williams's attempt to reach a fusion of self and other as one entailing a total suspension of the exploring consciousness. The poems often enact a *movement toward* climactic moments of intensive interaction or "interpenetration" that require an active participation of the exploring mind, or, better, self, since the interpenetration is a

kinesthetic process involving mind and body, head and heart. This self, in a dramatically unfolding and unfolded process, assimilates nature's energies and turns the work of art into an extension or reflection of those energies, by "imitating" or recreating them until "we become nature or . . . discover in ourselves nature's active part" (*A*, 241).

57 See Rosenblum, *Cubism and Twentieth Century Art*, pp. 44, 106, 129–31.

58 See Gombrich, *Art and Illusion*, p. 281: "Cubism, I believe, is the most radical attempt . . . to enforce one reading of the picture – that of a man-made construction, a colored canvas. If illusion is due to the interaction of clues and the absence of contradictory evidence, the only way to fight its transforming influence is to make the clues contradict each other and to prevent a coherent image of reality from destroying the pattern in the plane."

59 Rosenblum, *Cubism and Twentieth-Century Art*, p. 66. One of these pictorial devices in Picasso's collage is the unusual frame in the form of a mariner's rope. This rope, as Christine Poggi has shown, is a complex device with several functions, one of which consists in undercutting the difference between high art (or highbrow culture) and low art, and thus recalls Williams's own attempts at debunking traditional notions of poetry by so-called antipoetic elements. "The rope," writes Christine Poggi, "is a ready-made, mass-produced material associated with popular rather than fine art and is employed by Picasso to simulate artisanal skill. The rope, a low or even non-art material, serves to parody the beveled wooden frames that traditionally signify high art, just as the inclusion of oil-cloth parodies the value accorded the medium of oil painting. The prominent gestural smears of oil paint across the smooth surface of the oilcloth further emphasize this ironic juxtaposition of means" (*In Defiance of Painting*, p. 62).

Both the debunking of high art notions and the insistence on the equal validity of nonpainterly means can be seen as homologues to the manner in which Williams includes bits and pieces of ready-made language in his poems, a device culminating in the collage structure of *Paterson* with its newspaper clippings, excerpts of local histories, personal letters, and the like. Williams, inspired by the Cubist challenge to the fundamental convention of Western painting that the artist achieve his works with paint and pencil alone, fought throughout his life against the opposition of artistic and nonartistic devices, poetic and so-called antipoetic means. One may recall in this context what he wrote about the prose in *Paterson* (which is largely used as an unmodified or modified collage item): "It is *not* an anti-poetic device. . . . It *is* that prose and verse are both *writing*, both a matter of the words and an interrelation between words" (*SL*, 263).

60 William Carlos Williams, "Notes from a Talk on Poetry," *Poetry*, 14 (July 1919), p. 214.

61 Ibid.

62 See Charles Doyle's excellent article, "Kora and Venus."

CHAPTER 4: SOOTHING THE SAVAGE BEAST: CUBIST REALISM AND THE
URBAN LANDSCAPE

1   *Contact,* 1 (Dec. 1920): 1; *Contact,* 2 (Jan. 1921): 11–12.
2   Letters to Alfred Stieglitz, 31 August 1921 and 10 October 1921, The Alfred Stieglitz
    Collection, YALC.
3   Letter to William Carlos Williams, 13 October 1921, L, SUNY.
4   Letter to Alfred Stieglitz, 28 November 1921, YALC.
5   In what is apparently the first extant version of the poem, which Williams enclosed
    in a letter to his publisher, Brown, the impact of the number 5 is not so directly
    connected to its technological contemporary environment but concentrates more
    on form and color in isolation: "Among the rain / and lights / I saw the figure 5 /
    gold on red / moving / to gong clangs / siren howls / and wheels rumbling / tense
    / unheeded / through the dark city" (Williams files, YALC. This version corrob-
    orates Rod Townley's suggestion that Williams may have been inspired by one of
    the prose poems that Kandinsky included in *Concerning the Spiritual in Art,* beginning
    "Es war eine große 3 – weiß auf dunkelbraun" (*CSA,* 82). The immediate inspi-
    ration came from the well-known incident of the firetruck racing by when Williams
    was on Marsden Hartley's doorstep, as recounted in the *Autobiography* (Townley,
    The Early Poetry of William Carlos Williams [Ithaca: Cornell University Press, 1975],
    p. 198).
6   An unpublished letter to Henry Wells in 1955 reveals that both the pun in the title
    and the epiphanic moment, linked to the special sensitivity of the artist for a new
    kind of beauty, were indeed of foremost importance to Williams: "In the case of
    The Great Figure," he wrote to Wells, "I think you missed the irony of the word
    great, the contemptuous feeling I had at the moment for all '[g]rea[t] figures' in
    public life compared with that figure 5 riding in state with full panoply down the
    streets of the city ignored by everyone but the artist." See Christopher J. MacGowan,
    "William Carlos Williams' 'The Great Figure' and Marsden Hartley," *American Lit-
    erature,* 53:2(May 1981): 303. Williams's letter, quoted from MacGowan, is part of
    the General Manuscript Collection, Rare Book and Manuscript Library, Columbia
    University.
7   Breslin, "Williams and Demuth," p. 260. Breslin, to my knowledge, was also the
    first to point out the ambiguity of the title.
8   Letter to Alfred Stieglitz, The Alfred Stieglitz Archives, YALC.
9   See Donald B. Kuspit, "Individual and Mass Identity in Urban Art: The New York
    Case," *Art in America,* 65 (Sept.–Oct. 1977):68 and passim; Neil Myers, "William
    Carlos Williams' *Spring and All,*" in *William Carlos Williams,* ed. Charles Tomlinson
    (Harmondsworth: Penguin, 1972), pp. 215–32.
10 *William Carlos Williams,* p. 72. In contrast to Breslin's reading (and my own), Peter
    Schmidt, in a compelling interpretation of the poem, emphasizes the satirical and
    ironic elements: "Williams' Dadaist mocking of the language of church, government
    and the press . . . becomes a mockery of all those who would use the movies to
    enforce conservative and repressive middle class values; he sees the movies . . . as a
    predominantly *repressive* force, determinedly translating dangerous materials into
    proper ones, class conflict into conformity, resulting in crowds 'with the closeness
    and / universality of sand' " (*Williams, the Arts, and Literary Tradition,* p. 169).

Schmidt argues for a more pessimistic and caustic reading of a whole group of poems in *Spring and All*, a group which he regards as essentially Dadaistic. Among these he includes (besides "Light Becomes Darkness") "Flight to the City" (Poem IV), "The Agonized Spires" (Poem XIII), "Composition" (Poem XII), and "At the Faucet of June" (Poem VIII).

11 Christopher MacGowan (*William Carlos Williams's Early Poetry*, p. 106) believes that the reference in "Young Love" to Marin's "soup-like expressionism" is disparaging, and he quotes the critical statement on Marin that Williams made later in an interview with Emily Farnham. Marin was "not a draughtsman," Williams said; "I could never see Marin as an artist. Surely drawing is a basic thing in painting?" (Emily Farnham, "Charles Demuth, His Life, Psychology, and Works," Dissertation, Ohio State University, 1959, p. 990).

These remarks show that Williams's feelings about Marin were at least ambivalent; to put them in perspective, one would have to take into consideration his appreciation of Marin's work in the Foreword to the *Catalogue of the John Marin Memorial Exhibition* (Art Galleries, University of California, Los Angeles, 1955). In "Young Love," the reference to Marin appears in a context that contains cryptic references to a spring affair "fifteen years ago" with "Kiki," "at the hospital"; the futile attempts to remain aloof or "clean" are set off against the vortex of the city that seems to demand total commitment, even at the price of failure or guilt: "What about all this writing? // O 'Kiki' / O Miss Margaret Jarvis / The backhandspring // I: clean / clean / clean: yes . . . New York // Wrigley's, appendicitis, John Marin: / skyscraper soup – // Either that or a bullet!" (*CP1*, 200). Marin's art, whether successful or not, is an answer to the challenge of the big city, a product of his involvement. The specific guilt of the narrator, on the other hand, is his lack of commitment: "You sobbed, you beat your pillow / you tore your hair / you dug your nails into your sides // I was your nightgown / I watched! // Clean is he alone / after whom stream / the broken pieces of the city –."

12 Williams's outlook is also particularly interesting in the context of the current attempts to come to a clearer understanding of the fundamental phenomenological differences between the Modernist and the Postmodernist viewpoint. Seen from this angle, Williams remains on the one hand – inevitably – within the traditional thought patterns of Western metaphysics when he thinks in such oppositions as dream and disillusionment, truth and mystification, goal and pursuit of the goal. On the other hand, he moves beyond this when he identifies goal and pursuit, here and there ("here is everywhere"!), ideas and things, process and end, object as thing and object as force. The moment in which thinking in such opposites *as distinct entities* is transcended, the moment they become forces in a field instead of split elements of an original whole, opposites are ultimately aspects of the same. In place of the traditional idea of opposites we get, in J. Hillis Miller's words, "the idea of degrees of difference, differentiated forces which are not opposites but points on the same scale, distinctions of the same energy" ("Tradition and Difference," *Diacritics*, 2:4 [Winter 1972]: 13).

13 Quoted in André Breton, "Manifesto of Surrealism" (1924), in *Manifestoes of Surrealism*, trans. by Richard Seaver and Helen R. Lane (Ann Arbor: University of Michigan Press, 1972), p. 36.

14 Quoted in André Breton, "Surrealist Situation of the Object" (1935), in *Manifestoes of Surrealism*, p. 275.

15 Breton, "Manifesto of Surrealism," p. 37.

16 Roman Jakobson, *Studies in Child Language and Aphasia* (The Hague: Mouton, 1971), pp. 69–70.

17 Compared to the subject matter of Williams's poem – the contemporary world it refers to – the subject matter of a Cubist painting, such as a portrait or a still life, is on the whole much more unified. There are, however, some highly interesting exceptions, such as Picasso's *Au Bon Marché*, which combines an interior, a still-life, a portrait, and fragments of life in the modern city, and which uses puns and visual games that one could in several ways relate to the games Williams plays in "At the Faucet of June."

18 The term is indebted to Peter Schmidt's "modernist pastoral." Schmidt, too, in a compelling reading of the poem, stresses the importance of dissonance and heterogeneity, but relates them primarily to Dadaist practices. For Schmidt, the poem consists of an intriguing mixture of high and low, of the serious and the burlesque, in a wild concatenation of European high-brow culture, American commerce, advertising jargon, and sententiousness (*Williams, the Arts, and Literary Tradition*, pp. 158 ff).

19 Robert Creeley, *Contexts of Poetry: Interviews 1961–1971* (Bolinas, Cal.: Four Seasons Foundation, 1973), p. 17; my emphasis.

20 David Lodge, *The Modes of Modern Writing* (London: Edward Arnold, 1977), p. 93.

21 One might contrast Williams's conjunctions in this poem or in *Spring and All* in its entirety with those of Eliot in *The Waste Land*, published the year before. Where Eliot juxtaposes the barrenness of the present with a flowering past, Williams, answering with his own myth of Kora – the myth of cyclic return, the myth of the spatial and temporal *conjunctio oppositorum* – presents a world in which everything interacts with everything else: the timeless with the timebound, the sublime with the ordinary, the local with the universal.

22 See Hans Robert Jauss, "Poiesis," trans. Michael Shaw, *Critical Inquiry*, 8:3 (Spring 1982): 603 and passim; Max Nänny, *Ezra Pound: Poetics for an Electric Age* (Bern: Francke, 1973), pp. 90–114.

23 Williams Files (Za-Williams, misc., n.p.), YALC.

24 Wallace Stevens, *Collected Poems* (New York: Alfred A. Knopf, 1954), p. 423.

25 Reinhold Hohl, "Die heitreren Facetten des Kubismus," in *Kubismus: Künstler, Themen, Werke, 1907–1920* (Cologne: Joseph-Haubrich-Kunsthalle, 1982), p. 72; my translation.

26 William Carlos Williams, Introduction to Charles Henry Ford, *The Garden of Disorder and Other Poems* (London: Europa, 1938), p. 9.

27 I use the term "iconic" in its extended sense here, as referring to a language that is imitative by directly including visual and/or aural aspects of the signified. Auditory iconicity in that sense includes much more than onomatopoeia proper, once we look for it not only in individual words but include the relational or diagrammatic dimension – once we move, in Williams's words, from "single words" to their "association in groups." For an excellent discussion of iconicity in the context of literature and the visual arts, see Wendy Steiner, *The Colors of Rhetoric*.

28 Such an interpretation could be placed within the context of Williams's frequent attacks on the conservative universities and backward critics who "know everything and must keep everything under control" and who are therefore unable to accept the "undisciplined power of the *unimaginable* poem" (*SL*, 193–94; my italics). In this context, the word "impossible" could even directly foreshadow Williams's later references to the "impossible poem *Paterson*."

29 I am indebted to a colleague of mine, Ms. Barbara Sträuli, for drawing my attention to Thayer's painting.

30 The theory of mimicry or protective coloration in animals that Gerald H. Thayer explored together with his father, the painter Abbott Henderson Thayer, was expounded by them in their publication *Concealing-Coloration in the Animal Kingdom* (1909).

31 The lines may allude not only to Thayer's watercolor but also, as Peter Schmidt points out, to a passage on partridges in Thoreau's *Walden:* "The young suddenly disperse on your approach, at a signal from the mother, as if a whirlwind has swept them away, and they so exactly resemble the dried leaves and twigs that many a traveller has placed his foot in the midst of a brood, and heard the whir of the old bird as she flew off" (*The Norton Anthology of American Literature*, eds. Francis Murphy et al., Vol. 1, New York, 1979, p. 1672, quoted in Schmidt, *Williams, the Arts, and Literary Tradition*, p. 161).

32 See in this context Marjorie Perloff's *The Poetics of Indeterminacy*, in which she divides modernism into two "rival strains, the Symbolist or 'High Modern' and the 'Other Tradition'." Williams, according to Perloff, belongs to the latter strain, which goes back not only to Rimbaud and later French poets but is also related to the revolutionary movements in the visual arts. In painting and sculpture, Perloff maintains, "the stage in which surface is preferred to 'depth,' *process* to *structure*, is much more readily identifiable than it is in poetry. From the early days of Cubism in 1910 through Vorticism and Futurism, Dada and Surrealism, down to the Abstract Expressionism of the fifties, and the Conceptual Art, Super-Realism, assemblages, and performance art of the present, visual artists have consistently resisted the Symbolist model in favor of the creation of a world in which forms can exist 'littéralement et dans tous les sens,' an oscillation between representational reference and compositional game" (pp. 33–34).

My own view differs from Perloff's in that her indeterminacy or "irreducible ambiguity" (p. 34) is at the heart of Williams's poetics, whereas I regard it as only one of many means by which he keeps the reader aware of the irreducible doubleness of the sign and the nature of the poem as artifact.

CHAPTER 5: THE VIRGIN AND THE DYNAMO

1 *Skyscraper Primitives*, pp. 210–11; the quotation by Williams is from "Belly Music," *Others*, 5 (July 1919), Supplement, p. 30.

2 Bram Dijkstra has shown that Williams's opening paragraphs in *Spring and All* take up directly some of the programmatic statements in Rosenfeld's essays on some of the painters and writers of the Stieglitz circle. Williams thus pays homage to several of his artist friends at one and the same time, as does Demuth when he dedicates a

painting to Williams which also nods in the direction of Duchamp, Picabia, and other artists of the New York Dada group.

3 Decades later, in an interview with Emily Farnham, Williams was quick to point out that Demuth was constantly preoccupied with the erotic in his still lifes. The tone of Williams's remarks suggests that the artist friends not infrequently teased each other about the fascination that the pan-sexual held for them. As Musja Sheeler mentioned to me in an interview, Charles Sheeler – who was obviously much more reserved in this respect – would say of Georgia O'Keeffe (in an apparent mixture of admiration and disapproval) that she was "crazy" to exhibit her vulva-flowers to a public that dared not name what it saw; Williams in turn would jokingly refer to "Marsden's breasts" when talking about the mountains in Hartley's pastel *Mountains in New Mexico*, which he owned. The phrase was apparently Hartley's own, as Tashjian found out (*Williams and the American Scene*, p. 148). Obviously pan-eroticism, although a serious issue, was also the subject of bantering and self-directed irony.

4 Pierre Cabanne, *Dialogues with Marcel Duchamp* (New York: Viking, 1971), p. 88.

5 Apparently, there is no direct influence of Adams on the ideas that Williams voices in *In the American Grain*. Williams read *The Education of Henry Adams* (1918; New York: Random House, 1931) for the first time around 1930 at the instigation of Louis Zukofsky, who had written his M.A. thesis on Adams.

6 Tashjian's *Skyscraper Primitives* contains an excellent chapter on this aspect of the New York Dada movement ("291 and Francis Picabia," pp. 29–48).

7 "A Complete Reversal of Art Opinions by Marcel Duchamp, Iconoclast," *Arts and Decoration*, 5 (Sept. 1915): 427–28.

8 Untitled essay, *291*, 7–8 (Sept.–Oct. 1915):[1].

9 Lewis Mumford, "The Metropolitan Milieu," in *America and Alfred Stieglitz*, eds. Waldo Frank et al. (1934; New York: Octagon Books, 1975) p. 54.

10 Together with Williams's chapter "Jacataqua" in *In the American Grain*, Mumford's essay contains some of the most interesting and representative passages on how artists and critics of the avant-garde of that time viewed the plight of the American woman in the wake of the Puritan tradition: "Lusty men and passionate women of course remained in this society; but the whole tone of sex remained practically as low as it had been in the Victorian days. Although talk about sex, and even possibly physical indulgence, became more common, the actual manifestations often remained placidly anemic: a girl might have a dozen lovers without having known an orgasm, or have a dozen orgasms without having achieved any fundamental intimacy with her lover. On the surface, decorum or defiance of decorum; beneath it, irritation, frustration, resentment – resentment on the part of the male for the unarousableness of the female, about whom the faint aroma of anxious antisepsis clung like an invisible petticoat; resentment on the part of the female against the male both for his bothersome insistence and his lack of really persuasive aggression" ("The Metropolitan Milieu," p. 55).

11 As I tried to show before, Williams indicates in this poem by means of the pun *core/Kora* that Kora, the virginal goddess of growth and fruition, is replaced by the fascination held by the "core" of whirling flywheels – and in both instances (Greek mythology and contemporary America) the male principle dominates the female.

12 Miller, "Tradition and Difference," p. 13.

13 Joseph N. Riddel, *The Inverted Bell: Modernism and the Counterpoetics of William Carlos Williams* (Baton Rouge: Louisiana University Press, 1974), p. 107.

14 "The So-Called So-Called," *The Patron* (Bergen College, N.J., May 1937), pp. 37–40. Quoted from Miller, *Poets of Reality*, p. 322.

15 Rilke, *Gesammelte Gedichte*, p. 313; my translation.

16 Ernest Fenollosa, *The Chinese Written Character as a Medium for Poetry*, ed. Ezra Pound (1936; San Francisco: City Lights Books, 1968), p. 10.

17 Quoted in Dorothy Norman, *Alfred Stieglitz: An American Seer* (New York: Random House, 1960), pp. 80, 240n; no further source given.

18 Williams's word "bareheaded" is basically the same as Stieglitz's "without hats," but of course there are overtones in "bareheaded" – such as *exposed, naked, unprotected, open, simple, without ornament* – which are absent in Stieglitz's more neutral expression. Thus the term "bareheaded" itself contains implicitly several of the words – "free," "simple," "alive" – that appear in Stieglitz's recollection as part of a contextually explicit definition of what "without hats" connotes for him.

19 Statement by Stieglitz quoted in Dijkstra, *Hieroglyphics*, p. 102.

20 For Dijkstra, Williams's achievement as an avant-garde artist was "in large measure due to his careful study of the writings of the Stieglitz group" (*Hieroglyphics*, p. 110). Moreover, Dijkstra regards these writings themselves (by Rosenfeld, Waldo Frank, Marsden Hartley, and others) as a straightforward adoption of Stieglitz's convictions. But Stieglitz's importance was less that of the *sole* originator of the whole movement as that of a charismatic figure with a messianic sense which led him to become the tireless promoter of an indigenous American art. What came out of it was as much a collective achievement as that of any single person, with many forces joined and many voices and art works influencing, stimulating, enforcing, rivaling, and reinfluencing each other. In this many-faceted enterprise of early American Modernism, Stieglitz was as important a man of the first hour as Williams was of the second.

One also has to take into account that at the time when Williams began to frequent Stieglitz's gallery 291, the formation of the avant-garde was far from complete; it went on for more than a decade, and the two other important circles around Kreymborg and Arensberg were just forming. (It was only in 1915 that Duchamp set foot in America for the first time.) Williams's achievement in particular is due, among other things, to his enormous capacity to absorb influences and stimuli from all three circles, as well as from many other sources, individual artists and movements alike. He was able to do so because, throughout his life, he not only followed Pound's motto "Make It New" but remained conscious of the fact that originality was not creation *ex nihilo* but repetition with a difference, as the opening section of *Spring and All* and many other statements prove.

21 "The quality of *touch* in its deepest living sense is inherent in my photographs," said Stieglitz. "When that sense of touch is lost, the heartbeat of the photograph is extinct." (Quoted in Dijkstra, *Hieroglyphics*, p. 102.)

22 Quite apart from the pictorial elements in his own earlier work, Stieglitz's affinities to Pictorialism are strikingly visible in his editorial policy with *Camera Work* as well as the taste displayed in his private collection of photographs now in the possession of the Metropolitan Museum of Art. The full swing over to straight photography

in *Camera Work* came only in 1916–17 with the publication of Paul Strand's early work in the last two numbers of the magazine.

23 See for instance *Dancing Trees*, 1921; *Barn, Lake George*, 1922; *Apples and Gable, Lake George*, 1922; *Tree*, 1933; *Grasses*, 1933; all reproduced in Dorothy Norman, *Alfred Stieglitz*, plates XXX, XLVII, XLVIII, LII, LIV.

24 See the excellent analysis of this device in Pound's early poetry by Max Nänny, in "Context, Contiguity and Contact in Ezra Pound's Personae," *English Literary History*, 47 (1980):386–98.

25 This attempt to write poems that are more or less condensed fragments cut out of a larger continuum accounts well for the fact that they are basically metonymical and not metaphorical, in Jakobson's sense of the word. In this respect Williams's poems are directly related to those of the early Pound, whose influence he often acknowledged. Thus Herbert Schneidau's and Max Nänny's highly interesting accounts of the role of metonymy in Pound's poetry are also of direct relevance to Williams's poems. Pound, says Nänny, "had the true metonymist's preference for external phenomena *in presentia*, a preference that also accounts for his stress on 'presentation' in his poetics and poetry. It is in line with this stress on 'presentational immediacy' (Schneidau) that Pound . . . tends to prefer *icons* and *indices* to verbal symbols" ("Context, Contiguity and Contact in Ezra Pound's Personae," p. 389). Since "presentational immediacy" is an essential quality of the visual arts, it is obvious that both the early Pound and Williams try to achieve a similar pictorial immediacy through linguistic means of "presencing." See also Schneidau, "Wisdom Past Metaphor: Another View of Pound, Fenollosa, and Objective Verse," *Paideuma*, 5 (Spring–Summer 1976): 15–29.

26 Braque, Interview in *Zodiaque*, 18–19 (1954), p. 12.

27 See Don Ihde, *Listening and Voice: A Phenomenology of Sound* (Athens: Ohio University Press, 1976), pp. 13–14; William V. Spanos, "Charles Olson and Negative Capability: A Phenomenological Interpretation," *Contemporary Literature*, 21:1 (1980), p. 46 and passim.

28 Gary Snyder, "The Yogin and the Philosopher," in *The Old Ways: Six Essays* (San Francisco: City Lights, 1977), p. 9.

CHAPTER 6: THE SEARCH FOR A SYNTHETIC FORM

1 Quoted in Wendy Steiner, *Exact Resemblance to Exact Resemblance: The Literary Portraiture of Gertrude Stein* (New Haven, Conn.: Yale University Press, 1978), p. 204.

2 Wallace Stevens, *The Necessary Angel: Essays on Reality and the Imagination* (New York: Alfred A. Knopf, 1957), p. 175.

3 Steiner, *The Colors of Rhetoric*, p. 183; *Structure, Sign and Function: Selected Essays by Jan Mukařovský*, trans. and ed. John Burbank and Peter Steiner (New Haven, Conn.: Yale University Press, 1978), pp. 129–49.

4 See David Antin, "Modernism and Postmodernism: Approaching the Present in American Poetry," *boundary 2*, 1 (Fall 1972), pp. 132–33. Quoted in Perloff, *The Poetics of Indeterminacy*, p. 35.

5 Joseph N. Riddel, " 'Keep Your Pecker Up' – *Paterson Five* and the Question of Metapoetry," *Glyph, 8: Johns Hopkins Textual Studies* (Baltimore: Johns Hopkins University Press, 1981), p. 206.

6   William Carlos Williams, "America, Whitman, and the Art of Poetry," pp. 29–31.

7   Quoted in Dorothy Norman, *Alfred Stieglitz,* p. 76. Sarah Greenough argues convincingly that Stieglitz's excited report of how he came to make the photograph was recounted in 1942 and is not reliable as an account of what Stieglitz really thought of the photograph when he made it in 1907. Greenough mentions that Stieglitz exhibited it neither at the Dresden exhibition of 1909 nor at the Albright Gallery exhibition in 1910. She finds Steichen's different account more plausible, according to which it was de Zayas who discovered the photograph around 1910 while looking through some of Stieglitz's proofs. Steichen's account seems more plausible in view of Stieglitz's own artistic development: "[B]ecause of the stylistic similarity between *The Steerage* and Stieglitz's photographs from 1910, it appears that that was the year in which he first understood its significance" (Sarah Greenough and Juan Hamilton, eds., *Alfred Stieglitz: Photographs and Writings* [Washington, D.C.: National Gallery of Arts, 1983], p. 30). Moreover, it was exactly in that period between 1907 and 1910 that Stieglitz discovered and began exhibiting modern art, a discovery that changed not only his style but apparently also his attitude toward *The Steerage.*

8   Eric Himmel, "Change of Heart," *Camera Arts* 1:5 (Sept.–Oct. 1981): 38.

9   Paul Rosenfeld, *Port of New York* (1924; Urbana and London: University of Illinois Press, 1966), p. 272.

10 Jonathan Green, ed., *Camera Work: An Anthology* (Millerton, N.Y.: Aperture, 1973), p. 266.

11 Ibid., p. 268.

12 William Carlos Williams, "Studiously Unprepared: Notes for Various Talks and Readings, May 1940 to April 1941," MS, YALC. Quoted from Sayre, *Visual Text,* p. 44.

13 Green, ed., *Camera Work: An Anthology,* p. 264.

14 "Heaven's First Law," in J. Hillis Miller, ed., *William Carlos Williams: A Collection of Critical Essays* (Englewood Cliffs, N.J.: Prentice Hall, 1966), pp. 49–50.

15 Edward Weston, *Daybooks* (Millerton, N.Y.: Aperture, 1973), p. 55.

16 Green, ed., *Camera Work: An Anthology,* p. 326.

17 Paul Mariani, *William Carlos Williams: A New World Naked* (New York: McGraw Hill, 1981), p. 210; Matthew Josephson, *Life Among the Surrealists* (New York: Holt, Rinehart and Winston, 1962), pp. 253–54.

18 Rourke, *Charles Sheeler,* p. 143. Sheeler's Precisionist paintings are as closely related in intention and impact to his own photographs as are some of the hyper-realist paintings in the 1970s and 1980s (of Richard Estes, for instance) to the urban landscapes of such photographers as Steven Shore, Joel Meyerowitz, or Joe Maloney. It seems that in America, throughout this century, there have been again and again close ties between various movements which are all striving for an indigenous art that would reconcile the need for form with a respect for the mundane subject. It is interesting to note in such a context that a definition of photography, given by Barbara Rose in an article that argues for a basic continuity from Precisionism to Photorealism and Minimal Art, becomes a perfect definition of the Precisionist aesthetics of the avant-garde in the twenties and thirties. Photography, writes Barbara Rose, "can transform any subject, no matter how banal, into a classic formal ar-

rangement. Moreover, it can do so without denying the significance or identity of the subject. In a photograph, formal and subject meanings can have equal value; and the abstract must remain indivisibly wed to the concrete" ("The Politics of Art," Part 2, *Artforum*, 7:5 [Jan. 1969]:45).

It seems that in spite of these common characteristics Williams would rather acknowledge this fusion of the abstract and the concrete when he found it in painting than in photography. Still, he responded favorably to a number of photographers, such as Stieglitz, Sheeler, Atget, Walker Evans, Louis Lozovick, Berenice Abbot, and Barbara Morgan. He must also have been fully aware of the achievement of Paul Strand, but perhaps the estrangement between Sheeler and Strand after the mid-1920s (which involved Stieglitz, too, who began ignoring Sheeler after the latter had done fashion photography for *Vogue*) had also influenced Williams.

But more than questions of loyalty are involved in this issue, of course. At times Williams related photography to a "simply physical, external realism." Often, he stated in a letter in 1934, the photographic camera would record external facts without "[setting] them down with a view to penetration." To record the external fact was helpful only "if we are able to *see* general relationships in a local setting" (*SL*, 146). Even in such a moment in which he adopted a critical stance, however, he mentioned his awareness of the *potential* value of the camera which prevented the artist from resorting to too facile an abstraction.

19   Sutton, "A Visit with William Carlos Williams," pp. 321–22.

20   For masculine and feminine line endings, see Derek Attridge, *The Rhythms of English Poetry* (London: Longman, 1982), p. 8.

21   Only a few of the critics show a clear awareness of this crucial tension in Williams's aesthetics between the referential and the self-referential, most notably J. Hillis Miller, Charles Altieri, and Albert Gelpi. "[I]t is by now abundantly clear," writes Gelpi in *A Coherent Splendor*, "that although Williams stoutly maintained the integrity of the verbal object, he also maintained an unshakable respect, even at the height of his Modernism in *Spring and All*, for the integrity of the object being rendered into words. For Williams . . . the signifier still *does* signify. In his famous poem about the red wheelbarrow, the opening couplet, "so much depends / upon," immediately posits the mind as the source of connections and signification, and the mental act of signification depends upon an actual configuration of barrow, rain, and chickens. The poem assumes an independent existence but *acknowledges a dependence on natural phenomena as the point of origin and relevance* (p. 342; italics in the last sentence quoted are mine).

22   See Mariani, *A New World Naked*, pp. 339–40.

23   Paul Valéry, *Oeuvres* (Paris: Pléiade, 1960), vol. 1, pp. 1165–67.

24   Reported by Duret and quoted in Max Raphael, *Von Monet zu Picasso* (Munich, 1919), p. 62.

25   Roy Miki, *The Prepoetics of William Carlos Williams: Kora in Hell* (Ann Arbor: UMI Research Press, 1983), p. 35.

26   Meyer Schapiro, "The Apples of Cézanne: An Essay on the Meaning of Still-life," *Art News Annual*, 34 (1967): 44.

27   It is thus first of all this questioning of basic traditional assumptions about "high" and "low" that links many of Williams's poems to still-life painting, which, accord-

ing to Norman Bryson, makes us again aware of the fact that all values are the products of a specific culture: " . . . we need to be clear that the decision to regard some levels of human action as exalted and noble and others as trivial or base is the product of a series of cultural pressures; one is not dealing here with the *donnés* of nature. Every one of us lives our life in the orbit of basic routines of self-maintenance: cooking and eating, shopping, seeing to domestic chores, keeping our creatural habitat in viably good repair. Such activities are objectively necessary for our welfare and respond to inescapable conditions of human life. But how these activities are viewed and appraised – what value is *placed* on the life of creaturely routine – is very much a matter of culture, and of history. Whether these activities are respected or dismissed, valued or despised, depends on the work of ideology. . . . [T]he painting of what is 'mundane' or 'sordid' . . . is negative only from a certain viewpoint, in which the 'lowness' of a supposedly low-plane reality poses a threat to another level of culture that regards itself as having access to superior or exalted modes of existence. And if that humble line is evaluated negatively, we need to enquire what *kind* of threat it could conceivably pose (if it is indeed so lowly), and for whom" (*Looking at the Overlooked: Four Essays on Still Life Painting* [London: Reaktion Books, 1990], p. 137).

28   Herbert Schneidau outlines the concept of "sacramentalism" by placing such Modernist writers as Joyce in the larger context of the Judeo-Christian tradition: "Even in the early humorless examples of the notion of 'epiphany' the defining element is Joyce's ability to see more in clichés than anyone else would see. Familiar, trivial objects or snatches of random mundane conversation can be made to reverberate with significance, according to the doctrine; it is Joyce's version of seeing the world in a grain of sand. Behind Blake we can glimpse a tradition of religious representation, which Joyce's word 'epiphany' points toward. A complex heritage centers on the Hebrew proscription of images, which was meant to rebuke the mythological habits of mind that go back to Lascaux and Altamira and beyond. In the West, the proscription was not taken literally; instead, compromises were worked out, one of which we may call sacramentalism. It allows representation of divine things only if, paradoxically, the signifying figures are sufficiently humble and unremarkable, so as to offset idolatry." ("Style and Sacrament in Modernist Writing," *Georgia Review*, 31 [1977]: 437–38.)

29   D. S. Carne-Ross, "The Music of a Lost Dynasty: Pound in the Classroom," *Boston University Journal*, 21:1 (Winter 1972): 25–41.

30   Schneidau, "Style and Sacrament in Modernist Writing," p. 440.

31   Roman Jakobson and Morris Halle, *Fundamentals of Language*, rev. ed. (The Hague: Mouton, 1971), Part II: "Two Aspects of Language and Two Types of Aphasic Disturbances," p. 83.

32   D. S. Carne-Ross, "The Music of a Lost Dynasty," quoted in Schneidau, "Wisdom Past Metaphor," p. 19.

33   Roland Barthes, *Empire of Signs*, trans. Richard Howard (London: Jonathan Cape, 1982), p. 74. "[L]e haiku opère du moins en vue d'obtenir un language plat, que rien n'assied (comme c'est immanquable dans notre poésie) sur des couches superposées de sens, ce que l'on pourrait appeler le "feuilleté" des symboles. . . . Tout le Zen, dont le haikai n'est que la branche littéraire, apparaît ainsi comme une

immense pratique destinée à arrêter le langage, à casser cette sorte de radiophonie intérieure qui émet continûment en nous, jusque dans notre sommeil . . . " (Roland Barthes, *L'empire des signes* [Paris: Albert Skira, 1970], pp. 98–99).

34 *Empire of Signs*, p. 75; *L'empire des signes*, p. 100.

35 *Empire of Signs*, p. 74; *L'empire des signes*, p. 99.

36 Barthes, *Empire of Signs*, p. 83. "Ne décrivant ni ne définissant, le haiku . . . s'amincit jusqu'à la pure et seule désignation. *C'est cela, c'est ainsi*, dit le haiku, *c'est tel*. Ou mieux encore: *Tel!* dit-il, d'une touche si instantanée et si courte (sans vibration ni reprise) que la copule y apparaîtrait encore de trop, comme le remords d'une définition interdite, à jamais éloignée" (Barthes, *L'empire des signes*, p. 113).

37 Geoffrey H. Hartman, *Criticism in the Wilderness: The Study of Literature Today* (New Haven, Conn.: Yale University Press, 1980), pp. 120–21.

38 Michael Riffaterre, "Intertextual Representation: On Mimesis as Interpretive Discourse," *Critical Inquiry*, 11:1 (Sept. 1984): 145–46.

39 Ibid., p. 146.

40 Bryson, *Looking at the Overlooked*, p. 145.

41 The early "Pastoral" ("When I was younger"; quoted on p. 17–18, this volume) is a particularly interesting poem in that respect; the speaker, in the characteristic manner outlined here, openly asserts his own values in contradistinction to the conventional views of his society, but he does so by challenging these traditional views of "high" and "low" on two levels: on the level of the still life (traditional notions of beauty vs. his own appreciation of the trite or banal) and on the level of the pastoral (traditional values vs. a more contemplative life).

CHAPTER 7: THE POEM ON THE PAGE

1 See Marianne Teuber's excellent article, "Formvorstellung und Kubismus, oder Pablo Picasso und William James," which convincingly demonstrates that the experiments of physiologists like Helmholtz and psychologists like William James, introduced to Picasso by Gertrude Stein, influenced the Cubists to the point where they consciously played in their paintings with the laws of perception as outlined by these theorists (*Kubismus: Künstler, Themen, Werke, 1907–1920*, Catalog, Joseph-Haubrich-Kunsthalle, Cologne, 1982, pp. 9–57).

2 The standard work for an in-depth analysis of these laws of perception is of course Gombrich's *Art and Illusion*.

3 Quoted in Charles O. Hartman, *Free Verse: An Essay on Prosody* (Princeton: Princeton University Press, 1980), p. 92.

4 "Interview with Donald Hall," in *A Marianne Moore Reader* (New York: Viking, 1961), p. 263. Moore describes herself as "governed by the pull of the sentence."

5 Louis Zukofsky, "Program: 'Objectivists' 1931," *Poetry*, 37 (Feb. 1931): 268.

6 Sayre, *Visual Text*, p. 72.

7 John Hollander, *Vision and Resonance* (New York: Oxford University Press, 1975), p. 111.

8 An excellent analysis of this dimension in "Spring and All" is to be found in John Vernon, *Poetry and the Body* (Urbana: University of Illinois Press, 1979), pp. 123–26.

9   Rainer Maria Rilke, *Duino Elegies*. The German text, with an English translation, introduction, and commentary by J. B. Leishman and Stephen Spender (London: Chatto and Windus, 1939, 1963), p. 85.

10   "Dans le langage classique, ce sont les rapports qui mènent le mot puis l'emportent aussitôt vers un sens toujours projeté; dans la poésie moderne, les rapports ne sont qu'une extension du mot, c'est le Mot qui est "la demeure," . . . c'est le Mot qui nourrit et comble comme le dévoilement soudain d'une vérité; . . . il brille d'une liberté infinie et s'apprête à rayonner vers mille rapports incertains et possibles. Les rapports fixes abolis, le mot n'a plus q'un projet vertical, il est comme un bloc, un pilier qui plonge dans un total de sens, de réflexes et de rémanences: il est un signe debout" (Barthes, *Le degré zéro de l'écriture*, pp. 69–70; *Writing Degree Zero*, trans. Annette Lavers and Colin Smith [Boston: Beacon Press, 1970], p. 47).

11   Steiner, *The Colors of Rhetoric*, p. 204.

12   Unfortunately the iconic dimension is often all but lost in the new *Collected Poems*, since even many of the very short poems run over two pages. From the point of view of the layout – which here entails so much more than the question of an appealing presentation – the old edition is incomparably superior to the new one, which, needless to say, is a vast improvement in all other respects.

13   Max Nänny, "Imitative Form: The Modernist Poem on the Page," in *Poetry and Epistemology: Turning Points in the History of Poetic Knowledge*, eds. Roland Hagen-büchle and Laura Skandera (Regensburg: Friedrich Pustet, 1986), p. 219. In *The Collected Poems* (Vol. 1, p. 150), the iconic dimension is completely lost because of the page break after the first two lines.

14   Nänny, "Imitative Form," p. 216.

15   Roman Jakobson, "Quest for the Essence of Language," *Selected Writings*, Vol. 2, p. 349. For a basic discussion of the problems involved, see also Steiner, *The Colors of Rhetoric*, pp. 19–32 and Chapter 1, passim.

16   Max Nänny, "The Need for an Iconic Criticism," *Journal of Literary Criticism*, 1:1 (June 1984): 30–31.

17   Ibid., p. 31. The quotation is from Roman Jakobson, "Closing Statement: Linguistics and Poetics," in *Style in Language*, ed. Thomas Sebeok (Cambridge, Mass.: MIT Press, 1960), p. 356.

18   Thomas H. Jackson, "Positivism and Modern Poetics: Yeats, Mallarmé, and William Carlos Williams," *English Literary History*, 46 (1979): 536.

19   *Spring Showers* is reproduced in Dijkstra, *Hieroglyphics*, and in Norman, *Alfred Stieglitz*.

CONCLUSION

1   In his "Quest for the Essence of Language" (*Selected Writings*, Vol. 2) Jakobson demonstrates that it is less the iconic sign per se that resembles the signified than the sign whose *relations* reflect those of the object(s) referred to. This means that the icon is basically operative within the relational or "diagrammatical" (C. S. Peirce) structures of language; that is, as we have seen, within such oppositions as top–bottom, presence–absence, coherence–fragmentation, and so on.

2   Sutton, "A Visit with William Carlos Williams," pp. 321–22.

3 J. Hillis Miller, "Williams' *Spring and All* and the Progress of Poetry," *Daedalus*, 99: 2 (Spring 1970): 422.

4 Erwin Panofsky, "Die Perspektive als symbolische Form" (1927), in *Aufsätze zu Grundfragen der Kunstwissenschaft*, rev. ed. (Berlin: Bruno Hessling, 1974), p. 122.

5 "[In diesem psychophysiologischen Raum] gibt es keine strenge Gleichartigkeit der Orte und Richtungen, sondern jeder Ort hat seine Eigenart und seinen eigenen Wert. Der Gesichtsraum wie der Tastraum kommen darin überein, daß sie im Gegensatz zum metrischen Raum der Euklidischen Geometrie 'anisotrop' und 'inhomogen' sind: die Hauptrichtungen der Organisation: vorn-hinten, oben-unten, rechts-links sind in beiden physiologischen Räumen übereinstimmend ungleichwertig" ("Ernst Cassirer, *Philosophie der symbolischen Formen, II: Das mythische Denken* (Leipzig, 1925), pp. 107–08; my translation).

6 m "Mit dieser Formel [d.h. der Objektivierung des Subjektiven] ist nun aber die Tatsache bezeichnet, daß die Perspektive, gerade als sie aufgehört hatte, ein technisch-mathematisches Problem zu sein, in umso höherem Maße beginnen musste, ein künstlerisches Problem zu bilden. Denn sie ist ihrer Natur nach gleichsam eine zweischneidige Waffe: sie schafft den Körpern Platz, sich plastisch zu entfalten und mimisch zu bewegen – aber sie schafft auch dem Lichte die Möglichkeit, im Raum sich auszubreiten und die Körper malerisch aufzulösen; sie schafft Distanz zwischen dem Menschen und den Dingen ('das Erst ist das Aug, das do sicht, das Ander ist der Gegenwürf, der gesehen wird, das Dritt ist die Weiten dozwischen' sagt Dürer nach Piero Della Francesca) – aber sie hebt diese Distanz doch wiederum auf, indem sie die dem Menschen in selbständigem Dasein gegenüberstehende Ding-Welt gewissermaßen in sein Auge hineinzieht. . . . So lässt sich die Geschichte der Perspektive mit gleichem Recht als *ein Triumph des distanzierenden und objektivierenden Wirklichkeitssinnes, und als ein Triumph des distanzverneinenden menschlichen Machtstrebens . . . begreifen*" (Panofsky, "Die Perspektive als Symbolische Form," p. 123; my emphasis).

7 Approached from this angle, linear perspective can be regarded as the direct outcome (and subsequently as a strengthening) of the logocentric tradition, rooted in the inherent urge in logocentrism to envision the *primum movens* as an all-determining and all-encompassing center to which everything can be related and from which everything falls into perspective: "Whether the logos is the unmoved mover or man, God or human reason – *logos* as *ratio* – being in this 'onto-theological' tradition,' as Heidegger calls it, is perceived from a determining center, a 'still point,' which means, of course, from the end rather than from the beginning. We recall here Heidegger's term 'metaphysics,' which etymologically means . . . the perception of things-as-they-are from after, or beyond, or above the things themselves. That is to say, metaphysics, both theological and humanistic, is a spatializing process, or rather a spatializing of process. It perceives *physis* from the vantage point of a privileged center, from a distance that allows the perceiver to *see* everything at once – panoramically – as an object or, better, as a picture, i.e. a work of ordered Art. As Kierkegaard says about Hegel's metaphysical perspective, it allows the perceiver to see and comprehend being aesthetically, which is to say, adopting Foucault, to coerce or discipline things-as-they-are by means of the 'panoptic eye' " (William Spanos, "The De-struction of Form in Postmodern American Poetry: The Examples

of Charles Olson and Robert Creeley," *Amerikastudien / American Studies,* 25:4 [1980]: 383).

8 Williams, rejecting all art rooted in "logicality," is thus a prime example of the kind of poet who, according to Heidegger, is a kindred spirit to the philosopher who discards the will to power over existence inherent in Cartesian rationalism. George Steiner succinctly summarizes this important aspect of Heidegger's philosophy: "For Descartes, truth is determined and validated by certainty. Certainty, in turn, is located in the *ego.* The self becomes the hub of reality and relates to the world outside itself in an exploratory, necessarily exploitative way. As knower and user, the ego is predator. For Heidegger, on the contrary, the human person and self-consciousness are *not* the centre, the assessors of existence. Man is only a privileged listener and respondent to existence. The vital relation to otherness is not, as for Cartesian and positivist rationalism, one of 'grasping' and pragmatic use. It is a relation of audition. We are trying to 'listen to the voice of Being.' It is, or ought to be, a relation of extreme responsibility, custodianship, answerability to and for. Of this answerability, the thinker and the poet, *der Denker und der Dichter,* are at once the carriers and the trustees. This is because it is in their openness to language (to the *logos*), in their capacity to be *spoken* rather than to speak . . . that the truth, or can we say with Wordsworth and Hölderlin, that 'the music of being,' most urgently calls for and summons up response" (George Steiner, *Heidegger* [Glasgow: Fontana/Collins, 1978], p. 36). For a pertinent essay on the relation between Heidegger and Postmodernist American poetry, see William Spanos, "Breaking the Circle: Hermeneutics as Dis-closure," *boundary* 2, 5:2 (Winter 1977): 421–57.

9 Vernon, *Poetry and the Body,* p. 133; Doran, ed., *Conversations avec Cézanne,* p. 109.

10 Quoted in Gibbons, "Cubism and 'The Fourth Dimension,' " p. 144.

11 Marshall McLuhan and Harley Parker, *Through the Vanishing Point: Space in Poetry and Painting* (New York: Harper and Row, 1968), p. 20.

12 Reported by Duret and quoted by Max Raphael, *Von Monet zu Picasso,* p. 62.

Selected Bibliography

Adams, Henry. *The Education of Henry Adams.* In Henry Adams, *Novels, Mont St. Michel, The Education.* New York: Viking (The Library of America), 1983.

Altieri, Charles. "Abstraction as Act: Modernist Poetry in Relation to Painting." *Dada / Surrealism,* 10–11 (1982): 106–34.

"From Symbolist Thought to Immanence: The Ground of Postmodern American Poetics." *boundary* 2, 2:1 (1973): 605–37.

Painterly Abstraction in Modernist American Poetry. The Contemporaneity of Modernism. Cambridge: Cambridge University Press, 1989.

"Picasso's Collages and the Force of Cubism." *Kenyon Review,* 6 (Spring 1984): 8–33.

" 'Ponderation' in Cézanne and Williams." *Poetics Today,* 10:2 (Summer 1989): 373–99.

Angoff, Charles, ed. *William Carlos Williams.* Leverton Lecture Series. Rutherford, N.J.: Fairley Dickinson University Press, 1975.

Arnheim, Rudolf. *Art and Visual Perception: A Psychology of the Creative Eye.* New Version. Berkeley and Los Angeles: University of California Press, 1974.

Toward a Psychology of Art: Collected Essays. Berkeley and Los Angeles: University of California Press, 1966.

Bachelard, Gaston. *La terre et les rêveries du repos.* Paris: José Corti, 1948.

Badt, Kurt. *The Art of Cézanne,* trans. Sheila Ann Ogilvie. Berkeley and Los Angeles: University of California Press, 1965.

Barthes, Roland. *Le degré zéro de l'écriture.* Paris: Edition du Seuil, 1953.

L'empire des signes. Paris: Albert Skira, 1970.

Empire of Signs, trans. Richard Howard. London: Jonathan Cape, 1982.

Writing Degree Zero, trans. Annette Lavers and Colin Smith. Boston: Beacon Press, 1970.

Berger, John. *The Success and Failure of Picasso.* Harmondsworth: Penguin, 1965.

Berry, Eleanor. "Williams' Development of a New Prosodic Form – Not the 'Variable Foot,' But the Sight-Stanza." *William Carlos Williams Review,* 7:2 (Fall 1981): 21–30.

Braque, Georges. *Illustrated Notebooks, 1917–1955.* With a translation by Stanley Appelbaum. New York: Dover, 1971.

Breslin, James E. B. *William Carlos Williams: An American Artist.* New York: Oxford University Press, 1970.

"William Carlos Williams and Charles Demuth: Cross-Fertilization in the Arts." *Journal of Modern Literature,* 6:2 (April 1977): 248–63.

Breton, André. "Manifesto of Surrealism" (1924). In *Manifestoes of Surrealism,* trans. Richard Seaver and Helen R. Lane. Ann Arbor: University of Michigan Press, 1972.

"Surrealist Situation of the Object" (1935). In *Manifestoes of Surrealism,* trans. Richard Seaver and Helen R. Lane. Ann Arbor: University of Michigan Press, 1972.

Brooks, Van Wyck. *America's Coming-of-Age.* Rev. ed. Garden City, N.Y.: Doubleday, 1958.

Brown, Milton. *American Painting from the Armory Show to the Depression.* Princeton: Princeton University Press, 1955.

"Cubist-Realism: An American Style." *Marsyas,* 3 (1943–45): 138–60.

Bruns, Gerald L. "De Improvisatione: An Essay on *Kora in Hell.*" In *Inventions: Writing, Textuality and Understanding in Literary History.* New Haven, Conn.: Yale University Press, 1982, pp. 145–59.

Bryson, Norman. *Looking at the Overlooked: Four Essays on Still Life Painting.* London: Reaktion Books, 1990.

Burbick, Joan. "Grimaces of a New Age: The Postwar Poetry and Painting of William Carlos Williams and Jackson Pollock." *boundary 2,* 10:3 (Spring 1982): 109–23.

Burke, Kenneth. "William Carlos Williams: Two Judgments." In *William Carlos Williams: A Collection of Critical Essays,* ed. J. Hillis Miller. Englewood Cliffs, N.J.: Prentice Hall, 1966, pp. 47–61.

Cabanne, Pierre. *Dialogues with Marcel Duchamp.* New York: Viking, 1971.

Carne-Ross, D. S. "The Music of a Lost Dynasty: Pound in the Classroom." *Boston University Journal,* 21:1 (Winter 1972): 25–41.

Cassirer, Ernst. *Philosophie der symbolischen Formen, II: Das mythische Denken.* Berlin: B. Cassirer, 1925.

Cézanne, Paul. *Letters,* ed. John Rewald. New York: Hacker Art Books, 1976.

Champa, Kermit. "Charlie Was Like That." *Artforum,* 12 (March 1974): 54–59.

Charbonnier, Georges. *Le monologue du peintre.* Paris: René Julliard, 1959.

Contact. Ed. Robert McAlmon and William Carlos Williams. New York. Nos. 1–5 (1920–23).

Cook, Albert. *Figural Choice in Poetry and Art.* Hanover, N.H.: University Press of New England, 1985.

Creeley, Robert. *Contexts of Poetry: Interviews 1961–1971.* Bolinas, Calif.: Four Seasons Foundation, 1973.

Cureton, Richard D. "E. E. Cummings: A Case Study of Iconic Syntax." *Language and Style,* 14:3 (Summer 1981): 183–215.

Diepeveen, Leonard. "Shifting Metaphors: Interart Comparisons and Analogy." *Word & Image,* 5 (April–June 1989): 206–213.

Dijkstra, Bram. *The Hieroglyphics of a New Speech: Cubism, Stieglitz, and the Early Poetry of William Carlos Williams.* Princeton: Princeton University Press, 1969.

Doran, P. M., ed. *Conversations avec Cézanne.* Paris: Macula, 1978.

Doty, Robert. *Photo-Secession: Photography as a Fine Art.* Rochester: George Eastman House, 1960.

Doyle. Charles. "Kora and Venus: Process and Object in William Carlos Williams." *Perspective*, 17:3 (Winter 1974): 189–97.

William Carlos Williams: The Critical Heritage. London: Routledge and Kegan Paul, 1980.

Duchamp. Catalog; Museum Ludwig. Cologne: Museen der Stadt Köln, 1984.

Duchamp, Marcel. "The Richard Mutt Case." *The Blind Man*, 2 (May 1917): 5.

Duffey, Bernard. *A Poetry of Presence: The Writing of William Carlos Williams*. Madison: University of Wisconsin Press, 1986.

Eiseman, Alvord L. *Charles Demuth*. New York: Watson-Guptill, 1982.

Fahlman, Betsy, ed. *Pennsylvania Modern: Charles Demuth of Lancaster*. Catalog; Philadelphia Museum of Art, Philadelphia, 1983.

Farnham, Emily. *Charles Demuth: Behind a Laughing Mask*. Norman: University of Oklahoma Press, 1971.

Fenollosa, Ernest. *The Chinese Written Character as a Medium for Poetry*, ed. Ezra Pound. 1936; San Francisco: City Lights Books, 1968.

Frank, Joseph. *The Widening Gyre: Crisis and Mastery in Modern Literature*. Bloomington: Indiana University Press, 1968.

Frank, Waldo, et al., eds. *America and Alfred Stieglitz*. 1934; New York: Octagon Books, 1975.

Fredman, Stephen. "The Generative Sentence: William Carlos Williams's *Kora in Hell: Improvisations*." In Fredman, *Poet's Prose: The Crisis in American Verse*. New York: Cambridge University Press, 1983, pp. 12–54.

Friedman, Martin. *Charles Sheeler: Paintings, Drawings, Photgraphs*. New York: Watson-Guptill, 1975.

Fry, Edward F. *Cubism*. 1966; New York: Oxford University Press, 1978.

Fure, Rob. "The Design of Experience: William Carlos Williams and Juan Gris." *William Carlos Williams Newsletter*, 4:2 (Fall 1978): 10–19.

Gallup, Donald. "The Weaving of a Pattern: Marsden Hartley and Gertrude Stein." *Magazine of Art*, 41 (1948): 256–61.

Gay, Peter. "The Apples of Cézanne: An Essay in the Meaning of Still Life." In *Modern Art: 19th and 20th Centuries*. New York: Braziller, 1982.

Gelpi, Albert. *A Coherent Splendor: The American Poetic Renaissance, 1910–1950*. Cambridge: Cambridge University Press, 1987.

Genette, Gérard. "Valéry and the Poetics of Language." In *Textual Strategies: Perspectives in Post-Structuralist Criticism*, ed. Josué V. Harari. Ithaca, N.Y.: Cornell University Press, 1979, pp. 359–73.

Gibbons, Tom. "Cubism and 'The Fourth Dimension' in the Context of the Late Nineteenth-Century and Early Twentieth-Century Revival of Occult Idealism." *Journal of the Warburg and Courtauld Institutes*, 44 (1981): 130–47.

Golding, John. *Duchamp: The Bride Stripped Bare by Her Bachelors, Even*. New York: Viking, 1972.

Gombrich, E. H. *Art and Illusion: A Study of the Problem of Pictorial Representation*. Princeton: Princeton University Press, 1961.

Meditations on a Hobby Horse and Other Essays on the Theory of Art. London and New York: Phaidon, 1963.

Gowing, Lawrence. "The Logic of Organized Sensations." In *Cézanne: The Late Work*, ed. William Rubin. New York: Museum of Modern Art, 1977, pp. 55–72.

Green, Jonathan, ed. *Camera Work. An Anthology*. Millerton, N.Y.: Aperture, 1973.

Greenough, Sarah. "From the American Earth: Alfred Stieglitz's Photographs of Apples." *Art Journal*, 41:1 (Spring 1981): 46–53.

Greenough, Sarah, and Juan Hamilton, eds. *Alfred Stieglitz: Photographs and Writings*. Washington, D.C.: National Gallery of Art, 1983.

Gris, Juan. "Des possibilités de la peinture." *transatlantic review*, 1:6 (June 1924): 482–86; 2:1 (July 1924): 75–79. Reprinted in Kahnweiler, *Juan Gris: Sa vie, son oeuvre, ses écrits*; trans. in Kahnweiler, *Juan Gris: His Life and Work*.

Grogan, Ruth. "The Influence of Painting on William Carlos Williams." In *William Carlos Williams: A Critical Anthology*, ed. Charles Tomlinson. Harmondsworth: Penguin, 1972, pp. 265–98.

Guimond, James. *The Art of William Carlos Williams*. Urbana: University of Illinois Press, 1968.

Halter, Peter. "Expression in Color: The Theory of Wassily Kandinsky and the Poetry of William Carlos Williams." In *SPELL, 2: On Poetry and Poetics*, ed. Richard Waswo. Tübingen: Gunter Narr, 1985, pp. 137–54.

" 'How Shall I Be a Mirror to This Modernity?' William Carlos Williams, Alfred Stieglitz, and the Artists of the Stieglitz Circle." In *Poetry and the Fine Arts*, ed. Roland Hagenbüchle and Jaqueline S. Ollier. Eichstätt: Friederich Pustet, 1989, pp. 77–100.

"Paul Strand: The Search for a Synthetic Form." *Cercles*, 2 (Winter 1991): 139–50.

"Soothing the Savage Beast: William Carlos Williams' and Charles Demuth's Urban Landscapes." In *Modes of Interpretation: Essays Presented to Ernst Leisi*, ed. Richard J. Watts and Urs Weidmann. Tübingen: Gunter Narr, 1984, pp. 71–92.

Hartley, Marsden. *Adventures in the Arts*. New York: Boni and Liveright, 1921.

Hartman, Charles O. *Free Verse: An Essay on Prosody*. Princeton: Princeton University Press, 1980.

Hartman, Geoffrey H. *Criticism in the Wilderness: The Study of Literature Today*. New Haven, Conn.: Yale University Press, 1980.

Haskell, Barbara. *Charles Demuth*. New York: Harry N. Abrams, 1989.

Marsden Hartley. New York: Harry N. Abrams, 1987.

Hermans, Theo. *The Structure of Modernist Poetry*. London: Croom Helm, 1982.

Himmel, Eric. "Change of Heart." [On Alfred Stieglitz's *The Steerage*.] *Camera Arts*, 1:5 (Sept–Oct. 1981): 38–39, 104.

Hohl, Reinhold. "Die heitreren Facetten des Kubismus: Ueber die scheinillusionistischen Bildinhalte kubistischer Gemälde." In *Kubismus: Künstler, Themen, Werke, 1907–1920*. Catalog; Cologne: Joseph-Haubrich-Kunsthalle, 1982, pp. 71–91.

Holden, Jonathan. "The 'Found' in Contemporary Poetry." *Georgia Review*, 23:2 (Summer 1979): 329–41.

Hollander, John. "Figures of Interpretation. Notes on Picture and Text." *Poetry East*, 13–14 (Spring–Summer 1984): 23–30.

Vision and Resonance. New York: Oxford University Press, 1975.

Homer, William Innes. *Alfred Stieglitz and the American Avant-Garde*. Boston: New York Graphic Society, 1977.

Huelsenbeck, Richard. *En Avant Dada: A History of Dadaism,* trans. Ralph Manheim. Reprinted in *The Dada Painters and Poets,* ed. Robert Motherwell. New York: Wittenborn, 1967.

Hunt, John Dixon, ed. *Encounters: Essays on Literature and the Visual Arts.* London: Studio Vista, 1971.

"Sight and Song Itself. Painting and Poetry of William Carlos Williams." *Strivers Row,* 1 (1974): 77–106.

Imdahl, Max. *Bildautonomie und Wirklichkeit: Zur theoretischen Begründung moderner Malerei.* Mittenwald: Mäander, 1981.

Jackson, Thomas H. "Positivism and Modern Poetics: Yeats, Mallarmé, and William Carlos Williams." *English Literary History,* 46 (1979): 509–40.

Jakobson, Roman. *Selected Writings,* vol. 2. The Hague: Mouton, 1971.

Studies in Child Language and Aphasia. The Hague: Mouton, 1971.

Jakobson, Roman, and Morris Halle. *Fundamentals of Language.* 2nd rev. ed. The Hague: Mouton, 1971.

Jauss, Hans Robert. *Kleine Apologie der ästhetischen Erfahrung: Mit kunstgeschichtlichen Bemerkungen von Max Imdahl.* Konstanz: Universitätsverlag, 1972.

"Poiesis," trans. Michael Shaw. *Critical Inquiry,* 8:3 (Spring 1982): 591–608.

Josephson, Matthew. *Life Among the Surrealists.* New York: Holt, Rinehart and Winston, 1962.

Kahnweiler, Daniel-Henry. *Juan Gris: His Life and Work,* trans. Douglas Cooper. 1947; rev. ed. New York: Abrams, 1968.

Juan Gris: Sa vie, son oeuvre, ses écrits. Paris: Gallimard, 1946.

The Rise of Cubism, trans. Henry Aronson. New York: Wittenborn, Schultz, 1949.

Kandinsky, Wassily. *Concerning the Spiritual in Art,* ed. Robert Motherwell. New York: Wittenborn, 1947.

Essays über Kunst und Künstler. With an introduction by Max Bill. Bern: Benteli, 1974.

"Inner Necessity," trans. Edward Wadsworth. *Blast,* 1 (1914): 119–25.

"On the Question of Form." In *The Blaue Reiter Almanac,* ed. Klaus Lankheit, trans. Henning Falkenstein. New York: Viking, 1974.

Über das Geistige in der Kunst. With an introduction by Max Bill. Bern: Benteli, 1973.

Kenner, Hugh. *A Homemade World: The American Modernist Writers.* New York: William Morrow, 1975.

The Pound Era. Berkeley and Los Angeles: University of California Press, 1971.

Kermode, Frank, ed. *English Pastoral Poetry from the Beginnings to Marvell.* New York: Norton, 1972.

Korg, Jacob. *Language in Modern Literature: Innovation and Experience.* New York: Barnes and Noble, 1979.

Krauss, Rosalind. "Stieglitz/Equivalents." *October,* 11 (Winter 1979): 129–40.

Kreymborg, Alfred. *Troubadour: An American Biography.* 1925; New York: Sagamore Press, 1957.

Kubismus: Künstler, Themen, Werke, 1907–1920. Catalog; Joseph-Haubrich-Kunsthalle Köln. Bonn: Bildkunst, 1982.

Kuspit, Donald B. "Individual and Mass Identity in Urban Art: The New York Case." *Art in America,* 65 (Sept.–Oct. 1977): 67–77.

Levin, Gail. "Wassily Kandinsky and the American Avant-garde." *Criticism*, 21 (1979): 347–61.

Lewis, Wyndham. *Time and Western Man*. London: Chatto and Windus, 1927.

Lodge, David. *The Modes of Modern Writing*. London: Edward Arnold, 1977.

Lucic, Karen. *Charles Sheeler and the Cult of the Machine*. London: Reaktion Books, 1991.

MacGowan, Christopher J. *William Carlos Williams' Early Poetry: The Visual Arts Background*. Ann Arbor, Mich.: UMI Research Press, 1984.

McLuhan, Marshall, and Harley Parker. *Through the Vanishing Point: Space in Poetry and Painting*. New York: Harper and Row, 1968.

Mariani, Paul. *William Carlos Williams: A New World Naked*. New York: McGraw Hill, 1981.

   William Carlos Williams: The Poet and His Critics. Chicago: American Library Association, 1975.

Marling, William. *William Carlos Williams and the Painters, 1909–1923*. Athens: Ohio University Press, 1982.

Masheck, Joseph, ed. *Marcel Duchamp in Perspective*. Englewood Cliffs, N.J.: Prentice Hall, 1975.

Mazzaro, Jerome. *William Carlos Williams: The Later Poems*. Ithaca: Cornell University Press, 1973.

Miki, Roy. *The Prepoetics of William Carlos Williams: Kora in Hell*. Ann Arbor: UMI Research Press, 1983.

Millard, Charles. "The Photography of Charles Sheeler." In *Charles Sheeler*. Catalog; National Collection of Fine Arts, Smithsonian Institution, Washington, D.C., 1968, pp. 80–89.

Miller, J. Hillis. *The Linguistic Moment: From Wordsworth to Stevens*. Princeton: Princeton University Press, 1985.

   Poets of Reality: Six Twentieth Century Writers. Cambridge, Mass.: Harvard University Press, 1965.

   "Tradition and Difference." *Diacritics*, 2:4 (Winter 1972): 6–13.

   ed. *William Carlos Williams. A Collection of Critical Essays*. Englewood Cliffs, N.J.: Prentice Hall, 1966.

   "Williams' *Spring and All* and the Progress of Poetry." *Daedalus*, 99: 2 (Spring 1970): 405–34.

Moore, Patrick. "Cubist Prosody: William Carlos Williams and the Conventions of Verse Lineation." *Philological Quarterly*, 65 (Fall 1986): 515–36.

Mukařovsky, Jan. *Structure, Sign and Function: Selected Essays*, trans. and ed. John Burbank and Peter Steiner. New Haven, Conn.: Yale University Press, 1978.

Mumford, Lewis. "The Metropolitan Milieu." In *America and Alfred Stieglitz*, ed. Waldo Frank et al. 1934; New York: Octagon Books, 1975, pp. 33–58.

Myers, Neil. "William Carlos Williams' *Spring and All*." *Modern Language Quarterly*, 26: 2 (1965): 285–301.

   "Williams' 'Two Pendants: For the Ears'." *Journal of Modern Literature*, 1 (May 1971): 477–92.

Nänny, Max. "Context, Contiguity and Contact in Ezra Pound's Personae." *English Literary History*, 47 (1980): 386–98.

   Ezra Pound: Poetics for an Electric Age. Bern: Francke, 1973.

"Iconic Dimensions in Poetry." In *SPELL, 2: On Poetry and Poetics*, ed. Richard Waswo. Tübingen: Gunter Narr, 1985, pp. 111–35.

"Imitative Form: The Modernist Poem on the Page." In *Poetry and Epistemology: Turning Points in the History of Poetic Knowledge*, ed. Roland Hagenbüchle and Laura Skandera. Regensburg: Friedrich Pustet, 1986, pp. 213–31.

"The Need for an Iconic Criticism." *Journal of Literary Criticism*, 1:1 (June 1984): 29–42.

Naumann, Francis M. "The Big Show: The First Exhibition of the Society of Independent Artists." Part I, *Artforum*, 17 (February 1979): 34–39. Part II, *Artforum*, 17 (April 1979): 49–53.

Norman, Dorothy. *Alfred Stieglitz: An American Seer*. New York: Random House, 1960.

North, Michael. "The Sign of Five: Williams' 'The Great Figure' and Its Background." *Criticism*, 30 (Summer 1988): 325–48.

Ostrom, Alan. *The Poetic World of William Carlos Williams*. Carbondale: Southern Illinois University Press, 1966.

Others. Ed. Alfred Kreymborg, William Carlos Williams, et al. New York, Chicago. Vols. 1–5 (1915–19).

Panofsky, Erwin. "Die Perspektive als symbolische Form" (1927). In *Aufsätze zu Grundfragen der Kunstwissenschaft*. Rev. ed. Berlin: Bruno Hessling, 1974.

Perloff, Marjorie. "The Invention of Collage." *Collage*, 10–11 (1983): 5–47.

The Poetics of Indeterminacy: Rimbaud to Cage. Princeton: Princeton University Press, 1981.

" 'To Give a Design': Williams and the Visualization of Poetry." In Perloff, *The Dance of the Intellect: Studies in the Poetry of the Pound Tradition*. Cambridge: Cambridge University Press, 1985, pp. 88–118.

Poggi, Christine. *In Defiance of Painting: Cubism, Futurism, and the Invention of Collage*. New Haven, Conn.: Yale University Press, 1992.

Pound, Ezra. *Gaudier-Brzeska: A Memoir*. New York: New Directions, 1970.

The Letters of Ezra Pound, 1907–1941, ed. D. D. Paige. New York: Harcourt, Brace, 1950.

Literary Essays of Ezra Pound, ed. T. S. Eliot. Norfolk, Conn.: New Directions, 1954.

Raphael, Max. *Raumgestaltungen: Der Beginn der modernen Kunst im Kubismus und im Werk von Georges Braque*. 1949; Frankfurt: Campus Verlag, 1986.

Von Monet zu Picasso. Munich: Delphin, 1919.

Richardson, John. *Georges Braque*. Harmondsworth: Penguin, 1959.

Riddel, Joseph N. "Decentering the Image: The 'Project' of 'American' Poetics?" *boundary 2*, 8:1 (Fall 1979): 160–88.

The Inverted Bell: Modernism and the Counterpoetics of William Carlos Williams. Baton Rouge: Louisiana State University Press, 1974.

" 'Keep Your Pecker Up' – *Paterson Five* and the Question of Metapoetry." *Glyph, 8: Johns Hopkins Textual Studies*. Baltimore: Johns Hopkins University Press, 1981, pp. 203–31.

"The Wanderer and the Dance: William Carlos Williams' Early Poetics." In *The Shaken Realist: Essays in Modern Literature in Honor of Frederick J. Hoffman*, ed. Melvin J. Friedman and John B. Vickery. Baton Rouge: Louisiana State University Press, 1970, pp. 45–71.

Riffaterre, Michael. "Intertextual Representation: On Mimesis as Interpretive Discourse." *Critical Inquiry*, 11:1 (Sept. 1984): 141–62.

Rilke, Rainer Maria. *Duino Elegies*. The German text, with an English translation, introduction, and commentary by J. B. Leishman and Stephen Spender. 1939; London: Chatto and Windus, 1963.

Gesammelte Gedichte. Frankfurt: Insel, 1962.

Robinson, Alan. *Poetry, Painting and Ideas, 1885–1914*. London: Macmillan, 1985.

Rose, Barbara. "The Politics of Art." Part 2, *Artforum*, 7:5 (Jan. 1969): 44–49.

Rosenblum, Robert. *Cubism and Twentieth Century Art*. Rev. ed. New York: Abrams, 1976.

Rosenfeld, Paul. *Port of New York*. 1924; Urbana: University of Illinois Press, 1966.

Rourke, Constance. *Charles Sheeler: Artist in the American Tradition*. New York: Harcourt, Brace, 1938.

Rubin, William. "Cézannisme and the Beginnings of Cubism." In *Cézanne: The Late Work*, ed. William Rubin. New York: Museum of Modern Art, 1977, pp. 151–202.

Sayre, Henry M. "Avant-Garde Dispositions: Placing *Spring and All* in Context." *William Carlos Williams Review*, 10 (Fall 1984): 13–24.

"Distancing 'The Rose' from *Roses*." *William Carlos Williams Newsletter*, 5:1 (Spring 1979): 18–19.

"Ready-mades and Other Measures: The Poetics of Marcel Duchamp and William Carlos Williams." *Journal of Modern Literature*, 8:1 (1980): 3–22.

The Visual Text of William Carlos Williams. Urbana: University of Illinois Press, 1983.

Schapiro, Meyer. "The Apples of Cézanne. An Essay on the Meaning of Still-life." *Art News Annual*, 34 (1967): 34–53.

"Rebellion in Art." In *America in Crisis*, ed. Daniel Aaron. New York: Knopf, 1952.

Schmidt, Peter. "Some Versions of Modernist Pastoral: Williams and the Precisionists." *Contemporary Literature*, 21:3 (1980): 383–406.

William Carlos Williams, the Arts, and Literary Tradition. Baton Rouge: Louisiana State University Press, 1988.

Schneidau, Herbert. "Style and Sacrament in Modernist Writing." *Georgia Review*, 31 (1977): 427–52.

"Wisdom Past Metaphor: Another View of Pound, Fenollosa, and Objective Verse." *Paideuma*, 5 (Spring–Summer 1976): 15–29.

Schwartz, Paul Waldo. *Cubism*. New York: Praeger Publishers, 1971.

Schwarz, Arturo. *new york dada: duchamp, man ray, picabia*, ed. Armin Zweite et al. (Text in German and in English.) Munich: Prestel, 1974.

Sedlmayr, Hans. *Kunst und Wahrheit: Zur Theorie und Methode der Kunstgeschichte*. Hamburg: Rowohlt, 1958.

Shattuck, Roger. *The Innocent Eye: On Modern Literature and the Arts*. New York: Farrar, Straus, and Giroux, 1984.

Sheeler, Charles. Sheeler Papers (NSh-1). Archives of American Art, Smithsonian Institution, Washington, D.C.

Shiff, Richard. "Seeing Cézanne." *Critical Inquiry*, 4:4 (Summer 1978): 769–808.

Snyder, Gary. *The Old Ways: Six Essays*. San Francisco: City Lights, 1977.

Spanos, William V. "Breaking the Circle: Hermeneutics as Dis-closure." *boundary 2*, 5: 2 (Winter 1977): 421–57.

"Charles Olson and Negative Capability: A Phenomenological Interpretation." *Contemporary Literature*, 21:1 (1980): 39–80.

"The De-struction of Form in Postmodern American Poetry: The Examples of Charles Olson and Robert Creeley." *Amerikastudien / American Studies*, 25:4 (1980): 375–404.

Spears, Monroe K. *Dionysus and the City: Modernism in Twentieth-Century Poetry*. New York: Oxford University Press, 1970.

Steiner, George. *Heidegger*. Glasgow: Fontana / Collins, 1978.

Steiner, Wendy. *The Colors of Rhetoric: Problems in the Relation Between Literature and Painting*. Chicago: University of Chicago Press, 1982.

Steinmann, Lisa. "Once More, with Feeling: Teaching *Spring and All*." *William Carlos Williams Review*, 10 (Fall 1984): 7–12.

Strand, Paul. "Photography." *Seven Arts*, 10 (August 1917): 525.

"Photography and the New God." *Broom*, 3 (November 1922): 252–58.

Sutton, Walter. "A Visit with William Carlos Williams." *Minnesota Review*, 1 (April 1961): 309–24. Reprinted in *Speaking Straight Ahead: Interviews with William Carlos Williams*, ed. Linda Welshimer Wagner. New York: New Directions, 1976, pp. 38–56.

Tapscott, Stephen. "Williams, Sappho, and the Woman-as-Other." *William Carlos Williams Review*, 11:2 (Fall 1985): 30–44.

Tashjian, Dickran. *Skyscraper Primitives: Dada and the American Avant-Garde, 1910–1925*. Middletown, Conn.: Wesleyan University Press, 1975.

William Carlos Williams and the American Scene, 1920–1940. New York: Whitney Museum of American Art, 1978.

Terrell, Caroll F., ed. *William Carlos Williams: Man and Poet*. Orono, Maine: National Poetry Foundation, University of Maine at Orono, 1983.

Teuber, Marianne. "Formvorstellung und Kubismus, oder Pablo Picasso und William James." In *Kubismus: Künstler, Themen, Werke, 1907–1920*. Catalog; Cologne: Joseph-Haubrich-Kunsthalle, 1982, pp. 9–57.

Thomas, F. Richard. *Literary Admirers of Alfred Stieglitz*. Carbondale: Southern Illinois University Press, 1983.

Thompson, Jan. "Picabia and His Influence on American Art, 1913–1917." *Art Journal*, *39* (Fall 1979): 15.

Tomlinson, Charles, ed. *William Carlos Williams: A Critical Anthology*. Harmondsworth: Penguin, 1972.

Townley, Rod. *The Early Poetry of William Carlos Williams*. Ithaca: Cornell University Press, 1975.

Uspensky, Boris. *A Poetics of Composition: The Structure of the Artistic Text and Typology of a Compositional Form*, trans. Valentina Zavarin and Susan Wittig. Berkeley: University of California Press, 1974.

Valéry, Paul. "Introduction à la méthode de Léonard de Vinci." In *Oeuvres*, Vol. 1, ed. Jean Hytier. Paris: Gallimard (Bibliothèque de la Pléiade), 1960.

"The Method of Leonardo." In *Leonardo Poe Mallarmé. Collected Works of Paul Valéry*, Vol. 9, ed. Jackson Mathews. Princeton: Princeton University Press, 1968.

Vallier, Dora. "Braque, la peinture et nous: Propos de l'artiste recueillis." *Cahiers d'art,* 29:1 (Oct. 1954): 13–24.

Vernon, John. *Poetry and the Body.* Urbana: University of Illinois Press, 1979.

Wallace, Emily M. *A Bibliography of William Carlos Williams.* Middletown, Conn.: Wesleyan University Press, 1968.

Weaver, Mike. *William Carlos Williams: The American Background.* Cambridge: Cambridge University Press, 1971.

Weisstein, Ulrich. "Collage, Montage, and Related Terms: Their Literal and Figurative Use in and Application to Techniques and Forms in Various Arts." *Comparative Literature Studies,* 15:1 (March 1978): 124–39.

Weston, Edward. *Daybooks.* Millerton, N.Y.: Aperture, 1973.

Whitaker, Thomas R. "*Spring and All*: Teaching Us the Figures of the Dance." *William Carlos Williams Review,* 10 (Fall 1984): 1–6.

William Carlos Williams. New York: Twayne, 1968.

Whittemore, Reed. *William Carlos Williams: Poet from Jersey.* New York: Houghton, Mifflin, 1975.

Willard, Nancy. *Testimony of the Invisible Man: William Carlos Williams, Francis Ponge, Rainer Maria Rilke, Pablo Neruda.* Columbia: University of Missouri Press, 1970.

Williams, William Carlos. "America, Whitman, and the Art of Poetry." *Poetry Journal,* 8:1 (Nov. 1917): 27–36.

"Appreciation." *John Marin Memorial Exhibition.* Catalog; Art Galleries, Los Angeles, University of California, 1955.

The Autobiography of William Carlos Williams. 1951; New York: New Directions, 1967.

The Collected Earlier Poems. New York: New Directions, 1966.

The Collected Later Poems. Rev. ed. New York: New Directions, 1963.

The Collected Poems of William Carlos Williams. Vol. 1: *1909–1939,* ed. A. Walton Litz and Christopher MacGowan. New York: New Directions, 1986.

The Collected Poems of William Carlos Williams. Vol. 2: *1939–1962,* ed. Christopher MacGowan. New York: New Directions, 1988.

The Embodiment of Knowledge. Ed. Ron Loewinson. New York: New Directions, 1974.

The Farmers' Daughters. New York: New Directions, 1961.

I Wanted to Write a Poem: The Autobiography of the Works of a Poet. Reported and edited by Edith Heal. 1958; rev. ed. New York: New Directions, 1978.

Imaginations, ed. Webster Schott. New York: New Directions, 1970.

In the American Grain. 1925; reprinted New York: New Directions, 1956.

"The Lost Poems of William Carlos Williams, or The Past Recaptured," ed. John C. Thirlwall. *New Directions,* 16. New York: New Directions, 1957, pp. 3–45.

"Notes from a Talk on Poetry." *Poetry,* 14 (July 1919): 211–16.

Paterson. New York: New Directions, 1969.

Pictures from Brueghel. New York: New Directions, 1962.

A Recognizable Image: William Carlos Williams on Art and Artists, ed. Bram Dijkstra. New York: New Directions, 1978.

Selected Essays. New York: New Directions, 1969.

The Selected Letters of William Carlos Williams, ed. John C. Thirlwall. New York: McDowell, Obolensky, 1957.

"The So-Called So-Called." In *The Patron*. Bergen, N.J.: Bergen College, 1937, pp. 37–40.

"Some Hints Toward the Enjoyment of Modern Verse." In *Contemporary Poetry: A Retrospective from the Quarterly Review of Literature*, ed. T. Weiss and Renée Weiss. Princeton: Princeton University Press, 1974, pp. 124–28.

Speaking Straight Ahead: Interviews with William Carlos Williams, ed. Linda Welshimer Wagner. New York: New Directions, 1976.

A Voyage to Pagany. New York: New Directions, 1970.

Zukofsky, Louis. *Prepositions: The Collected Critical Essays*. New York: Horizon Press, 1968.

Index

CPSIA information can be obtained
at www.ICGtesting.com
Printed in the USA
LVOW11s1606030317

526089LV00001B/55/P